J.W. WATERHOUSE

THE MODERN PRE-RAPHAELITE

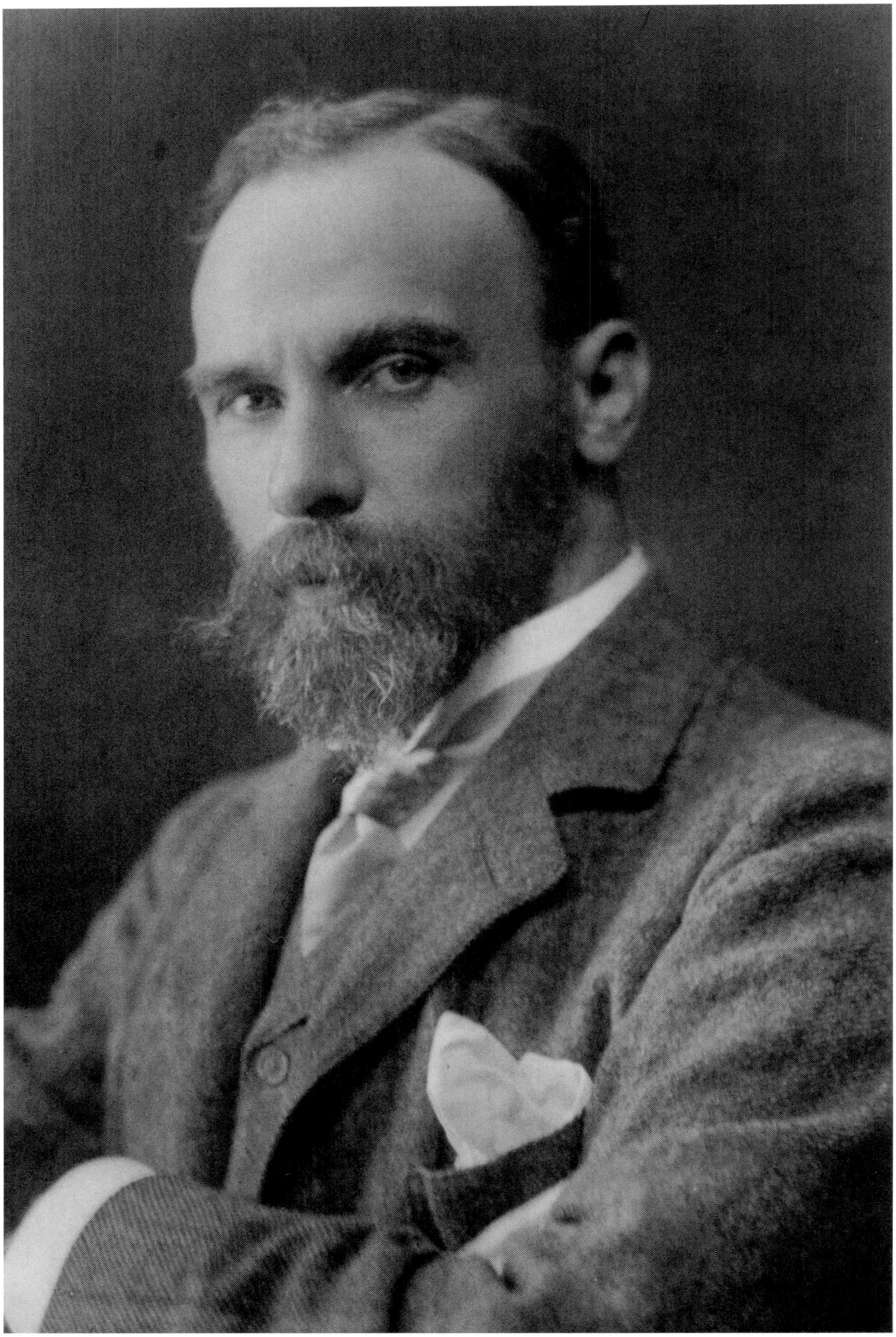

J.W. WATERHOUSE

THE MODERN PRE-RAPHAELITE

Elizabeth Prettejohn
Peter Trippi
Robert Upstone
Patty Wageman

GRONINGER MUSEUM - ROYAL ACADEMY OF ARTS - MONTREAL MUSEUM OF FINE ARTS

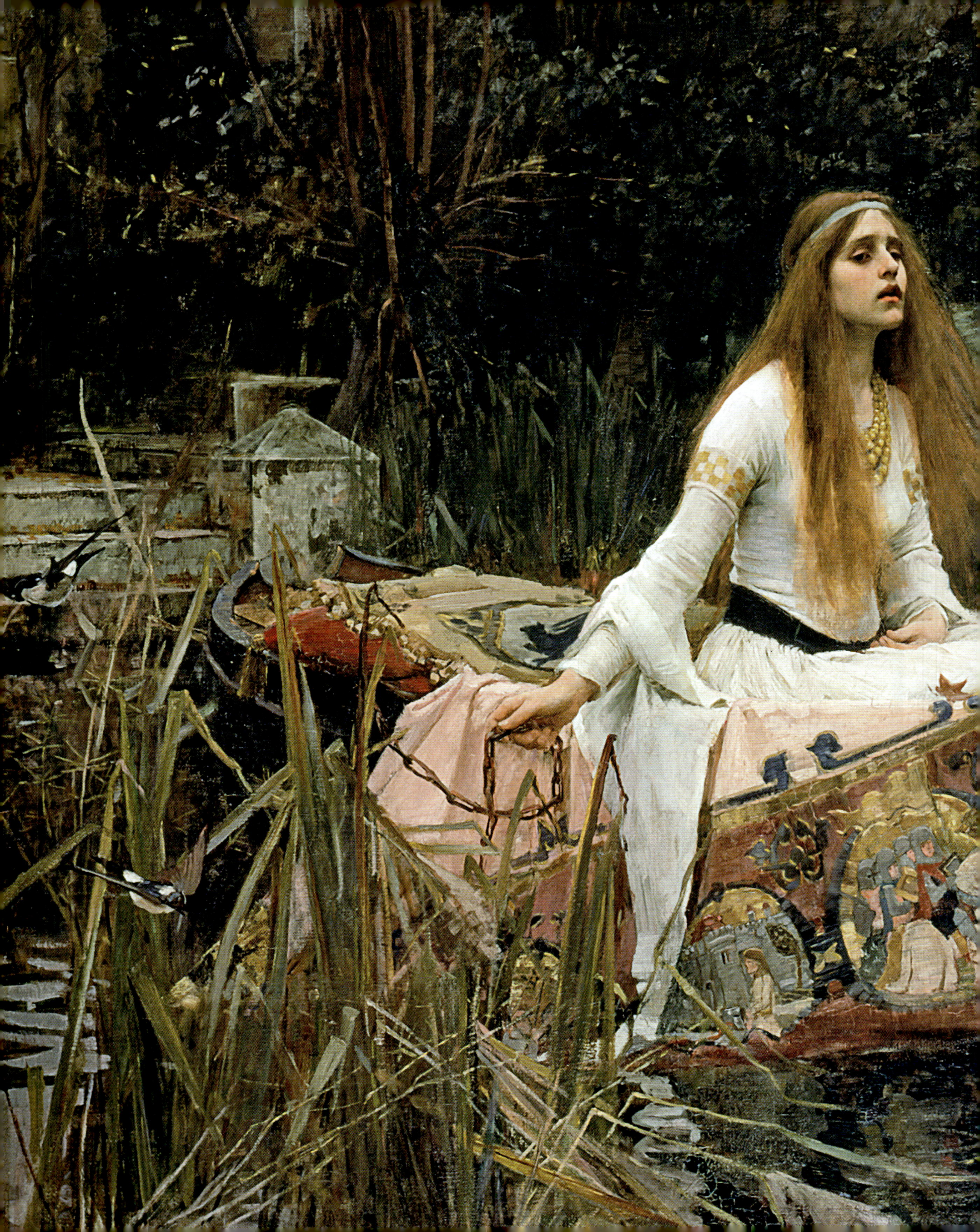

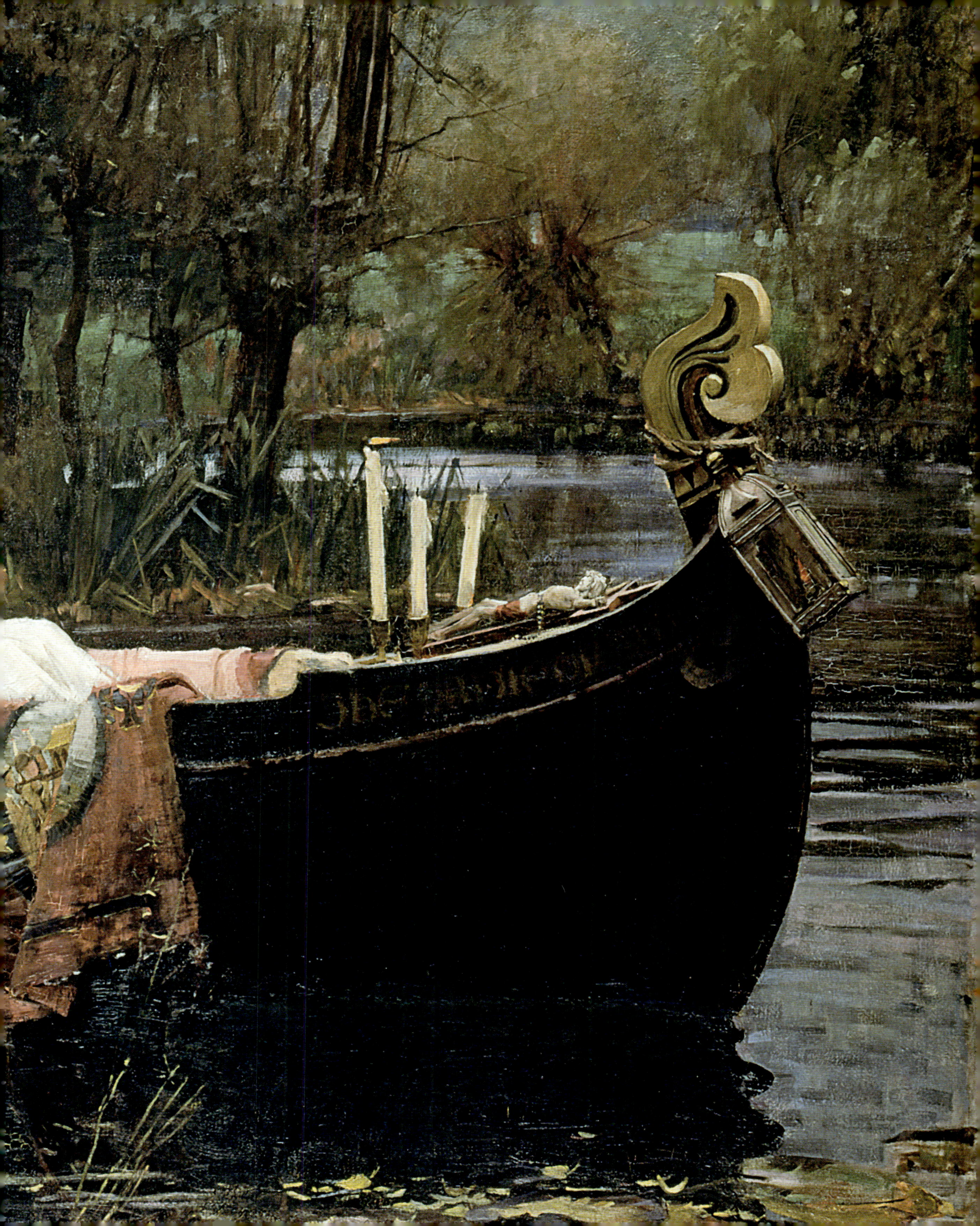

First published on the occasion of the exhibition
'J.W. Waterhouse: The Modern Pre-Raphaelite'

Groninger Museum, Groningen, the Netherlands, 14 December 2008 – 3 May 2009
Royal Academy of Arts, London, 27 June – 13 September 2009
Montreal Museum of Fine Arts, 1 October 2009 – 7 February 2010

Exhibition organised by the Groninger Museum, the Netherlands, with the collaboration of the Royal Academy of Arts, London, and the Montreal Museum of Fine Arts

SUPPORTED BY

BBL Company and GasTerra

The Royal Academy of Arts is grateful to Her Majesty's Government for its help in agreeing to indemnify the exhibition under the National Heritage Act 1980 and to the Museums, Libraries and Archives Council, for its help in arranging this indemnity.

EXHIBITION CURATORS
Elizabeth Prettejohn
Peter Trippi
Robert Upstone
Patty Wageman
with MaryAnne Stevens

EXHIBITION ORGANISATION
Groninger Museum, Groningen
Stijn ten Hoeve

Royal Academy of Arts, London
Cayetana Castillo
Caroline McCarthy

Montreal Museum of Fine Arts, Montreal
Nathalie Bondil
Pascal Normandin

The international exhibition program of the Montreal Museum of Fine Arts receives financial support from the Montreal Museum of Fine Arts Foundation and the Paul G. Desmarais Fund.

The research for this exhibition and catalogue carried out by Elizabeth Prettejohn and Christina Bradstreet was generously supported by the University of Bristol

University of BRISTOL

Copy-editing: Taal & Teken (Leo Reijnen/Hedie Meischke)
Translation from the Dutch: Donald Gardner
Book design: Rudo Menge
Printed in Belgium by Blondé Printing nv, Wommelgem

British Library Cataloguing-in-Publication Data
A catalogue record for this book is available from the British Library

ISBN 978-1-905711-36-9 (hardback)
ISBN 978-90-8586-489-9 (paperback)

Distributed outside the United States and Canada
by Thames & Hudson Ltd, London

Distributed in the United States and Canada
by Harry N. Abrams, Inc., New York

ILLUSTRATIONS

Contents

Acknowledgements

The organisers would like to thank the following for their generous assistance during the making of this exhibition and its catalogue:

all members of staff at the Groninger Museum, Seth Armitage, Maureen Attrill, Nicholas Bagshawe, Angela Barlow, Martin Barnes, Arik Bartelmus, Ria van Bastelaere, Jenny Beard, Julia Beaumont-Jones, Edwin Becker, David Beevers, Martin Beisly, Richard Beresford, Kathleen Borms, Susan Bourne, Christina Bradstreet, Alex Bratt, David Breuer, Pauline Broer, Myra Brown, Peter Brown, Scott Buckle, Godfrey Burke, Melissa Buron, Ina Busch, Edmund Capon, Lucy Cattell, Pauline Caulfield, Danielle Champagne, Caroline Collier, Olivia Colling, John Collins, Katherine Coombs, Kathryn Cope, Elspeth Dennison, Stephen Deuchar, Hamish Dewar, Rob Dickins, Sally Dobinson, Benjamin Doller, Sarah Drake, Amanda Draper, Harriet Drummond, Simon Edsor, Tim Egan, Jacques Erussard, Donato Esposito, Oliver Fairclough, The Lord and Lady Faringdon, Susanna Ferguson, Matthew Floris, Grant Ford, Robert Fowler, Genevieve Fox, Jennifer Francis, David Freeman, Daphne Frühmann, Nathalie Glaser, Hilliard Goldfarb, Simon Goldhill, Wendy Goldsmith, Anne Goodchild, Timothy Goodhue, Ted Gott, Sue Graves, Amanda Green, Jonathan Green, Tineke de Groot, Monica Grose-Hodge, Stephen Guy, Liz Haine, Jane Hall, Edward Halshaw, Andras Hamelberg, Yvonne Hardman, Simon Harper, Chris Harvey, Eileen Heinink, Ruth Hibbard, Sara Holdsworth, David Hopkins, Bernard Horrocks, Michael Houlihan, Christine Hourdé, Marijke Huijbregts, Ronald Hutton, David Jackson, Lynsey Jones, Mark Jones, Paul Jones, Flora Kaplan, Louise Kelly, Julia Kerr, Amy C. King, Reyahn King, Vivien Knight, Arjen Kok, Barbera van Kooij, Marcel Kramer, Ling-Ling Kuo, Jane and Aidan Langley, Gertjan Lankhorst, Jane Lawrence, Minou de Leeuw, Defanie Liao, Rachel Lloyd, Katharine Lochnan, Rupert Maas, Sally McIntosh, David McNeff, Charles Martindale, David Mason, Jennifer Melville, Christopher Menz, Amy Meyers, Thomas Miller, Julie Milne, Elizabeth Milton, Tim Moreton, Edward Morris, Hélène Nadeau, Peter and Renate Nahum, Sandy Nairne, Angela Nevill, Hans Nobel, Jim Nordstrom, Charles O'Brien, David Orcutt, Susan Owens, Matthew Paton, Hilde Paulussen, Alice Pearson, Sandra Penketh, Roxanne Peters, John and Eileen Physick, Tanja Pirsig-Marshall, Klaus-D. Pohl, Mark Pomeroy, Tom Tempest Radford, Fay Rawlinson, Christine Riding, Daniel Robbins, John Roles, Dolores and Terence Rowe, Dorothy Rowe, Polly Sartori, Phil Sayers, John Schaeffer, José Schraauwers, Frank Sharp, Juliet Simpson, Peyton Skipwith, Alison Smith, Barry Smith, Charles Saumarez Smith, Phillip Sowter, Brian Stewart, Reena Suleman, Virginia Tandy, Matthew Teitelbaum, Pierre Théberge, Heather Thomas, Nick Tite, Simon Toll, Julian Treuherz, Helen Valentine, Diana Vasquez, Gerard Vaughan, Hansch van der Velde, Henry Vivian-Neal, Rebecca Wallace, Nigel Walsh, Ben Warner, Christopher Webster, Lucy Wheeler, Stephen Whittle, Scott Wilcox, Amira Zahid; and all individuals who prefer to remain anonymous.

Lenders to the Exhibition

Aberdeen Art Gallery and Museums
Adelaide, Art Gallery of South Australia
Burnley, Towneley Hall, Burnley Borough Council
Cardiff, Amgueddfa Cymru/National Museum Wales**
Darmstadt, Hessisches Landesmuseum***
The Rob Dickins Collection, courtesy of Christie's
Falmouth Art Gallery*
Kirkcaldy Museum and Art Gallery, Fife Council Museums
Collection Dr Dennis T. Lanigan, Canada
Leeds Art Gallery*
National Museums Liverpool
London, Royal Academy of Arts
London, Tate
London, Victoria and Albert Museum
Manchester City Galleries
Melbourne, National Gallery of Victoria
New Haven, Yale Center for British Art
New York, Dahesh Museum of Art*
Newcastle upon Tyne, Laing Art Gallery, Tyne and Wear Museums*
Oldham, Gallery Oldham
Ottawa, National Gallery of Canada
Pasadena, Kelley Gallery
Collection John Physick CBE FSA and Mrs Eileen Physick
Plymouth City Museum and Art Gallery*
Preston, Harris Museum and Art Gallery
Prudential plc*
Rendei Township, Taiwan, Chi Mei Museum
Collection Sir Tim Rice
Rochdale, Touchstones Rochdale Art Gallery*
Collection Nicky and Roma Ryan, courtesy of the Maas Gallery*
Collection Anna Sui
Sydney, Art Gallery of New South Wales
Collection Michael Titterington****
Toronto, Art Gallery of Ontario****
Collection Stephen and Linda Waterhouse
Collection Robert and Ann Wiggins, USA
and others who wish to remain anonymous

* Lending to Groningen and Montreal only
** Lending to Montreal only
*** Lending to London only
**** Lending to London and Montreal only

FOREWORD

The British artist John William Waterhouse RA (1849–1917) is exceptional amongst major Victorian artists in that he has never been accorded a comprehensive retrospective exhibition. Given that he died during World War I, he did not receive the customary memorial exhibition at the Royal Academy of Arts, and the only presentation of his work prior to this current exhibition was a significant, but relatively modest show presented at Sheffield City Art Galleries in 1978.

Four years ago, encouraged by the success of its exhibition *Femmes Fatales,* in which Waterhouse figured significantly, the Groninger Museum decided to explore the possibility of making a comprehensive retrospective, drawing upon the considerable scholarship which had been undertaken in the field of Victorian art during the intervening years. Within Waterhouse studies this had been led by Peter Trippi, an independent art historian and the author of the biography of the artist published in 2002, who was joined by two experts in later Victorian art, Robert Upstone, Curator of Modern British Art at Tate, and Professor Elizabeth Prettejohn of the University of Bristol. Having entered into dialogue with them, the Groninger Museum was able to realise the project. Its international dimension, through its presentation at the Royal Academy of Arts, London, and at the Montreal Museum of Fine Arts, will ensure that J. W. Waterhouse RA not only returns to an institution with which he was closely involved throughout his career, but also receives thorough representation for the first time in North America. Here, a renewed interest in Pre-Raphaelite and Victorian art during the second half of the twentieth century has been as vital as that witnessed in Europe.

Born in the year that the Pre-Raphaelite Brotherhood exhibited for the first time, Waterhouse devoted his mature work to the pursuit of many of their aesthetic concerns: emotionally charged subject-matter drawn from archetypal myths and English literature; dense, claustrophobic compositions; richly worked surfaces, and a luxurious palette. Indeed, he was noted for the captivating theatricality radiating from his canvases, his engagement with important nineteenth-century themes and the superb quality of his craftsmanship.

Waterhouse's involvement with the Royal Academy of Arts was precocious but enduring. He entered the Royal Academy Schools in 1870. Four years later, at the age of 26, he saw his work hung at the annual Summer Exhibition, an honour accorded to him annually until his death in 1917. At the age of 36 he was elected an Associate Royal Academician and in 1895, aged 46, he ascended to the status of Royal Academician. He was also a regular teacher in the Schools. Such involvement with the institution fully justifies the Royal Academy's immediate response to the proposal to present this important retrospective at Burlington House, the building with which Waterhouse was familiar throughout his career.

Equally significant is the presentation of this exhibition at the Montreal Museum of Fine Arts. Despite apparently working within the context of late-nineteenth-century British art, and the Pre-Raphaelite tradition in particular, Waterhouse's association with those British artists who turned to French Naturalism in the 1870s led some of his compatriots to regard his work as cosmopolitan. His work from the mid-1880s onwards was accused of introducing into the Royal

Academy 'the mechanical art which has spread from Paris all over Europe, blotting out in its progress all artistic expression of racial instincts'. A heresy in its day, a major force today, the presence of Waterhouse's work will be an asset to the Museum of Fine Arts, whose foundation in 1860 places it at the intersection of two cultural identities, the Victorian and the French.

We wish to express our deep admiration of and sincere gratitude to the three guest curators, Peter Trippi, Robert Upstone and Elizabeth Prettejohn. Without their expertise on Waterhouse and his historical and cultural context, and their unrivalled knowledge of the current location of his works, this exhibition would not have been possible to realise. They have been assisted by the staff in our three institutions: Stijn ten Hoeve with Rianne Schoonderbeek at the Groninger Museum, MaryAnne Stevens with Caroline McCarthy and Katia Pisvin at the Royal Academy of Arts, and Paul Lavallée and Pascal Normandin at the Montreal Museum of Fine Arts.

This exhibition would not have been possible without the understanding, support and enthusiasm of the many museums and private individuals who have lent their works and, on many occasions, welcomed the guest curators and ourselves so hospitably. While our gratitude to each individual lender is expressed elsewhere in the catalogue, we would like to take this opportunity to express our especial thanks to those museums such as Tate Britain, who, by agreeing to part with their most famous paintings by Waterhouse, have deprived visitors of what are considered to be some of their favourite works.

No exhibition can be mounted without financial support from external sources. Both the exhibition and the catalogue at the Groninger Museum were generously supported by the Gasunie and GasTerra Fund for Cultural Events. Special thanks should be made to Hansch van der Velden and Ben Warner, whose enthusiasm for this project has meant that the generosity of Gasunie and GasTerra has been extended to provide support for the presentation of the exhibition at the Royal Academy of Arts.

Although one of the most popular paintings on display at Tate Britain is *The Lady of Shalott,* few of its numerous admirers know anything about its creator, John William Waterhouse RA. It is time to shed light on the paradox of this artist, highly acclaimed and popular in his day yet long since forgotten, to allow the corpus of his work to receive, at last, the full degree of admiration and recognition that it truly deserves.

Patty Wageman
Acting Director, Groninger Museum

Sir Nicholas Grimshaw CBE
President, Royal Academy of Arts

Nathalie Bondil
Director and Chief Curator, The Montreal Museum of Fine Arts

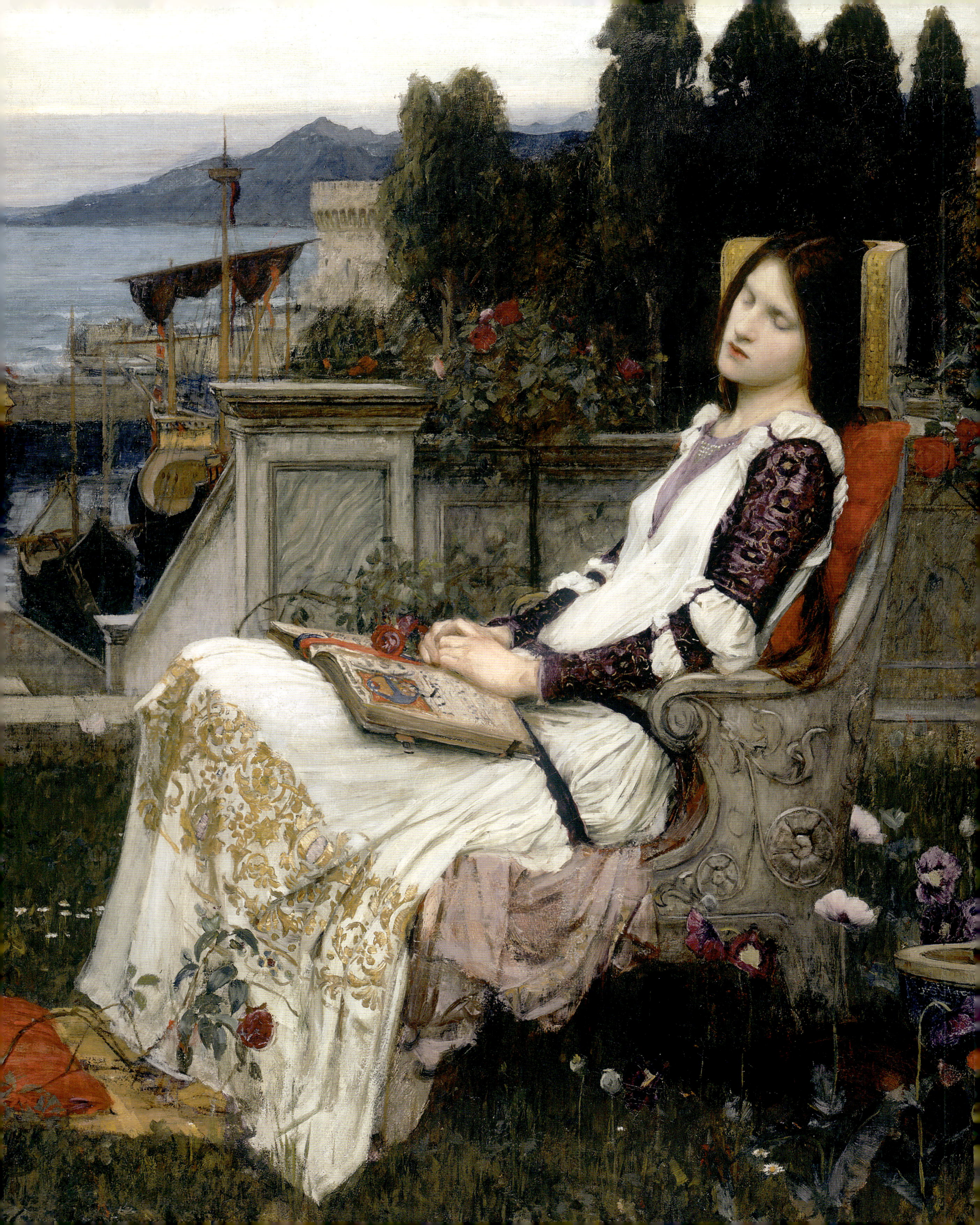

JOHN WILLIAM WATERHOUSE
A BIOGRAPHICAL OVERVIEW

Peter Trippi

Although his paintings were widely known in his day, and although he joined numerous artistic societies of high prestige, the personality of John William Waterhouse (1849-1917) was rarely mentioned by his contemporaries in their correspondence. His papers remain unlocated, and his scarce surviving letters to others suggest a man of few words. Was he painfully shy, or disagreeable? Perhaps he stuttered, or had a hearing impairment that no one dared note in writing?

Whatever the case, Waterhouse's paintings have survived to speak for him, and together they reveal a man who *felt* very deeply. Coursing through the pictures, across five decades, are Waterhouse's fascination with melancholy, magic, and the thrilling dangers of love and beauty. Several contemporary observers called his pictures poetic, not only because they are scenes imagined from poetry, but also because they are lyrical in the truest sense of the word – imbued with the same hypnotic power possessed by the ancient poets who sang their stories. This was also a man particularly enthralled with *female* beauty and the power of women over men, over nature, over each other – no matter how sturdy or fragile they might appear physically.

These questions and observations must be remembered as we examine the plain facts of Waterhouse's life. In many respects, his biography resembles that of other leading Academicians of the Victorian era, so there were probably other factors at play that cannot be traced in conventional ways.

AN ACADEMY MAN

It is appropriate that the present retrospective of Waterhouse's paintings will make one of its three appearances at the Royal Academy of Arts, the institution that lay at the centre of this painter's life. Waterhouse created most of his major pictures for display at the Academy, where he intended their glowing colours and lively brushwork to delight collectors, reviewers, and the public.

It was perhaps inevitable that Waterhouse's career should focus on the Academy, as both his parents exhibited there and they may even have met in its galleries. He was born and baptised in 1849 at Rome, the first child of the Yorkshire-born painter William Waterhouse (1816-1890) and his second wife, Isabella Mackenzie (c. 1821-1857). The child was given an Italian nickname ('Nino', short for 'Giovannino', or 'little John') that stayed with him all his life. In 1854 the family settled in Kensington (London), where his mother and two brothers later died of tuberculosis.

Within a year of his father's remarriage in 1860, Waterhouse was at school in Leeds, where he relished Roman history and contemplated engineering as a career. Back in London, he assisted his father with portraits and entered the Academy Schools as a Probationer in sculpture in 1870, at the age of 21. Six months later he was admitted as a Student, but soon began to exhibit paintings, not sculpture, at the Dudley Gallery, Society of British Artists, and elsewhere in London. These pictures ranged from *Undine* (private collection), which showed the eponymous water nymph pining by a fountain and was the first of Waterhouse's many female figures associated

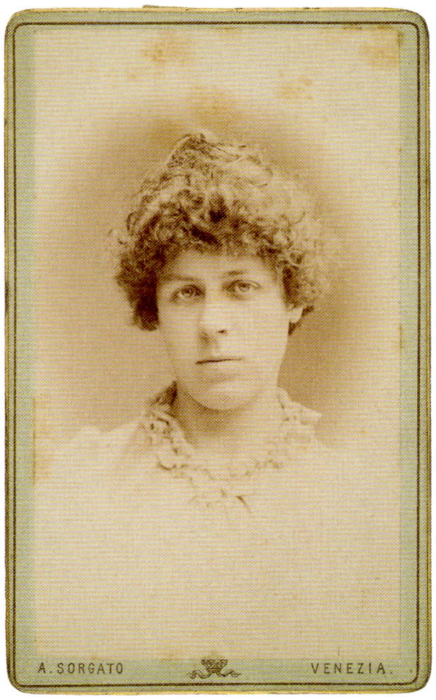

1. Esther Kenworthy Waterhouse, c. 1885, taken by Antonio Sorgato, Venice

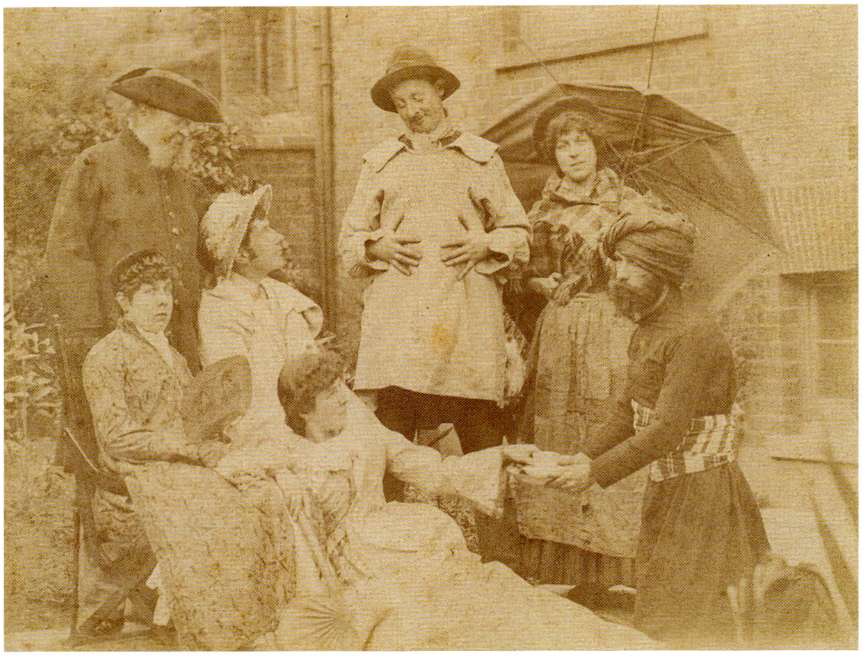

2. A fancy dress party, c. 1884-1888, Primrose Hill Studios, London. Standing: Joseph Wolf, Lance Calkin, Esther Waterhouse. Seated: Emily Kenworthy Feeney, Charles Whymper, Edith Kenworthy. Kneeling: J.W. Waterhouse in turban

with water, to an Orientalist beauty in *The Unwelcome Companion: A Street Scene in Cairo* (cat. 1).

In 1874 an allegory with Roman setting, *Sleep and his Half Brother Death* (fig. 9), became the first work by Waterhouse accepted for the Academy's Summer Exhibition, where he showed regularly until 1917. Two years later *After the Dance* (cat. 4) hung 'on the line' there, the first of his entries accorded this honour. The classicised pictures of this period echo Lawrence Alma-Tadema in their archaeological accuracy, yet their scale is larger and their mood more melancholy. Waterhouse produced genre scenes of ancient and modern life in 1877 while visiting Italy, where he was enthralled by Pompeii.

Acquisitions by municipal galleries began in 1883, when the Art Gallery of South Australia at Adelaide purchased *The Favourites of the Emperor Honorius* (cat. 12), which perfected Waterhouse's emerging fascination with the physical and psychological distance between a single figure and a group. In 1883 Waterhouse married a woman eight years his junior, the Ealing flower painter Esther Kenworthy (1857-1944), whose father was an artist and mother a school mistress. Although he was married in the Church of England, Waterhouse's ongoing depictions of ritual magic suggest that he was interested in occultism. The childless couple rented rooms near 3 Primrose Hill Studios, which Waterhouse had leased in 1878. Neighbours in this studio complex included the Antwerp-trained English painter, William Logsdail, who posed the Waterhouses and their siblings for three of his London street scenes of the late 1880s.

Waterhouse's large, dramatic pictures of supernatural women in antiquity found buyers and plaudits at the Academy: *Consulting the Oracle* (1884, cat. 15) and *St Eulalia* (1885, cat. 16) were acquired by Henry Tate, and *The Magic Circle* (1886, cat. 17) for the nation through the Academy's Chantrey Bequest. Waterhouse sent smaller genre pictures, including some of Venetian life, to the Grosvenor Gallery, Institute of Oil Painters, and Royal Institute of Painters in Water Colours; he became a member of the latter two institutions, as well as the Art Workers Guild and Arts Club. His much-noticed depiction of Eulalia's martyrdom ensured his election in 1885 as an Associate of the Royal Academy, where he proceeded to teach in the Life and Painting Schools intermittently from 1887 to 1908. Waterhouse must have enjoyed teaching generally, for he also served later as a 'Visitor' at the St John's Wood Art School, King's College School of Art for Women, and Baker Street School of Animal Painting.

TURNING POINTS

Waterhouse's prestige grew further after his enormous 1887 canvas of the Hebrew martyr *Mariamne* (cat. 18) earned medals at the world's fairs in Paris (1889), Chicago (1893), and Brussels (1897). Like the other women he painted in the 1880s, Mariamne is dramatic in her presence; even George Bernard Shaw perceived Waterhouse's fascination with the stage during this period, the heyday of Sarah Bernhardt and Ellen Terry. In 1887 the Waterhouses moved their workplace to the larger 6 Primrose Hill Studios. Through contact there with

Logsdail and the Newlyn painter Frank Bramley, Waterhouse experimented with the popular grey-toned painting techniques of the Frenchman Jules Bastien-Lepage (1848-1884). It is ironic that one of his few works in this naturalistic style, *The Lady of Shalott* of 1888 (cat. 20), has come to represent Waterhouse so prominently by virtue of its presence in the collection that Henry Tate gave the nation to form the National Gallery of British Art.

The Lady of Shalott constituted Waterhouse's first foray into Pre-Raphaelitism not only because it illustrates a scene from Tennyson's famous poem, but also because it demonstrates the powerful impact that John Everett Millais's drowning *Ophelia* of 1851-1852 (fig. 23) made when it was shown again in London in 1886. Under the spell of that meticulously detailed masterwork, Waterhouse suddenly saw that nature could – according to his 1909 biographer Rose E.D. Sketchley – 'hold out promise of an imaginative revelation to be won by sheer faithfulness of sight'.[1] Waterhouse clearly shared the widespread Victorian inter-association of water, women, and drowning: in 1889 he sent to the Academy his own naturalistic *Ophelia* (fig. 30), and ultimately exhibited two more treatments of Ophelia (figs 18, 39) and the Lady of Shalott (cats 30, 60).

Waterhouse's failure to sell the 1889 *Ophelia* may have persuaded him to try a different stylistic course. In 1890 his father died, and he did not exhibit at the Academy for the first time in sixteen years. Like so much of the artist's life, this hiatus is undocumented, but it seems to have encompassed a self-reinvention, possibly while visiting Italy: in 1891 he reappeared in the London exhibitions with a new fascination for classical enchantresses drawn from Homer and Ovid, and with a more jewel-toned palette.

This mature and very successful phase opened with *Ulysses and the Sirens* (cat. 22), acquired by the National Gallery of Victoria in Melbourne upon the advice of Academy President Frederic Leighton and other senior Academicians, who also recommended *Circe Invidiosa* (cat. 23) to the Art Gallery of South Australia in 1892.

THE HEYDAY

From this point, Waterhouse specialised in wistful, mildly eroticized maidens – their singular beauty both natural and unattainable – posed in timeless settings that evoke a vaguely melancholy other-world. Whether these women appear alone, supplicating or enchanting a man, or in pairs or groups, Waterhouse usually bypassed vigorous action for a stillness that conveys the stories' pivotal moments: *The Times* saw them as 'pre-Raphaelite pictures in a more modern manner' painted by 'a kind of academic Burne-Jones, like him in his types and his moods, but with less insistence on design and more on atmosphere'.[2]

A number of influential critics supported Waterhouse, especially at *The Studio,* which gave heavy coverage to

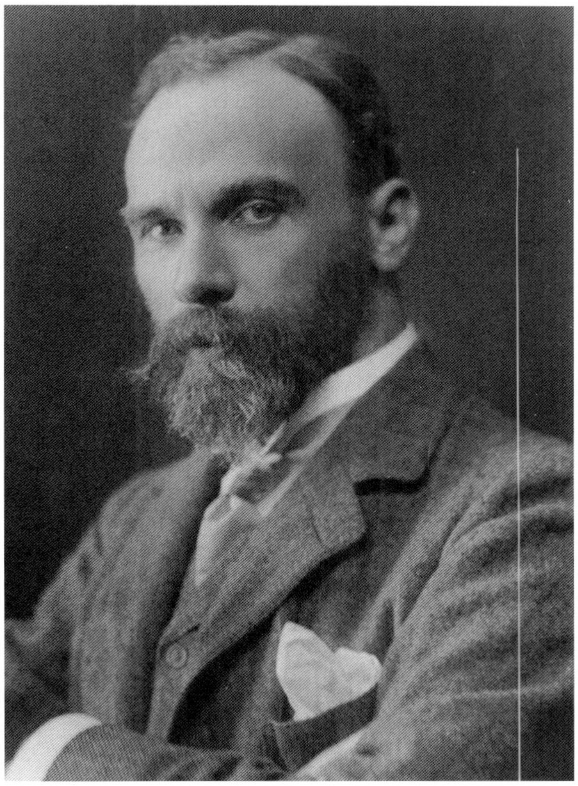

3. J.W. Waterhouse, c. 1886, taken by H.S. Mendelssohn, London

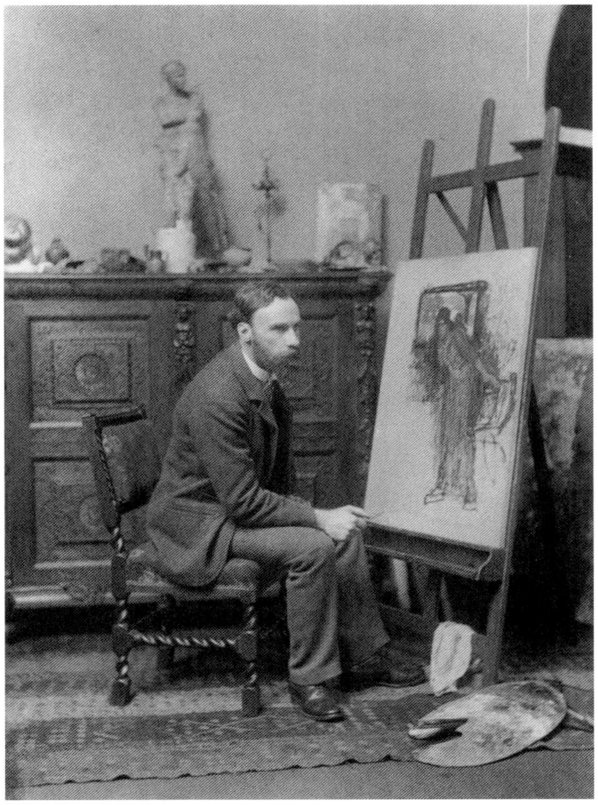

4. J.W. Waterhouse with a version of *The Lady of Shalott*, c. 1891, taken by Ralph Winwood Robinson, London

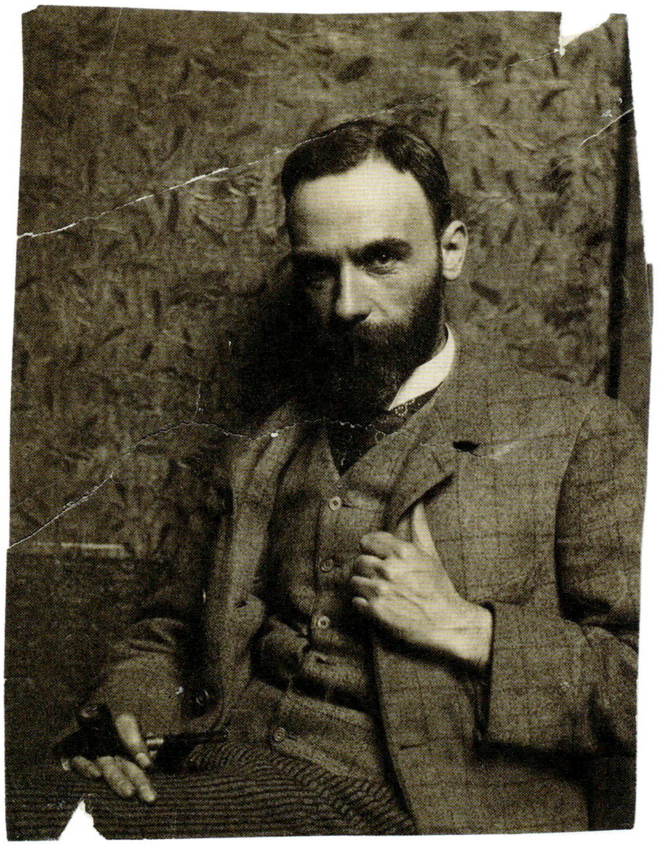

5. J.W. Waterhouse, c. 1890-1895, photographer unknown

St Cecilia (cat. 31), painted over a two-year period before it won acclaim at the Academy in 1895. Editor Gleeson White argued that this and other Waterhouse paintings were 'decorative panels of colour, less conventional than tapestry, less flat than if they were mural decoration, but all the same, not openings through a wall looking into the real world or the world of fancy, but panels self-replete with beauty of line, beauty of mass, and beauty of colour'.[3]

White deemed Waterhouse's 1894 *Ophelia* (fig. 39) 'wellnigh as typical of the forces that influence the younger school to-day as Millais' 'Ophelia' was in 1852. Then Pre-Raphaelitism was as much 'in the air', as decorative treatment has been for some years past.'[4] Indeed, many commentators perceived such decoration as the latest phase of Pre-Raphaelitism, which in the 1890s saw such founders as Ford Madox Brown, Millais, and Burne-Jones pass. Along with Frank Dicksee, Arthur Hacker, Maurice Greiffenhagen, Frank Brangwyn, and others in their thirties and forties, Waterhouse was therefore championed by some conservatives as one of their natural successors, heterogeneous though these younger men were.

The critic Claude Phillips counted Waterhouse among 'the moderates of modernity', those who embraced 'the modern French standpoint' without disregarding 'the face of English art'.[5] Harry Quilter hailed *St Cecilia* as 'one of the most brilliant and essentially modern performances of this eclectic age ... Mr. Waterhouse has chosen, so to speak, a pre-Raphaelite subject, and yet has treated it in a way that is not pre-Raphaelite any more than it is impressionist, or touched with any other affectation'.[6] Such allusions to individuality *and* eclecticism recurred throughout the 1890s; even today Waterhouse's mature pictures strike us as distinctive and yet somehow evocative of earlier masters.

Not everyone approved, however: The progressive D.S. MacColl attacked *Circe Offering the Cup to Ulysses* as 'half-realism, which is convincing neither as dream nor as daylight'.[7] A painter himself, MacColl overlapped with Waterhouse for two years in the decoration-minded Art Workers Guild, and it would be fascinating to know how they interacted there.

The sensation of the 1897 Summer Exhibition was *Hylas and the Nymphs* (cat. 32), in which *jeunes filles fatales* seduce a typically powerless young man. Its interlocking gazes, languid mood, moral ambiguity, and timeless setting mark it as one of Waterhouse's masterworks.

Because Waterhouse found beauty and emotional power in both classical and romantic literature, he could celebrate – within the same decade – Psyche, Ariadne, Keats's *La Belle Dame Sans Merci,* Tennyson's Mariana and Lady Clare, and Shakespeare's Juliet. Although he is best known for Tennysonian scenes, he actually painted more episodes from Ovid's superbly pictorial *Metamorphoses,* including *Echo and Narcissus* (cat. 43). Like Ophelia and the Lady of Shalott, Ovid's characters act out the passionate awakenings, deaths, and transfigurations that elevate their tales into myths conveying a hopeful message of regeneration.

This openness was duly noted by Claude Phillips: 'For a cold pseudo-classicism, which to-day convinces neither the painter nor his public, Mr. J.W. Waterhouse substitutes a romanticism with which his own artistic temperament, as well as that of his [English] race, is thoroughly in accord.'[8] Indeed, it would seem Waterhouse had found a way to please both the elite and the public: in 1895, another critic reported that, despite Waterhouse's status as 'a painter's painter, he has always enjoyed an astonishingly broad popularity'.[9] That year, still basking in the fresh acclaim for *St Cecilia,* Waterhouse was elected to the status of full Academician, after annual nominations since 1892. He served on the Academy's governing council intermittently between 1896 and 1911, and in 1899 was invited to join the socially exclusive Athenaeum Club.

A PAINTER'S PAINTER

From the 1880s onward, observers noted Waterhouse's capacity to compose without the exhaustive studies used by many other academicians. His thirteen surviving sketchbooks (see seven of them at cats 92-98) contain studies in pencil and compositions tested from different viewpoints, only some

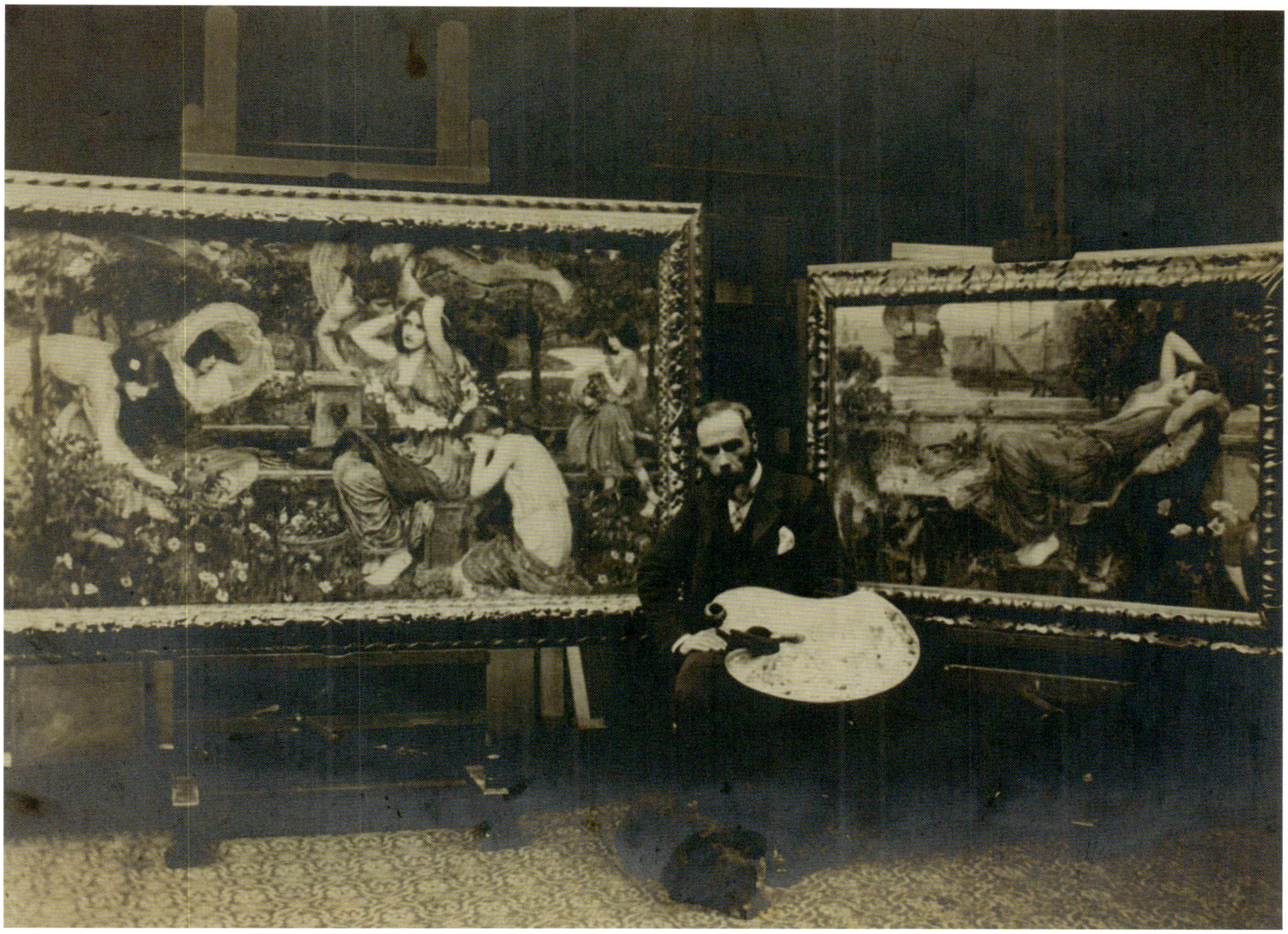

6. J.W. Waterhouse with his two Academy exhibits of 1898, *Flora and the Zephyrs* (left) and *Ariadne* (cat. 34). Its inscription in pencil ('With Mr. McCulloch's best wishes for a Happy Xmas and a Happy New Year, 25 Dec. '98') indicates this photograph was taken for the collector George McCulloch, who bought *Flora and the Zephyrs*, *St Cecilia*, and the 1894 *Ophelia*. On the reverse is a pencil sketch, possibly by Waterhouse, of what appears to be the nymph who holds Hylas's arm in cat. 32. Image: 40.5 x 56 cm, mounted on board and deteriorating from silver oxidization. Victoria and Albert Museum, London, E.526-2008.

of which led to finished canvases. In his studio with a model (usually female) and occasionally a lay figure, Waterhouse drew on sheets with pencil, charcoal, or chalk and made lively oil sketches on canvas, board, or panel.

Fortunately, Waterhouse scribbled the names of some models in his sketchbooks. Perpetuating an academic tradition, he transcended their particularities to create his own idealised, instantly recognizable type of female beauty. Scholars' attention has focused on the woman who appears in more than 60 paintings from 1889 to the artist's death in 1917. The search for her name has pivoted on a drawing for the 1905 *Lamia* (cat. 75) inscribed 'Miss Muriel Foster/ Buxton Rd/Chingford', but this annotation is problematic and the search remains open.[10] Given their three-decade relationship, this 'Waterhouse girl' surely functioned as the artist's muse.

Waterhouse purchased primed canvases and brushed upon them the main lines of his composition with dark, flowing paint mixed with an easy-to-handle medium. He then laid in the basic tonal relationships as blocks of thinned, translucent colour, such as pale green or fawn. Unfinished oils reveal that he did not fully articulate figures that would ultimately be covered with draperies, and that he devoted his keenest attention to faces and hair.

Waterhouse worked intensively at the easel, applying as many as twelve layers of paint to achieve his desired effect. Microscopic sampling shows that he gathered up to six different pigments in one brushload: for example, the metalwork he loved to depict (e.g., cat. 47) appears brownish yellow to the eye, but actually contains ultramarine, viridian, yellow ochre, charcoal black, sienna, and prismatic lead white.[11] *St Cecilia* is one of at least four canvases containing

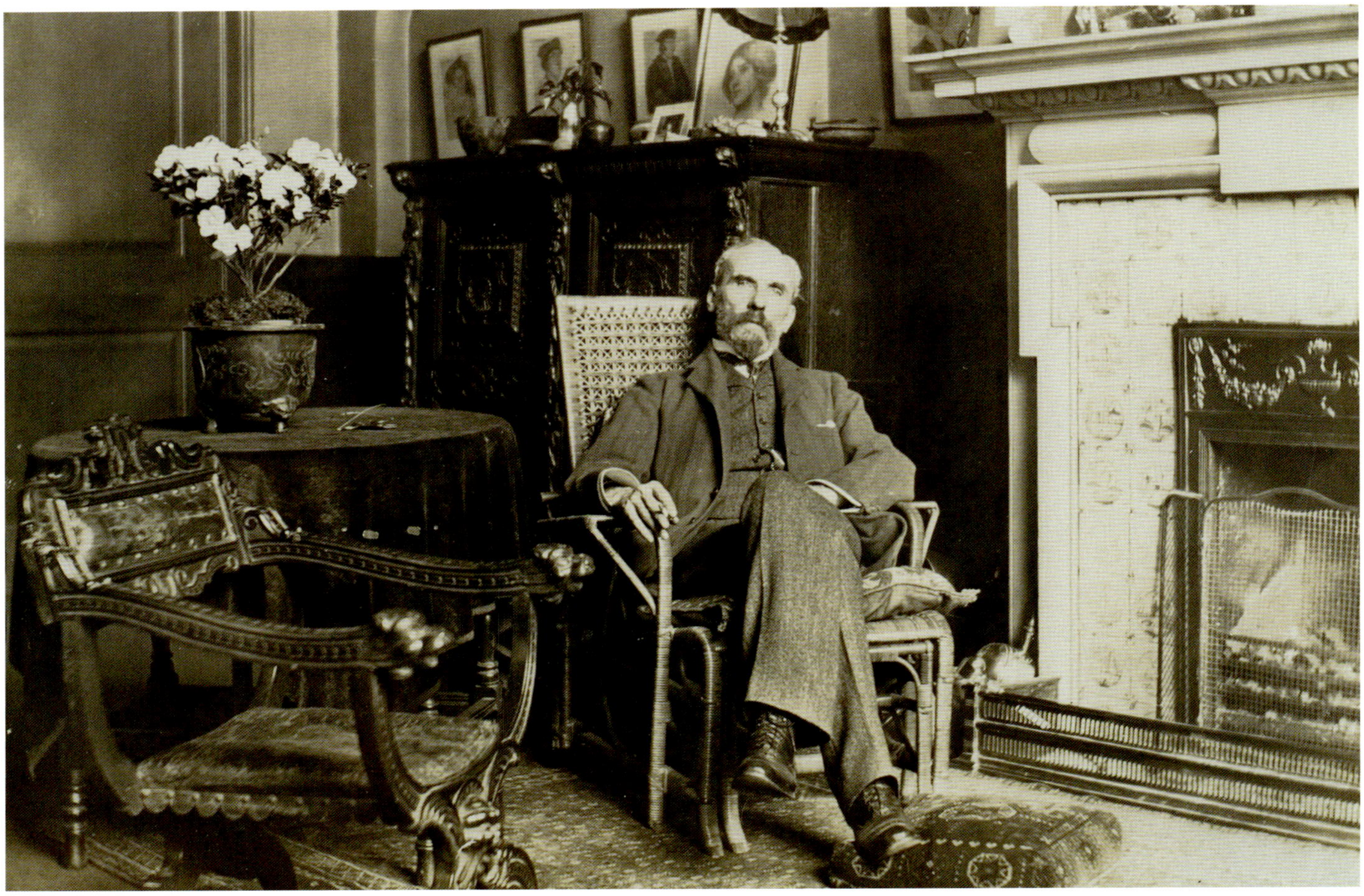

7. J.W. Waterhouse in his studio, 1913, taken by Holloway of Notting Hill

verdigris, and it also has an interleaving of ground gold leaf. The presence of such expensive materials where they cannot be seen confirms that Waterhouse compulsively added layers to refine his vision, and indeed several major canvases contain pentimenti. We know that he altered several pictures even after they were purchased, and for at least two others he extended the canvas to complete the composition.

In view of such perfectionism, one understands why the collector James Murray complained that 'W[aterhouse] & his wife have no sense of time'.[12] Letters show that he rushed to complete works for the Academy's 'sending-in day,' and his failure to let paint layers dry may account for the distinctive crackling of many pictures' surfaces. Waterhouse knew of this problem: in 1899 he recommended filling cracks with watercolours to reduce its visual impact.

We still do not know why Waterhouse told a census-taker in 1891 that he was both a 'painter' and a 'sculptist.'[13] He knew several of Britain's so-called New Sculptors, whose idealised images of women in contemplation resemble Waterhouse's both formally and in their Symbolist undercurrents. Particularly similar are those of his fellow Art-Worker Harry Bates ARA (1850-1899), whose large studio house, at 10 Hall Road in the prestigious London neighbourhood of St John's Wood, was acquired by the Waterhouses in 1900. Equally intriguing is Waterhouse's sparsely documented friendship with George Frampton RA (1860-1928): by 1911 he owned at least two bronze heads by Frampton.[14] The relatively large delegation of New Sculptors at Waterhouse's funeral points to his continuing interest in this area.

LATER YEARS, AND THE AFTERLIFE

As critics turned against explicit narrative during the 1900s, Waterhouse painted more and more women seated by streams or picking bright flowers. Seemingly plotless, several of these canvases actually allude to the Ovidian abductions of Oreithyia and Proserpina. Having once enclosed his women in gardens and glades, Waterhouse now opened his pictures to expansive meadows drenched in silvery light.

His recognizable – if not progressive – style still attracted (conservative) buyers. Waterhouse particularly cultivated the financier Alexander Henderson, later first Baron Faringdon. Henderson's extended family socialized with Waterhouse from the 1890s – ultimately owning more than 40 pictures by him, including commissioned portraits. In 1912 the Aberdeen Art Gallery paid £1,400 for *Penelope and the Suitors* (cat. 58), and the next year *St Cecilia* brought a remarkable £2,415 at the mining magnate George McCulloch's estate dispersal. *The Annunciation* (1914, private collection), Waterhouse's only biblical scene, marked a renewed emphasis on narratives in historical settings closely associated with early Pre-Raphaelitism, and thus with Englishness. Other such themes included Shakespeare's Miranda from *The Tempest* (cat. 62), Tristram and Isolde from Thomas Malory's *Morte d'Arthur* (cat. 63), and episodes from Giovanni Boccaccio's *Il Decameron* (cats 65, 66). Several of these late works were acquired by the soap magnate W.H. Lever: he later bought *The Enchanted Garden* (cat. 66), which was on the easel when Waterhouse died of liver cancer in 1917.

In retrospect, Waterhouse's passing in the midst of a cataclysmic world war seems almost timely. In its memorial tribute, *The Studio* classed Waterhouse 'among the best of our romanticist painters' for 'the right atmosphere of poetic suggestion', yet *The Times* thought eclecticism had limited Waterhouse's originality – a modernist perspective anticipating the rapid decline in his reputation.[15] Attending Waterhouse's funeral in St John's Wood were patrons such as James Murray and H.W. Henderson; the artists included Academy President E.J. Poynter, Herbert Draper, Briton Riviere, and William Strang.

He was interred at Kensal Green Cemetery in London, where his widow was also buried in 1944. Instead of receiving his own memorial exhibition at the Royal Academy, as Alma-Tadema had in 1913, Waterhouse was represented in a 1922 show of recently deceased Academicians. His widow held a 100 lot studio sale at Christie's in 1926, when Waterhouse's work was so unfashionable that the 1889 *Ophelia* sold for only £450.

The nadir in Waterhouse's reputation actually came in the 1940s and 1950s, when two British galleries de-accessioned his works and a privately owned masterwork (cat. 46) went to auction unrecognised. Since the 1960s, more Waterhouses have been reproduced commercially, and the 1888 version of *The Lady of Shalott* has become Tate's best-selling postcard. An important advance was made by the scholar Anthony Hobson (1920-2000), whose 1989 monograph is still in print, and who co-organized, with Anne Goodchild, the first retrospective at Sheffield and Wolverhampton in 1978-1979.

The revival of interest in Waterhouse moved to a new level in 2000 when headlines worldwide announced that the Andrew Lloyd Webber Art Foundation had acquired *St Cecilia* for £6.6 million, still the highest price known to be paid for a Victorian painting. Waterhouse would surely be pleased by the growing acclaim, and hopefully by the present retrospective, the largest gathering of his works ever.

1 R.E.D. Sketchley, *The Art of J.W. Waterhouse, R.A.*, Christmas Number of *The Art Journal*, 1909, p. 15.
2 *The Times*, 12 February 1917, p. 6.
3 Gleeson White, *The Master Painters of Britain*, London, 1898, vol. 4, p. 10.
4 *Ibid.*
5 *Academy* 1201, 11 May 1895, p. 407.
6 *The Times*, 4 May 1895, p. 12.
7 *Spectator*, 16 May 1891, p. 693.
8 *Academy* 1255, 23 May 1896, p. 432.
9 *The Art Journal*, June 1895, p. 176.
10 James K. Baker and Cathy L. Baker, 'Miss Muriel Foster: The John William Waterhouse Model', *Journal of Pre-Raphaelite Studies* 8, autumn 1999, pp. 70-82; and 'The Lamia in the Art of J.W. Waterhouse', *British Art Journal*, vol. V, no. 2 (Autumn 2004), pp. 15-22.
11 Technical analysis was conducted for the author in 2000 by Libby Sheldon of University College London.
12 Aberdeen Art Gallery Archive; annotation by Murray on a letter dated 25 December 1911 that he had received from Waterhouse.
13 1891 Census, St Pancras parish, sheet RG12/118, 44 Chalcot Cres. Thanks to Michael Kelley.
14 *International Fine Arts Exhibition Rome 1911, British Section Catalogue* (London, 1911, 2nd ed.), p. 71. JWW lent these to the Sculpture section (cats. 1116, 1117).
15 A.L. Baldry, 'The Late J.W. Waterhouse, R.A.', *Studio*, Vol. LXXI, June 1917, p. 10; and *The Times*, 12 February 1917, p. 6.

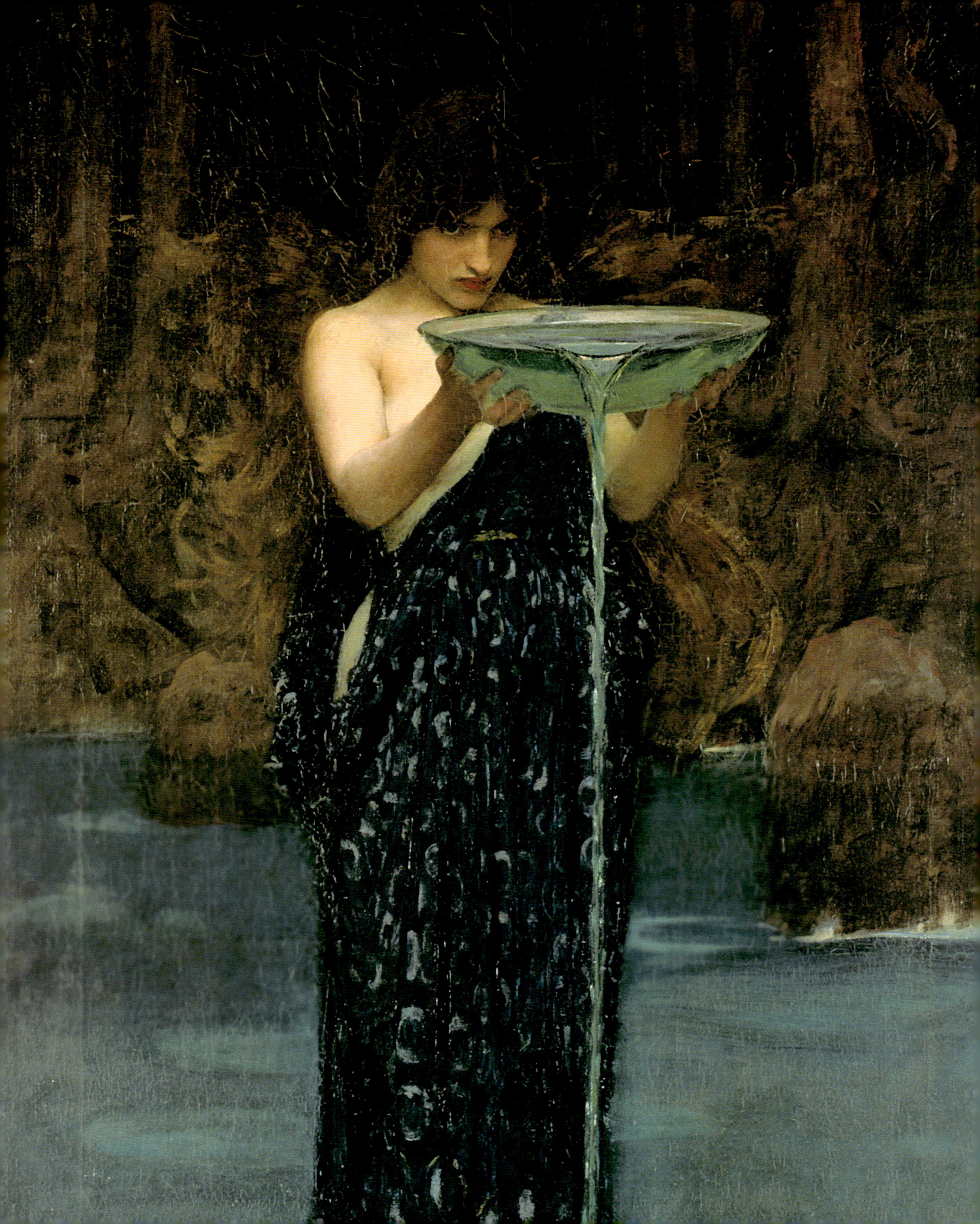

WATERHOUSE'S IMAGINATION

Elizabeth Prettejohn

'He lives in a world of his own imagining', wrote the critic Alfred Lys Baldry of Waterhouse in 1908;[1] the next year, in the longest account of Waterhouse's art published during his lifetime, Rose E.D. Sketchley described a 'distinct imaginative system' in which all the work of his artistic maturity cohered.[2] Both phrases seem to point to something more thoroughgoing than mere inventiveness in Waterhouse's work; indeed, both critics freely acknowledged that he drew his themes from the most traditional of sources, ancient and medieval history and legend. Some of Waterhouse's most famous paintings – *The Lady of Shalott*, *Ophelia*, *Ariadne* – dealt with subject-matter that had already inspired countless paintings on the walls of the annual Royal Academy exhibitions. Yet Waterhouse's imagination seemed not merely to produce new readings of old stories. For these and other critics, Waterhouse was able to create a world of his own, a world in which nothing was commonplace and yet everything made sense, where saints or naiads, witches or heroes appeared at home. Indeed, for the French painter Edmond Aman-Jean, writing in 1896, Waterhouse's world was, if anything, *too* plausible; it seemed 'to lack that air of mystery, befitting the weird old myths of the days of the gods'.[3] How did Waterhouse's imagination work this magic, to make the 'weird' stories of the remote past look only natural?

Waterhouse's exhibiting career lasted forty-five years, from his first attempt to sell three modest pictures at a minor London exhibition in 1872 (unusually for a first-time exhibitor, he sold all three) to his final, posthumous showing at the Royal Academy, just months after his death in 1917. Over this long period, the character of his subject-matter changed appreciably, and critics in the later decades of his career delighted in dividing it into phases. But one feature remained constant: apart from the occasional portrait, and a few pictures of scenes encountered in his travels, Waterhouse painted only subjects set in the distant past. As Baldry put it, his pictorial world was one 'which knows nothing of the stress and turmoil of modern life'.[4] Unlike so many painters of his generation, including some of his close friends, he was never tempted to capture the transient appearances of fashionable society, urban development, or contemporary rural life. It does not follow, however, that his art was impervious to modern ideas: on the contrary, each new phase in his career engaged in some way with the latest thinking on some issue of contemporary concern. Too little is known about Waterhouse's life to be sure about which books or journals he may have read, which of London's social circles he may have frequented, or what kinds of art he may have seen on journeys abroad. But his paintings clearly demonstrate that he was alive to the exciting new developments of the later nineteenth and early twentieth centuries in archaeology, anthropology, comparative mythology, the study of ancient and modern religions, occultism, and the revival of paganism.

SCENES OF ANCIENT LIFE

Victorian critics, as well as more recent scholars, have often called attention to the influence of Lawrence Alma-

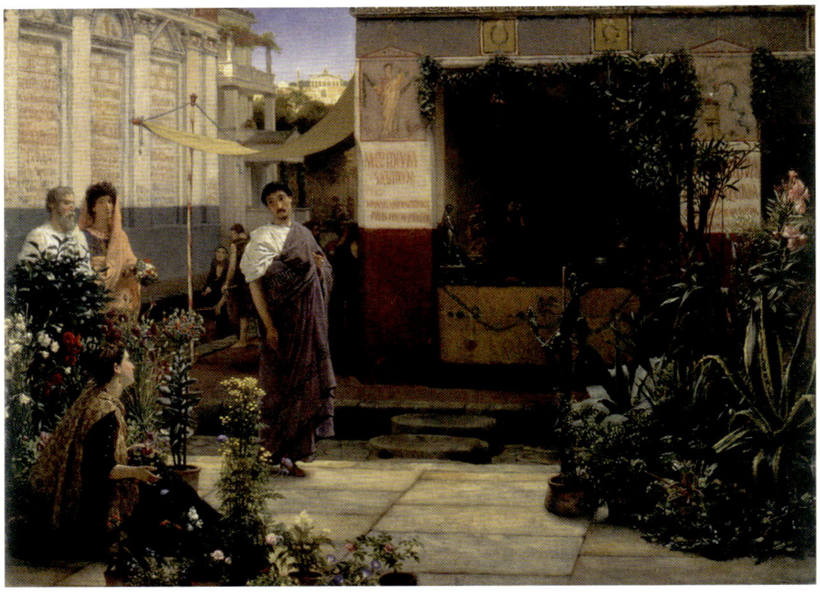

8. Lawrence Alma-Tadema, *The Flower Market*, 1868, Oil on panel, 42.1 x 58 cm, Manchester City Galleries

Tadema, the Dutch painter who settled in London in 1870, on Waterhouse's early work. Alma-Tadema was the pioneer of a new approach to classical subject-matter, which concentrated on the lives of ordinary people in the ancient world, rather than the heroic deeds of generals and statesmen. His first biographer, the German archaeologist and historical novelist Georg Ebers, clearly indicated the democratic political resonances of this range of subject-matter:

> The student leaves the gymnasium with the knowledge of numerous political events, many names of kings, and dates. Not until, released from school restraint, he goes back independently to the sources of information, does he discover that he has learned little of the character and life of the peoples he has been shown.... [H]e joyfully perceives how much more delightful it is to make himself familiar with the homes of the people to be investigated, the regulation of their government, their civil and social life, their religion and science, than to know the names and bloody deeds of their kings and the battles they fought.[5]

Alma-Tadema was inspired to embark on this project by a visit to Pompeii in 1863-1864, when he saw the first results of a new phase of excavation in the ancient town, under the innovative direction of the archaeologist Giuseppe Fiorelli. While Pompeii and its twin site, Herculaneum, had been continuously excavated since the mid-eighteenth century, Fiorelli initiated a dramatic new approach: instead of recovering artefacts from the site, for display in a museum setting, Fiorelli concentrated on clearing debris from the site itself so that Pompeii's streets, public buildings, and private houses could be experienced as a lived environment. The vividness of this experience, as well as the abundant discoveries of household objects in the course of excavation, encouraged Alma-Tadema to elaborate his pictures of ancient life with an unprecedented wealth of circumstantial detail. The first time he exhibited at the Royal Academy, in 1869, the critic for the leading British art periodical, *The Art Journal*, responded with astonishment: 'The picture restores to life what has been dead in antiquarian detail; the old Roman citizen now walks before us, treading on ancient mosaics and surrounded by antique bronzes and classic columns'.[6]

Waterhouse followed in Alma-Tadema's footsteps when he visited Pompeii in 1877. According to J.A. Blaikie, in the first published article on Waterhouse, 'his imagination was kindled by reading in the ruined streets of Pompeii the melodramatic romance of its last days', Edward Bulwer Lytton's bestselling novel of 1834, *The Last Days of Pompeii*.[7] Waterhouse sketched the reconstructed streets and dwellings of the ancient town, which his paintings would repopulate with their lost inhabitants, much as the historical novelist had done in words; the watercolour *Scene at Pompeii* (cat. 6), for example, records the distinctive red-painted columns that would reappear in such works as *Dolce Far Niente* of 1880 (cat. 8). Waterhouse shared Alma-Tadema's politically progressive fascination with the lives of ordinary people, and many of his early subjects parallel those of the older painter: scenes of domestic religion, such as *The Household Gods* of 1880 (cat. 9), or of humble commercial transactions, as in *A Flower Stall* of the same

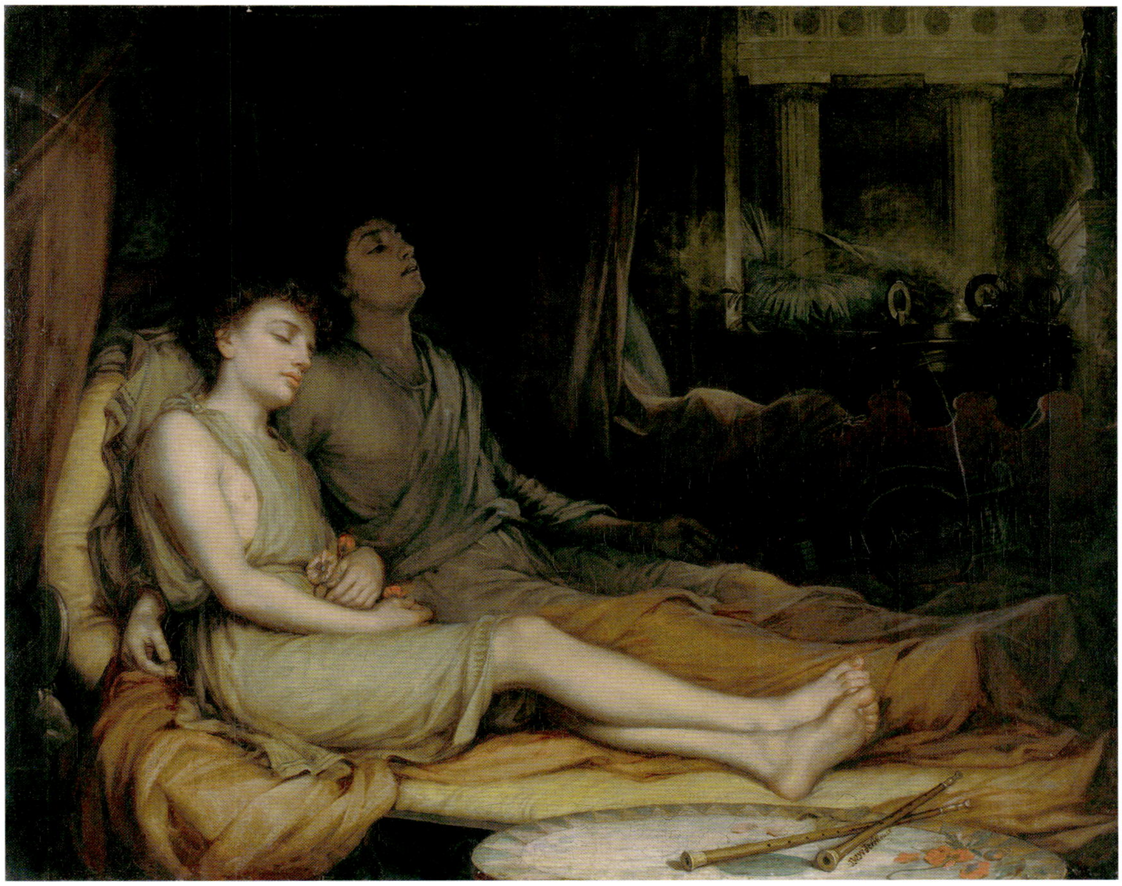

9. J.W. Waterhouse, *Sleep and his Half-Brother Death*, 1874, Oil on canvas, 72 x 92 cm, Private collection courtesy of Sotheby's

year (cat. 10), reminiscent of Alma-Tadema's *The Flower Market* of 1868 (fig. 8). But even in these early paintings, Waterhouse was developing his own, distinctive approach. Like Alma-Tadema, he carefully researched the material culture of the ancient Roman world, but from the start Waterhouse's scenes were more spacious and more sparing of antiquarian detail. The square brazier before the domestic shrine in *The Household Gods* recalls an example from the House of the Faun in Pompeii, which Waterhouse could have seen in the Naples Archaeological Museum (no. 72991), but its decorative details, in which Alma-Tadema would surely have delighted, are notably simplified in Waterhouse's painting, so that attention is clearly focussed on the ritual actions of the two figures. Alma-Tadema's *Flower Market* weaves the encounter between the flower-seller and her patrician client, in the foreground, together with a wealth of additional information about the social and commercial life of Pompeii: the wine-shop to the right, the notice-board teeming with advertisements on the building to the left, workers unloading wine-jars and drawing water from a well in the left background. Waterhouse's *Flower Stall* concentrates, instead, on a single incident of women choosing flowers, set against the clean, sunlit lines of a street corner. Moreover, the profusion of fragrant roses recalls the emphasis on sensuous delight of the contemporary Aesthetic Movement.[8]

Waterhouse's allegiance to the ideal of 'art for art's sake' reaches its culmination in *Dolce Far Niente* of 1879 (cat. 7), with its striking golden sunflower, one of the quintessential symbols of the Aesthetic Movement. As in many paintings by Alma-Tadema, the ancient Roman world appears as one of opulence and leisure, yet Waterhouse introduces distinctive touches of his own. The foreshortened pose of the figure, turned obliquely into depth, adumbrates such later works as *St Eulalia* (cat. 16), and helps to capture the ephemeral moment of the title – 'sweet doing nothing' – as the white feathers flutter in mid-air, brilliant highlights against the marble wall. With utmost delicacy, the painting hints at a contrast between the momentary pleasures of the young girl and the remote antiquity of the Roman marble setting.

Even in these unpretentious scenes, then, Waterhouse creates his own special style; his pictures are notably simpler and more concentrated in design than Alma-Tadema's, and present only a few piquant artefacts, such as the accurately rendered hanging lamp in *Dolce Far Niente*. But Waterhouse's principal works of the period, the ones he showed at the Royal Academy (the most prestigious exhibiting venue in London), develop a more serious range of concerns, and they do so with unusual ambition for an artist still in his twenties. *Sleep and his Half-Brother Death*, Waterhouse's first Royal Academy exhibit in 1874 (fig. 9), *After the Dance* of 1876 (cat. 4), and *A Sick Child Brought into the Temple of Aesculapius* of 1877 (cat. 5) all represent scenes of childhood in the ancient world with a sense of wistfulness or melancholy. These are not playful anecdotes about children, of the kind familiar in Victorian painting; instead they engage with sober questions about childhood illness, death, and (in the case of *After the Dance*) labour. Moreover, they are increasingly large in scale, reaching genuine monumentality in *A Sick Child*, at just over two metres wide larger than almost all of Alma-Tadema's paintings to date, and on the scale of the grandest paintings by Frederic Leighton, the foremost English painter of classical subjects who would be elected President of the Royal Academy in 1878. According to such accounts as have survived, Waterhouse was an unassuming man; certainly he never aspired to hold public office in the British art world. Already, however, in his first decade as a Royal Academy exhibitor, he was staking a claim to become one of the leading painters of the generation after Leighton.

HISTORY PAINTING

Towards the end of the 1870s, Waterhouse embarked on a series of paintings that, while they drew on the same archaeological research that informed his scenes of ancient life, attempted something highly unusual in the British art world of the day, although it was a longstanding tradition in the continental painting of the centuries since the Renaissance: the depiction of important events from Greek, Roman, and Early Christian history. This was exactly the traditional range of subject-matter from which Alma-Tadema, according to Ebers, deliberately distanced his work, and for Baldry, reviewing Waterhouse's career in 1895, the move 'was in a measure retrograde, in the direction of Academic painting'.[9] Baldry's reservation is understandable, coming from a critic who championed the progressive art associated with the slogan 'art for art's sake', but it fails to acknowledge the considerable daring involved in choosing a range of subjects that, while they held the highest status in traditional art theories, had never achieved any great popularity, or commercial success, in England. Furthermore, the historical subjects Waterhouse chose were complex and challenging; they drew on erudite sources well beyond the standard range of education and reading among the audiences that encountered them at exhibition, and involved powerful moral, psychological, political, or religious issues.

The series began in 1878, just the year after *A Sick Child*, with *The Remorse of Nero after the Murder of his Mother* (fig. 10). The Roman Emperor Nero was, of course, a household name, a watchword for the utmost in Imperial cruelty and depravity; the scene of Nero playing the lyre while the city of Rome burned had often been painted, notably by Benjamin Robert Haydon in a painting exhibited in 1846. Indeed, Haydon's name remained famous throughout the Victorian period precisely because of the utter failure of his ambition to achieve success as a historical painter in the grand manner, widely reputed as the cause of his suicide in 1846 – just after painting his *Nero*. In choosing Nero as the subject of his first exhibited history painting, Waterhouse was perhaps declaring a determination to carry on Haydon's project, or to succeed where Haydon had failed. Yet Waterhouse did not choose the stock scene of Nero with his lyre; instead he invented an episode, drawing on reports by Roman historians of Nero's deranged mental state after he had ordered the assassination of his own mother.[10] The event is equally shocking, and in Waterhouse's interpretation it becomes psychologically and morally intense. Is the viewer meant to sympathise with the still boyish Emperor, who has thrown himself on his couch in an agony of remorse, his fists clenched to support an anguished – or petulant – face? Or is this a sinister comment on the potential of absolute power to corrupt absolutely, with possible contemporary relevance to the growing imperial power of Victorian Britain? The cool classical elegance of the palace interior, and the absence of additional clues to the surrounding narrative, leave the answer uncertain.

Similar complexities animate each of the succeeding paintings of historical events. *Diogenes* of 1882 (cat. 11) juxtaposes the Cynic philosopher who spent his life in the fruitless search for an honest man with a bevy of attractive women; should we admire his rectitude or shudder at the self-imposed squalor of the tub in which he insisted on living, as a declaration of his contempt for riches? *The Favourites of the Emperor Honorius* of 1883 (cat. 12) shows a later Emperor (reigned 395-423 A.D.) feeding his birds while his courtiers fawn; does the painting censure Honorius's dereliction of duty, the courtiers' sycophancy, or both? *Consulting the Oracle* of 1884 (cat. 15) represents an ancient Jewish custom of seeking prophetic utterances from a mummified human head; is this an anthopological exploration of an interesting ancient custom, or an indictment of superstition? *St Eulalia* of 1885 (cat. 16) draws on the fourth-century Latin poet Prudentius to show a girl-martyr, her body pathetically abandoned in the forum; should the viewer feel uneasy about enjoying the half-nude body with its flowing hair, in the context of a scene of violent death? Finally, *Mariamne* of 1887 (cat. 18) presents the rejected wife of the Jewish king Herod the Great, a story from the Jewish historian of the first century A.D., Flavius Josephus. But Josephus gives two very different versions

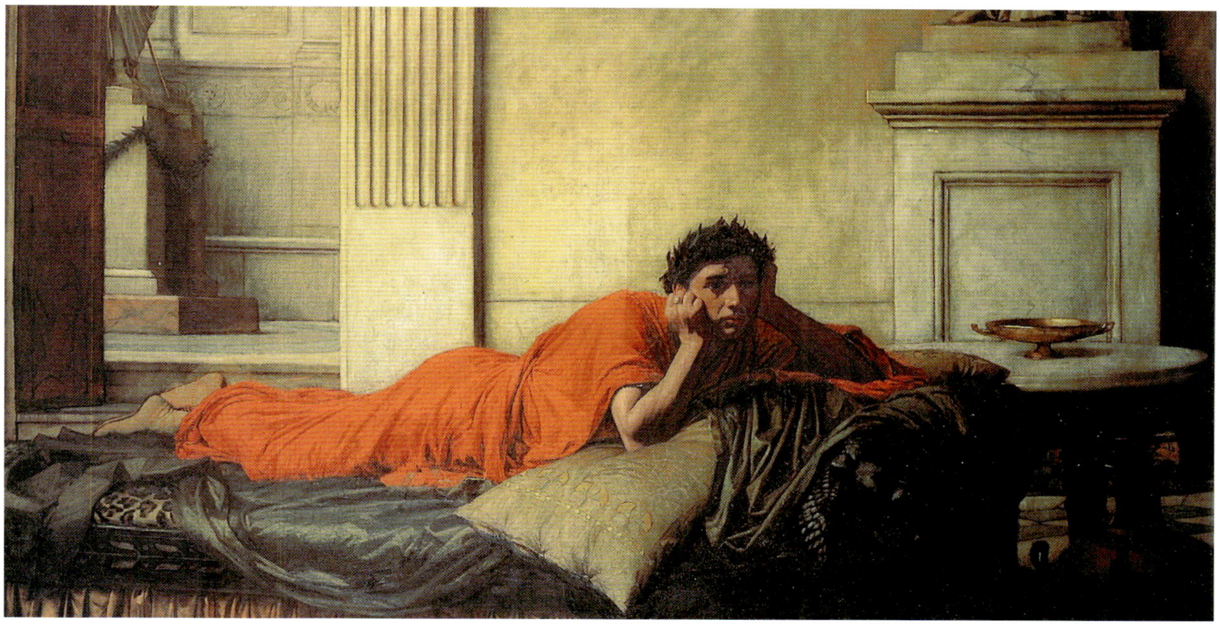

10. J.W. Waterhouse, *The Remorse of Nero after the Murder of his Mother,* 1878, Oil on canvas, 94 x 168 cm, Private collection

of Mariamne's story: is she a tragic victim, or an arrogant schemer?[11] In all of these subjects there is a dark or sinister edge; how should the viewer square that with the material splendour and artistic elegance of the sumptuous ancient setting represented in each painting?

In this sequence of paintings, all of them unusually large in scale and ambitious in subject-matter for the British Royal Academy, Waterhouse honed his skill as a pictorial dramatist. The catalogues of Royal Academy exhibitions routinely included quotations from the texts from which painters drew their subjects, in an art world notorious throughout Europe for its literary predilections. Waterhouse occasionally included a reference to one of his erudite sources, but he seldom quoted a lengthy passage, and for good reason: his paintings did not illustrate their sources with the minute fidelity of so much Victorian painting. Instead Waterhouse painstakingly invented a pictorial composition which, in each case, wholly transformed the literary subject into visual drama. We can often trace the process through sketchbooks, drawings, and oil sketches, which experiment now with one, now another grouping of figures, or placement of architectural and landscape elements, to arrive gradually at a composition that could convey its complex story with utmost clarity. The two surviving oil sketches for *The Favourites of the Emperor Honorius* provide a striking example of how Waterhouse, after deciding on a basic plan that juxtaposed the Emperor with his courtiers, adjusted the precise relationships among the figures and architectural elements several times, to arrive finally at a supremely lucid balance between the figure groups (cats 13, 14).

Mariamne, the culminating work in Waterhouse's series of history paintings, is also the largest picture he ever made, more than two-and-a-half metres high by nearly two metres wide. If the aim of the series was to establish Waterhouse's credentials as a worthy successor to the High Art tradition in European painting, it was successful: Waterhouse was elected Associate of the Royal Academy in 1885, immediately after the exhibition of *St Eulalia*, at the age of only thirty-six. Whether or not Baldry was right, that this phase in Waterhouse's career was something of an anomaly, it is certainly the case that *Mariamne* was the last painting in which he attempted a scene from a historical text. Perhaps a new sense of security, after his election to the Associateship, freed him to pursue themes closer to his heart; perhaps he was responding to new experiences and new influences, which we shall explore below. Whatever the reasons, though, a significant shift occurred some time towards the end of the 1880s.

THE TURNING-POINT

Both Baldry and Sketchley, the two critics who produced summative accounts of Waterhouse's career, identified a turning-point at about that date, but their different agendas

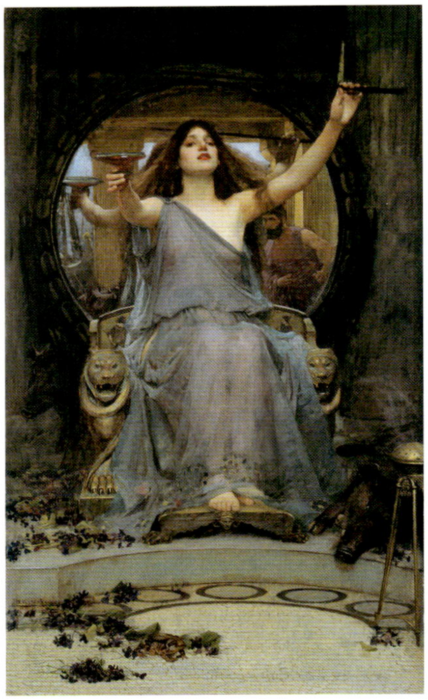

11. J.W. Waterhouse, *Circe Offering the Cup to Ulysses*, 1891, Oil on canvas, 149 x 92 cm, Gallery Oldham

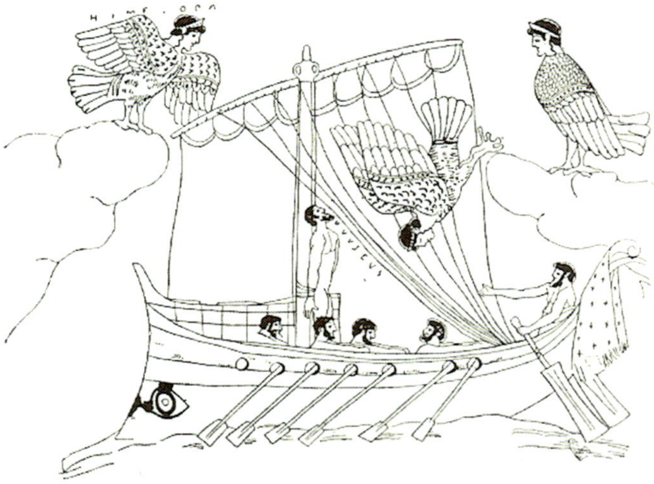

12. Unidentified artist, Line drawing of 'Ulysses and the Sirens' vase at British Museum (cat. E.156), from *Magazine of Art*, vol. 10, 1887, p. 135

led them to select different paintings as decisive. For Baldry, the important step was a turn away from narrative or literary subjects, in favour of a more exclusive attention to formal considerations along with the expression of archetypal human emotions.[12] Baldry, himself a painter and always attentive in his criticism to technical matters, also laid considerable stress on Waterhouse's decision to abandon painting in the open air, and instead to develop a new method of colouring and lighting his pictures based on the conditions within the studio; while we have only Baldry's word that this was a conscious decision on Waterhouse's part, it makes some sense in relation to his changing style at this period (discussed more fully in Robert Upstone's essay, pp. 37-49). Baldry therefore paid no attention to what later became Waterhouse's most famous painting, *The Lady of Shalott* of 1888 (cat. 20), with its story from a poem by Tennyson and its outdoor setting. He dated the turning-point in Waterhouse's work to the paintings of mythological subjects that began in 1891, after a year in which, for the first time since his debut, Waterhouse did not exhibit at the Royal Academy.

There is some biographical logic to this view: Waterhouse's father, himself a painter, died at the beginning of 1890, and even before that date Waterhouse had begun to travel extensively in Italy. The emotional impact of his father's death, the new experiences of his travels, or simply the break in his pattern of work may well have caused Waterhouse to reconsider his artistic mission. A sketchbook (cat. 94) shows a set of new ideas beginning, intriguingly, to develop: alongside sketches of buildings, landscapes, and peasant girls on the picturesque island of Capri, Waterhouse begins to experiment with sketches for the compositions that would eventually become *Ulysses and the Sirens* (fig. 13, cat. 22) and *Circe Offering the Cup to Ulysses* (fig. 11, cat. 21). The sketchbook also includes drawings of the wings of birds, but the figures of the Sirens themselves do not appear; these must have been added to Waterhouse's idea for the composition later, back in London, when he drew on a vase in the British Museum for their distinctive forms, half-bird and half-woman (fig. 12). The sketchbook is fascinating for showing the painter's imagination at work, in a series of experiments that only gradually crystallise as the compositions of the great paintings of 1891.

Baldry also alludes to what he calls a 'newer conviction' of Waterhouse's, 'this definite inclination towards a picturesque mysticism'; later in the article he calls him 'a painter of mystic suggestions'.[13] It remains unclear whether Baldry meant to point to anything more definite than a general interest in subjects with magical or supernatural associations. Rose Sketchley, on the other

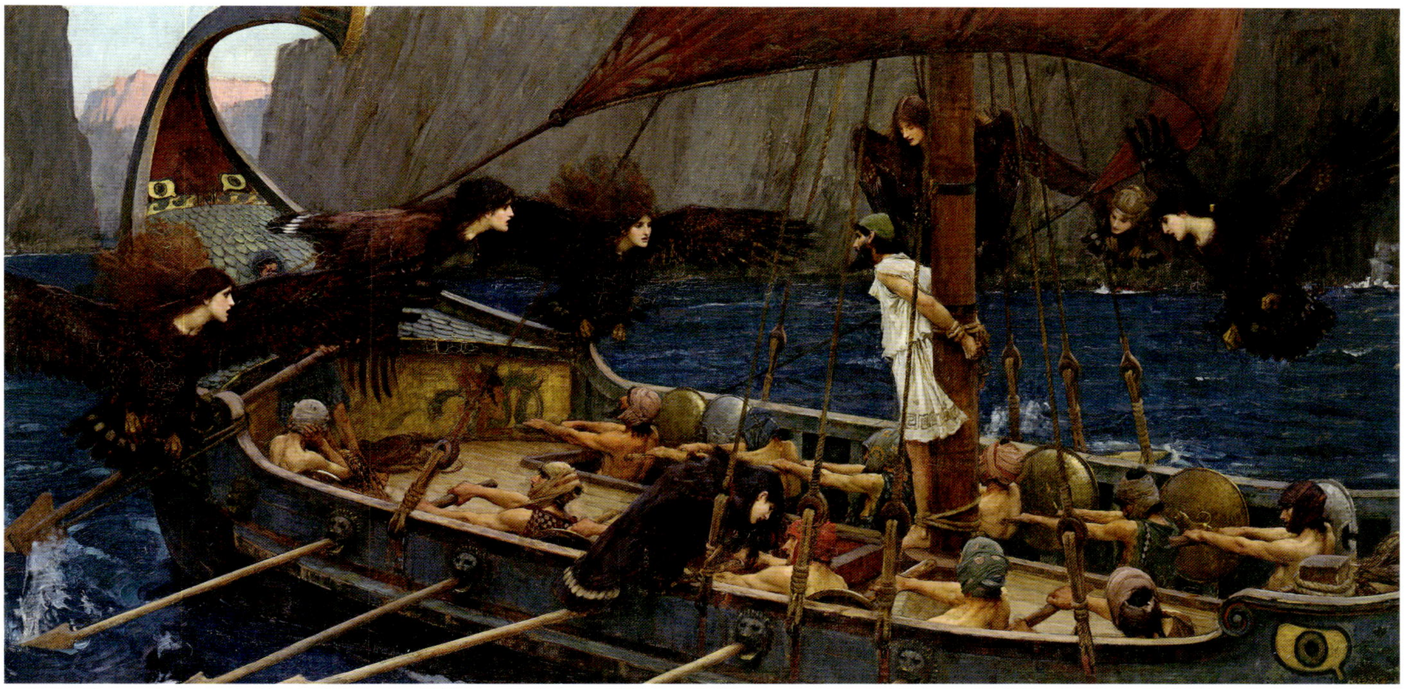

13. J.W. Waterhouse, *Ulysses and the Sirens*, 1891, Oil on canvas, 100.6 x 201.7 cm, National Gallery of Victoria, Melbourne

hand, offers a specific interpretation of Waterhouse's later work in relation to the tradition of the occult, much under discussion in certain London circles in the 1890s and beyond.[14] In contrast to the earlier vogue for spiritualism, a popular movement which emphasised contact between a living medium and the spirits of the deceased, the occult movements of the fin-de-siècle and early twentieth century tended to elitism and arcane learning, founded on a series of key literary texts extending from classical antiquity through to modern poetry in the Romantic tradition.[15] Sketchley structures her account of Waterhouse through reference to one such text, *De Raptu Proserpinae* ('The Rape of Proserpina'), by the Latin poet Claudian (born c. 370 A.D.) – coincidentally or not, Claudian was also the author of a series of panegyrics to Honorius which, while not the immediate source for Waterhouse's painting of 1883, might have formed part of his research for that work. Sketchley begins by describing *De Raptu Proserpinae* as 'the last poem of living paganism'. Perhaps the phrase implies a post-classical cessation of pagan belief, but Sketchley goes on unmistakably to point to its revival in the modern world. She describes Waterhouse in terms that clearly link him to such a revival: 'The true interpreter of these essential things', she writes, 'must himself have turned to them as to an inner dream'.[16]

It is no surprise, then, that Sketchley gives special significance to Waterhouse's painting of 1886, *The Magic Circle* (cat. 17), for her the first work that 'belongs more closely to the artist himself'. She presents the work as transitional: probably, she says, it was first conceived 'only as a striking incident, particularly vivid to the artist, but not pointing beyond itself to allied ends'.[17] In it, though, Waterhouse begins to realise 'the personal element ... not simply as well-considered choice of this or that appropriate device, but in discernment of what the visible aspect may imply, beyond the immediate effect. The picture denotes the attitude in which occultism is founded'. The decisive turning-point comes with *The Lady of Shalott*: 'Definitely', in this painting of 1888, 'the change from receptive to reflective consciousness is fulfilled'.[18] While there are many reasons for regarding *The Lady of Shalott* as a specially significant event in Waterhouse's development, not least its enduring fascination for generations of viewers, Sketchley's emphasis on this painting, rather than the more obviously mystical *Magic Circle*, may seem puzzling at first. But there is a coded logic to it, although Sketchley leaves it to her initiated readers to work it out for themselves. Tennyson first published the poem on which Waterhouse's painting is based in 1832; by then he had already made a schoolboy translation of the first 93 lines of Claudian's *De*

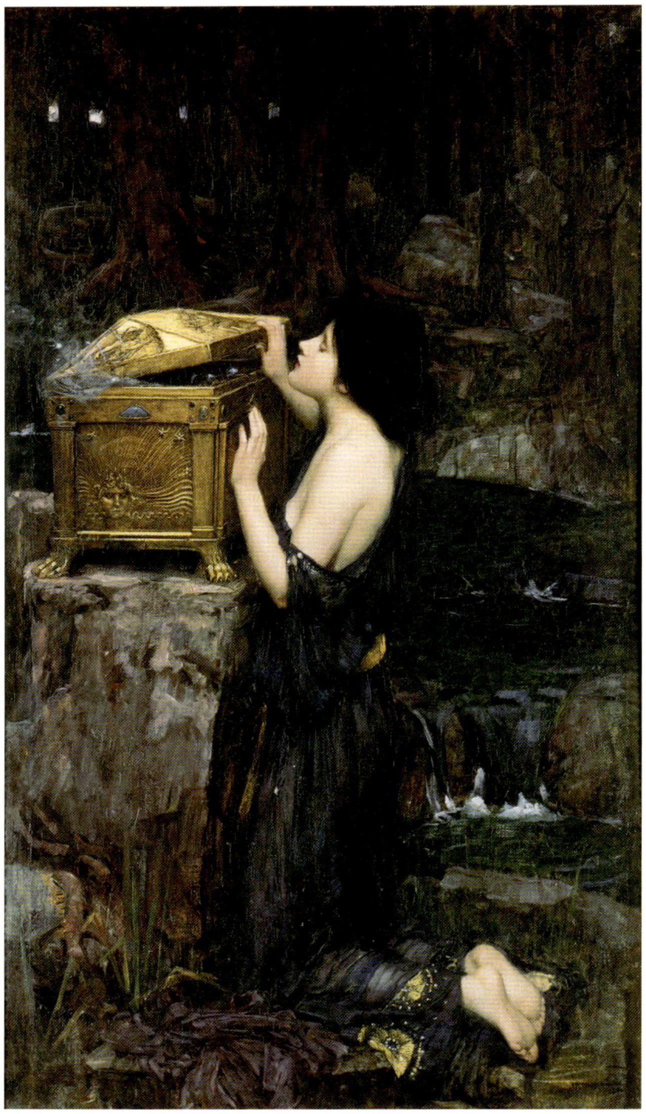

14. J.W. Waterhouse, *Pandora*, 1896, Oil on canvas, 152.4 x 91.4 cm, Collection Lord Lloyd Webber

Raptu Proserpinae, and literary scholars have suggested that the myth of Proserpina made a strong impact on Tennyson's subsequent verse, such as 'The Lady of Shalott'.[19] A scene in Claudian's poem, where Proserpina sings while she weaves, may have been one inspiration for 'The Lady of Shalott'; the Lady's fatal journey to Camelot can be seen as a parallel for Proserpina's descent to the underworld. Thus there is a secret linkage among Claudian's poem, Tennyson's poem, and Waterhouse's painting through the figure of the woman weaver, a motif that recurs not only in Waterhouse's later representations of *The Lady of Shalott* (cats 30, 60), but also in *Penelope and the Suitors* of 1912 (cat. 58) and in a late oil sketch for a picture representing Circe (cat. 57).

MYTH

Can we, then, attribute the 'distinct imaginative system' of Waterhouse's later work to a fascination with the occult? It is tempting to suggest that the strange dearth of surviving documentation on Waterhouse is evidence of a secret life, perhaps as member of an occult movement, but this must remain pure speculation; since occult movements are by definition secret, they are resistant to research. Perhaps the most that can be said is that Waterhouse's later works consistently represent the same myths that were seen as specially revelatory in occultist circles of the same period. In that respect, it is important to emphasise that – despite the claims of the occult tradition to immemorial antiquity – this choice of subject-matter marks Waterhouse's project as distinctively modern, and very much in keeping with the experimentation of literary modernism in the next few decades. W.B. Yeats explicitly avowed his devotion to the occult; other modernists, notably Ezra Pound, T.S. Eliot, James Joyce, and D.H. Lawrence, incorporated elements of the occult tradition into their works, although debate continues to rage among scholars about the import of these allusions.[20] Whether these writers, or Waterhouse, were actually initiates in the many occult societies that were thriving in London around the turn of the twentieth century, they drew on stories and motifs, associated with the occult, to powerful effect. Moreover, occultism in the strict sense was only one strand in a wider pattern of interest in pagan religion, comparative mythology, nature mythology, classical archaeology, and anthropology, gathering momentum at exactly the moment when Waterhouse took up mythological subject-matter.[21] Waterhouse's choices of mythological subjects correspond broadly to the range of myths treated in such works as Sir James George Frazer's *The Golden Bough* (1890-1915), often described as a founding work of modern anthropology, and the writings of the Cambridge classicist Jane Harrison, whose work from 1890 onwards emphasised the grounding of myth in ancient ritual practice.[22] In the years around the turn of the century, then, there was a vast spectrum from the most sober scholarship on ancient religion and anthropology, at one end, to the wildest devotees of occult lore at the other; we may never know precisely where to situate Waterhouse on this spectrum.

Pound began his *Cantos* (1917-1970) with Ulysses' journey to the mouth of the underworld, a key story in occultist lore since it involves a palingenesis, or spiritual rebirth. In Canto I he alludes repeatedly to the role of the sorceress Circe, whose instruction guides Ulysses on his journey; Ulysses' affair with Circe can also be figured, in occultist terms, as a *hieros gamos* or mystic marriage.[23] James Joyce's *Ulysses* of 1922 draws on both occult motifs in satirical vein. Three decades earlier, Waterhouse too had begun his exploration of mythology with Ulysses and Circe, in two paintings of episodes that precede and follow Ulysses' journey to the underworld in Homer's *Odyssey*:

Circe Offering the Cup to Ulysses, seen at the New Gallery in 1891 (fig. 11, cat. 21), and at the simultaneous Royal Academy exhibition, *Ulysses and the Sirens* (fig. 13, cat. 22). At the Academy the next year, he showed *Circe Invidiosa* ('jealous Circe', cat. 23) – the same mythological sorceress, but this time drawn from Ovid's *Metamorphoses*, another key text for the occult tradition, and one to which Waterhouse would return again and again (see for example cats 34, 41, 43). Yet Waterhouse, as we have already seen, was not an illustrator of ancient texts, and he does not closely follow the narratives of either Homer or Ovid. Instead he is concerned with creating his own, distinctively modern pictorial drama: where Homer's *Odyssey*, Book XII, has just two Sirens, singing from their island, Waterhouse represents seven of them (a magic number) and brings them close, swooping on their bird-wings to menace Ulysses' ship. Moreover, the scene comes to life in a landscape reminiscent of those Waterhouse himself had visited and sketched in recent years, on Capri and the Bay of Naples; similarly, the blue-green waters of *Circe Invidiosa* recall the famous caves of Capri and the Amalfi coast.[24]

As noted above, Waterhouse borrowed the distinctive bird-forms of his Sirens from a vase in the British Museum, to which his attention might have been drawn by line drawings of the vase in either Jane Harrison's book of 1882, *Myths of the Odyssey in Art and Literature*, or her article in the *Magazine of Art* for 1887, 'The Myth of Odysseus and the Sirens' (fig. 12).[25] Perhaps, indeed, Harrison's book was one prompt for Waterhouse's interest in the story of Ulysses; the book called novel attention to visual representations on ancient vases and gems, alongside the more familiar literary treatments of the myths. But, again, Waterhouse's project was to create a fresh pictorial drama, not an antiquarian exploration of the ancient visual evidence. Although Harrison's book illustrated several ancient representations of Ulysses' first encounter with Circe, Waterhouse imagines the scene anew. Significantly, he rejects the most common ancient composition, which shows Circe embracing Ulysses' knees in supplication.[26] In each of Waterhouse's representations, Circe is a powerful sorceress, not a defeated woman. It may be, indeed, that Circe's role as sage and spiritual guide is the key to Waterhouse's paintings of the story of Ulysses. Moreover, Waterhouse's fascination with the figure of Circe lasted throughout his lifetime; after 1910 he made two large-scale oil sketches for a new composition showing Circe seated at a table, ruminating on her magic designs (cats 56, 57).

In recent scholarship, when Waterhouse's work has been discussed at all, it has usually been to castigate him for his misogyny in representing the female figure as evil in her very beauty. Certainly the *femme fatale* is a constant presence: as a mermaid, she lures men with her singing (cat. 35); water-nymphs entice Hylas (cat. 32); *Lamia* (cat. 46) and *La Belle Dame Sans Merci* (cat. 28) stray from Keats's poems

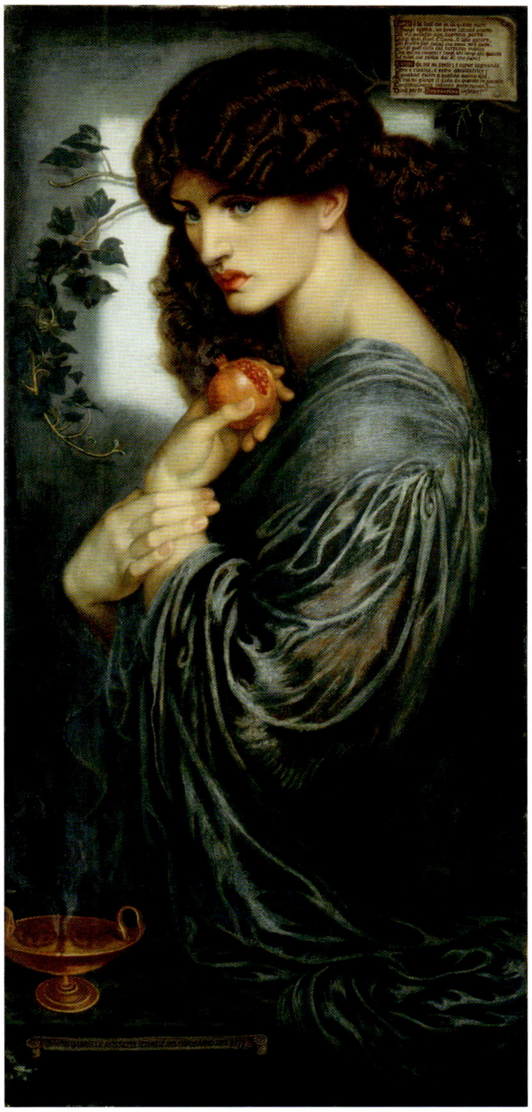

15. Dante Gabriel Rossetti, *Proserpine*, 1873-1877, Oil on canvas, 119.5 x 57.8 cm, Private collection

into Waterhouse's magic woods, there to entrap hapless knights. Yet these fatal encounters may also be figured as palingeneses or mystic marriages, and perhaps Waterhouse's women are not so much *femmes fatales* as wise sorceresses, with Circe as their archetype. Often they are rebels who refuse to obey the men (or male gods) in authority; for example, Waterhouse painted two parallel myths of women who open forbidden boxes, *Pandora* in 1896 (fig. 14) and *Psyche Opening the Golden Box* in 1903 (cat. 44). These women defy the gods, yet their deadpan faces give no clue to their motives and no guide to the spectator's moral response: should we admire their resistance to patriarchal authority or fear their irresponsible power over men? In opening the box, Pandora releases all the evils into the world; thus she is worse than Nero, whose cruelty was at

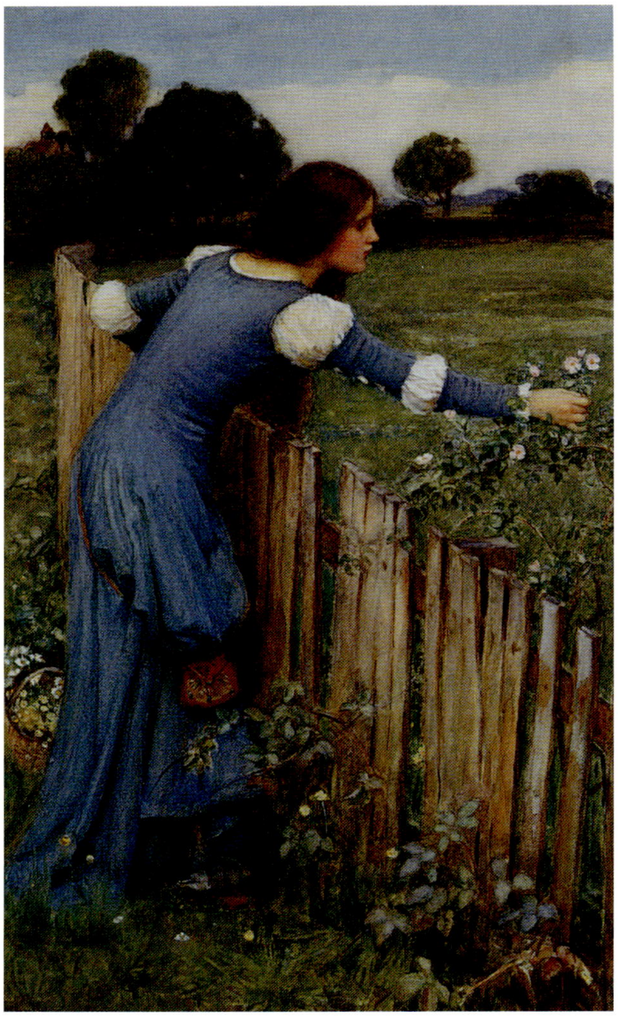

16. J.W. Waterhouse, *Spring* (*The Flower Picker*), c. 1900, Watercolour heightened with white on paper, 46.2 x 29.2 cm, Collection Lord Lloyd Webber

least limited to Rome. But there is a crucial tension here, for the occult may reverse good and evil. The secret knowledge within Pandora's box (or Psyche's) is evil if we side with the gods; but it may be good if we refuse to accept their sway over us. The box, in *Pandora*, presents perhaps the clearest occult symbol in Waterhouse's work: the relief decoration, in pure gold, showing the sun dawning over water immediately brings to mind the secret society of which Yeats was a member, the Hermetic Order of the Golden Dawn.[27]

Sketchley casts the development of Waterhouse's mythological subjects in parallel to Claudian's description of the tapestry woven by Proserpina, and traces a sequence of natural elements, from water (in *Ulysses and the Sirens* through to *Hylas and the Nymphs* and *Echo and Narcissus*) to earth and finally to 'human flowers'.[28] The scheme perhaps underplays the importance of water in all phases of Waterhouse's work, and the presence of the word in his name may not be a coincidence. But it points to the central importance of nature in Waterhouse's mythological world: after 1890 woodlands, flowery meadows, ponds and streams largely replace the built environment of Waterhouse's earlier classical scenes. These are not pastoral landscapes, or classical landscapes ordered for human cultivation; rather they are the magic forests and enchanted gardens of folklore or fairy tale. Thus they participate in a widespread revival of interest in the rustic god Pan and his followers – fauns, satyrs, nymphs – as representatives of a universal nature mythology, explored in English and American poetry from 1890 onwards;[29] a parallel development appears in the painting of Arnold Böcklin and other continental Symbolists. An oil sketch (cat. 25) made in preparation for one of Waterhouse's first woodland subjects, *A Naiad* of 1893 (cat. 27), suggests that the artist was now drawing inspiration from the English countryside. As Yeats wrote many years later: 'when I prepared [Sophocles's play] 'Oedipus at Colonus' for the Abbey stage [in Dublin] I saw that the wood of the Furies ... was any Irish haunted wood'.[30] Waterhouse's English woods and waters are haunted by naiads, dryads, satyrs, and mermaids; perhaps they offer routes to the underworld, through the depths of water, the forest undergrowth, or the flowery meadow that (as in the story of Proserpina) may open up a chasm to the world below. Moreover, the figures within them – Sketchley's 'human flowers' – are most commonly represented at the age of adolescence, on the threshold between childhood and maturity.

Oddly, one myth that never appears overtly in Waterhouse's work is the very one Sketchley saw as the key: the myth of Proserpina, the goddess (known as Persephone in Greek) who was gathering flowers in the vale of Enna when Pluto carried her through a chasm to the underworld; after some vicissitudes she was released for half of each year. Her annual return to the world of the living can be explained as a nature myth about the cyclical return of spring, or (in occult terms) as a palingenesis; allusions to Proserpina are frequent in modernist literature.[31] Given this context, it seems surprising that Waterhouse did not paint the subject. Yet it may be possible, nonetheless, to configure Waterhouse's mythological world as a vast tapestry with the figure of Proserpina at its centre, mysteriously unseen, but from whom threads radiate to weave together all of the other myths. We have already seen how the figure of Proserpina as weaver may draw in the Lady of Shalott, Penelope, and the late composition of Circe. Her descent to the underworld recalls the journeys of Ulysses and Dante, Orpheus and Psyche, and the punishment there of the Danaïdes (cat. 47). As flower-gatherer she is the sister of Ophelia, represented in three of Waterhouse's paintings (figs 18, 30, 39), and of numerous figures with other names, or no name at all, in a sequence of paintings from 1900 onwards, where the flowers are those enumerated in Claudian – springtime anemones (as in *Windflowers*, cat. 42), roses, violets, hyacinths and narcissi. Claudian calls the anemone the sign of Venus's grief, with reference to the flower that sprang from the blood of Adonis, her mortal lover; like Proserpina (a parallel noted in Frazer's *Golden Bough*), Adonis is reborn every spring, as in Waterhouse's painting of 1899, *The Awakening of Adonis* (fig. 19). A flower marked the death of another beautiful youth, Narcissus, who is invoked in Claudian's *De Raptu Proserpinae* and represented in Waterhouse's haunting painting, *Echo and Narcissus* of 1903 (cat. 43). Perhaps the most intriguing parallel to the Proserpina myth is found in one of Waterhouse's last pictures, unfinished at his death (cat. 64). Even in its sketchy state, it is possible to discern the precise scenario of Dante's *Purgatorio*, canto XXVIII: the poet, Dante, appears on the near side of the river Lethe, beyond which is the figure of Matilda, gathering flowers. Dante tells us that Matilda is singing, like Claudian's Proserpina and the Lady of Shalott, and he even compares her to Proserpina in the vale of Enna (see p. 196). Dante, whose *Divine Comedy* traces a descent to the underworld (*Inferno*) before proceeding through Purgatory to Paradise, was another point of reference in occult literature, along with the troubadour poets and Boccaccio, seen to create a medieval link between the ancient and modern secret traditions; two of Waterhouse's very last paintings are drawn from Boccaccio (cats 65, 66). Interestingly, the medieval link was promoted in the writings of Gabriele Rossetti, the Dante scholar and father of the painter Dante Gabriel Rossetti, whose powerful paintings of Proserpina (fig. 15) would have been well-known to Waterhouse.[32]

It may, then, be possible to weave threads among all of Waterhouse's mythological paintings, and even among the later works that seem to lack specific subject-matter. But do these multifarious linkages simply reflect the period's enthusiasm for comparative mythology, or do they outline an occult system, as Sketchley implies? Roses are everywhere in Waterhouse's art, often as an accessory, sometimes as the central focus. In *The Soul of the Rose* (cat. 50), the figure breathes deeply of the scent of the rose, confounding the traditional hierarchy of the senses, in which smell is an animal or degraded sense, to suggest a spiritual experience.[33] Roses are also among Proserpina's flowers, and they are ubiquitous in occult literature and ritual, for example in the poetry and prose of Yeats and in Rosicrucianism, revived in the later nineteenth century, notably by the French occultist Joséphin Péladan, whose writings were known in England and who invited English artists to participate in his Salons de la Rose + Croix.[34] Yet roses can have any number of associations: they are the flowers of love, symbols of pure beauty, attributes of the Virgin Mary and of the goddess Venus.

We have already seen that the French painter Aman-Jean, a participant in Péladan's Salon de la Rose + Croix, failed to find 'mystery' in Waterhouse's work of 1896. Similarly, in a

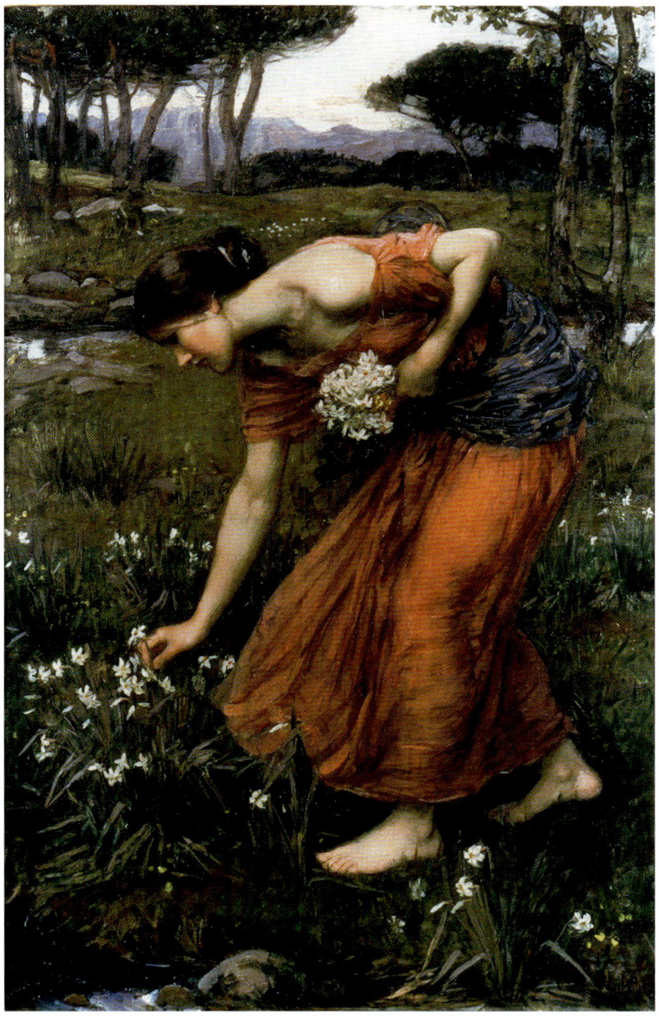

17. J.W. Waterhouse, *Narcissus*, 1913, Oil on canvas, 94.5 x 64 cm, Private collection courtesy of Sotheby's

private letter of 1909, Pound made reference to the beauty of Waterhouse's paintings, but denied them precisely the further dimension that distinguished them for Sketchley, in her article of the same year.[35] In a revised version of the passage from the letter, published in 1910, Pound substitutes the name of Burne-Jones for that of Waterhouse, but makes the same distinction: 'there are works of art which are beautiful objects and works of art which are keys or passwords admitting one to a deeper knowledge, to a finer perception of beauty'.[36] For Pound, then, Waterhouse and Burne-Jones had not made the transition from Aestheticism, the creation of beautiful objects for their own sake, to the deeper significance he finds in the art of his own compatriot, James McNeill Whistler, and the poetry of Dante.

Perhaps the reservations of both Pound and Aman-Jean reflect a reluctance to admit Waterhouse's art to the inner circle of the occult tradition. Yet their comments

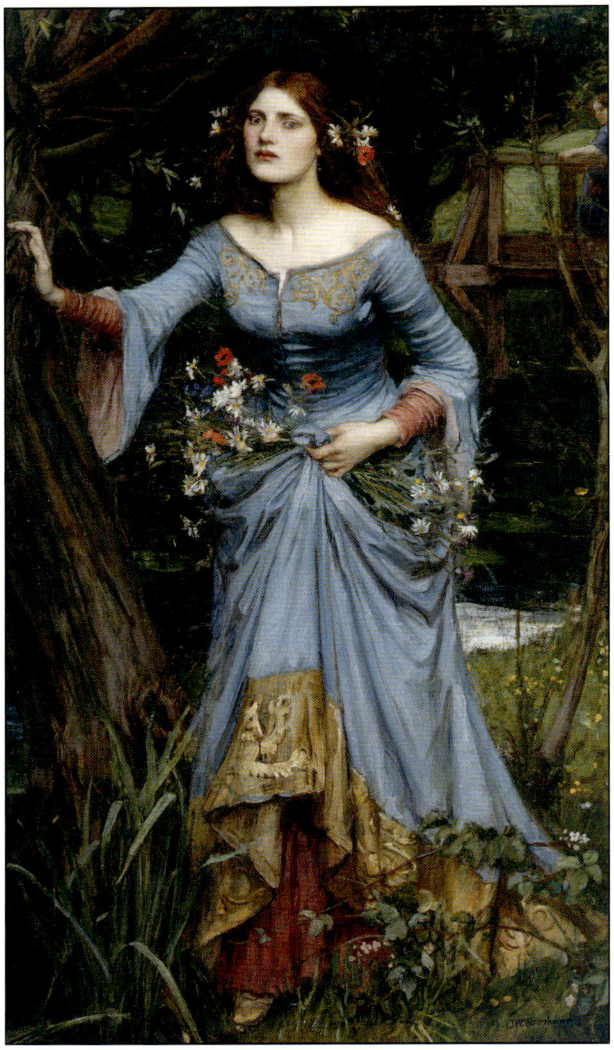

18. J.W. Waterhouse, *Ophelia*, 1910, Oil on canvas, 100.3 x 62.2 cm, Collection Lord Lloyd Webber

are perceptive in another sense: they call attention to Waterhouse's special skill in dramatising a pictorial narrative so lucidly that it is intelligible at once, however complex its literary affiliations or secret messages. It is perhaps this skill, developed as we have already seen in the sequence of history paintings and carried on in the mythological pictures, that accounts for Waterhouse's exceptional popularity with exhibition and museum audiences. For Pound and the modernist generation, such lucidity became a fault, and popular appeal a demerit. Thus Waterhouse's cultural status underwent a strange reversal in the modernist criticism of the twentieth century. During his own lifetime, his art unequivocally represented high culture: for Blaikie, his election to the Associateship in 1885 was 'the more notable because his work has ever been distinguished by qualities that appeal more to painters than to popular tastes', and a writer in *The Studio* for 1897 noted that 'He has never given way to the temptation by which modern artists are beset, to gain popularity by concessions to the general demand for triviality of subject and showy cleverness of technical expression'.[37] Yet for most of the twentieth century, precisely the opposite view prevailed, as Waterhouse's art came to seem middlebrow or popularising.

In later twentieth-century criticism, Waterhouse's devotion to subject-matter from the remote past marked him, additionally, as conservative, something that would have made little sense to Pound or the other first-generation modernists, immersed as they were in the Western cultural tradition. For Sketchley, Waterhouse's sense of the past is a matter, not of antiquarianism, but rather of 'poetical sensation': 'Therein lies the source of the tender vividness of his art, its power to renew for modern sight and imagination a beauty lost from the common apprehension of life'.[38] Waterhouse, born in 1849, did not make the transition to the modernist artistic styles that were already beginning to appear in the work of much younger artists at the end of his lifetime. Yet as Sketchley's phrasing suggests, his pictorial dramatisations of ancient myths partake of the early twentieth-century mood expressed in Pound's own famous slogan, 'make it new'.[39]

Since the connections divined by occultists are by definition secret or hidden, there is no way to disprove them (except to enter the hermetic world oneself, to claim superior insight into the secret lore). To an extent, then, Sketchley's occult interpretation of Waterhouse's work becomes a self-fulfilling prophecy: once the basic occult premise is in play, virtually anything can be seen to have a secret significance. Thus the occult is too promiscuous to offer a definitive account of Waterhouse's subject-matter and imagery. Yet in another sense its frame of reference may be too impoverished. Sketchley is surely right to see a 'distinct imaginative system' in Waterhouse's art, but his paintings are not simple ciphers, to be decoded for their concealed messages. When the paintings are seen in their complex and interlocking relationships, they reveal secrets more various and more intriguing in that they cannot be reduced to mere occult symbols. The tapestries that link *The Lady of Shalott* and *Penelope*, the lyres of Orpheus and the Siren, the flowery meadows inhabited by Adonis, Narcissus, Ophelia, Matilda, and numerous nameless surrogates of Proserpina – any of these may be interpreted for their secret meanings. But perhaps it is more important that they interpret one another, as irreducible components of Waterhouse's haunting imaginative world.

Many thanks for the generous help of Christina Bradstreet, Simon Goldhill, David Hopkins, Ronald Hutton, Charles Martindale, Edward Morris, and Peter Trippi.

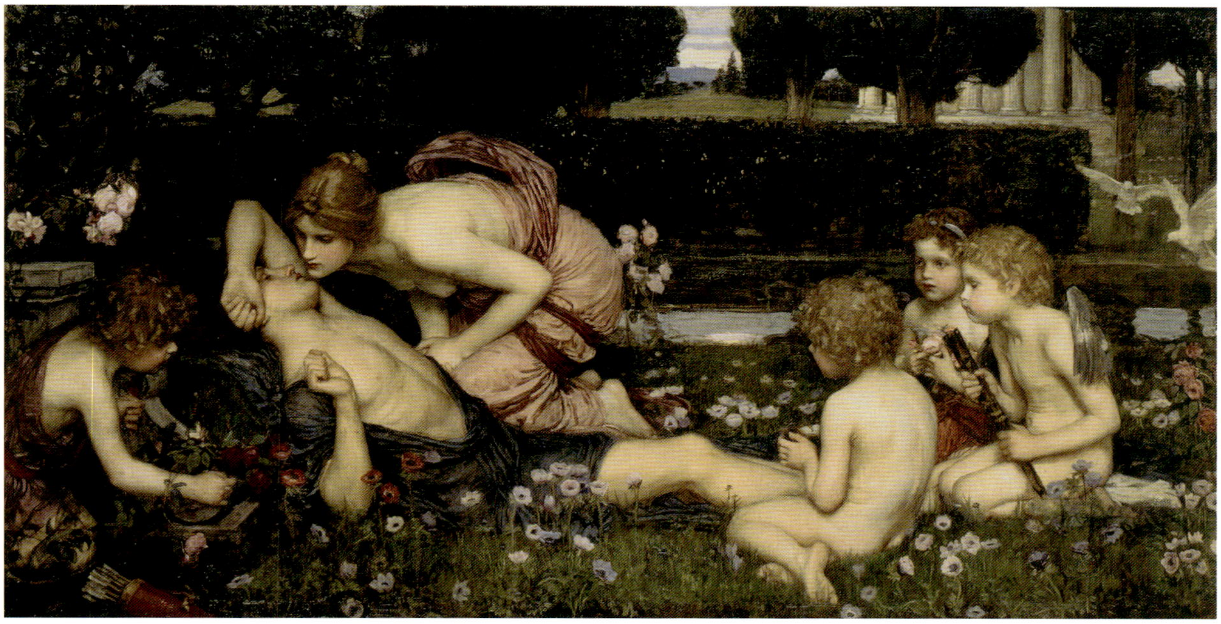

19. J.W. Waterhouse, *The Awakening of Adonis*, 1899, Oil on canvas, 95.9 x 188 cm, Collection Lord Lloyd Webber

1 Unsigned article, probably by Alfred Lys Baldry, 'Some Drawings by J.W. Waterhouse, R.A.', *Studio*, vol. XLIV, September 1908, p. 250. Baldry was the author of three signed articles on Waterhouse in *The Studio* (1895, 1911, 1917), which are closely related to the article of 1908 in argumentation and phraseology; compare, for example, Baldry's statement: 'Artistically he belonged to a world of his own creation' (A.L. Baldry, 'The Late J.W. Waterhouse, R.A.', *Studio*, vol. LXXI, June 1917, p. 4).
2 R.E.D. Sketchley, *The Art of J.W. Waterhouse, R.A.*, Christmas Number of *The Art Journal*, 1909, p. 11.
3 [Edmond] Aman-Jean, 'Some Pictures at the Royal Academy. Criticised by a French Painter', *Studio*, vol. VIII, 15 July 1896, p. 110.
4 Unsigned article, probably by Alfred Lys Baldry, 'Some Drawings by J.W. Waterhouse, R.A.', *Studio*, vol. XLIV, September 1908, p. 250.
5 Georg Ebers, *Lorenz Alma Tadema: His Life and Works*, trans. Mary J. Safford, New York: William S. Gottsberger, 1886, pp. 27-28.
6 'The Royal Academy', *The Art Journal*, vol. n.s. VIII, 1 June 1869, p. 168. On Alma-Tadema see Edwin Becker and others, eds, *Sir Lawrence Alma-Tadema*, exhibition catalogue, Amsterdam: Van Gogh Museum and Liverpool: Walker Art Gallery, 1996.
7 J.A. Blaikie, 'J.W. Waterhouse, A.R.A.', *Magazine of Art*, vol. IX, 1886, p. 2.
8 See Elizabeth Prettejohn, *Art for Art's Sake: Aestheticism in Victorian Painting*, New Haven and London: Yale University Press, 2007.
9 A. Lys Baldry, 'J.W. Waterhouse and his Work', *Studio*, vol. IV, January 1895, p. 108.
10 For the accounts of Dio Cassius, Tacitus, and Suetonius see Rosemary Julia Barrow, *The Use of Classical Art and Literature by Victorian Painters, 1860-1912: Creating Continuity with the Traditions of High Art*, Lewiston, NY, Queenston, Ontario, and Lampeter, Wales: The Edwin Mellen Press, 2007, p. 30.
11 I am indebted to Simon Goldhill for this insight.
12 A. Lys Baldry, 'J.W. Waterhouse and his Work', *Studio*, vol. IV, January 1895, pp. 108-112.
13 *Ibid*, pp. 111, 115.
14 Little is known of Rose Sketchley, a journalist who wrote on a wide variety of subjects, but she may have had a special interest in the occult; in 1908, she contributed an article to *The Art Journal* on the artist and psychic Austin Osman Spare, an influential figure in occult circles. It is also unknown whether Sketchley based her account of Waterhouse on personal acquaintance or interviews with him, although it is likely that she had his cooperation, or even his assistance, in obtaining permission to reproduce a large number of his works in her article.
15 See Alex Owen, *The Place of Enchantment: British Occultism and the Culture of the Modern*, Chicago and London: The University of Chicago Press, 2004.
16 R.E.D. Sketchley, *The Art of J.W. Waterhouse, R.A.*, Christmas Number of *The Art Journal*, 1909, p. 1.
17 *Ibid*, pp. 11-12.
18 *Ibid*, p. 15.
19 See for example Margot K. Louis, 'Proserpine and Pessimism: Goddesses of Death, Life, and Language from Swinburne to Wharton', *Modern Philology*, vol. 96, no. 3, February 1999, p. 326.
20 See Leon Surette, *The Birth of Modernism: Ezra Pound, T.S. Eliot, W.B. Yeats, and the Occult*, Montreal & Kingston, London, and Buffalo: McGill-Queen's University Press, 1993.
21 For a particularly lucid survey of the entire field see Ronald Hutton, *The Triumph of the Moon: A History of Modern Pagan Witchcraft*, Oxford University Press, 1999, chapters 1-10.
22 As Harrison put it in 1890, 'My belief is that in many, even in the large majority of cases *ritual practice misunderstood* explains the elaboration of myth' (Jane E. Harrison and Margaret deG. Verrall, *Mythology and Monuments of Ancient Athens*, London and New York: Macmillan, 1890, p. iii). On Harrison see Mary Beard, *The Invention of Jane Harrison*, Cambridge, Mass., and London: Harvard University Press, 2000; Annabel Robinson, *The Life and Work of Jane Ellen Harrison*, Oxford University Press, 2002; Sandra J. Peacock, *Jane Ellen Harrison: The Mask and the Self*, New Haven and London: Yale University Press, 1988.
23 See Leon Surette, *The Birth of Modernism: Ezra Pound, T.S. Eliot, W.B. Yeats, and the Occult*, Montreal and Kingston, London, and Buffalo: McGill-Queen's University Press, 1993, pp. 15-16, 115.
24 In a letter to his patron Julia Ellsworth Ford, dated 18 March (without a year, but probably from 1903 or later), Waterhouse confirms that the subjects of *Ulysses and the Sirens* and *Circe Invidiosa* were suggested by the landscapes of Capri (Beinecke Library, Yale University, Za//Ford (Julia Ellsworth)//Corresp/Mb-Z; thanks to Peter Trippi for discovering this letter). Julia Ellsworth Ford bought Waterhouse's other Royal Academy exhibit of 1892, *Danaë*, which featured a landscape similar to that of *Ulysses and the Sirens*; the painting was stolen from her New York house in 1947 and remains untraced.
25 J.E. Harrison, *Myths of the Odyssey in Art and Literature*, London: Rivingtons, 1882, plate 37; Jane E. Harrison, 'The Myth of Odysseus and the Sirens', *Magazine of Art*, vol. X, 1887, p. 135.
26 See J.E. Harrison, *Myths of the Odyssey in Art and Literature*, London: Rivingtons, 1882, plates 23-25 and Autotype V.
27 There is a large literature on the Golden Dawn, founded in 1888, and Yeats's involvement with it (he was initiated in 1890); see for example Ronald Hutton, *The Triumph of the Moon: A History of Modern Pagan Witchcraft*, Oxford University Press, 1999, pp. 74-83; Alex Owen, *The Place of Enchantment: British Occultism and the Culture of the Modern*, Chicago and London: The University of Chicago Press, 2004, pp. 51-84.
28 R.E.D. Sketchley, *The Art of J.W. Waterhouse, R.A.*, Christmas Number of *The Art Journal*, 1909, pp. 21-23.
29 See Patricia Merivale, *Pan the Goat-God: His Myth in Modern Times*, Cambridge, Mass.: Harvard University Press, 1969.
30 Russell K. Alspach assisted by Catharine C. Alspach, eds, *The Variorum Edition of the Plays of W.B. Yeats*, London, Melbourne, and Toronto: Macmillan, 1966, p. 899.
31 See Leon Surette, *The Birth of Modernism: Ezra Pound, T.S. Eliot, W.B. Yeats, and the Occult*, Montreal and Kingston, London, and Buffalo: McGill-Queen's University Press, 1993, pp. 16, 214-215.
32 On Gabriele Rossetti, see Leon Surette, *The Birth of Modernism: Ezra Pound, T.S. Eliot, W.B. Yeats, and the Occult*, Montreal and Kingston, London, and Buffalo: McGill-Queen's University Press, 1993, pp. 45-49, 108-122, and *passim*.
33 See Christina Bradstreet, '"Wicked with Roses": Floral Femininity and the Erotics of Scent', *Nineteenth-Century Art Worldwide*, spring 2007, at http://19thc-artworldwide.org.
34 See Leon Surette, *The Birth of Modernism: Ezra Pound, T.S. Eliot, W.B. Yeats, and the Occult*, Montreal & Kingston, London, and Buffalo: McGill-Queen's University Press, 1993, pp. 127-142 and *passim*; Robert Pincus-Witten, *Occult Symbolism in France: Joséphin Péladan and the Salons de la Rose-Croix*, New York: Garland, 1976.
35 See Rebecca Beasley, 'Ezra Pound's Whistler', *American Literature*, vol. 74, no. 3, 2002, pp. 498-499.
36 Ezra Pound, *The Spirit of Romance*, London: J.M. Dent & Sons, 1910, p. 162. Perhaps, in the published version, Pound was avoiding a disparaging reference to a living artist (Burne-Jones had died in 1898).
37 J.A. Blaikie, 'J.W. Waterhouse, A.R.A.', *Magazine of Art*, vol. IX, 1886, p. 1; 'Mr. J.W. Waterhouse's Painting, "Hylas and the Nymphs"', *Studio*, vol. X, 15 May 1897, p. 243.
38 R.E.D. Sketchley, *The Art of J.W. Waterhouse, R.A.*, Christmas Number of *The Art Journal*, 1909, p. 18.
39 The phrase is the title of an influential volume of essays (Ezra Pound, *Make It New*, London: Faber and Faber, 1934).

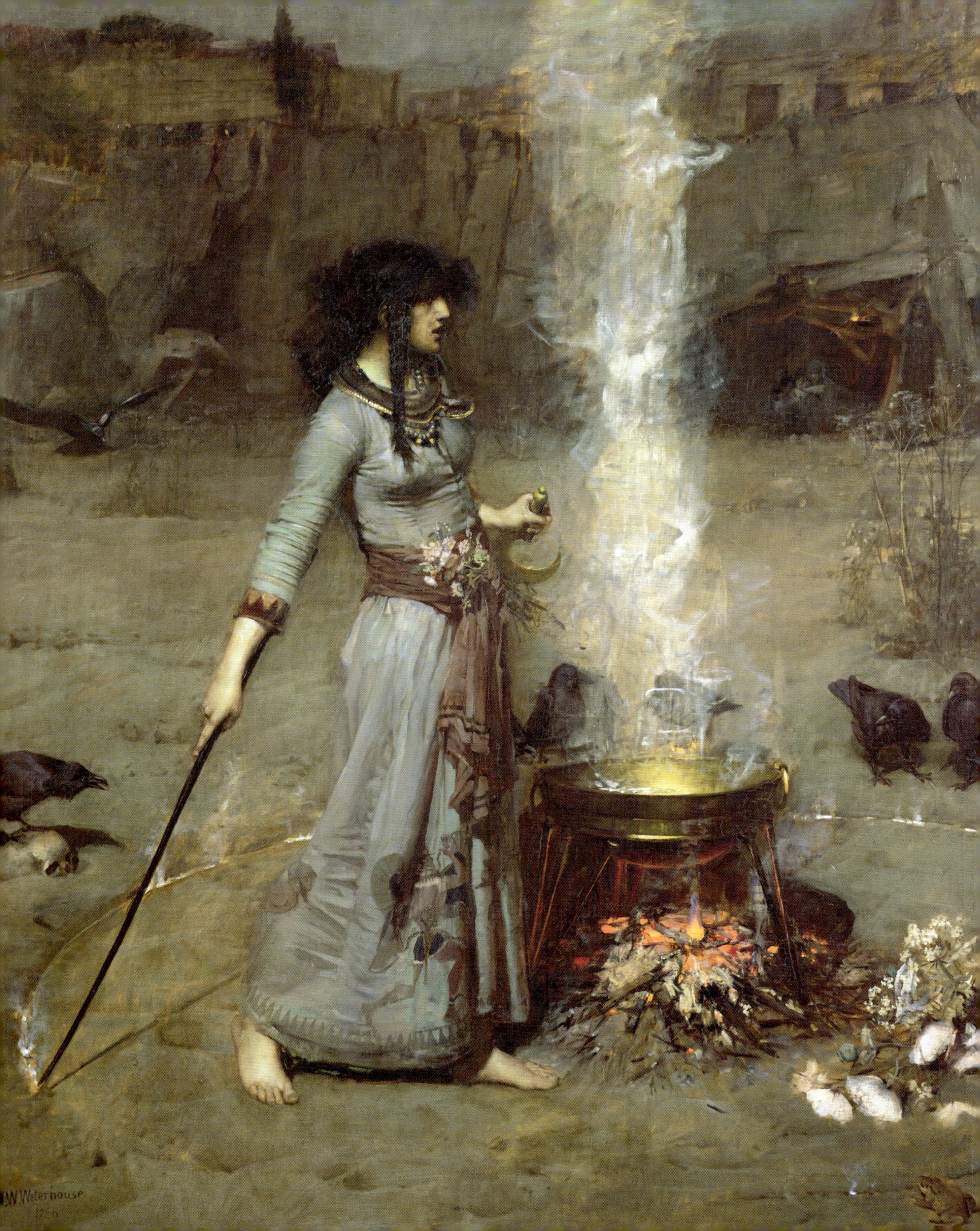
W.Waterhouse

BETWEEN INNOVATION AND TRADITION
WATERHOUSE AND MODERN FRENCH PAINTING

Robert Upstone

The modern hunger to classify, categorise, and enumerate sometimes struggles to define precisely what sort of painter Waterhouse was, or to which stream or genus of British nineteenth-century art he should be aligned. His work has different phases that subtly shift and mutate, while retaining a highly individual character and an identity that is immediately recognisable. There is a certain temptation to identify him as some species of 'Academic' painter. This is a comfortingly broad categorisation, and seems to be supported by Waterhouse's enduring commitment to exhibiting at the Royal Academy over a lifetime's career, and also by his tendency until the later 1880s to select primarily subjects derived from ancient Greek and Roman myth or history. But the somewhat reductive connotations that 'Academic' brings with it give no sense of his originality and invention, or of his transgression of Academic typological conventions. The frequently dark undercurrents that underpin Waterhouse's work can be investigated rewardingly by viewing him in context with the pan-European phenomenon of Symbolist painting, and again this weighs against any straightforward categorisation as simply an 'Academic' painter.[1]

Perhaps the most common description of Waterhouse is that he is a certain variety of 'high' Pre-Raphaelite, and this is a classification that has been supported by his occasional inclusion in modern books and exhibitions about the Brotherhood and their successors.[2] In its obituary in 1917 *The Times* was quite clear in how it defined Waterhouse: 'He painted pre-Raphaelite pictures in a more modern manner. He was, in fact, a kind of academic Burne-Jones, like him in his types and his moods, but with less insistence on design and more on atmosphere.'[3] That he was a form of Pre-Raphaelite was a classification also suggested in Waterhouse's lifetime, and which appeared for instance in the major assessment of his career that was written by R.E.D. Sketchley in 1909, and presumably published with the artist's involvement.[4] Sketchley examined this classification specifically in relation to what was one of Waterhouse's most famous pictures, *The Lady of Shalott* (fig. 20, cat. 20), and noted how it marked a dramatic new direction for Waterhouse's art. If Waterhouse chose a subject favoured by the Pre-Raphaelites, he did not follow their meticulous signature technique. Instead he evolved a thoroughly personal mode of expression that contentiously looked to modern French art for inspiration.[5] Of *The Lady of Shalott* Sketchley wrote:

> Nature seemed to the painter to hold out promise of an imaginative revelation to be won by faithfulness of sight. Thus intense admiration for the early pictures of Millais seen by him for the first time at the Grosvenor Gallery in 1886, prompted him to think. Already, by sympathy with the work of the French plein-airists, he had been brought to consider whether the right fulfilment of ideal subject might not lie in rendering to the utmost the aspect of the selected model. No change in technique was implied by his acceptance of Pre-Raphaelite theory … 'The Lady of Shalott' is specially broad and sustained in execution, and neither in colour nor in design is there any approximation to the missal-like intensity of Pre-Raphaelitism … [it] has the cool open-air unity of French naturalism.[6]

The moment at which Waterhouse began to shift away into a new mode of expression and subject can be precisely identified, and it was a move prompted both by personal and broader considerations. The second half of the 1880s was a tumultuous period in contemporary British art, in which the value of French practices was bitterly contested. It was also a moment at which Waterhouse grew tired of criticism of the principally Greek and Roman scenes he showed at the Academy each year, and sought to reinvent himself. Alma-Tadema was a painter whom Waterhouse greatly admired, and influenced his earlier canvases. But discerning this, critics occasionally made unfavourable comparisons and, much to Waterhouse's irritation, pedantically found fault with minor details of archaeological accuracy rather than absorbing the dramatic subject-matter of the picture itself. 'Giving reminders of other artists', George Bernard Shaw wrote waspishly in 1886, 'is quite a speciality with Mr Waterhouse'.[7] The revelatory experience of the retrospective of Millais's paintings in 1886 marked the genesis of Waterhouse's commitment to Pre-Raphaelite type subjects. His experiments with French naturalist techniques – square brushing, and enlivening the surface with broken touches of colour – were first ventured in *The Magic Circle* (cat. 17) which Waterhouse sent to the Royal Academy in 1886. Its reception was generally good, and few critics seemed to take offence at this very public employment of French methods. Indeed it was purchased for the nation by the Chantrey Trustees for £650 but, in a highly unusual break with protocol, the vote was split seven for and three against. This might have given some slight warning for the reception of Waterhouse's more complex painting in a French idiom, *The Lady of Shalott*.

Waterhouse's *Lady of Shalott* marked a departure for him in several ways. The theme of a doomed, punished woman who meets a violent end is of course an uncomfortably recurrent leitmotif in his work, and it was evidently one of his preferred and very favourite subjects. In the years leading up to *The Lady of Shalott* he sent to the Academy *St Eulalia* (cat. 16) in 1885 – a picture which depicted the corpse of the twelve year old virgin Christian martyr who endured having her flesh torn with hooks and then had fires lit under her to increase her suffering – and in 1887, *Mariamne* (cat. 18), the beautiful queen falsely accused of adultery, and put to death by Herod, whom Waterhouse showed being led away in chains to her execution, proud but mute. These pictures were punctuated at the Royal Academy by *Consulting the Oracle* (cat. 15) in 1884 and *The Magic Circle* (cat. 17) in 1886, both exoticised characterisations of woman as mystic or witch.

The Lady of Shalott continued the theme of doomed femininity, and combined both these Waterhouse feminine 'types' – for, as Tennyson relates in his poem, the Lady of Shalott was a 'fairy Lady' engaged in weaving 'A magic web', the tapestry itself having magical properties. Instead of Classical antiquity, the Bible, or Christian history, Waterhouse turned to Tennyson's version of the Arthurian myths. These were at the height of their popularity but, in the context of Waterhouse's output, it might be interpreted as deliberately shifting towards an authentically British subject. The year after, in 1889, his Academy contribution was another home-grown female victim, *Ophelia* (fig. 30). Waterhouse's choice might simply have capitalised on areas that sold well – Arthurian legend, Tennyson, and Shakespeare were always popular and there was a great growth in the number of Arthurian pictures exhibited in the 1880s and 1890s.[8]

The 1880s in Britain was a period of intense speculation about the direction the 'National School' should take. Conservatives looked to uphold the traditions and values of British art of the past, and the manner in which these had been taught. But younger painters saw in the development of naturalism and impressionism in Paris an exciting example of the potential plurality that art could take. It should be noted that neither contemporary artists nor critics in Britain were seemingly precise in their application of the two terms, naturalism and impressionism, with the latter being the least understood, the least accurately applied and the most inflammatory. Discontent among the younger generation gathered around the appropriate teaching of art, in some degree a debate that had been ignited by successive government inquiries and the establishment of a national curriculum in the state art schools. As the premier teaching and exhibiting institution, but exempt from government reform, the Royal Academy came in for particular criticism by young artists who favoured French prototypes. The quality and direction of Royal Academy training was challenged, and by the 1880s there was a chorus of criticism, claiming the Academy's traditions and strict rules were out of touch with modern artistic requirements. Moreover its selection processes for the prestigious annual exhibitions and elections of its members were openly accused of being at best dogmatic and reactionary, and at worst openly corrupt. By 1885 criticism was getting so outspoken that *The Magazine of Art* was able to state:

> The Royal Academy is no longer a name to charm with. The public have recognised that it is in no wise equal to its responsibilities, and that its constitution is as glaring an anachronism as the laws by which it is governed. As an educational institution it has little or nothing to teach; and its students, as soon as they have passed the curriculum it imposes on them make haste to betake themselves to France, to learn, not only how to paint and draw, but to forget as much as they can of the theory and practice acquired in its schools. In Paris they are taught to see and to represent; no painter warns them back from the unholy and unnecessary study of the nude; they may profit by the example of men who are primarily not idealists, but craftsmen. They have found out that to be a painter you must first of all be able to paint; that you may practice the academical tradition for years, and find yourself worse off at the end than at the beginning; that such Englishmen as could

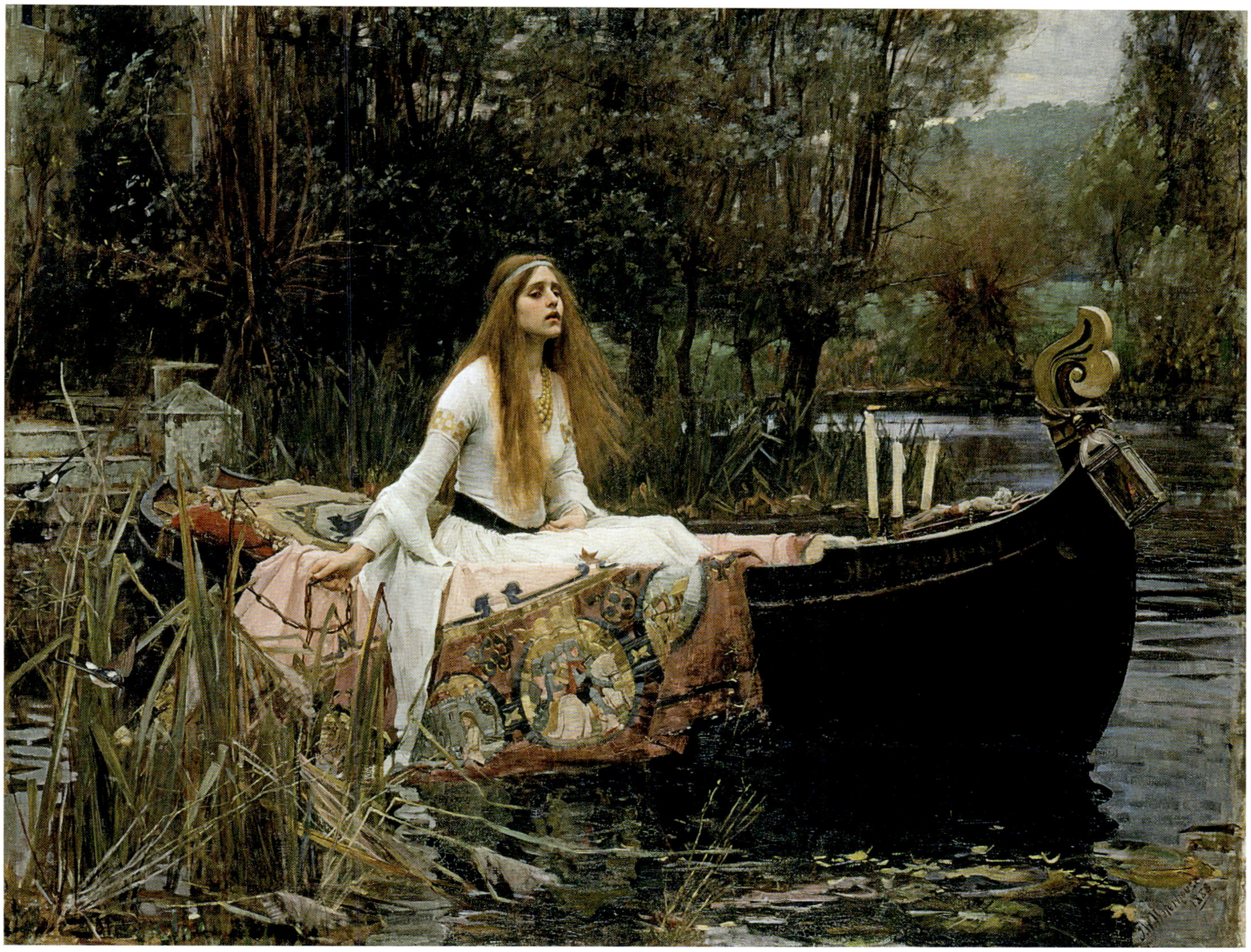

20. J.W. Waterhouse, *The Lady of Shalott*, 1888, Oil on canvas, 153 x 200 cm, Tate

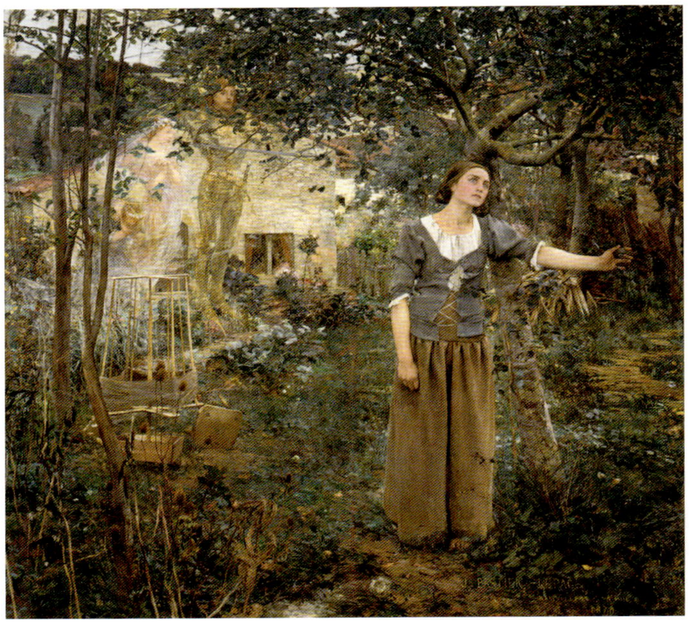

21. Jules Bastien-Lepage, *Joan of Arc Listening to the Voices,* 1879, Oil on canvas, 254 x 279.4 cm, Metropolitan Museum of Art, New York

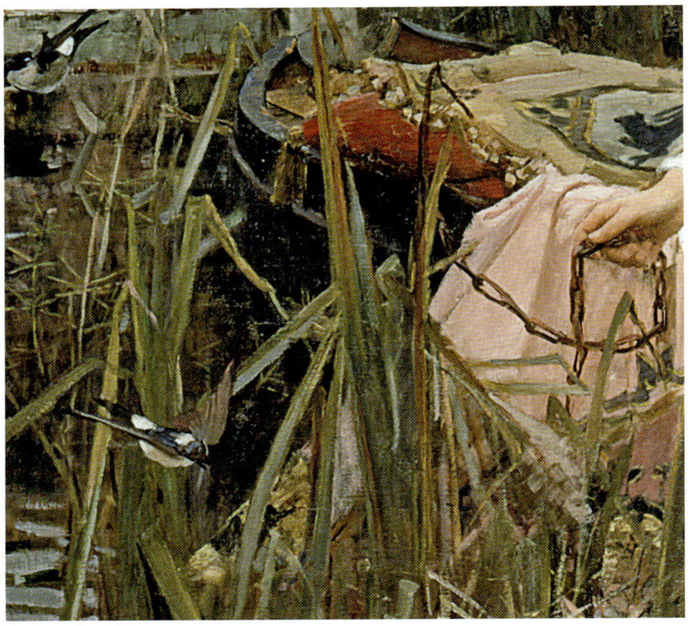

22. J.W. Waterhouse, *The Lady of Shalott* (detail), 1888, Oil on canvas, Overall 153 x 200 cm, Tate

show them anything are far too busy money-making to give them a single thought; and the result is that French influences are strengthening and multiplying year by year, and year by year the Academy is falling farther into the past. It cannot teach, and it will not learn.[9]

Waterhouse was a stalwart Academy exhibitor, as this was the premier venue for securing lucrative sales. Yet his friendships in the 1880s suggest that he may have held a more complex range of sympathies than we might at first imagine. Financially well off from brisk Academy sales, in 1878 Waterhouse was able to move into one of the Primrose Hill Studios, which was a key event for the development of the style and ambition of his art. Purpose built by the architect Alfred Healey as artists' studio-houses, they still survive off Fitzroy Road in London NW1. They consisted of twelve apartments around a central courtyard and housed a rich diversity of artistic talent. Here the Waterhouses were particular friends of Maurice Greiffenhagen and William Logsdail and their wives, and Waterhouse and Logsdail both revelled in a jolly bohemian camaraderie that recalls George Du Maurier's novel *Trilby* of 1894. (See fig. 47) 'We formed a happy family', Logsdail recalled in his manuscript memoirs, 'in and out of each other's studios during the day, and in the evening swapping stories over the cards and whisky or dining at the Bull and Bush on Hampstead Heath'.[10] Logsdail was busy painting monumental plein-air records of modern London life seen in the streets, and employed Waterhouse and his wife as models in some of them. Logsdail regularly worked in the studio courtyard, and Waterhouse may have followed his example, as his move to Primrose Hill coincided with his production of larger-scale pictures. And Waterhouse was also on warm terms with the plein-airiste Frank Bramley, a friend he seems most likely to have made through Logsdail, as Bramley and Logsdail were contemporaries at both the Lincoln School of Art and the Antwerp Academy. Bramley and Logsdail had been painting in Venice in the first half of the 1880s, and Waterhouse too spent time there, painting intimate, loose oils which recorded canal scenes and fisher girls in a manner greatly at variance with the finished formality of his Academic machines. Bramley exhibited at the Royal Academy for the first time in 1884, showing some canvases of Venetian women close in idiom to Waterhouse's paintings of the same subject-matter. The following year saw the sensation of Stanhope Forbes's *Fish Sale on a Cornish Beach* at the Academy, and this persuaded Bramley to join Forbes in setting up an art school at Newlyn, where Forbes was already ensconced. Together they formed the nucleus of the Newlyn School, a group of painters committed to painting naturalist, everyday rural scenes in the manner of

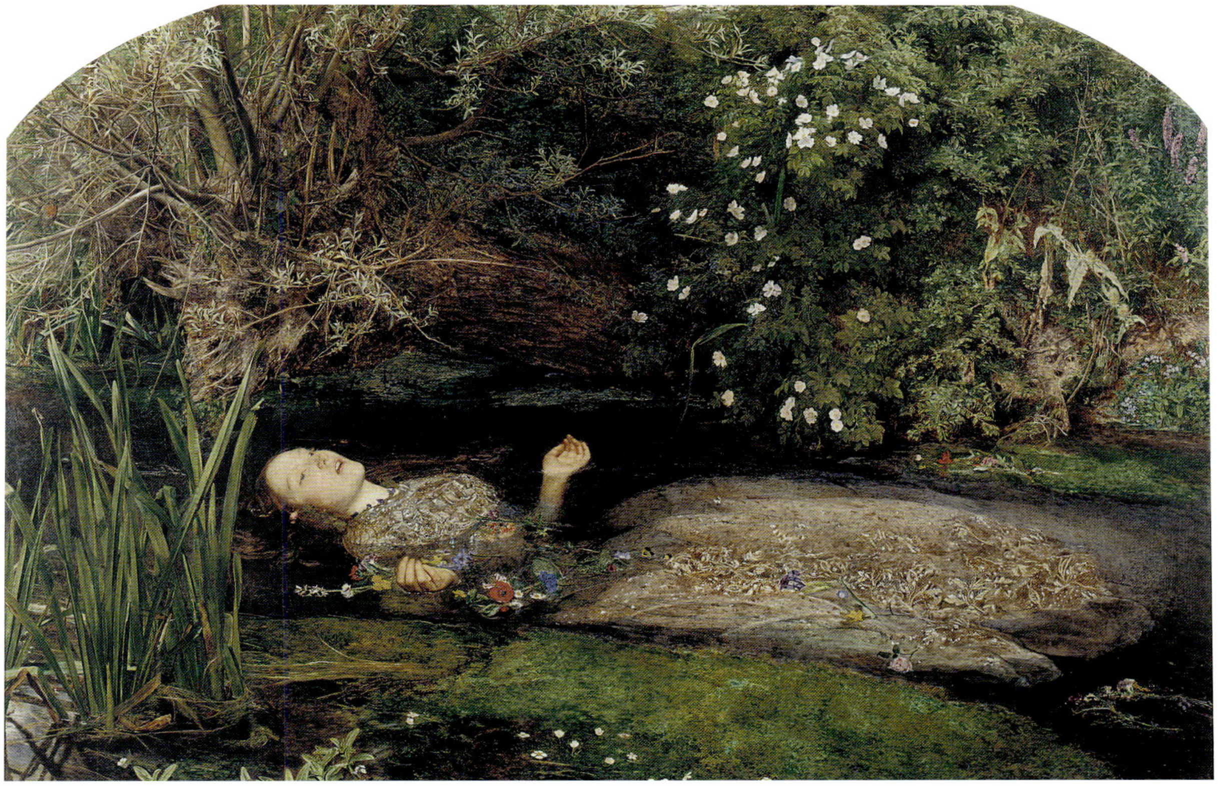

23. John Everett Millais, *Ophelia,* 1851-1852, Oil on canvas, 76.2 x 111.8 cm (arched), Tate

the French painters Jules Bastien-Lepage and Jules Breton. Forbes had spent two years training in Paris under Léon Bonnat and here had developed his admiration for subjects and styles which ran counter to what many of the senior Royal Academicians believed was the true and proper destiny of the National School.

In 1886 Forbes, Bramley, Henry Herbert La Thangue, George Clausen, and others formed their own breakaway exhibiting society, the New English Art Club, dedicated both to the creation of a new kind of English art and the championing of French painting techniques and rural naturalist subjects. Whether they might have asked Waterhouse or Logsdail if they were interested in joining is unknown, but Waterhouse's election as an Associate of the Royal Academy the year before might make this unlikely, as did his continuing commitment to large Academic subject pictures. But both Waterhouse and Logsdail were touched by New English Art Club technique. The naturalists imitated Bastien-Lepage's way of working, and in *The Lady of Shalott* Waterhouse seems to have partly had in mind their rapid dabs of paint and square-brushing to give a lively rendering of nature. At the Academy such technical practices were anathema and were condemned in the RA Schools. Its invention attributed to Bastien, square brushing was described by a British critic as a technique where paint was put on rapidly with a square brush:

> those who practice it in its simplest form leave the brushmarks and do not smooth away the evidence of the method, thus sometimes insisting on the way the picture is painted, perhaps at the sacrifice of subtleties in the subject.[11]

Waterhouse's new style had nothing to do with the sleek finish of Leighton or the precision of Alma-Tadema. Instead Waterhouse opted for the virile 'naturalist' style then being used by NEAC painters. This was a bold attempt to combine a Pre-Raphaelite subject with painting in a naturalist manner, and it must be viewed in the context of the bitter row that was now sweeping the London art world between the conservatives of the Royal Academy and the avant-garde impressionists of the New English Art Club.

Bad feeling between naturalists and Academics reached a frenzy in 1887-1888, and was fought out bitterly in the pages of *The Magazine of Art*. In March 1887 Sir James Linton, President of the Royal Institute of Painters in Water-Colours, wrote an article which denounced naturalist tendencies in British art. This was followed by the French critic Ernest Chesneau's startling article 'The English School in Peril' which warned British painters against abandoning their own native prototypes and following French styles and training.[12] 'It is a grave error', Chesneau warned: 'Not only should we never allow the sacred flame of nationalism in art to die

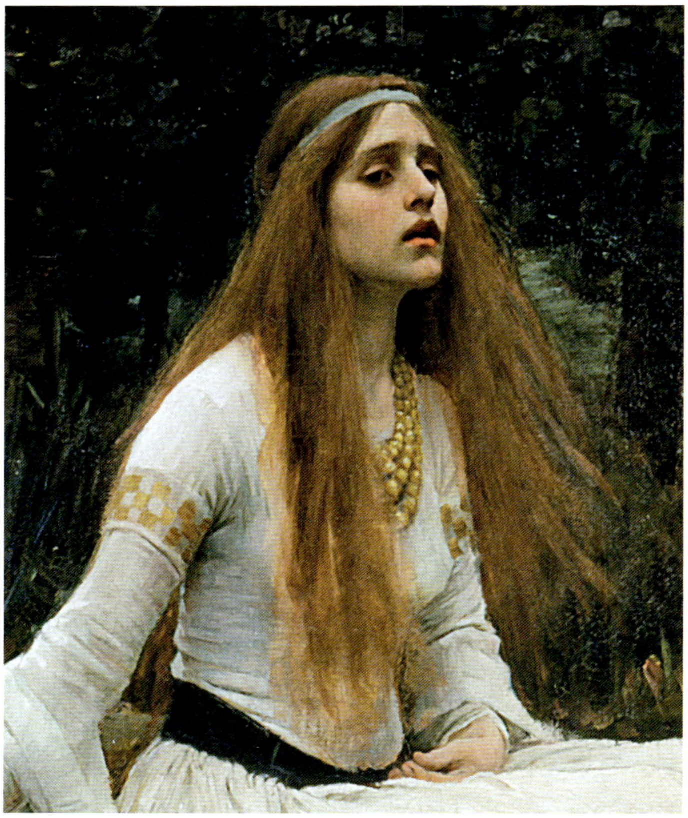

24. J.W. Waterhouse, *The Lady of Shalott* (detail), 1888, Oil on canvas, Overall 153 x 200 cm, Tate

out, but, on the contrary, we should cherish it with jealous zeal'.[13] The critic Claude Phillips took the absence of British naturalist and impressionist work from the Manchester Jubilee Exhibition to signal a veto of French tendencies in British art. It was, he wrote:

> Like the ostrich hiding from danger … it is to such influences, and to those of the many branches of the French naturalistic school of this later generation that we shall owe the next development of English art. It is, we think, a subject for sincere regret that this should be the case; not because we would undervalue the extraordinary merit and genuineness of much that is produced in these same schools, but because it appears doubtful whether the English genius can ever more than superficially accommodate itself to such methods, of which it is easy to acquire the trick without the truth … Yet is young England to be blamed for its revolt from stagnation and cheap conventionality?[14]

A founder member of the New English Art Club, George Clausen wrote a brilliantly argued rebuttal of Linton and Chesneau's articles, criticising the RA and pointing out that British art had always been re-energised by foreign artists and it was to this that it owed its success. 'On what grounds should we not study and profit by all that is open to us?', Clausen wrote.

> Why close our eyes to the works, say, of French contemporary artists? … Is it because they are aliens? And yet they are not so far removed from us as are the great masters, whom we study for our profit, and who were not only aliens, but of a past age. We have assimilated them, we read their thoughts, and we admit, in our admiration of their works, that the central truths of nature and human life are common to all ages and lands. Let us be candid in this matter. Art is but the expression of thought; and we have the right to hold ourselves open to every thought that appeals to us.[15]

Clausen wrote how it was evidently the failure of art teaching in Britain to modernise, most notably in the Royal Academy, which drove young artists to Paris. The secret of 'Laborious and persistent study of the nude, under the continuous personal influence of the best artists' was the French method for success, and one at odds with the Royal Academy's insistence on spending years drawing only from the Antique.[16] Clausen stated baldly that British teachers were not artists of the first order, as too few of the best would deign to teach, and furthermore that

> blame, if any, must rest with those guardians of our art who for long years allowed the teaching of our art schools to be little better than a farce. Have they preserved and handed down the traditions of our early painters? What and where are they? Lost! … They and their school are dead, while the Royal Academy … has sat dozing over its money bags.[17]

These were serious allegations which saw the argument slipping away from the traditionalists. The pugnacious Academician William Powell Frith intervened with an article entitled 'Crazes in Art' which vilified both Pre-Raphaelitism – which Clausen identified as having been a revitalising force – and Impressionism.[18] Frith struck at the heart of the Impressionist agenda by maintaining that only the standards of an Academic training could possibly deliver great art. He opened his article: 'A thorough knowledge of drawing (only to be acquired by severe early training) is an absolute necessity for all who desire to arrive at excellence in art.'[19] Launching himself at the Pre-Raphaelites, who had begun this culture of disrespectfully questioning tradition, Frith wrote:

> While … others were putting into practice true principles of art – principles founded upon the great examples of the greatest masters – there suddenly arose amongst us a band of young men who called themselves 'Pre-Raphaelite Brethren', and who proceeded to prove the justice of their nomenclature by refusing the guidance of any painter who had the misfortune in their wise young eyes, of being born after, or contemporary with Raphael ... Ugliness and angularity took the place of grace … when the wiseacres amongst the public could count all the leaves on a plant, could see the light in a bird's eye … the new school was right and the old one wrong. We [the RAs] were taunted with

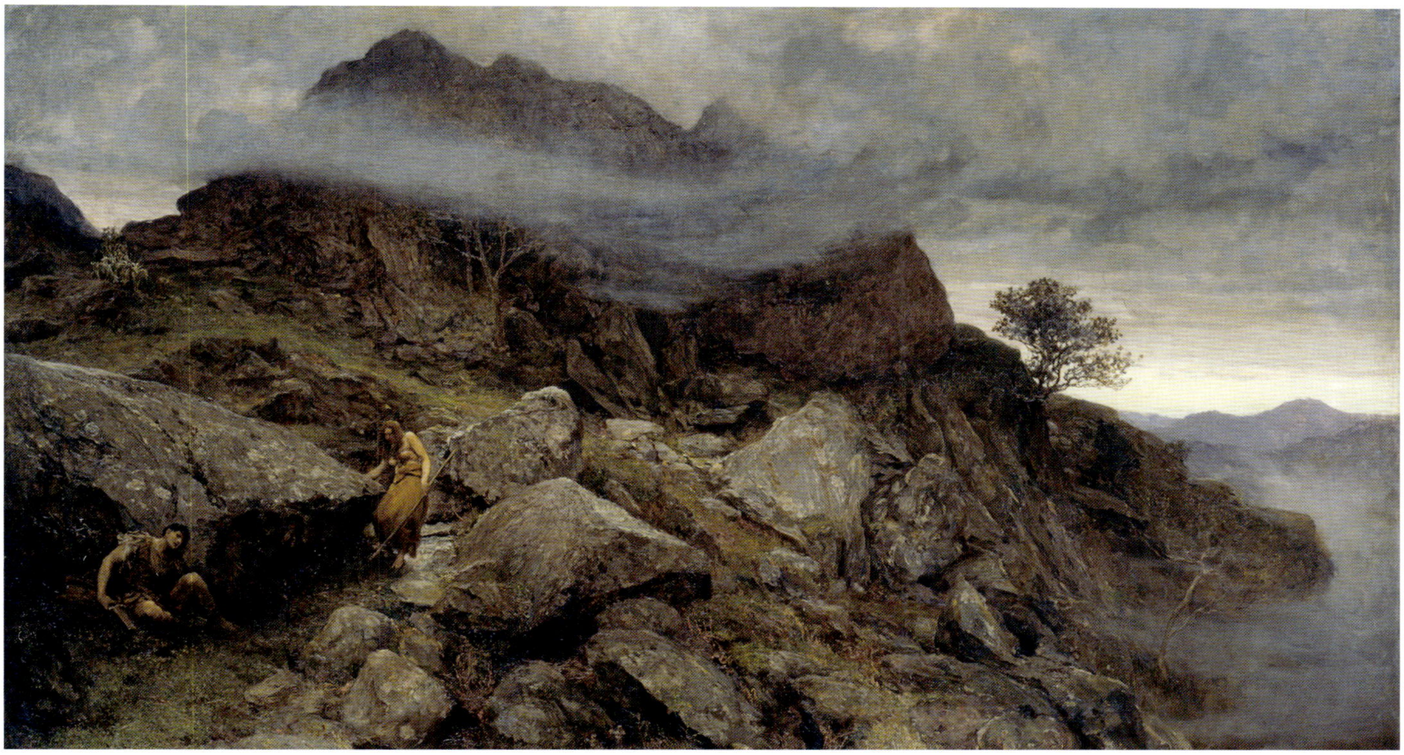

25. Hubert von Herkomer, *Found,* 1884-1885, Oil on canvas, 137.2 x 230.5 cm, Tate

> sloppiness and carelessness, and the absence of honesty in our painting of Nature … this ridiculous movement received the support of a brilliant writer [ie Ruskin] … [who] is, I hold, often utterly mistaken and wrong …[20]

Turning his attention to more recent developments, Frith continued:

> The Pre-Raphaelite craze ran its course like a fever … and another, far more dangerous craze has come upon us. Born and bred in France, what is called Impressionism has tainted the art of this country … the 'Impressionists' will not be allowed to play their pranks in the Royal Academy exhibition; we have enough evidence there of the seeming forgetfulness of the good that may be acquired from foreign training … but the [Impressionist] craze itself will as assuredly pass away as everything foolish and false does sooner or later.[21]

Frith was laying down a warning to anyone who might be tempted by French practices to introduce them to the Academy, and using terminology that equated them with sickness and contagion. Even Millais echoed him, warning alarmingly of a loss of national identity:

> There is among us a band of young men who, though English, persist in painting with a broken French accent, all of them much alike, and seemingly content to lose their identity in their imitation of French masters.[22]

Against the background of these very public battles, Waterhouse's decision to adopt a more modern technique for his 1888 Academy machine was a brave move. In *The Lady of Shalott* nature was carefully observed and recorded, appearing like a real riverbank, not a studio construction, and indeed, certain passages were reputedly painted outside. Without the central subject of the fairy Lady herself, this could be a superbly naturalistic, evocative impression of landscape. Yet to all this freely rendered observation Waterhouse added the Lady of Shalott, mixing naturalism with magic and myth. While his style was at the cutting edge of current British aesthetic developments, his subject looked backwards, both to an Arthurian story and to an old and generally respected generation of British artists, the Pre-Raphaelites, whom he so greatly admired. The picture contains a number of references to Pre-Raphaelite pictures, and it is tempting to see *The Lady of Shalott* as advancing an argument for a revitalisation of the Pre-Raphaelites' famous dictum of 'truth to nature' expressed in naturalist terms, while maintaining their seriousness of subject matter. It is as if Waterhouse were suggesting a programme to resolve the opposing arguments around naturalism and tradition. If so, *The Lady of Shalott* was an attempt to bring together past and

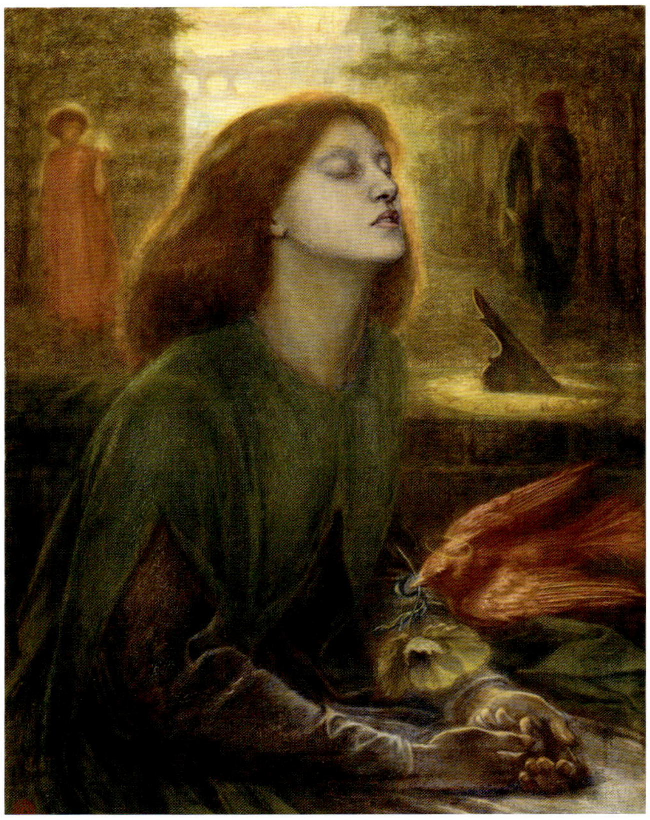

26. Dante Gabriel Rossetti, *Beata Beatrix,* 1864-1870, Oil on canvas, 86.4 x 66 cm, Tate

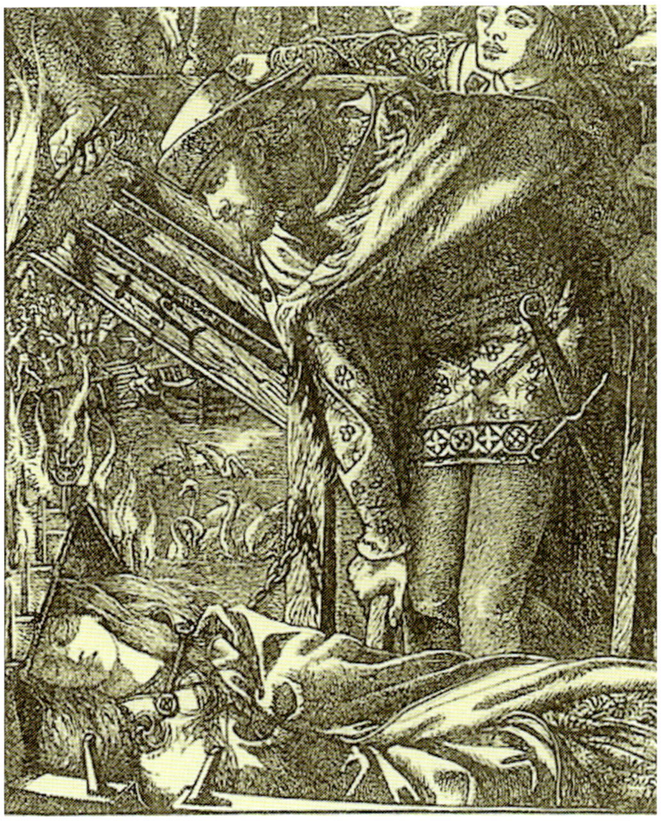

27. After Dante Gabriel Rossetti, 'The Lady of Shalott', Wood engraving in Alfred Tennyson, *Poems,* published by Edward Moxon, London, 1857

present, reconciling tradition and innovation to find a 'third way' which mediated between what were seen as the two extremes of the Academy and the naturalist impressionists. To a younger, less conservative generation, *The Lady of Shalott* was certainly seen as a rallying call for the possibility of unifying these opposing demands of naturalism and narrative. The critic R.E.D. Sketchley recalled that 'The picture was received with much enthusiasm by young painters, as a successful reconciliation of the claims of the imagination and realism in art'.[23]

In choosing a native myth, Waterhouse was bolstering the 'Britishness' of his picture, and the general revival of interest in pictures of Arthurian legends at the end of the century can be seen in the context of contemporary concerns about nationalism and race. Eugenics, immigration, and analysis of English and British racial and cultural identity all meant that Arthur's ethnicity, and the authenticity of homogeneous native myth came under scrutiny and question. By the 1880s the tales of Arthur and his knights were generally considered specifically Celtic, and this awareness is perhaps indicated in Waterhouse's picture by the Lady's red hair. For a late Victorian audience, Celtic denoted mysticism, and ancient, 'authentic' Britons, inextricably bound up with, for them, positive concepts of racial purity and integrity. Celtic-style jewellery and decoration became highly popular. However, racial self-examination and awareness also brought uncertainty to non-Celts. The closing decades of the century saw ethnic nationalist movements emerging politically, some openly separatist and republican. Pan-Celtic and folklore societies were formed to study the culturally distinct constituents of Great Britain; in Wales the Eisteddfod was flourishing, and a group was formed to foster links between traditional Welsh and Breton cultures. The question of whether Camelot was in Cornwall, Northumbria, or Scotland, as various projects set out to answer, held distinct political connotations, laying claim to the past as well as the present. Interest in the 'original' racial make-up of Britain can be seen as the subtext behind a range of Academic pictures of the time, such as Herkomer's *Found* (fig. 25) showing an 'Ancient' British woman's discovery of a wounded Roman soldier. Such pictures indicate concern about national and racial identity, of which the resurgence of Arthurian images was further evidence. Waterhouse's switch in 1888 to a story identified as native and authentic, after a career devoted to painting Greek or Roman scenes, could appear almost an act of nationalist cultural assertion.

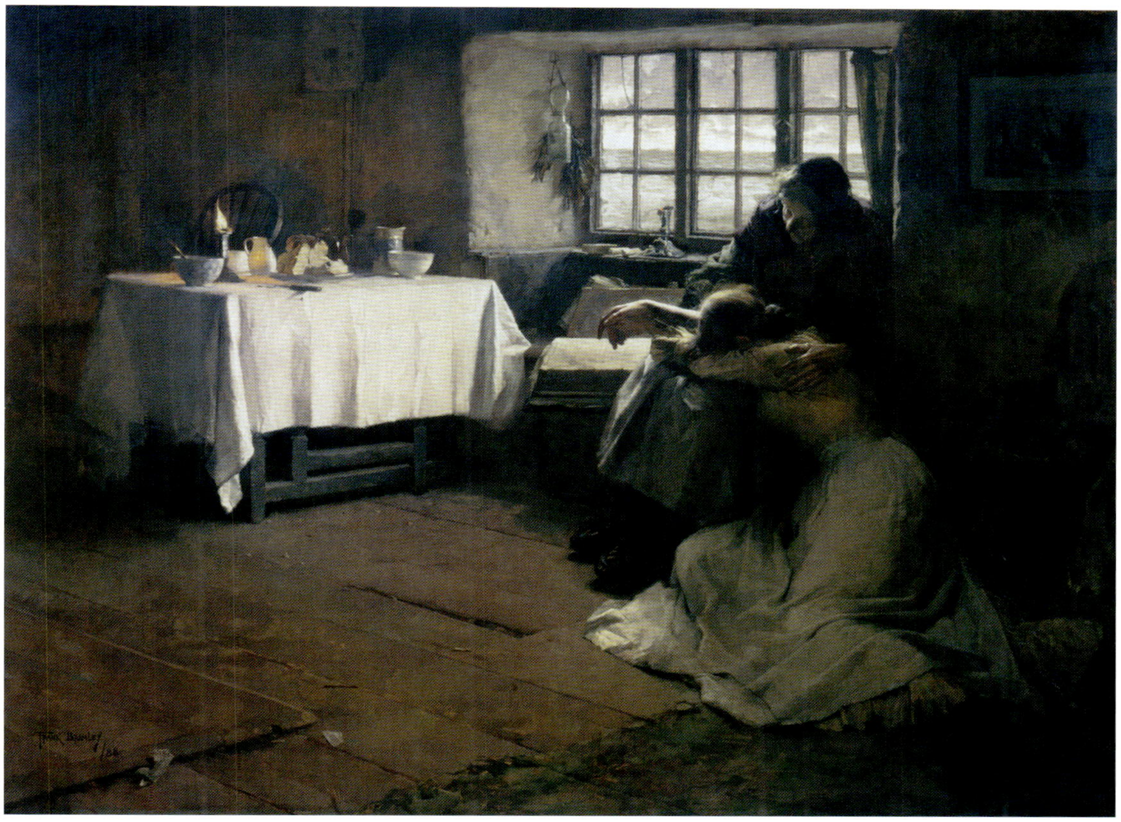

28. Frank Bramley, *A Hopeless Dawn,* 1888, Oil on canvas, 122.6 x 167.6 cm, Tate

A close antecedent for Waterhouse's picture was very evidently Millais's *Ophelia* (fig. 23), which he saw at the Grosvenor Gallery in 1886. Ophelia floating singing to her death has clear narrative parallels with the Lady of Shalott, but Waterhouse appears to have also borrowed or adapted certain pictorial passages. The rushes occupying the left foreground of *The Lady of Shalott* are close in arrangement to those in the same position in *Ophelia*, and willows, emblems of weeping and sadness, appear in both texts and pictures. For the figure itself, Waterhouse looked to another Pre-Raphaelite, Dante Gabriel Rossetti. Poised between life and death, the half-turned face, flowing red hair, parted lips, up-tilted head, and positioning of the left arm are all adapted from Rossetti's *Beata Beatrix* (fig. 26), which Waterhouse saw at the Royal Academy memorial display of his pictures in 1883. Waterhouse's wife Esther modelled for his own picture, and there is something slightly uncomfortable in the fact that he set her in the pose of Rossetti's own, dead wife.

Millais's *The Bride* seems to have been a further more peripheral source of inspiration, but Waterhouse also used another, more modern source for the Lady. He turned to the arch exponent of French naturalism Jules Bastien-Lepage, and specifically to his picture *Joan of Arc* of 1879 (fig. 21). The rapt expression and intensity of the pose evidently owe something of a debt to Bastien's canvas, although it is interesting that of all his many pictures, most of them ruralist in one way or another, Waterhouse chose a subject picture, and an historical one at that.

Other more peripheral elements were also poached from the Pre-Raphaelites. Rossetti had contributed to an illustrated edition of Tennyson's poems published by Moxon in 1857 with which Waterhouse was evidently familiar. The prominent candles on the prow of Waterhouse's boat in *The Lady of Shalott* are not mentioned anywhere by Tennyson, and these and the prow's decoration were lifted from Rossetti's small Moxon design which showed the discovery of the Lady of Shalott's body at Camelot (fig. 27).

But the symbolism of the candle guttering to extinction, indicating imminent death, also appeared in a painting of a modern subject. Frank Bramley used exactly the same device to denote the flickering away of a lost sailor's life as his wife mourns at home in *A Hopeless Dawn* (fig. 28) which was the sensation of the 1888 Academy. As Bramley was a friend of Waterhouse and Logsdail it must seem possible that Waterhouse saw or heard about Bramley's picture, giving him the idea to appropriate its central symbolic

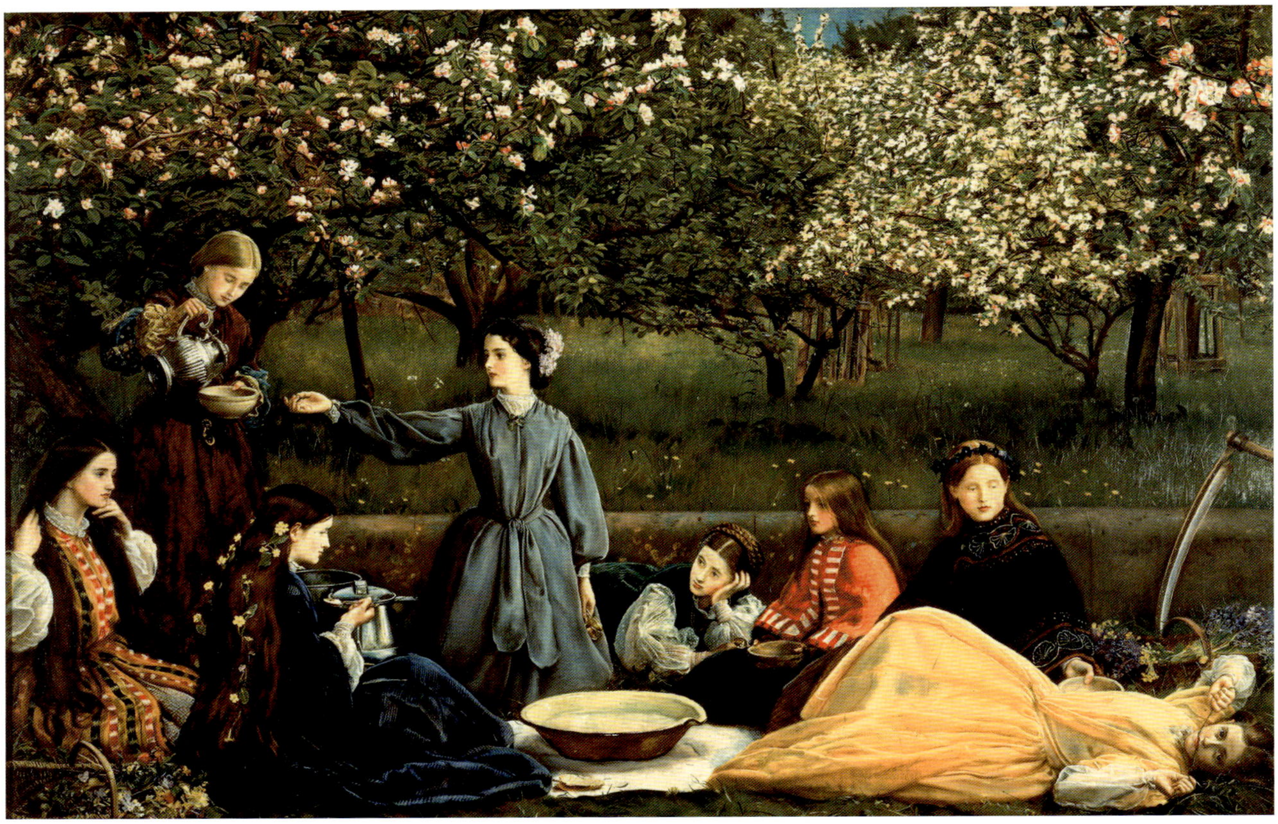

29. John Everett Millais, *Spring (Apple Blossoms)*, 1859, Oil on canvas, 113 x 176.3 cm, Lady Lever Art Gallery, Port Sunlight, National Museums Liverpool

motif for his own very different picture. Waterhouse's trinity of candles, blowing out one by one in a countdown to death, combined with the crucifix on the prow of the boat, introduced a religious element into *The Lady of Shalott* that was entirely absent from Tennyson's poem. The swallows on the left are symbols of salvation, and Waterhouse may perhaps be suggesting that the Lady's faith will redeem her, and that, as in Rossetti's *Beata Beatrix*, death is only a transition to the next world.

The Academy demonstrated its magnanimity and admiration by displaying Waterhouse's picture, despite its naturalist style, at the centre of the main wall in Room 6, where it was visible to every visitor at the end of the enfilade at the top of the staircase at Burlington House. Other works in the same room included another Arthurian subject, *Sir Galahad* by Charles Edward Johnson, and Logsdail's plein-airiste *St Martin-in-the-Fields* which he had spent some weeks painting in a cart in Trafalgar Square. *The Lady of Shalott*, however, did not receive the praise that Waterhouse had begun to expect. The critics noted his turn to a naturalist style and its reception clearly suffered from the row between conservative and avant-garde factions in the press.

M.H. Spielmann in *The Magazine of Art* judged the picture 'a disappointment; with a change of style and treatment there has come about a check in his onward course. Not that there is any lack of invention or drawing: but the French flatness of tones takes much of the quality out of the colour'.[24] The *Saturday Review* complained of it being 'brutal and unromantic in treatment', the *Portfolio* described it as 'curiously realised' and 'weird',[25] and the *Athenaeum* sneered:

> A greater mistake than Mr Waterhouse's *Lady of Shalott* is not in the Academy … Hackneyed as the subject is, it was never so poorly treated. A dyspeptic and commonplace young female sits, with all the self-consciousness of the stage, in a boat … Commonplace and pretentious as this insult to the poem is, the execution is as insincere as the composition is tame.

The Art Journal, however, praised the picture, and drew attention to the new direction the picture took Waterhouse's art:

> Mr Waterhouse, whose excellent work, with its singular artistic method, was still fresh in its interest, made a sudden change in this beautiful picture, so that those best versed in his work

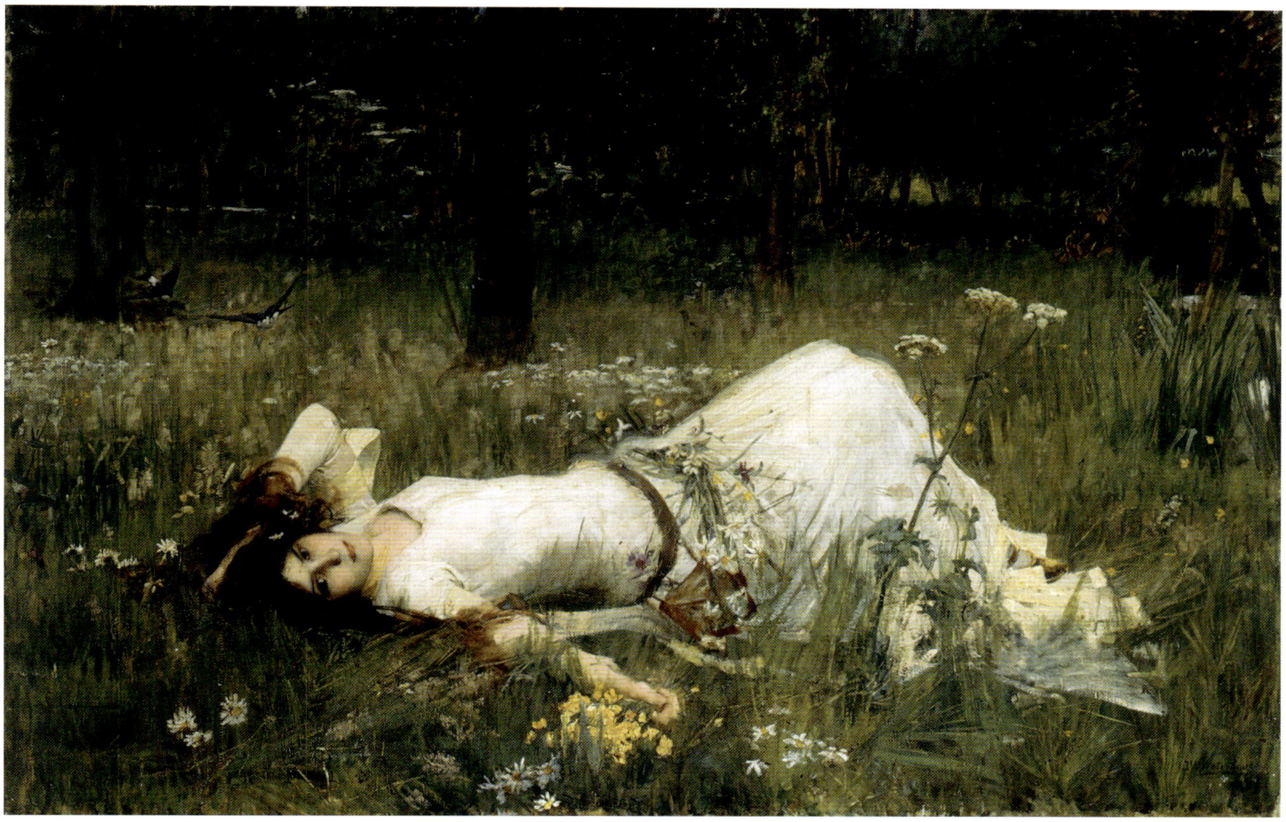

30. J.W. Waterhouse, *Ophelia,* 1889, Oil on canvas, 98 x 158 cm, Collection Lord Lloyd Webber

> were probably the last to recognise his hand in the new manner. The type he chose for the spell-controlled lady, her action, and the garments in which he has arrayed her, bring his work into kinship with that of the Pre-Raphaelites of the middle of this century, but the difference of the execution is thereby all the more marked; the almost impressionary delicacy of the rendering of willows, weeds, and water is such as claims harmony with French work rather than what was so intensely English. Mr Waterhouse's sincerity saves the picture absolutely from the charge of affectation, or at any rate self-consciousness, which clings to so much that has been done under the same impulse.[26]

This last observation was important, because many of the most extreme pictures, which had been shown at the New English Art Club, especially those by Steer, had been criticised for being wilfully mannered in their technique and colouring.

Waterhouse did not need to worry unduly about the rash of poor criticism of his picture as he already had a buyer. Henry Tate, an admirer of Waterhouse's work, purchased the picture for somewhere in the region of 1,000 guineas, a vast sum. For the next year's Royal Academy exhibition Waterhouse stuck to his guns and painted a picture even more technically adventurous and openly French in its execution, *Ophelia* (fig. 30). This was again a traditional, native subject and one most famously treated by Millais. But Waterhouse took for it another precedent by Millais, *Spring* (fig. 29). This again he had seen at the 1886 Grosvenor retrospective, and *Ophelia* was based on the recumbent figure on the right of Millais's picture, threatened famously by Death's scythe. Perhaps alluding to this borrowing, *The Art Journal* complained he 'displays the mad maiden in no novelty of attitude'.[27] Interestingly, Waterhouse's Ophelia is reversed suggesting that some element of tracing or translation from Millais may have been involved in his initial studies for the figure. But while the subject and its modelling made overt reference to a Pre-Raphaelite prototype, Waterhouse again used a virile modern style which saw him smear the paint over the canvas in a series of dashes and flicks that relied on abstraction for their effect (fig. 31).

But Waterhouse's *Ophelia* was not greeted as a success. Opinion was hardening against the influence of Bastien and French techniques, and as it moved towards a more radical

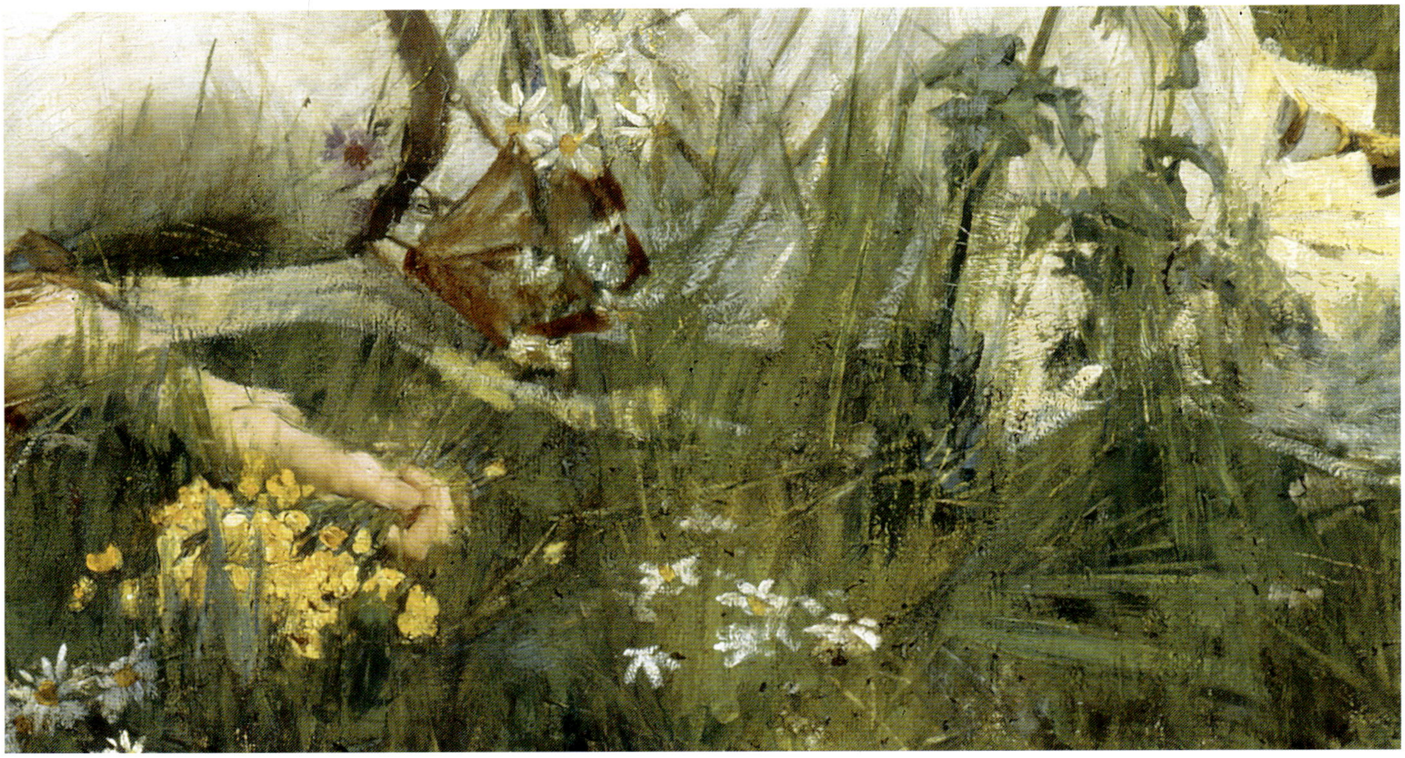

31. J.W. Waterhouse, *Ophelia* (detail), 1889, Oil on canvas, Overall 98 x 158 cm, Collection Lord Lloyd Webber

phase the New English Art Club was beyond the pale. Forbes and Bramley, who cannily maintained connection with the Academy by continuing to send their pictures there as well as the New English Art Club, were eventually to abandon the latter altogether and return to the conservative embrace of their Academic colleagues.

Claude Phillips saw Waterhouse's picture in overtly nationalistic terms, complaining of *Ophelia* that:

> If the English painter is to attempt the interpretation of English humanity and English nature … from the French standpoint, art of serious and enduring work can hardly be the result. It is not possible to emulate the pictorial thoroughness, the technical energy and inventiveness of our neighbours without sacrificing national sincerity.[28]

And indeed, rather oddly, *Ophelia* had a certain resonance with a New English Art Club picture by an American, Alexander Harrison, which was exhibited in 1887, *In Arcadia* (fig. 32), a nude subject painted at Grez on an epic scale. For the first time in many years Waterhouse could not find a buyer. He had surely hoped that Henry Tate might acquire *Ophelia*, but this was not to be and the painting remained on his hands, as did another picture he sent in 1889 to the RA, *Under the Olives*. Always one with an eye on sales, this must have hurt badly. In 1890 Waterhouse failed to send anything at all for exhibition at the Royal Academy. This was the first time the Academy had not held one of his pictures since 1874. His father had died in January 1890 and, while he nursed his wounds, he prepared for another, distinctive phase of painting which he launched publicly in 1891 with his startling canvases *Ulysses and the Sirens* (cat. 22) and *Circe Offering the Cup to Ulysses* (cat. 21), and which saw him retreat from naturalist technique for good. The criticism of painting at the New English Art Club based on French prototypes had become too extreme. Such vitriol and moral opprobrium were heaped upon Philip Wilson Steer that reputedly he seriously considered abandoning art. Instead he adapted his painting to imitate Turner and Constable and found immediate critical favour. Waterhouse similarly changed his style and never looked back.

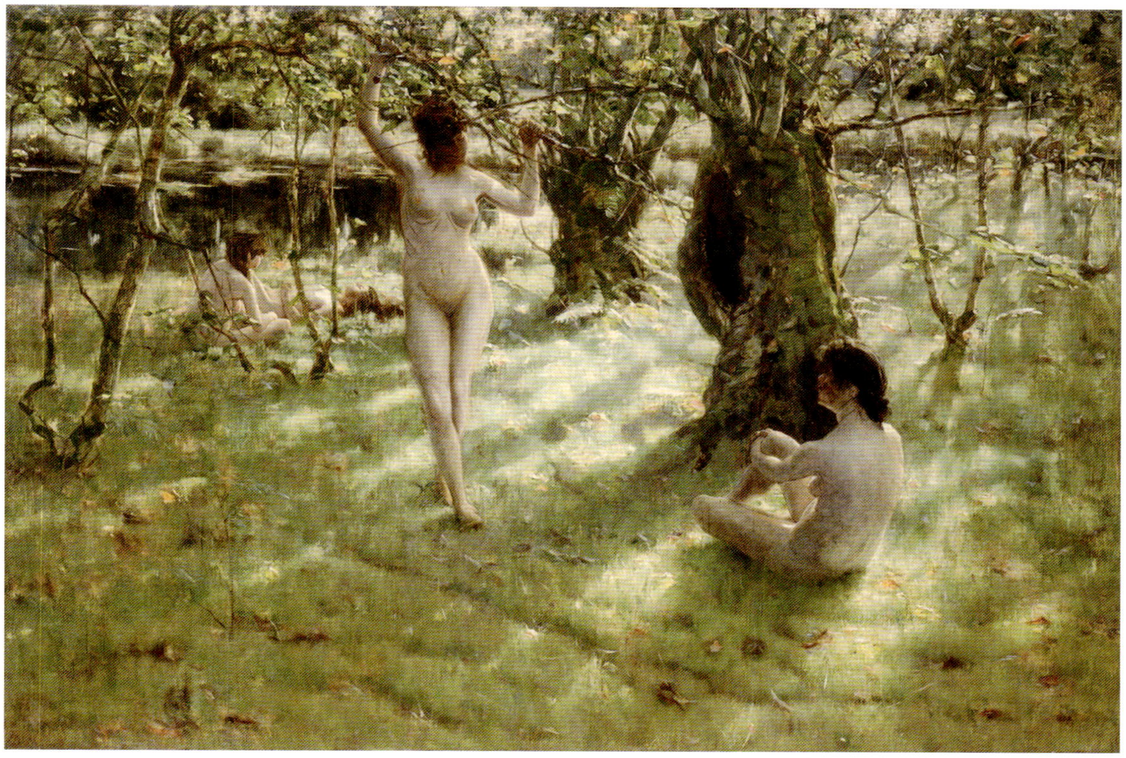

32. Alexander Harrison, *In Arcadia,* 1886, Oil on canvas, 197 x 290 cm, Musée d'Orsay, Paris

1 See Patty Wageman's essay, pp. 51-61.
2 See for instance *The Last Romantics*, exhibition catalogue, Barbican Art Gallery, 1989, pp. 117-118.
3 *The Times*, 12 February 1917, p. 6.
4 R.E.D. Sketchley, *The Art of J.W. Waterhouse, R.A.*, Christmas Number of *Art Journal*, 1909, p. 15.
5 *Ibid.*
6 *Ibid.*
7 George Bernard Shaw, *The World*, 12 May 1886.
8 See Christine Poulson, *The Quest for the Grail: Arthurian Legend in British Art 1840-1920*, Manchester 1999.
9 'Current Art IV', *The Magazine of Art*, 1885, p. 470.
10 Private collection.
11 Morley Roberts, 'A Colony of Artists', *The Scottish Art Review*, 1889, p. 72.
12 Ernest Chesneau, 'The English School in Peril: A Letter from Paris', *The Magazine of Art*, 1887, pp. 25-28.
13 *Ibid*, p. 28.
14 Claude Phillips, 'The Progress of English Art as shown at the Manchester Exhibition', *The Magazine of Art*, 1887, p. 46.
15 George Clausen, 'The English School in Peril: A Reply', *The Magazine of Art*, 1887, p. 223.
16 *Ibid*, p. 224.
17 *Ibid.*
18 William Powell Frith, 'Crazes in Art: Pre-Raphaelitism and Impressionism', *The Magazine of Art*, 1887, pp. 187-191.
19 *Ibid*, p. 187.
20 *Ibid*, pp. 189-191.
21 *Ibid*, p. 191.
22 John Everett Millais, 'Thoughts on the Art of Today', *The Magazine of Art*, 1887, p. 290.
23 R.E.D. Sketchley, *The Art of J.W. Waterhouse, R.A.*, Christmas Number of *Art Journal*, 1909, p. 15.
24 M.H. Spielmann, 'Current Art', *The Magazine of Art*, 1888, p. 271.
25 *The Portfolio*, 1888, p. 123.
26 'The Lady of Shalott', *The Art Journal*, 1889, p. 142.
27 *The Art Journal*, 1889, p. 188.
28 *Academy*, no. 35, 11 May 1889, p. 328.

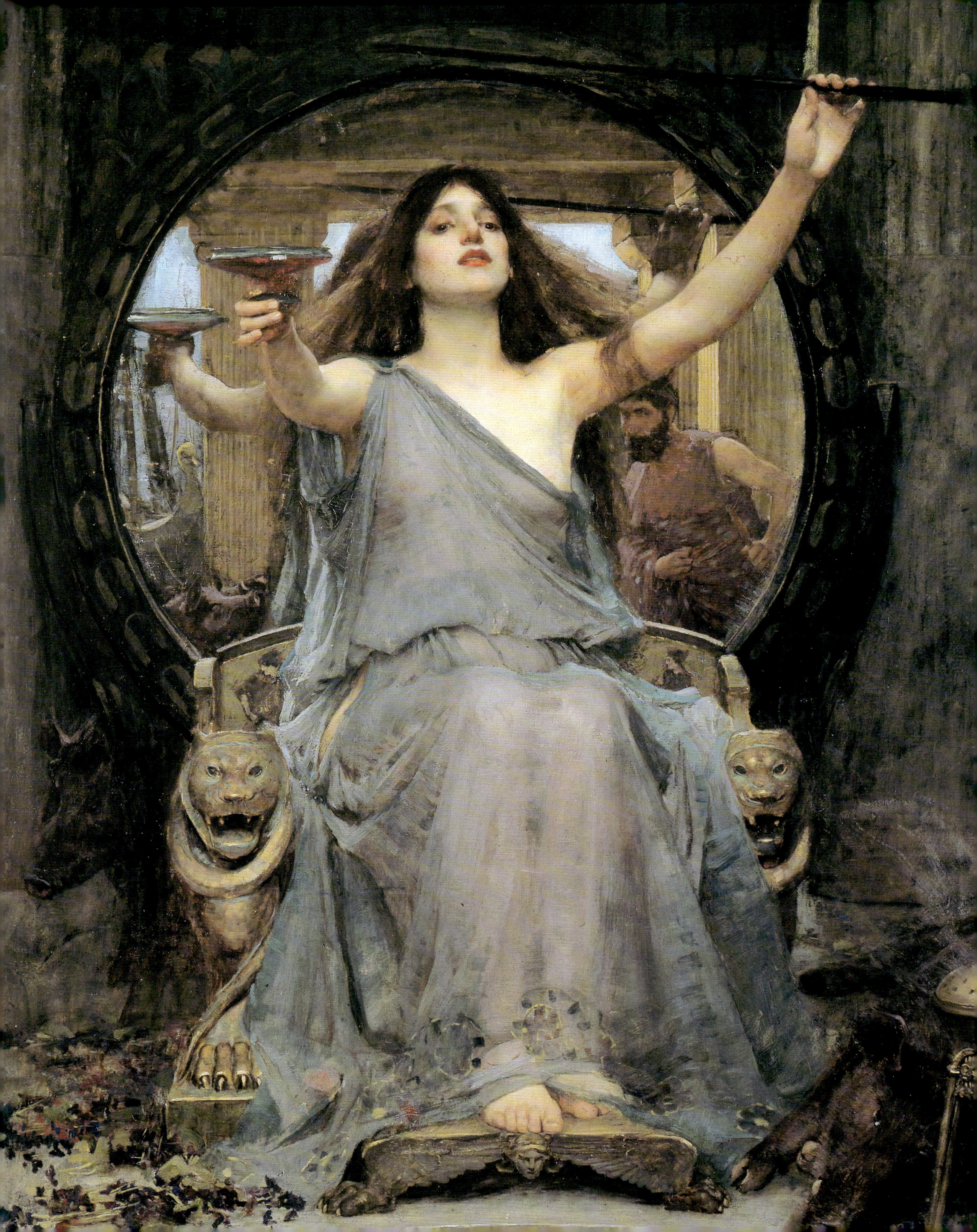

DREAM OR REALITY? WATERHOUSE'S WOMEN AND SYMBOLISM

Patty Wageman

We know so little about the life of John William Waterhouse that any interpretation of his work will suffer from lacunae that can never be filled with any certainty. When we consider the development of his paintings, in which certain features and subjects recur constantly, it is clear, as Peter Trippi writes in the biographical overview in this catalogue, that Waterhouse felt a fascination with women.

With the exception of the odd sketch and one great work, *The Favourites of the Emperor Honorius* (cat. 12), there is not a single painting in the exhibition in which women do not appear, often as the principal focus of attention. We see in turn passive women, sensual women, melancholy women, domestic women, not to mention strong women, both gorgeous and dangerous. They are the protagonists of their own stories, in a world that derives sometimes from mythology and sometimes from poetry and literature. Dressed in costumes from classical antiquity or the Renaissance, Waterhouse's women usually wear long robes that both conceal and reveal their physical form, in some cases exposing part of their bodies. Waterhouse painted them in a way that is almost palpable, so that the viewer can easily identify with them. They seem to be of flesh and blood, but they live in another, bygone time. A comparison of even a small selection of his paintings taken from different periods of his career shows that his image of femininity was an idealized one. He had a clear preference for a certain type of woman, who crops up each time in a different context. Who was she then; who was his model and muse? Despite some notes in his sketchbooks, we are lost for an answer.

Besides the model as muse, there are other striking features that recur regularly in Waterhouse's paintings – for instance, his frequent use of mirrors and circles and of women in or near stretches of water. Is it possible to attribute a deeper meaning to these motifs, apart from the fact that they lend the composition great beauty and excitement, reinforcing the tales they depict with exquisite imagery? Was Waterhouse just following a trend or was he completely original? How did nineteenth-century viewers look at his paintings? My aim in this essay is to enquire as to how far his work belonged to the spirit of the age in Europe, with reference to some of his paintings and examples of his contemporaries.

With regard to his preference for mythological tales and events from classical antiquity, and also for Pre-Raphaelite themes, Waterhouse was definitely a man of his time.[1] His choice of subject matter ties in perfectly with various trends in nineteenth-century painting. Is it also possible, however, to view his work in relation to continental Symbolism? Apart from the almost annual presentations in the summer exhibitions of the Royal Academy, his paintings were also shown at the world's fairs in Paris (1889 and 1900) and Brussels (1897). He is known to have travelled to the continent regularly, where it is very likely that he encountered French academic classicism early in his career, Impressionism from the 1870s onward, and Symbolism in the 1880s and 1890s.[2]

If we want to locate Waterhouse in this broader art-historical context we should realize that, in terms of social history, the nineteenth century was a period of industrial progress that gave rise to great prosperity and secularisation, and also to

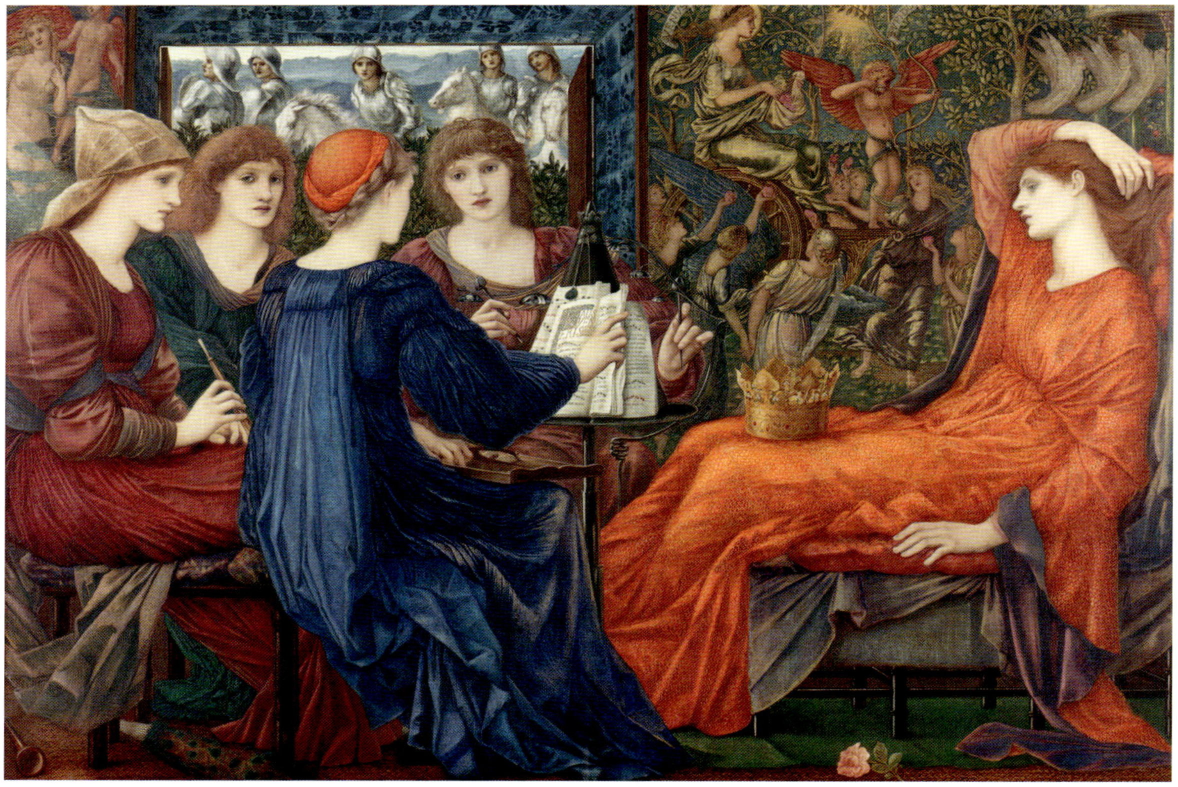

33. Edward Burne-Jones, *Laus Veneris*, 1870-1878, Oil on canvas, 122.6 x 183.2 cm, Laing Art Gallery, Tyne and Wear Museums, Newcastle upon Tyne

an increased mental distance from life in the country. These developments led in turn to shifts in social opinions and cultural values. One such shift led to Symbolism. Although it cannot be described as having a single coherent style, Symbolism can be seen as the intellectual trend that left a deep imprint on the arts and literature from the mid-1880s to the early twentieth century. Striking features in this trend are its ideas about women, the position of literature and mythology in painting and vice versa, the struggle against rationalism, and deriving from this, the quest for an unconscious creativity and an appreciation of the importance of the spiritual.[3]

Another change that occurred in the nineteenth century concerned the position of women. This was an issue of constant debate, and opinions were sharply divided; the growing campaigns for women's property rights and women's suffrage had both ardent supporters and vigorous opponents.[4] These different notions can be seen in the way that different artists depicted women in their paintings. Both Symbolism, as an artistic movement, and the debates over women's roles in society may have made an impact on Waterhouse's work.

WATERHOUSE'S WOMEN

Youthful, slender women with pale skin and dark brown or dark red hair were clearly Waterhouse's ideal. The rosy blushes on their cheeks give their pale faces a gentle expression and authenticity. Their gaze is often dreamy and inward-looking, or else concentrated on the action in which they are engaged, as in *Circe Invidiosa* (1892, cat. 23).

The Waterhouse woman, depicted as a young girl – then still a child – makes her first appearance in the painting *After the Dance* of 1876 (cat. 4); she is relaxing in a Roman palace after her performance. Waterhouse painted her in a reclining pose that he reintroduces in a similar fashion in works such as *Dolce Far Niente* (1879 and 1880, cats 7, 8), *Ophelia* (1889, fig. 30), *Ariadne* (1898, cat. 34), *'Listening to My Sweet Pipings'* (1911, cat. 55), and *Sweet Summer* (1912, private collection).

Although the story is different in every painting and the model changes over the course of time from a Mediterranean-looking woman to one with a more English appearance, it is fascinating to see that right up to *Sweet Summer*, painted five years before the death of the artist, these reclining women retain a certain languor and lethargy, forming a

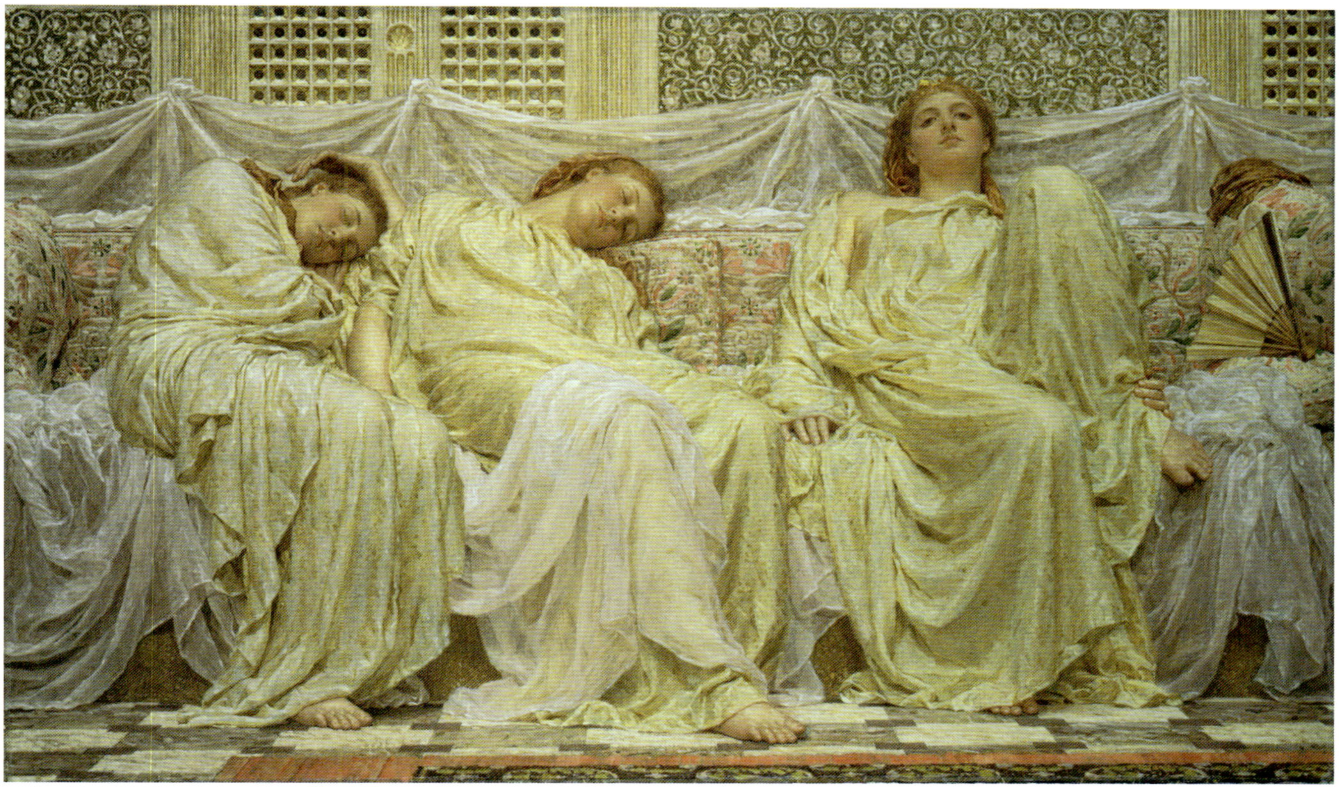

34. Albert Moore, *The Dreamers*, 1882, Oil on canvas, 72 x 121 cm, Birmingham Museums & Art Gallery

recurring element in the compositions. A title like *Dolce Far Niente* literally underscores this attitude; the expression, popular at the time, gave Waterhouse the possibility of representing beauty by way of a harmonious balance in form, lines, and colour with an Italian-Roman setting in the style of Lawrence Alma-Tadema. *Ariadne* alludes to the myth of that name and the leopards, flowers, and background are portents of Ariadne's marriage to the god Bacchus.[5] Of course Waterhouse's choice of the moment in the story defines the composition, but her dormant pose, with her arms behind her head, gives her the same air of languor, sensuality, and helplessness as the young women in the *Dolce Far Niente* pictures. The question arises here of whether the painting is actually concerned with the story or whether it is merely an excuse to paint beautiful women, with the symbols surrounding them being left to tell the story. The same can be said of the ladies reclining in the grass in *Ophelia* and '*Listening to My Sweet Pipings'*. Despite the fact that they are far removed from each other in time and content, these pensive women reposing in the closed composition of an idyllic landscape – where every trace of daily life is excluded – remain the common denominator.

Although these reclining women are only one of Waterhouse's approaches to treating his female subjects, they are also typical of the way that many nineteenth-century painters depicted them. His paintings relate to those of contemporaries, with *Laus Veneris* (1870-1878, fig. 33) by Edward Burne-Jones and *The Dreamers* (1882, fig. 34) by Albert Moore being just two examples; each shows striking similarities with the compositions of Waterhouse, who was clearly inspired by the older men's works yet brought to the easel his own pictorial approach. The sensual power conveyed by these scenes remains today. The way he depicted women reflected a notion that had been widespread since the mid-nineteenth century. This idea, however, when linked to the cliché of Victorian society in which every open expression of sexuality was taboo and where women lacked every vestige of independence, could be related to Bram Dijkstra's constructs of the domestic nun and the *femme fragile*, in which a woman stayed at home to serve her husband or sacrificed herself for her husband by becoming ill and fragile.[6] If one views Waterhouse's sensual, sleeping women in this way, it explains the enormous popularity that his paintings enjoyed during his lifetime since they meant an escape from reality. Based on this argument, the Edwardian shift in gender relations would be one reason for the decline in the appreciation of his paintings at the end of his life and immediately after his death. Moreover, the renewed concern with the body at the end of the twentieth and the beginning of the twenty-first century may account for the recent resurgence of interest in his work.

Prompted by the literary expressions of figures as varied as the poet Charles Baudelaire and the esoteric art critic, occultist, and Rosicrucian Joséphin Péladan in France, and the Belgian poet Grégoire Le Roy, the new ideas about women led Frenchmen and Belgians toward the extreme Symbolist fantasies of the satanic women of Félicien Rops (fig. 35) and on the other hand to the fascination with woman as a mysterious and inscrutable creature in the work of Fernand Khnopff (figs 36, 38).

Although his work is different in style and execution, Khnopff displays a similar fascination with his model as well as a preference for a certain type of woman. One important feature is the way his mysterious female figures stare at their viewers without really appearing to see them. The most noticeable elements are the eyes and mouth. Their faces are surrounded by huge tresses of hair that frame the composition or fade into an indefinite background. The flowers they clasp are often the detail that would seem to explain the content of the work. Khnopff's concern with faces can also be seen in the sketches and drawings of Waterhouse, who shared his liking for a certain type of face, even when he was portraying society ladies. Waterhouse's faces always have the same pensive expression, and, like the women in the portraits of Khnopff, they appear self-absorbed. We see women like this in sketches such as *Head of a Girl* (cat. 37), *Medea* (cat. 49), *Study for the Head in 'The Rose Bower'* (cat. 73) and *The Love Philtre* (cat. 59).

Khnopff was a shining example for the French and Belgian Symbolists, but although he never acknowledged a direct connection with them in his writings, he did show his work in the exhibitions of La Rose + Croix organized by Péladan.[7] Emile Verhaeren, Khnopff's first biographer, wrote in 1886: 'In the end he had to resort to the symbol, this ultimate union of observation and feeling'.[8] The Symbolist movement aimed at achieving meaning and beauty in a modern world in which the spiritual had to take on the challenge of materialism. The reason for linking Khnopff with Waterhouse is that – apart from their similar approaches to the female model – Khnopff aimed to unite the visual with the literary, as so many British painters did. Khnopff was, for instance, profoundly affected by the work of Edward Burne-Jones, which he first saw in exhibitions in Paris in 1878 and 1889 (the year Waterhouse showed *Mariamne* at the Exposition Universelle). He also admired the earlier Pre-Raphaelites and the poetry of Christina Rossetti, the sister of Dante Gabriel Rossetti. It was his fascination with English art that led Khnopff to make his first visit to London in 1891. He went on to give lectures about English art in Brussels and between 1894 and 1914 wrote regularly on the artistic climate in Brussels for *The Studio* and *The Magazine of Art*. These magazines also occasionally featured reviews of Waterhouse's work, a fact indicating that Waterhouse might have been aware of developments not only in England but in Europe as well.[9] In this way Khnopff brought the English-speaking world in contact with artistic developments in France and Belgium (particularly that of *La Libre Esthétique*[10]), and vice versa.[11]

REALITY OR REFLECTION?

Besides his fascination with women, the use of circular mirrors, and of circles in general, is a recurrent feature of Waterhouse's scenes. Two early works in which circles draw the viewer's attention to the centre are *Consulting the Oracle* of 1884 (cat. 15) and *The Magic Circle* (cat. 17), painted two years later.

Consulting the Oracle is set in a Near Eastern space where women have come together to listen to the oracle. The women are grouped around the priestess in a semicircle. Each woman is recognizable as a distinct individual whose attention is fixed on the priestess while she interprets the oracle and gestures towards them. Waterhouse has chosen the climax – the moment when the oracle is pronounced. The whole work is imbued with a mystical atmosphere and the women are totally absorbed in the moment, apparently in a state of trance. For Victorian women the oriental female was everything they were not – strong, passionate, seductive, irrational, and unknown.[12] Although the circle is incomplete, it seems to extend beyond the painting, placing us viewers, as it were, on its edge. Thus we become part of the scene, especially because the priestess who receives the oracle has turned her face towards us.

The Symbolists, interested as they were in all that was spiritual and occult, saw circles as the perfect form representing the cosmic supernatural power (God), in which spirit, intellect, and the material world descended in concentric stages. Waterhouse had used this occult symbol for the first time in 1881 in a sepia sketch of a priestess with wild locks who traces a circle on the ground in a moonlit landscape (cat. 79).

The large oil painting that emerged from this sepia five years later, *The Magic Circle,* brims with magical symbols. The priestess stands inside the almost compete circle; outside are seven black ravens and a toad whose presence hints at the misfortune to be suffered by those also outside the circle. The snake round her neck represents the Ouroboros, the Egyptian symbol of the cycle of life.[13] Apart from the spiritual and symbolic meaning of the circle, Waterhouse presents us with a strong, independent, and mysterious woman. *Consulting the Oracle* and *The Magic Circle* did not fail to attract the attention of the press and Waterhouse gained a reputation for ambition.

After 1891 Waterhouse applied the circle in another way as well. He continued to use it in relation to women who

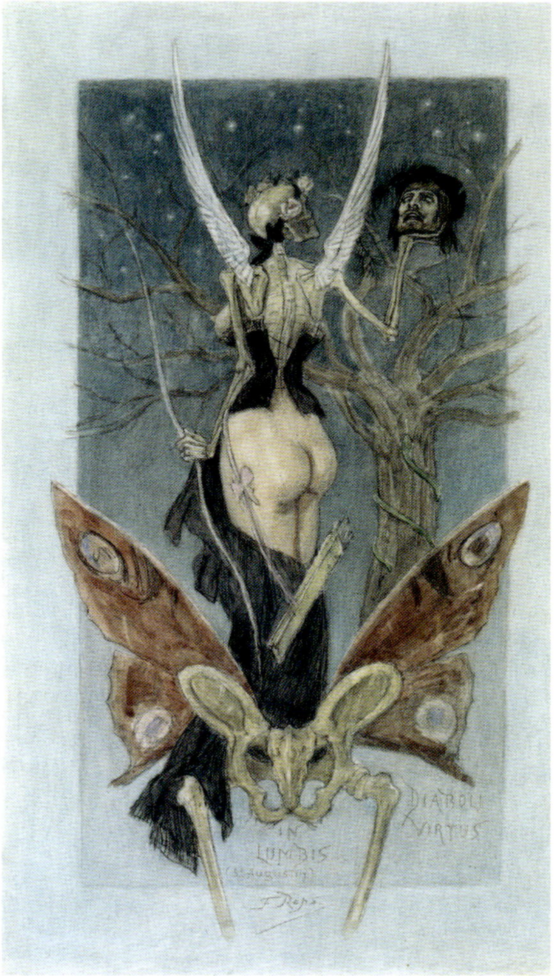

35. Félicien Rops, *L'Initiation sentimentale*, Mixed media on paper, 29.2 x 18.2 cm, Musée provincial Félicien Rops à Namur

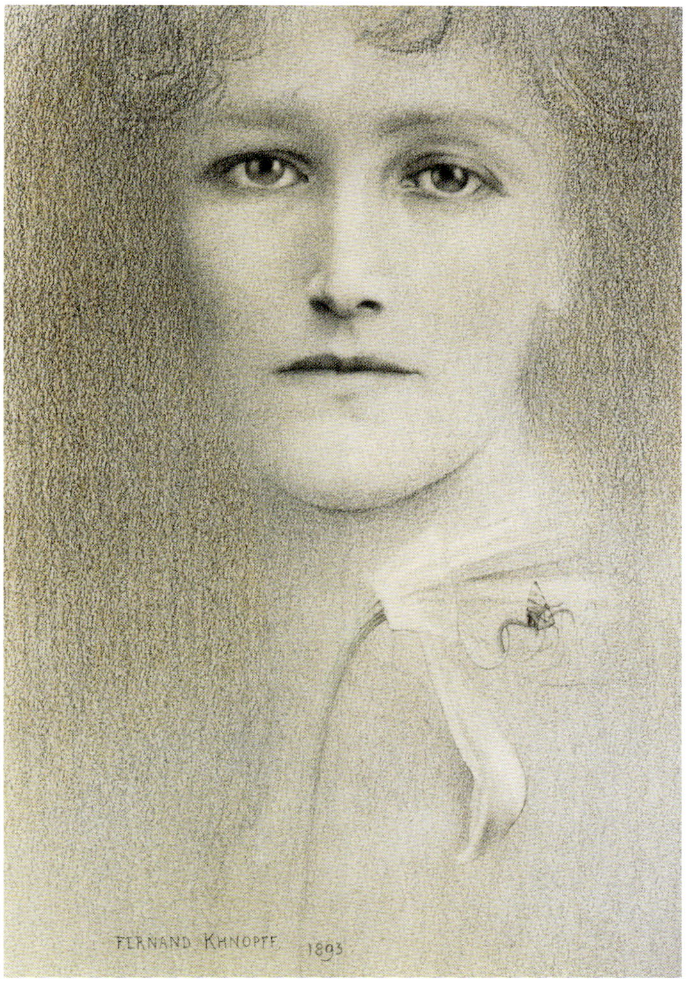

36. Fernand Khnopff, *Diffidence (Lilie)*, 1893, Graphite and coloured pencil on paper, 25.5 x 17.5 cm, Private collection

were skilled in the magic arts, but besides that made explicit references to myths. What was involved was no longer magic circles painted literally. Instead he concentrated on a circular mirror that gave reality back in the form of a reflection. In *Circe Offering the Cup to Ulysses* (1891, cat. 21) Circe, daughter of the sun god Helios, holds a poisoned chalice in one hand, while with the other, raised arm, she clasps the wand that is perhaps required to ensure the success of the spell with which she threatens Ulysses. The semicircle in front of her throne is completed in the round mirror behind her. In it one sees Ulysses approaching her while in the background the ships can be discerned moored in the harbour. The swine in the foreground are Ulysses' crew who have been bewitched by the potion that Circe now offers Ulysses. The throne on which she sits is decorated with stylized lions that again wear the Ouroboros symbol around their necks like a mane, while her feet rest on a bench decorated with a winged head. In the foreground the toad alludes to approaching calamity.

The circular mirror served in many of Waterhouse's paintings to reflect the real world that, in a manner of speaking, is situated behind us viewers. This makes us part of the work and in the case of *Circe Offering the Cup to Ulysses* places us in the same submissive role as Ulysses. Waterhouse has positioned Circe with regard to the mirror in such a way that she seems to tower above the viewer as she sits on her throne. Unlike the sensually reclining women discussed above, the works just mentioned involve women who are powerful *femmes fatales*, capable of transforming men into beasts or doing other sorts of evil. They possess supernatural powers and are exceptionally beautiful. The beauty is clearly an aspect here

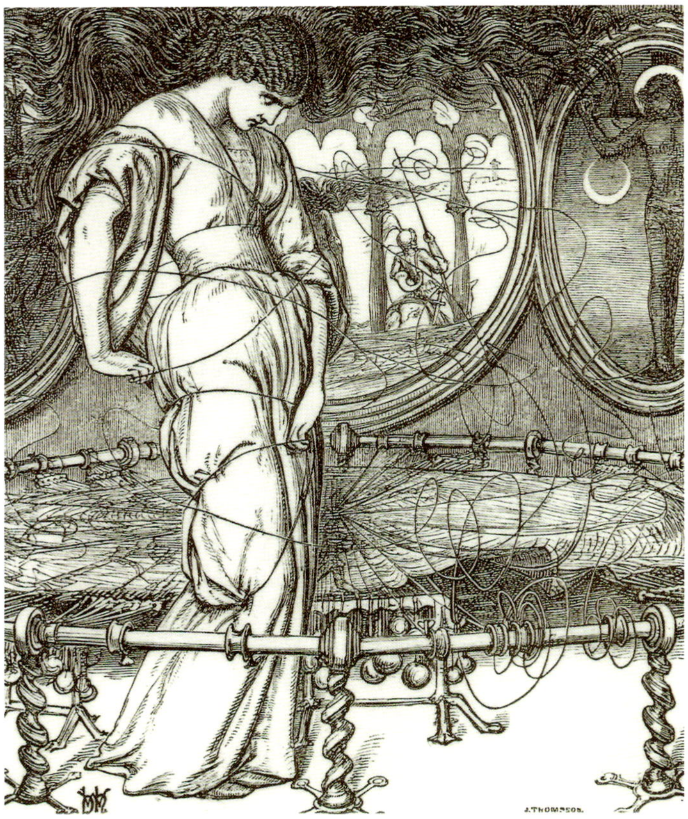

37. After William Holman Hunt, 'The Lady of Shalott', Wood engraving in Alfred Tennyson, *Poems*, published by Edward Moxon, London, 1857

of their fatal attraction. In *Circe Offering the Cup to Ulysses* Waterhouse has depicted a supremely good-looking woman in an almost transparent robe. Trippi points out that the Homeric women in Waterhouse's work derive their power not only from their physical beauty but also from their sex appeal. To take this argument a step further, the Victorians used the words Sirens and Circe as euphemisms for prostitutes.[14] Circe, too, however 'fatal' she may have been, was also Ulysses' lover but immortal because she was a goddess. It was her magical power to transform men into beasts that appealed to the Symbolists, the theosophists, and the occultists alike.

Another, equally symbolic use of a mirror to provide a glimpse of reality occurs in *The Lady of Shalott* of 1894 (cat. 30). While the mirror of Circe allows the viewer to follow part of the scene, in *The Lady of Shalott* it has a sinister effect as well. When the Lady looks outside and sees Lancelot approaching, the curse comes upon her and will lead to her death. The mirror breaks and the threads from her magic loom wind about her dress. Waterhouse would have known the famous conception of this scene by the Pre-Raphaelite artist William Holman Hunt, used as an illustration in the Moxon edition of Tennyson's *Poems*, published in 1857 (fig. 37).

The poem by Tennyson was an important source of inspiration not just for the Pre-Raphaelites but also for Waterhouse and he returned to the subject at various points in his life up until two years before his death. The circle is used in various ways in his three versions of *The Lady of Shalott*. It serves as a mirror, but also as a motif in the mosaic in the floor. A striking feature is the state of confusion that overwhelms the Lady. This is expressed in her pose and her gaze as she is about to step out of the circle on the floor – a motion that deprives her of the protection of the spell. In short, the painting is full of symbolic allusions to her fall, which results from her looking out of the window instead of observing reality through its reflection in the mirror. In the version *'I am Half Sick of Shadows', said the Lady of Shalott* of 1915 (cat. 60) she is portrayed as a pensive woman reclining with an almost bored look in her eyes – exhausted by staring in the mirror, while the rose symbolizing love is reflected only in the mirror but is not visible in the foreground.[15] The tapestry she is weaving shows elements from her life. As Robert Upstone mentions in his entry, the story of the Lady of Shalott is clearly connected with the shifting position of women in society, and in particular, male concern about the growing independence of the 'New Woman'.[16] Dijkstra argues exactly the opposite here in relation to the *femme fragile* who meekly submits to death as a result of an unreciprocated love or serves her husband by sacrificing her life. Both interpretations contain a germ of truth, and the concept of a metaphor for the doom-ridden atmosphere of nineteenth-century domestic life is as valid as that of Dijkstra. On the other hand the aspect of the world passing by in the mirror might well be a reference to the allegory of Plato's cave.[17]

Although the mirror in these works reflects the outside world in the same way as the shadows in Plato's cave, it is also a symbol of the lives of women protected from reality. The latter situation was all too familiar in the nineteenth century. The symbolism of reflection goes even further, however: the character of woman is compared with a mirror that only reflects whatever it contains, or, still further, the mirror is needed to confirm her existence. In mythology women are therefore often compared with the moon, which reflects the light of the sun. Their mythological equivalent was Diana, whose symbol was the moon. Dijkstra is correct in saying that 'if woman was a reflector, a mirror, then the mirror itself was symbolic of woman: a 'ghost', a reflection of passion, an elusive image, a self-contained, self encircling entity'.[18] Furthermore the mirror symbolized truth and the Virgin Mary, yet it had also stood as a symbol of human vanity down the ages (see *Vanity*, cat. 54). In *The Lady of Shalott*, all of these symbolic aspects of reflection are involved. They can also be found in two other works by Waterhouse, *Mariana in the South* (1897, cat. 33) and *Destiny* (1900, cat. 40).

Waterhouse was not alone in his use of circles and mirrors, and the Symbolists were very interested in the potential of the mirror for multiple interpretation in their work as well.

Khnopff went even further and frequently portrayed his women in circular compositions, or leaning against a mirror, while seeming to caress their image with their lips. Khnopff's drawing *With Grégoire Le Roy, My Heart Weeps for Days of Yore* (fig. 38) of 1889 is a fine example. The woman has placed her face against the mirror and appears to be unaware of the world around her. The use of the circular mirror takes on narcissistic traits here because the woman seems to be kissing her own image. This view of a woman doing nothing but being absorbed in her own reflection acquired greater currency toward the end of the nineteenth century. According to the Symbolists, the mirror was not merely the literal reflection of the person as such, but also represented the reflection of one's inner *persona* – in other words, the mirror was the symbol of the quest for one's soul. Apart from the function of reflection or narcissism, Khnopff regarded the circle as the ideal shape and symbol of perfection; he painted a golden circle on his studio's floor and conducted all his work inside it.[19]

FATAL ATTRACTION? WOMEN AND WATER

It is a small step from the reflection in the mirror to one in the water. Waterhouse's obsession with water, as a metaphor of danger, but also as an impenetrable, magical, and mythical element, would seem obvious in light of the above. Water offered him a whole range of possibilities that were well suited to his love of mythology and other literary sources. Hadn't Venus risen out of the sea and wasn't she the pre-eminent symbol of woman? On the other hand there was the unattainable water nymph or mermaid who could lure a man down to her watery realm, and hence to his death. There are plenty of examples in Waterhouse's oeuvre that deal with the fatal attraction of water. *A Mermaid* (1900, cat. 35) and *Ophelia* (1894, fig. 39) are similar in composition, depicting a woman by the water. It is highly relevant that Shakespeare compared the drowning Ophelia to a mermaid.[20] Waterhouse's understanding of mermaids was surely informed by Hans Christian Andersen's famous fairy tale, and also by Tennyson's poem 'The Mermaid'.

Trippi points out that the Victorians fantasized about the mermaid who wanted to enjoy human love and thus gain a soul. She would however never be able to live on dry land among humans or experience true love, because this would mean her death. The symbolic appeal of an unattainable and beautiful woman threatened by death was a theme that gained huge popularity in painting throughout Europe in the 1890s, as we can see from works by Edward Burne-Jones, Herbert Draper, Waterhouse's friend Maurice Greiffenhagen, Frederic Leighton, Evelyn De Morgan (fig. 40), Arnold Böcklin, Franz von Stuck, Max Klinger, and Gustav Klimt.

An even more forceful symbolist and myth-based interpretation of the appeal of water is found in *A Naiad* (1893, cat. 27), *Hylas and the Nymphs* (1896, cat. 32) and *Echo and Narcissus* (1903, cat. 43). Here too seduction, vanity, reflection, death, and transformation are the main motifs. In *A Naiad* the water nymph rises from the stream and fixes her gaze on the sleeping youth whom she evidently sees as her prey. The goats in the background are an allusion to Bacchus, the divinity of the dissolute life.[21] The densely wooded landscape gives the scene a timeless setting, but it also points to the nineteenth-century fascination with woods, thought of as the dwelling-places of supernatural beings such as elves and fairies.

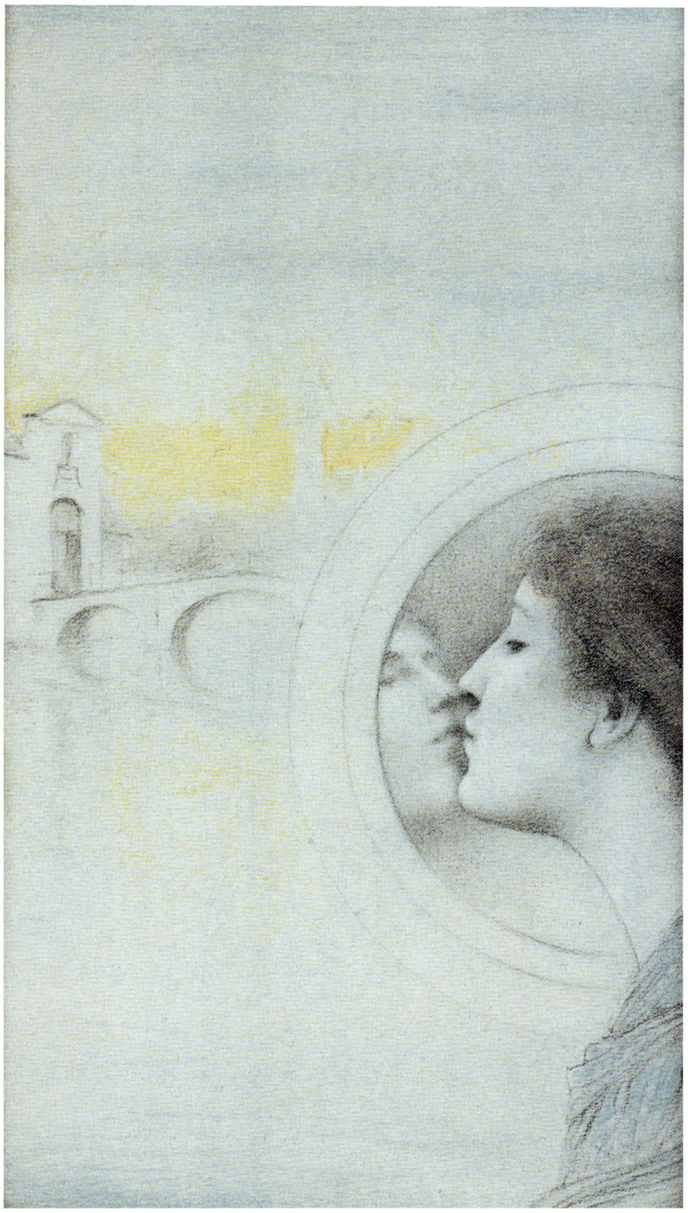

38. Fernand Khnopff, *With Grégoire Le Roy. My Heart Weeps for Days of Yore*, 1889, Coloured pencil and white highlights on paper, 25 x 14.2 cm, Private collection

In *Hylas and the Nymphs* the water lilies in the hair of the nymphs and the yellow irises on the shore allude in mocking fashion to their innocence and virginity. Among the many ancient versions of the myth of Hylas, Apollonius of Rhodes mentioned only one nymph, while Theocritus did not specify the number.[22] In his painting Waterhouse has increased the number to seven, all of whom are equally beautiful. The magic number seven meant that he could group them in a semicircle, thus reinforcing the theme of Hylas's falling under the spell of their beauty. They seem to be related not only to each other, but also to the water nymph Waterhouse painted three years earlier. It is remarkable that in both cases he gave a personal visual interpretation of the myth, by setting them in an almost English landscape and drawing our attention to the women instead of the man, despite the fact that Hylas's blue robe and red girdle have the most vibrant and striking colours in the composition. In the story the nymphs fall for the beauty of Hylas, but Waterhouse leaves it to the viewer and lets the nymphs lure Hylas into the water while mesmerising him with their charm. Once again the implication seems to be that beauty and sensuality are synonymous with illicit sexual desire – a notion that was familiar to many nineteenth-century men. Various interpretations of the myth make one wonder whether Hylas should not be seen here as a typical nineteenth-century decadent abandoning himself to pleasure.[23]

The works by Waterhouse that most immediately convey a possible Symbolist influence in combination with his fascination with water are *Nymphs Finding the Head of Orpheus* (1900, cat. 41) and *The Charmer* (1911, fig. 41).

The tale of Orpheus, like that of *Echo and Narcissus*, was one of many told by Ovid in his *Metamorphoses*. In the nineteenth century this Latin poet played an important role in theories about the transformation, rebirth, and survival of the soul after the death of the body. Themes like these may have appealed to Waterhouse, given his preference for occult and symbolic material.[24] The tale of Orpheus, moreover, was one of the most popular subjects for the Symbolists. They adored this poet-musician because he sang the truth, thus speaking to men's passions; he was also regarded as a misunderstood poet, a *poète maudit*. The Maeneads disapproved of Orpheus's grief because he was too passionate in mourning his wife Eurydice, whom he had to leave behind in the underworld. They tore him to pieces during one of their rites and threw his head and lyre into the water where he continued to float and sing until the nymphs, who pitied him, gave him a burial.[25] The fact that he did not sink in the feminine element of water is an interesting element in the story. Another unusual feature is that, in Waterhouse's treatment, the floating head is fairly androgynous and resembles the long-haired nymphs of *Hylas and the Nymphs* more than it does a male head. As always, Waterhouse picked out the most dramatic moment in the story – when the head and lyre are drifting past the nymphs who have come to collect water. The conjunction of music and emotion on canvas here may indicate that Waterhouse drew inspiration from Symbolism, especially from the fascination with Orpheus held by the French painter Gustave Moreau (1828-1898), whose *Thracian Girl Carrying the Head of Orpheus* of 1865 (fig. 42) was reproduced in *The Magazine of Art* the very year Waterhouse produced his painting.[26] Although Moreau's work is different from that of Waterhouse in technique and composition, the two artists shared a preference for this part of the tale. In 1877, Moreau's *L'Apparition* was shown at the Grosvenor Gallery in London, where Waterhouse would almost certainly have seen it.[27]

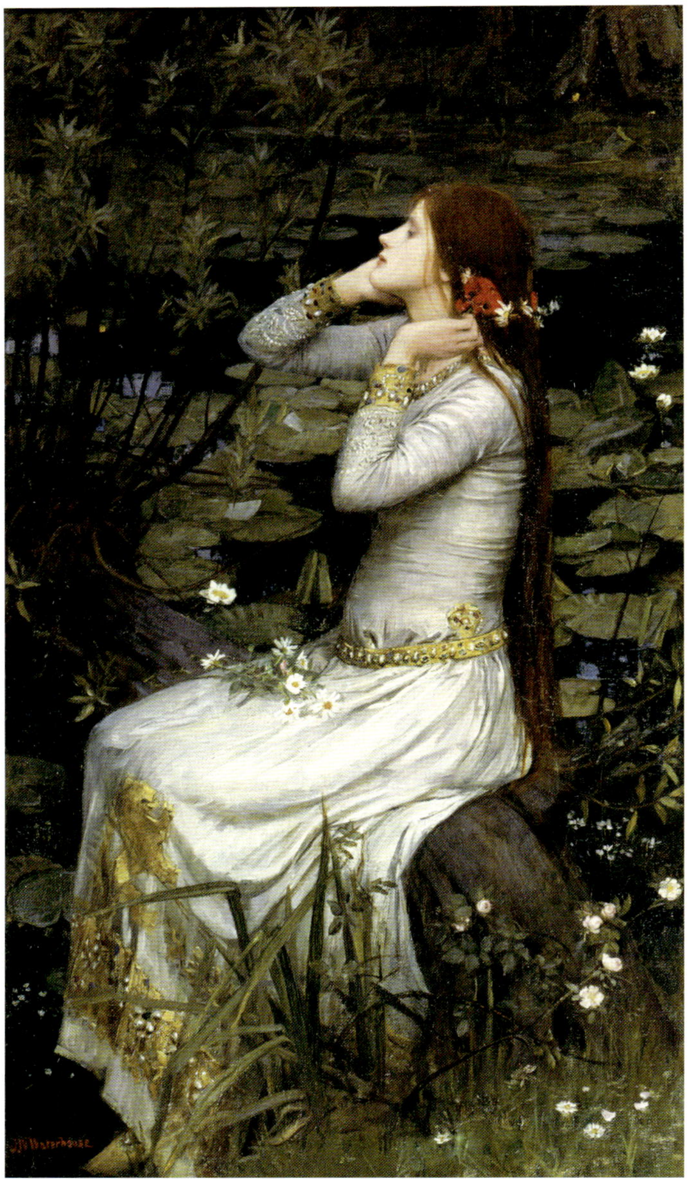

39. J.W. Waterhouse, *Ophelia*, 1894, Oil on canvas, 124.4 x 73.6 cm, Private collection

Moreau became the object of a cult in France in his own lifetime due to the fact that after 1880 he no longer exhibited his work at the Salon. Possibilities of seeing it therefore became increasingly rare, and he concentrated instead on creating his own universe in his studio, peopling it with figures from classical mythology. He wrote his ideas down in different notebooks, in which he explained that he wanted his

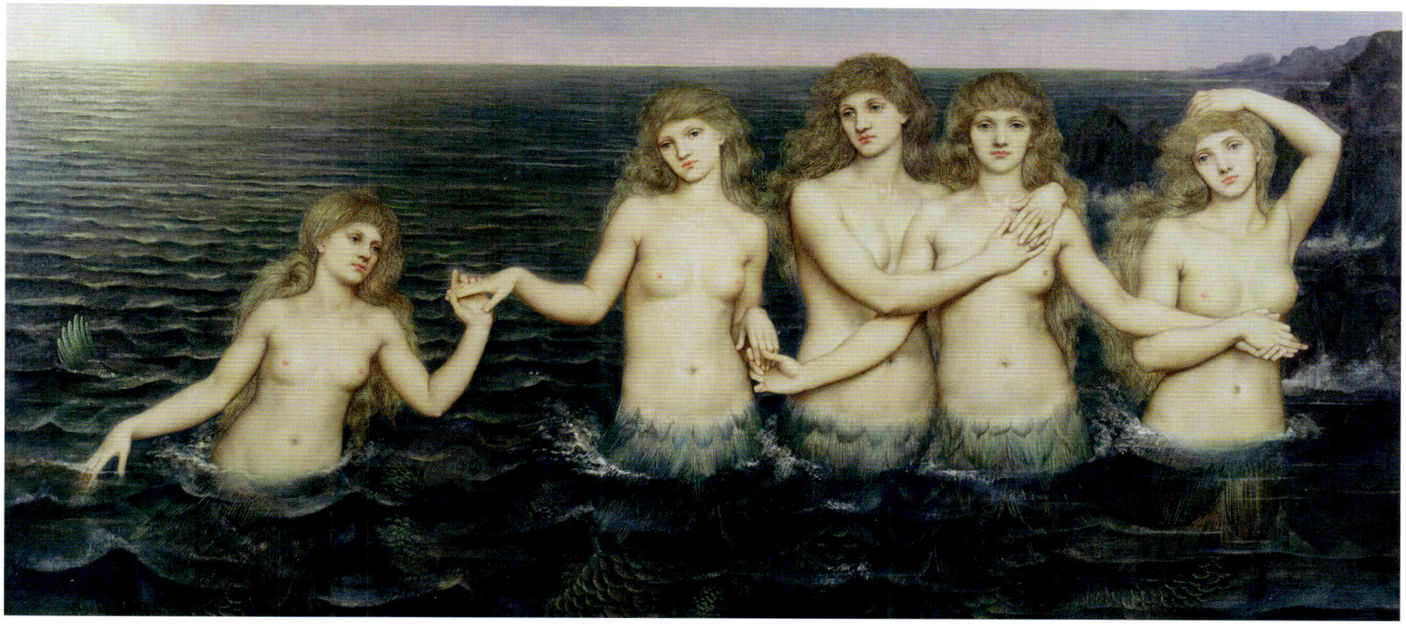

40. Evelyn De Morgan, *The Sea Maidens*, 1885-1886, Oil on canvas, 71.1 x 109.2 cm, The De Morgan Foundation, London

art to give expression to a 'motionless dream'.[28] Because he added to and altered his paintings on a daily basis, a process emerged of a never-ending work in progress. He regarded the painter as a 'craftsman who collected dreams' with emphasis on the imagination.[29] In his review of Moreau's work, Joris-Karl Huysmans mentioned the poem 'Parisian Dream' from Baudelaire's *Fleurs du Mal*. Subsequently in his novel *A Rebours*, Huysmans described Moreau and Odilon Redon (who painted the head of Orpheus with the lyre c. 1903-1910, fig. 43) as the only artists capable of achieving both spiritual and decadent extremes in their work. In this way, he said, they escaped the ugliness and immorality of the nineteenth century. This combination of beauty, theatricality, and death are elements also typical of the work of Waterhouse.

Bearing in mind the position of nineteenth-century women, one can appreciate that Waterhouse's sensual, magnificent, and seductive females must have had a particular power for his contemporaries, arousing feelings of both excitement and fear. Because he drew on literature that was widely known and selected compositions that resembled the work of his contemporaries, while using a Symbolist approach that everybody in his age could interpret, his paintings remained popular almost until his death. It was his freer manner of brushwork that distinguished his work from that of such contemporaries as Burne-Jones, De Morgan, Moreau, and Khnopff.[30]

The lack of information about Waterhouse's personal and social life means that we are dependent on his paintings and their subjects for any conclusions about his opinions. We cannot therefore state with certainty whether he can be counted among the Symbolists or whether his affinity lay more with occultism. Although he regularly makes use of a symbolic and Symbolist formal idiom, and shows a fascination with literary sources that allude to both Symbolism and occultism, Waterhouse's naturalistic technique gives his works a visual immediacy quite distinct from the Symbolists', one which complicates our reading of him. His preference for dramatic situations and emotions can be interpreted as Symbolist, yet no obvious esotericism can be found in his work, as there is in that of Khnopff or De Morgan, who firmly situated themselves outside everyday reality. By contrast, Waterhouse deliberately introduces reality, whether in the palpability of his women or the recognizably English landscapes in which he increasingly set his scenes. Through this combination of a desire for reality and a longing for another world, he attained the very highest level of artistry. His mysterious women continue to charm viewers, yet they never betray their secret, floating endlessly between dream and reality.

Many thanks for the generous help of Peter Trippi, Elizabeth Prettejohn, Barbera van Kooij, David Jackson, and Stijn ten Hoeve.

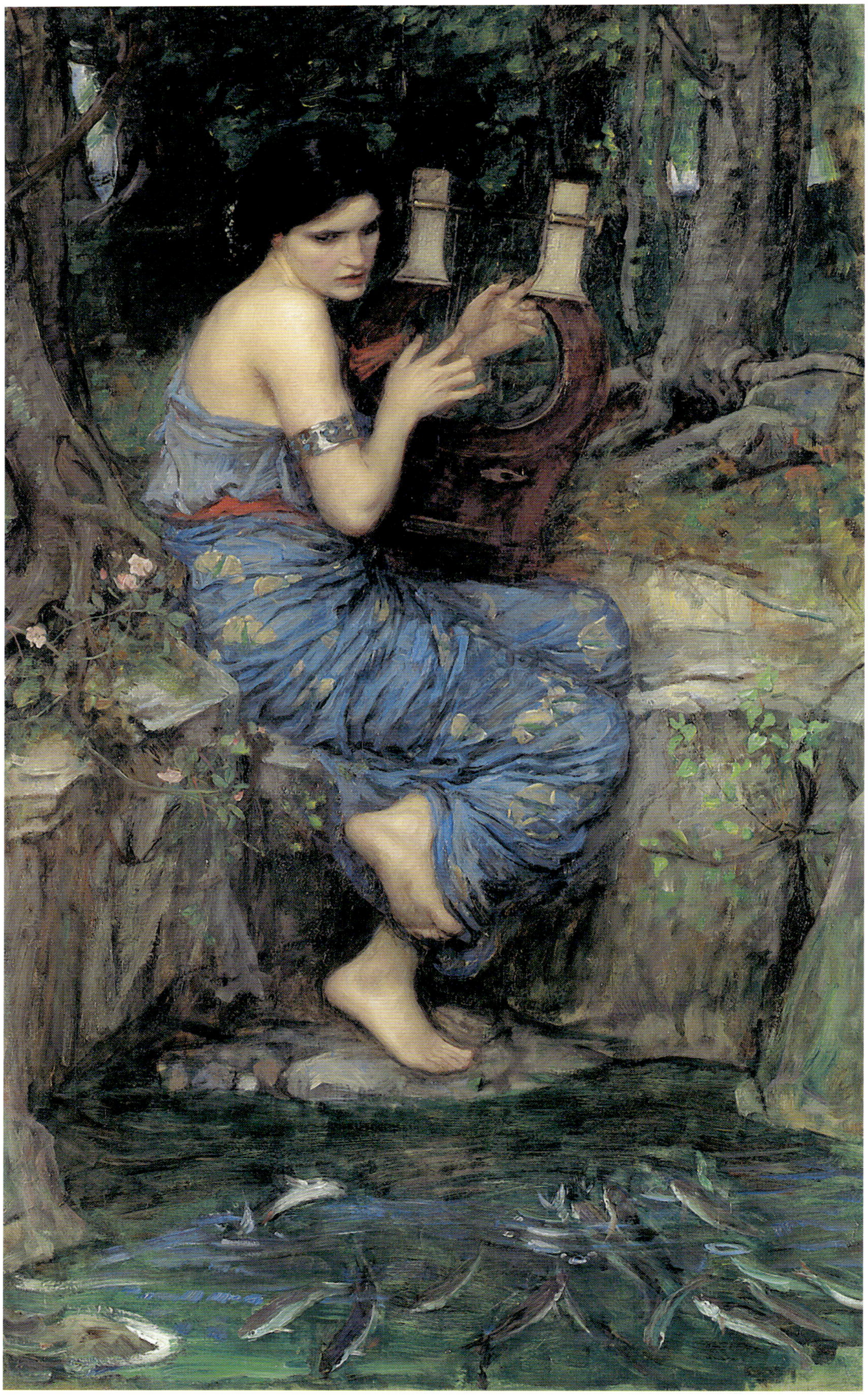

41. J.W. Waterhouse, *The Charmer,* 1911, Oil on canvas, 97 x 61 cm, Private collection courtesy of Christie's

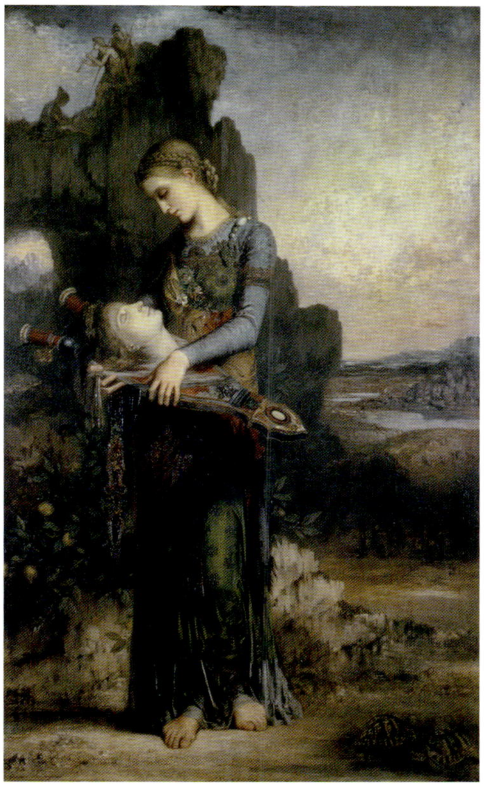

42. Gustave Moreau, *Thracian Girl Carrying the Head of Orpheus*, 1865, Oil on panel, 154 x 99.5 cm, Musée d'Orsay, Paris

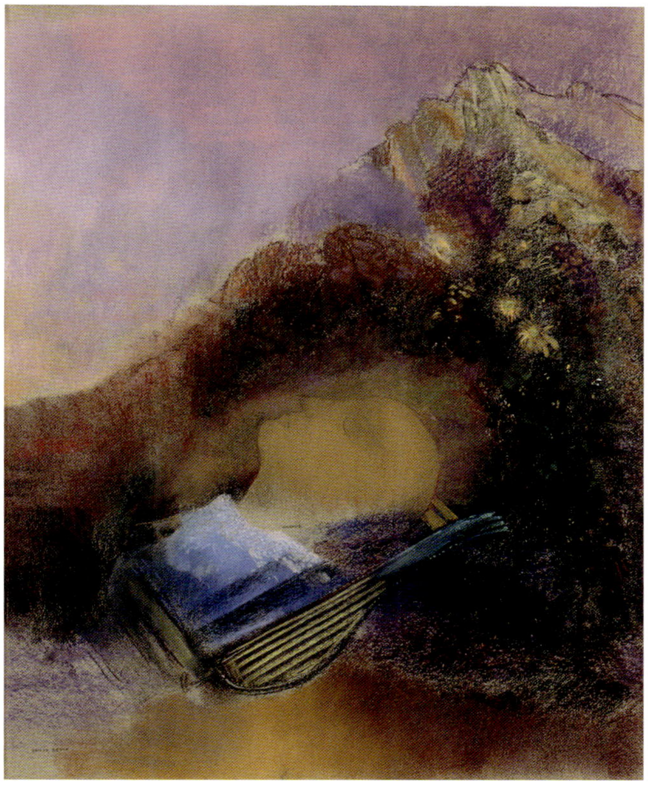

43. Odilon Redon, *Orpheus*, c. 1903-1910, Pastel on paper, 68.8 x 56.8 cm, The Cleveland Museum of Art

1 For a discussion in this catalogue of the use of mythological themes in Waterhouse's work, see Elizabeth Prettejohn, 'Waterhouse's Imagination', pp. 23-35.
2 For more information in this catalogue about the life of Waterhouse, see Peter Trippi, 'John William Waterhouse: A Biographical Overview', pp. 15-21. For Waterhouse's working method, see Robert Upstone's essay in this catalogue, 'Between Innovation and Tradition: Waterhouse and Modern French Painting', pp. 37-49.
3 Rodolphe Rapetti, *Symbolism*, Paris, 2005, pp. 11-15.
4 It is difficult to summarize the nineteenth-century women's movement here, but within its voluminous literature is an especially important resource: Deborah Cherry, *Beyond the Frame: Feminism and Visual Culture, Britain 1850-1900* (Routledge 2000).
5 Peter Trippi, *J.W. Waterhouse*, London, 2002, pp. 43, 153-156. For more information about *Ariadne*, see Elizabeth Prettejohn's entry, cat. 34.
6 Bram Dijkstra, *Idols of Perversity: Fantasies of Feminine Evil in Fin-de-Siècle Culture*, Oxford, 1986.
7 Péladan was a French writer and priest of an occult sect. He had made a study of the occult tradition, before going on to found the Rose + Croix group.
8 Exhib. cat., *Fernand Khnopff (1858-1921)*, Koninklijke Musea voor Schone Kunsten, Brussels 2004, p. 13 (note 3).
9 *Ibid.*, p. 45.
10 In 1894 *La Libre Esthétique* came out of the Société des Vingt (XX) which was founded by Edmond Picard and Octave Maus ten years earlier. Les XX served as an important association for international cultural and artistic exchange between artists in Europe. Bettina Spaanstra-Polak, *Het Symbolisme in de Nederlandse schilderkunst 1890-1900*, Bussum 2004, p. 87.
11 MaryAnne Stevens is correct in writing that it was Khnopff who built the bridge between the two worlds while conversely fostering a wider understanding of English contemporary art in Brussels. Similar to the way that English contemporary literature inspired English artists, Khnopff responded to the Symbolist texts of his Belgian and French contemporaries. MaryAnne Stevens, 'Symbolism – A French Monopoly' in exhib. cat., *The Age of Rossetti, Burne-Jones & Watts: Symbolism in Britain 1860-1910*, Tate Gallery, London 1997, pp. 58-59.
12 Trippi, *op.cit.* (note 5), pp. 60-64.
13 *Ibid.*, pp. 71-80. For a detailed description and explanation of *The Magic Circle*, see cat. 17.
14 *Ibid.*, p. 111.
15 *Ibid.*, p. 219.
16 See for a more detailed description Robert Upstone's entry on *The Lady of Shalott* in this catalogue, cat. 20.
17 In the allegory of Plato's cave, people sit in chains in a cave. They can only see the world outside in the form of shadows on the wall. This is their reality. On freeing themselves of their chains and stepping outside the cave they are unable to understand this new world and are blinded by the light of the sun. The same happens if they later return to the gloom of the cave. Freeing themselves of their chains symbolizes a long period of thinking about the Good, while resisting the temptation of earthly pleasures. The symbol of escaping from the cave stands for the soul rising to the world of abstractions, the real, recognizable world that we experience with our spirit. Plato, *The Republic*, Book 7 (514a–520a).
18 Bram Dijkstra, *op.cit.* (note 6), p. 127.
19 Khnopff, *op.cit.* (note 8), p. 220.
20 Trippi, *op.cit.* (note 5), pp. 122-123.
21 *Ibid.*, p. 127.
22 For the reference to Theocritus, see cat. 32. The one nymph can be found in Apollonius Rhodius, *Argonautica*, Book 1 (1207-1239).
23 This for instance is the view of the art critic M.H. Spielmann who thought that the nymphs had such languishing expressions and delicate shapes that it was a question whether we should feel sorry for Hylas. See Trippi, *op.cit.* (note 5), p. 149 (note 124).
24 Waterhouse was not alone in this, as Elizabeth Prettejohn describes in her essay 'Waterhouse's Imagination' in this catalogue, pp 23-35.
25 T.T. Kroon, *Mythologisch woordenboek*, 's Gravenhage 1875.
26 Trippi, *op.cit.* (note 5), p. 173.
27 I would like to thank Elizabeth Prettejohn for pointing this out to me.
28 Rapetti, *op.cit.* (note 3), pp. 40-42 (note 25).
29 *Ibid.*, p. 44 (note 29).
30 For more about Waterhouse's method of painting, see Robert Upstone, 'Between Innovation and Tradition: Waterhouse and Modern French Painting', in this catalogue.

CATALOGUE

Elizabeth Prettejohn (EP)
Peter Trippi (PT)
Robert Upstone (RU)

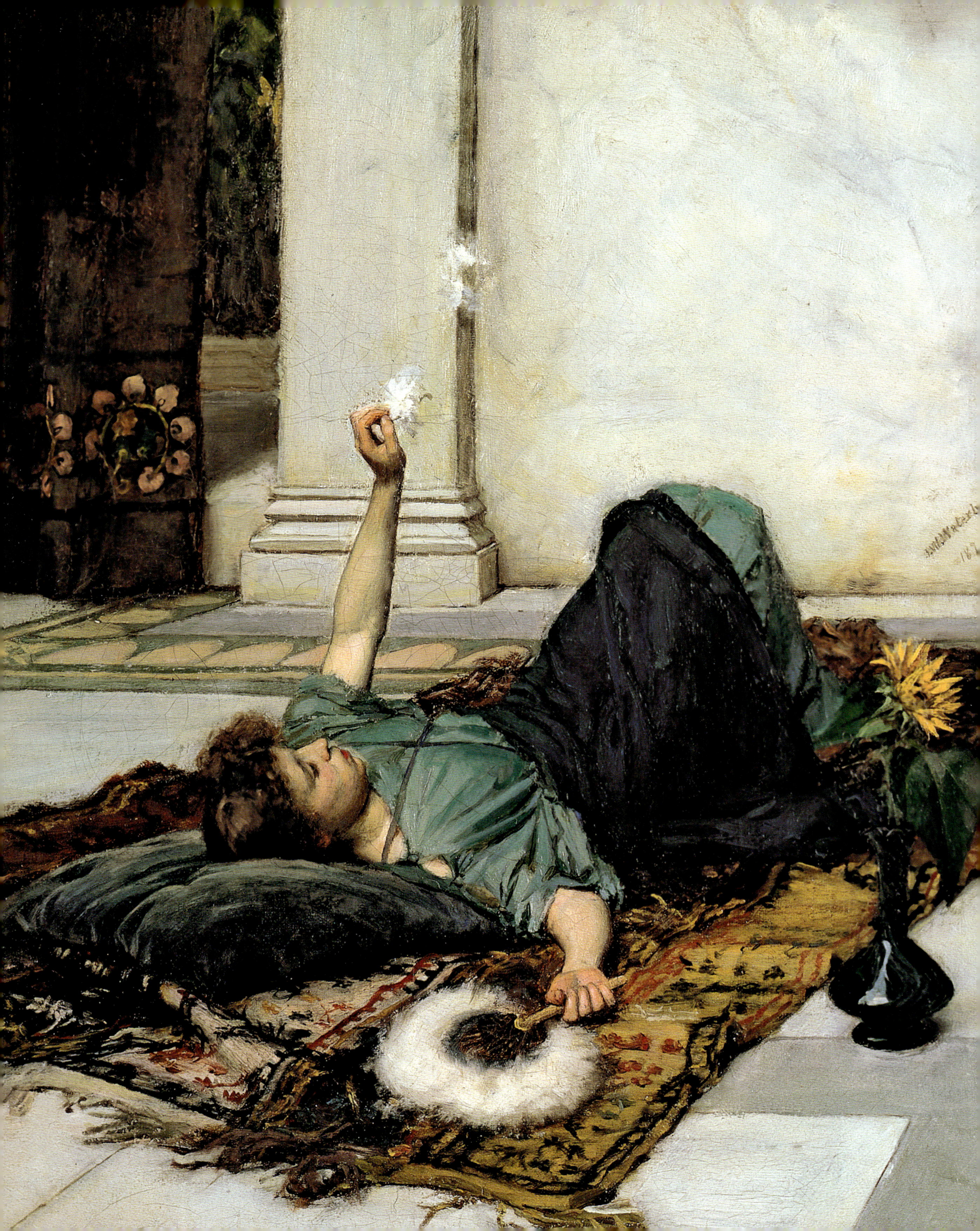

Youthful Experiments

1. The Unwelcome Companion: A Street Scene in Cairo 1873

OIL ON CANVAS, 59 X 49.5 CM - TOWNELEY HALL, BURNLEY BOROUGH COUNCIL, GIFT OF MRS. SARAH OLDMAN, 1951- EXHIBITED SOCIETY OF BRITISH ARTISTS, 1873

This is one of six Orientalist pictures known to have been made by Waterhouse during the 1870s. A year before he sent it to the Society of British Artists (along with *Vendeur à eau),* he had sold there *The Slave* and *Bedowin Woman.* In 1876 he sent *An Odalisque* to Glasgow, and by 1884 Sir John Aird owned Waterhouse's quite similar *Dancing Girl.*[1]

Englishmen's demand for Near Eastern images had intensified with the opening of the Suez Canal in 1869 and ongoing reportage of the Ottoman Empire's decline. The French Academician Jean-Léon Gérôme had achieved worldwide celebrity through reproductions after his Orientalist canvases, and it is noteworthy that Waterhouse's study at the Royal Academy Schools (from 1870) coincided with Gérôme's refuge in London from the Franco-Prussian War. The Frenchman was elected an Honorary Foreign Academician, and it is quite possible that Waterhouse met him at the Academy.

Much as this picture owes to Gérôme's famous Cairene women, Waterhouse's arch and column are actually derived from the Alhambra, the Moorish palace built in the Middle Ages near Granada. Too abbreviated to be legible, the Koranic inscriptions on the wall are carved in Andalusian *thuluth,* a monumental Arabic script found at the Alhambra. As there is no evidence that Waterhouse traveled to Spain this early in life, he probably visited the South Kensington Museum (near his family home) to sketch from its numerous architectural models of Alhambran interiors, or from the influential chromolithographic album of Alhambran drawings (1836-1845) published by South Kensington designer Owen Jones (1809-1874).

The title *Unwelcome Companion* infers that the model – whose tambourine indicates she is a dancer – has evaded an admirer. Despite the temptation to relate this to a famous work by William Holman Hunt, *A Street Scene in Cairo: The Lantern Maker's Courtship* (exhibited 1861), in which an Egyptian maiden prevents a lover from removing her mask, these pictures share only a title. Hunt's woman appears genuinely Egyptian; in *The Unwelcome Companion* and also *The Slave* a year earlier, Waterhouse used Western models with vaguely Near Eastern features – exoticised variations of 'keepsake' beauties. Keepsake books were sentimental early Victorian literature illustrated with engravings of bejeweled ladies, usually pictured standing alone. Presented for emulation by female viewers, keepsake beauties also indulged men's erotic fantasies. Like many Victorian images of women, Waterhouse's slave and tambourine girl cast an inconclusive gaze, suggesting both powerlessness and unfathomability. **PT**

1 Privately published *Collection of Pictures and Statuary: Catalogue prepared and arranged by Henry Blackburn, editor of 'Academy Notes', etc. Mr. John Aird, 14, Hyde Park Terrace, June, 1884*, p. 32.

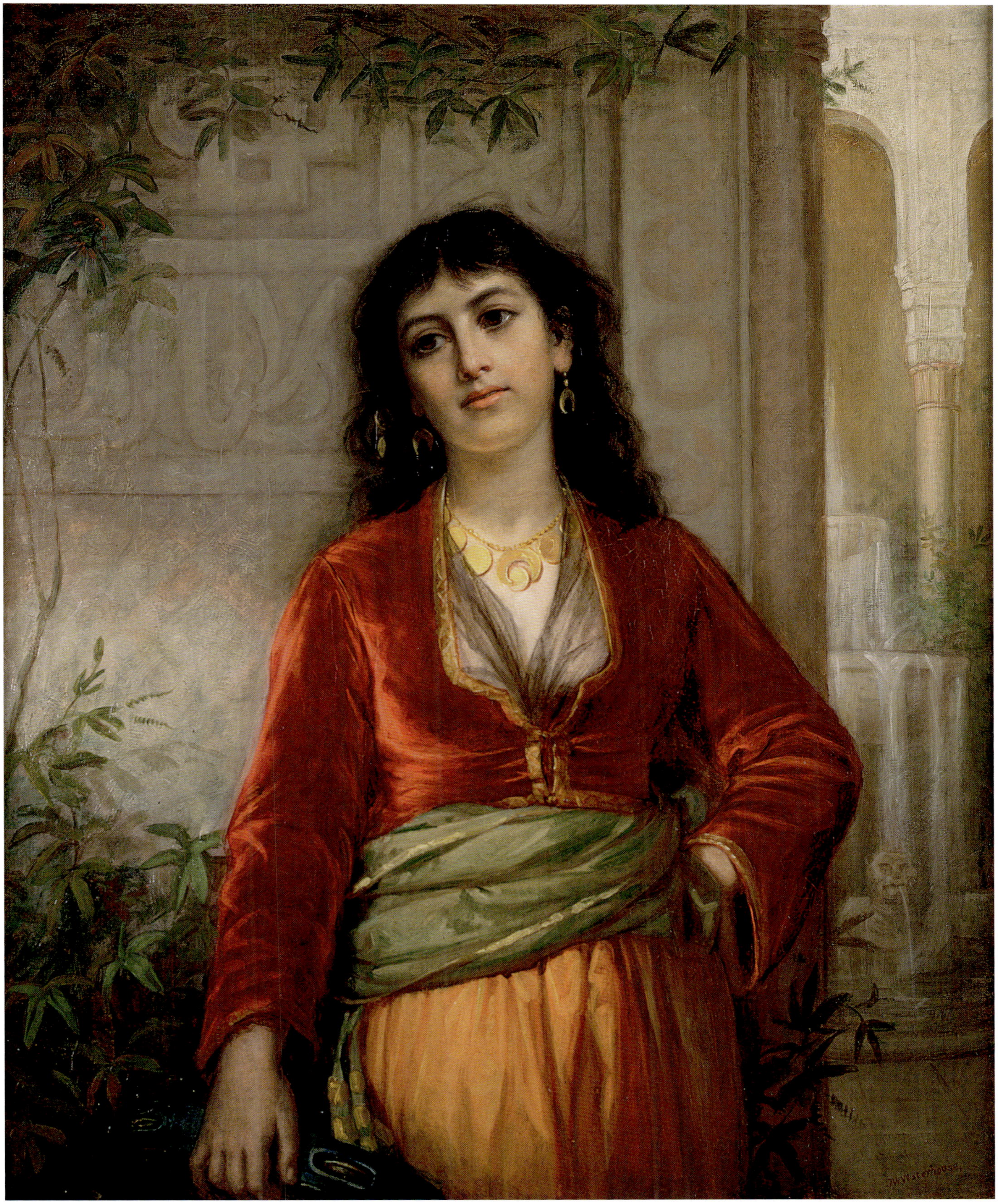

2. **In the Peristyle** 1874

OIL ON CANVAS, 67.3 X 52.1 CM - TOUCHSTONES ROCHDALE ART GALLERY, GIFT OF ROBERT TAYLOR HEAPE, 1908 - EXHIBITED DUDLEY GALLERY WINTER EXHIBITION, 1874

In the earliest years of his career, Waterhouse showed a number of works at the less pretentious London exhibitions. *In the Peristyle* appeared at the Dudley Gallery, an artist-run exhibiting society that was particularly hospitable to younger painters, in the winter of 1874, just a few months after Waterhouse made his Royal Academy debut with the more important painting, *Sleep and his Half-Brother Death* (fig. 9). Modestly priced at 35 guineas, *In the Peristyle* was painted over a previous composition, traces of which have emerged through the paint surface – a reminder of the young painter's need to economise. While the simple scene lacks the serious overtones of its Royal Academy counterpart, it represents another side of the painter's emerging fascination with childhood. The young girl's pose, as she turns to scatter grain from her basket, seems to have been caught from the life, as the birds flutter around her, or perch on the white marble architrave of the peristyle above. Waterhouse draws on the new fashion for scenes of everyday life from the ancient world, but without overemphasis on archaeological details. **EP**

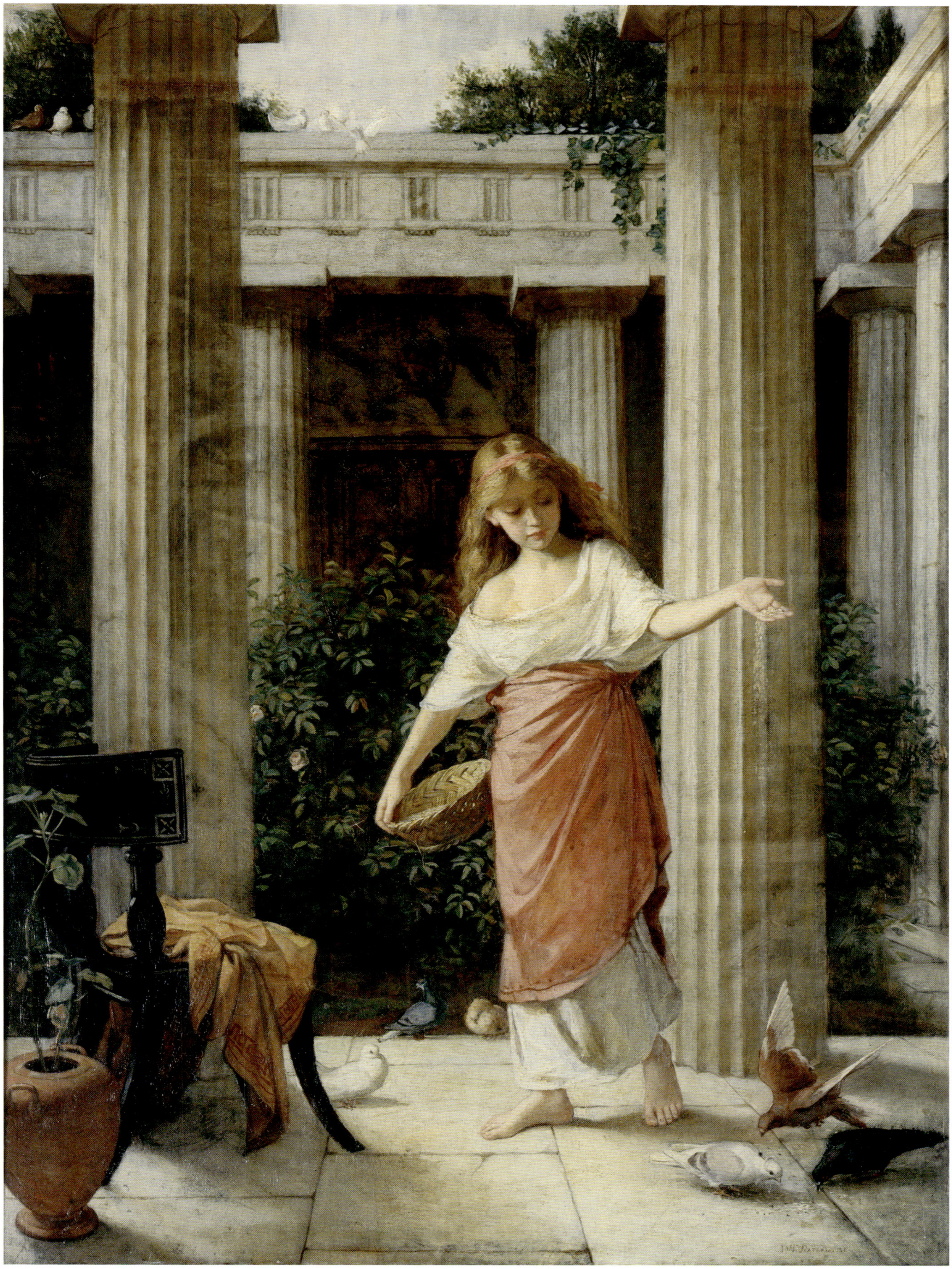

3. Miranda 1875

OIL ON CANVAS, 76 X 101.5 CM - COLLECTION ROBERT AND ANN WIGGINS, USA - EXHIBITED ROYAL ACADEMY, 1875

This painting, exhibited at the Royal Academy the year after Waterhouse's successful debut there (with *Sleep and his Half-Brother Death*, fig. 9), marks the artist's first experiment in representing a heroine from one of Shakespeare's plays – a familiar kind of subject in English painting of the period, and one to which Waterhouse would return, with striking effect, much later in his career, with *Cleopatra* of 1888 (cat. 19) and three versions of *Ophelia* (1889, 1894, and 1910, figs 18, 30, 39). In 1916, he returned to the heroine of this early painting: Miranda, the daughter of Prospero in Shakespeare's play of 1611, *The Tempest* (see cat. 62). Both depictions, from the very beginning and the very end of Waterhouse's career, show Miranda on the seashore gazing at the ship that will bring her eventual lover, Ferdinand, to the island on which she lives in exile. The later scene shows the ship tossed in the tempest with which the play begins (and which gives it its title), but this early work, more unusually, represents a moment before the beginning of the action: Miranda, seated gracefully on a rock, looks out to the distant ship, still untroubled, although ominous clouds are beginning to gather behind her back. Unusually, again, Miranda is not dressed in the costume of Shakespeare's time, but instead wears classical drapery carefully imitated from ancient Greek sculpture: cords cross between the breasts, and encircle the waist with an overfold of crinkling fabric. The hairstyle, with two bands of circling ribbon, is also classical, and the ends of the ribbon flutter in the wind, just beginning to rise as the storm approaches. The drapery and hairstyle resemble the work of such artists as Frederic Leighton, Albert Moore, or Edward John Poynter at this date, but the painting is novel in using these classical elements to characterise the pensive Shakespearean heroine. **EP**

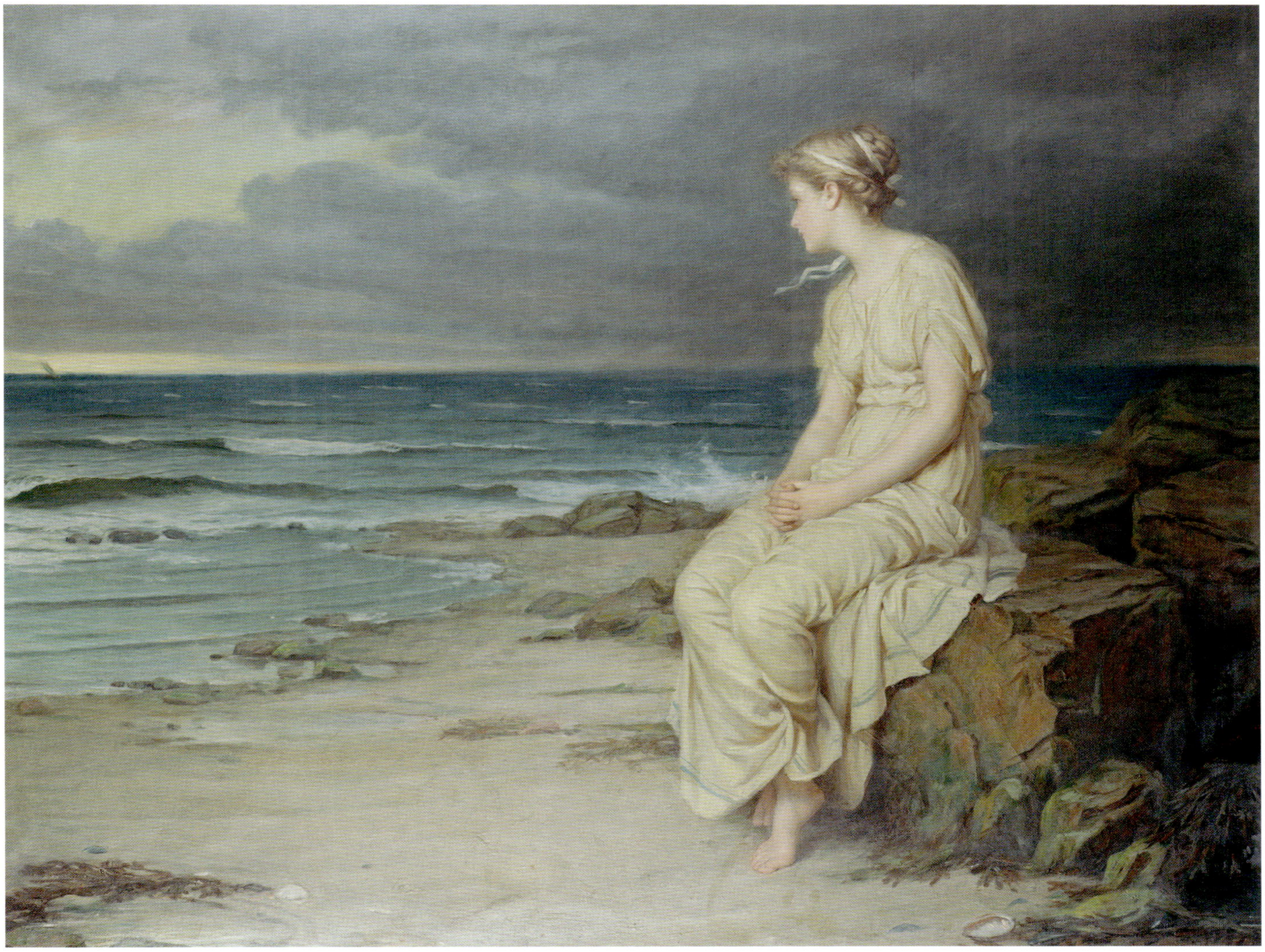

4. After the Dance 1876

OIL ON CANVAS, 76.2 X 127 CM - COLLECTION SIR TIM RICE - EXHIBITED ROYAL ACADEMY, 1876

In 1876, only the third year Waterhouse exhibited at the Royal Academy, this painting was displayed in a prominent position 'on the line', just above eye level where exhibition crowds could see it with ease; in the highly competitive arena of the Royal Academy exhibitions, this was a sign that the young artist was already achieving recognition. The composition, with its angled view into a complex interior space, reveals the influence of Lawrence Alma-Tadema, who coincidentally showed a painting with an identical title at the same exhibition (fig. 44), but Waterhouse makes the subject very much his own. Whereas Alma-Tadema's *After the Dance* featured a voluptuous nude bacchante, asleep after revelry, Waterhouse represents the children of the ancient world, seen from a viewpoint at their own level. From the title, and the tambourine lying next to the reclining girl, the spectator guesses that these are child dancers, resting after their labours. The mature male musicians, seated on a marble bench, are relegated to the background; one plays a tibia, or double pipe, while the other leans on his lyre, and a third figure surveys the scene from behind. The viewer can only guess what may be happening in the larger white marble room beyond the left edge of the painting, while attention is focussed on the secluded recess occupied by the children. The pensive expression of the young boy, the wilting flower in his hand, and the exhausted poses of both children add a tinge of melancholy, emphasised by the sombre tones of the background wall painting, which appears to represent a funeral procession. Perhaps the painting hints at the cruelty of child labour, or at the evanescence of childhood, but it does not offer a neat anecdote like those of so many Victorian paintings of children. At a metre and a quarter wide, this was an ambitious painting for the twenty-seven-year-old artist. The expert foreshortening of the mosaic and white marble floor, as well as details such as the lustrous glaze on the shallow red-figured bowl on the right, demonstrate the young painter's technical skill as well as his antiquarian learning. Yet this is not merely a bravura display. It offers a sidelong glimpse into an ancient world that is precise in every detail, yet still enigmatic to the modern observer. **EP**

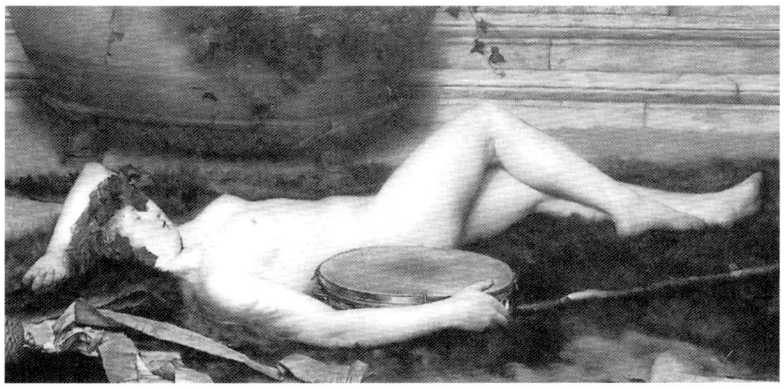

44. Lawrence Alma-Tadema, *After the Dance*, 1875,
Oil on canvas, 58.4 x 130 cm, Location unknown

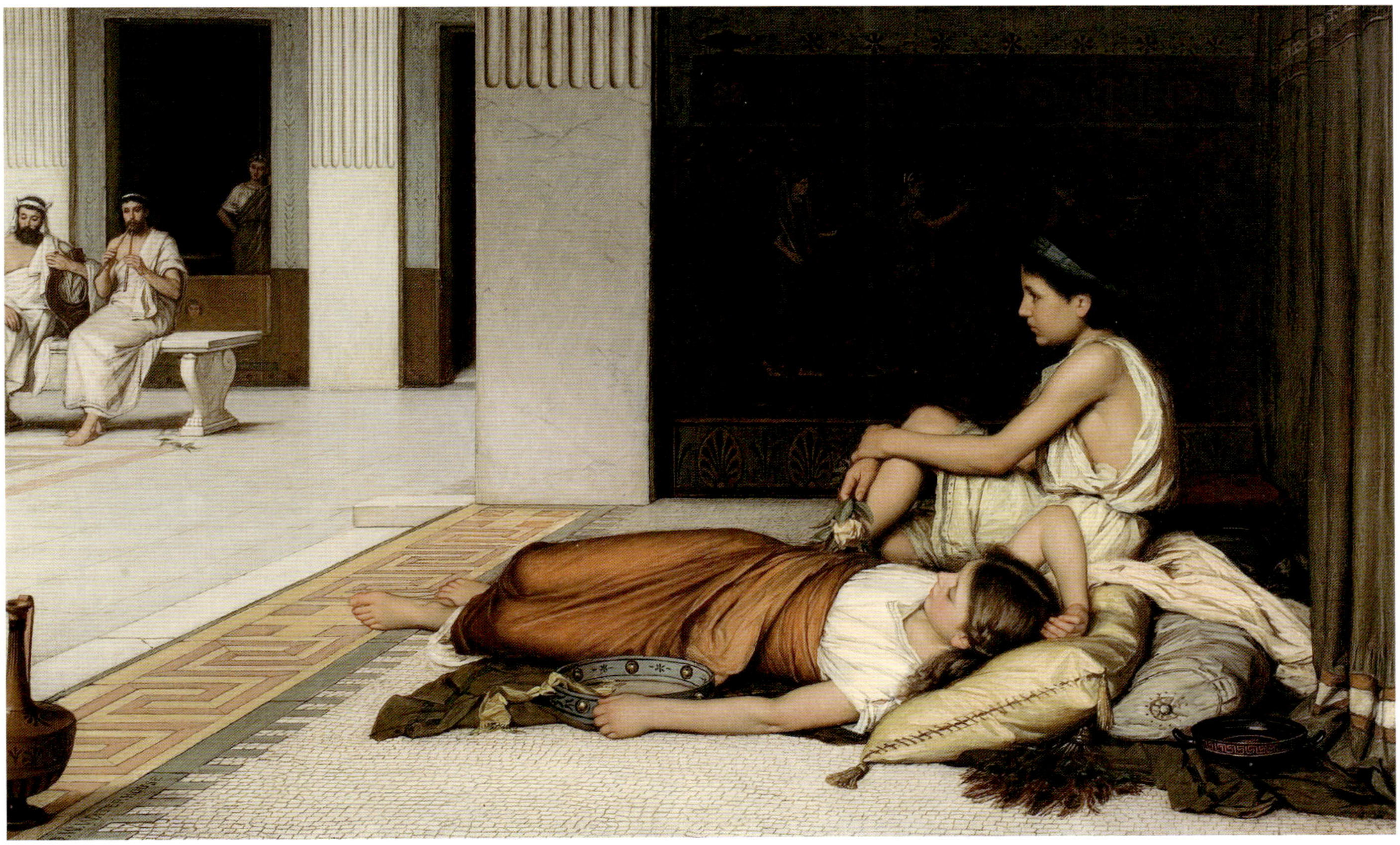

5. A Sick Child Brought into the Temple of Aesculapius 1877

OIL ON CANVAS, 170 X 208 CM - COLLECTION SIR TIM RICE - EXHIBITED ROYAL ACADEMY, 1877

Waterhouse continues to explore the world of ancient childhood in this painting of an ailing little girl, brought to the temple of Aesculapius, the god of medicine whose bronze statue looms above the scene on the right; the statue bears a staff entwined with the god's symbol, a serpent. The subject links Victorian concerns about child mortality with the ancient custom of seeking a cure by visiting one of the Asclepiea, temples devoted to the healing god Asclepius. Waterhouse's title uses the Latin name for the god (Aesculapius) and the grand marble architecture confirms the suggestion that the scene represents the cult established in 292 BC when Romans, afflicted by a plague, transferred Asclepius's snake from his temple at Epidaurus to Rome (the event is recounted in Book XV of Ovid's *Metamorphoses*, later a favourite text of Waterhouse's). Perhaps the classical scholar and critic, Walter Pater, took his cue from Waterhouse's painting for the scene in his novel of 1885, *Marius the Epicurean*, where the child Marius visits the temple of Aesculapius. In the novel, Pater elaborates the details of the ancient ritual of 'incubation', in which the sufferer sleeps in the temple to receive the god's healing messages in dreams. Perhaps because a sleeping figure would be unlikely to convey the narrative of healing, Waterhouse instead concentrates on the ministrations of the child, surrounded by her family, before the statue of the god. With a wan hand, supported by her mother, she holds a sprig of laurel towards the bronze tripod, from which wisps of smoke arise to suggest the burning of medicinal herbs. Laurel, sacred to Aesculapius's father Apollo (also a god of healing), wreathes the tripod and statue base, the heads of the sick child and white-robed priest, and the lap of the older sister who kneels in the foreground. The clean white lines of the temple architecture, the orderliness of the ritual, and the baskets of fruit and flowers may suggest hope, but this is delicately balanced with the pathos of the sick child. As in other paintings of this early period, Waterhouse leaves the conclusion of the story to the spectator's imagination; we cannot tell whether the child will recover or die. **EP**

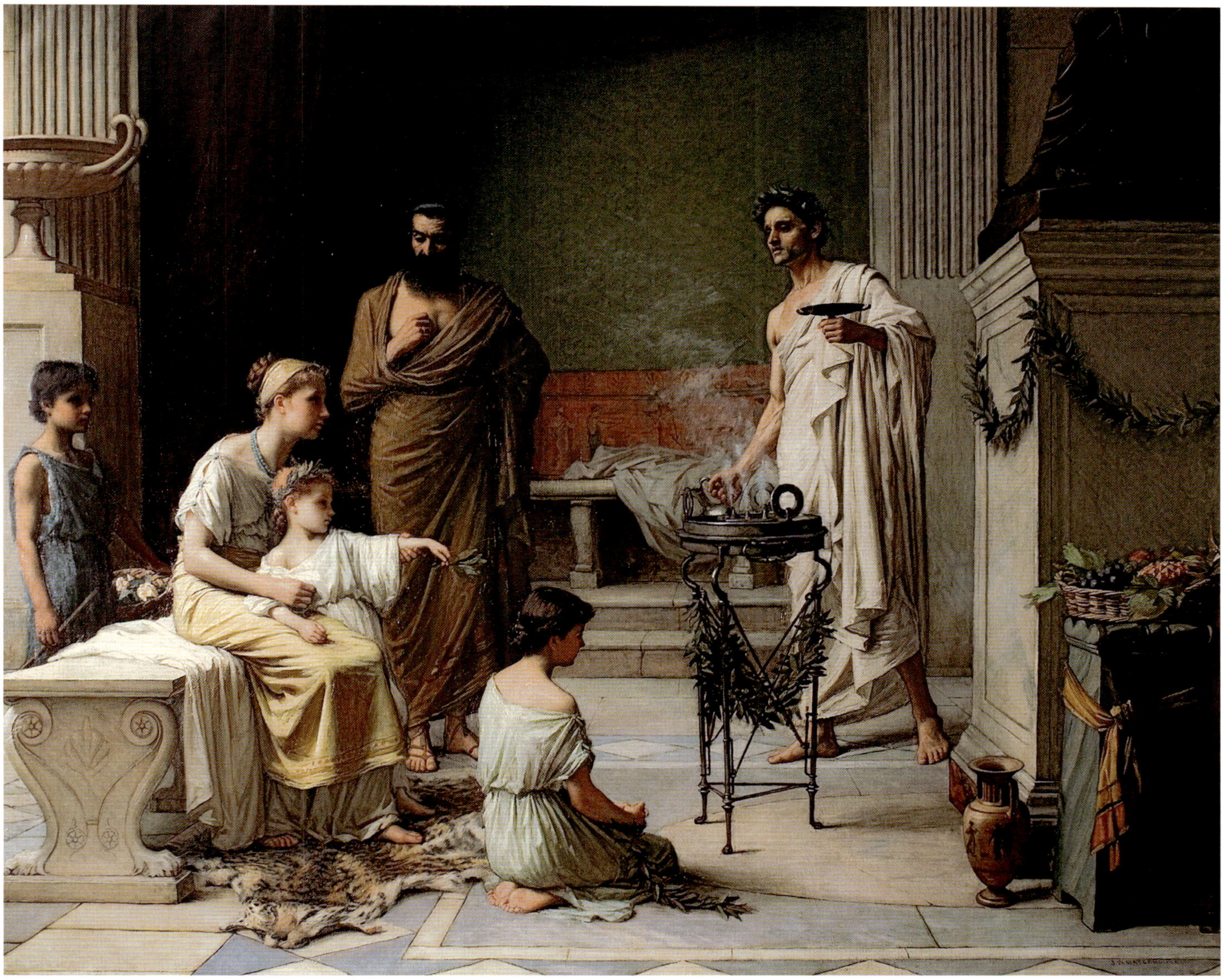

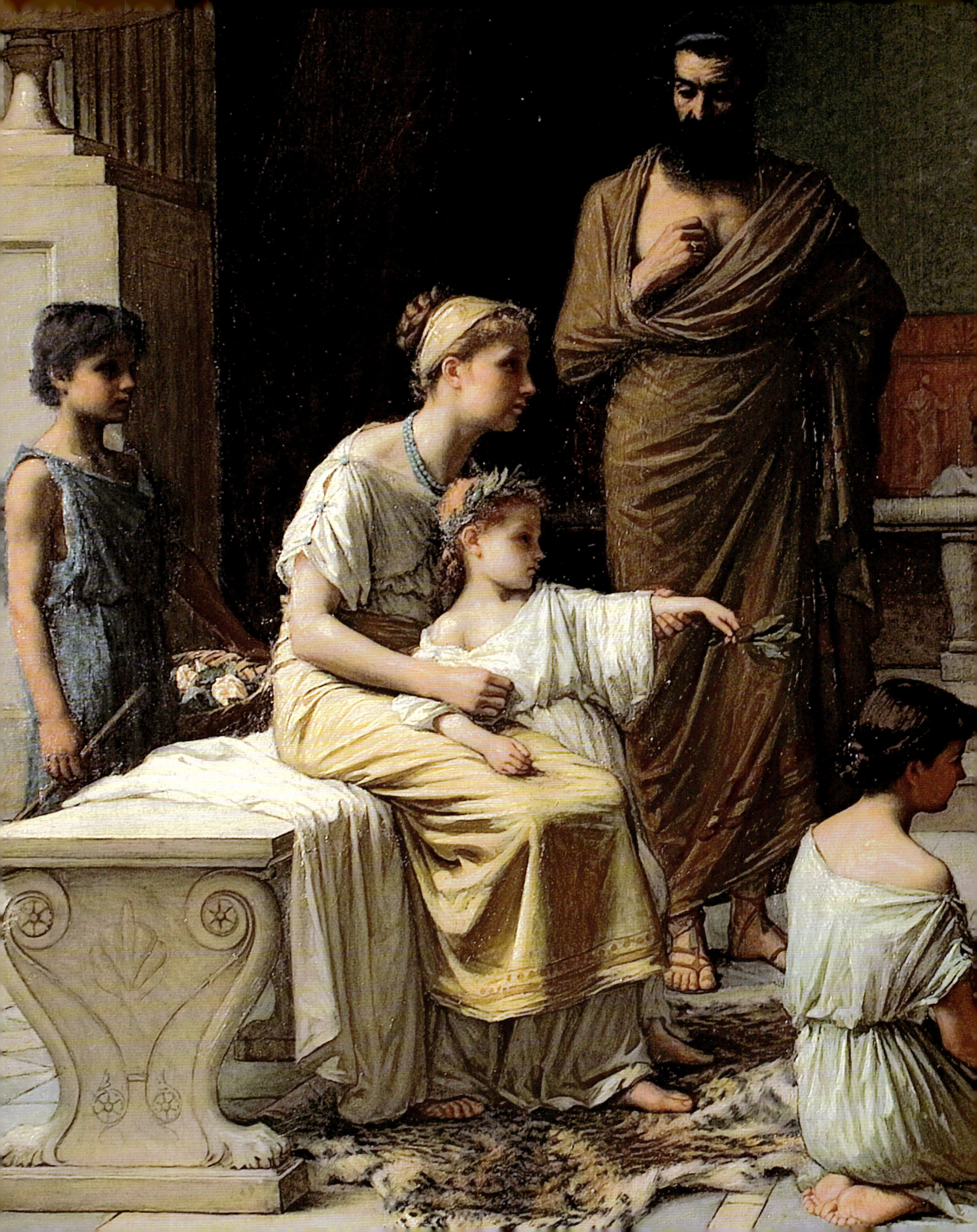

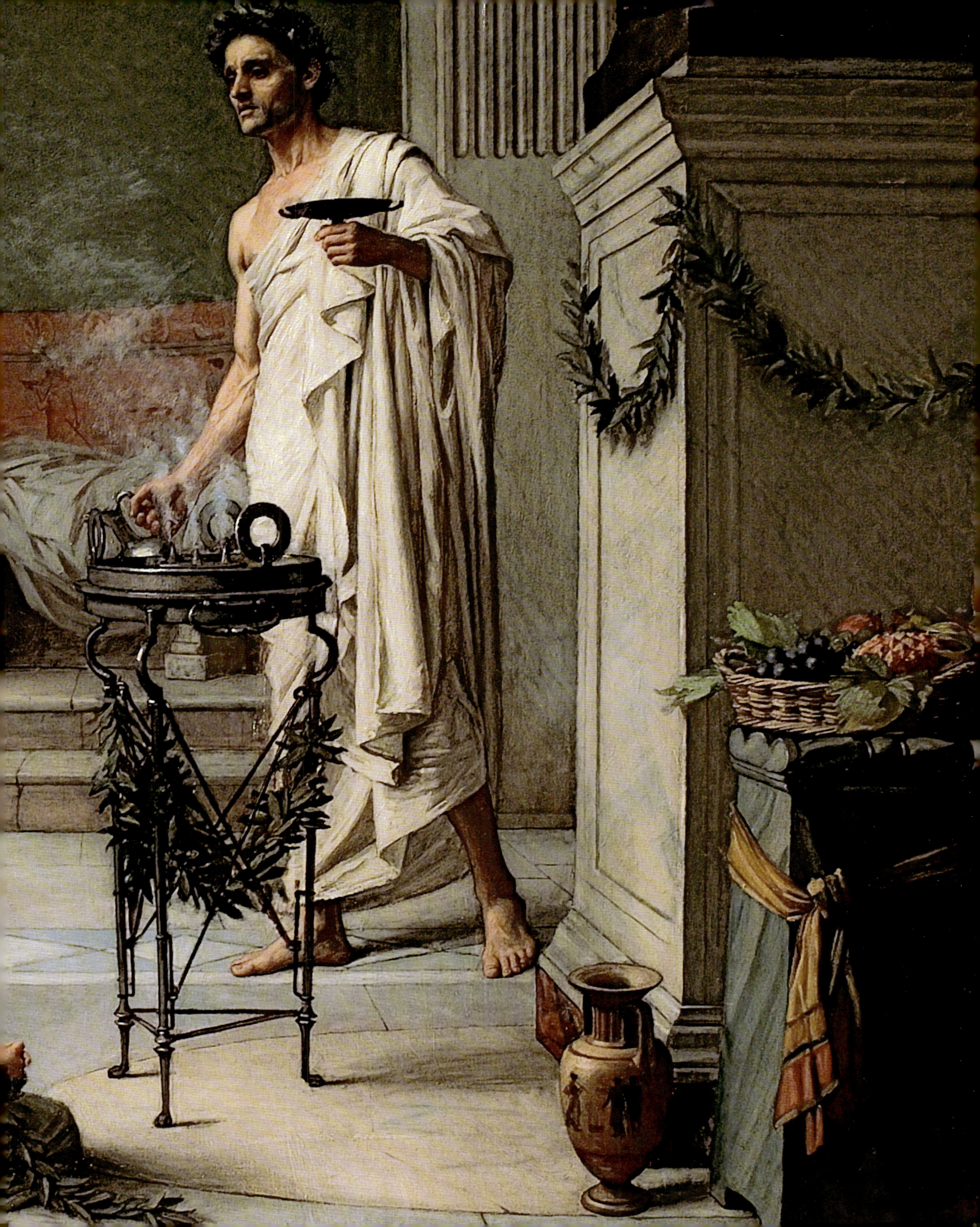

6. Scene at Pompeii c. 1877

WATERCOLOUR ON PAPER, 31 X 23.1 CM - COLLECTION JOHN PHYSICK

In 1877 Waterhouse revisited Italy, the country of his birth, apparently for the first time since his parents had brought him back to England, at the age of five. Like Alma-Tadema before him, he was fascinated by recent excavations at Pompeii, the streets and houses of which he sketched in watercolours such as this example. Since 1860, the archaeologist Guiseppe Fiorelli had been introducing novel excavation techniques, which concentrated on clearing rubble and restoring the architectural spaces of the town, rather than simply unearthing its artefacts. Waterhouse's watercolours capture this recent phase of Pompeii's history; here, for example, he shows the sunlit atrium of an excavated house, with columns supporting a reconstructed wooden roof. The atrium is unpretentious, moderate in scale and undecorated except for the red painting on the lower sections of the columns, found in many Pompeian houses. Although Pompeii at this date was a well-visited tourist attraction as well as a working excavation site, Waterhouse's scene, like many contemporary photographs of the site, is unpopulated. No doubt the artist wished principally to study and record the architectural setting, but the empty atrium also invites the viewer to speculate on its long-lost Pompeian inhabitants. On Waterhouse's visit of 1877, according to the first article on his career, 'his imagination was kindled by reading in the ruined streets of Pompeii the melodramatic romance of its last days'[1] – that is, the celebrated historical novel by Edward Bulwer-Lytton, *The Last Days of Pompeii* (1834), which repopulated the site with fictional characters. **EP**

1 J.A. Blaikie, 'J.W. Waterhouse, A.R.A.', *Magazine of Art*, vol. IX, 1886, p. 2.

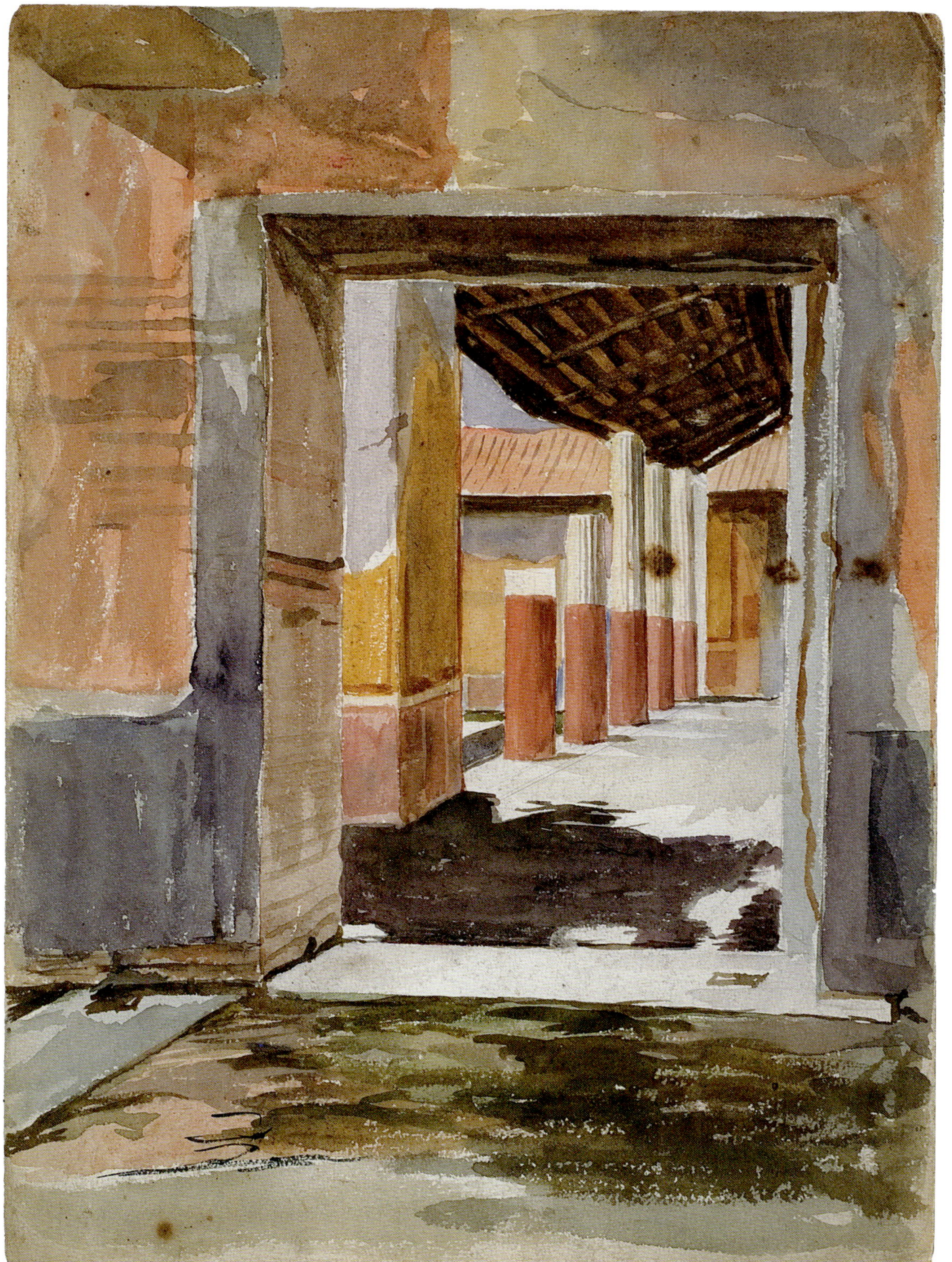

7. Dolce Far Niente 1879

OIL ON CANVAS, 49.5 X 36.5 CM - PRUDENTIAL PLC - EXHIBITED DUDLEY GALLERY, 1879

The title – 'sweet doing nothing' – was a popular phrase, used twice by Waterhouse, and before him by William Holman Hunt for a painting of a sensual and sumptuously dressed female model at life size, exhibited at the Royal Academy in 1867 (fig. 45). In 1871, the critic for *The Art Journal* used the phrase to describe a new group of painters who 'cherish in common, reverence for the antique, affection for modern Italy; they affect southern climes, costumes, sunshine, also a certain *dolce far niente* style, with a general Sybarite state of mind which rests in Art and aestheticism as the be-all and end-all of existence'.[1] Although Waterhouse had not yet begun to exhibit when this remark was published, his choice of title suggests that he was allying himself with the carefree, Italianate subjects of this group of painters, several of whom favoured settings on the island of Capri, later to assume special importance for Waterhouse as well. Waterhouse's fame would eventually eclipse that of any of the painters in this group.[2]

Waterhouse's two paintings are subtly differentiated despite their shared title. The larger work (cat. 8, pp. 82-83), dated 1880 but apparently not exhibited, is a scene of everyday life in the ancient world very much in the manner of Alma-Tadema, who often used a composition, derived from ancient vase-paintings representing symposia (or drinking parties), in which figures recline on couches, parallel to the picture surface; before them are small tables laden with flowers, fruit, statuettes, plates, or vessels. In this case Waterhouse places brilliant yellow daffodils and a small jug on an elegant marble and bronze table, similar to examples found at Pompeii which Waterhouse would have seen in the Naples Museum on his journey of 1877. The colonnade behind the figure, with its distinctive red and white colouring, is clearly inspired by Pompeian interiors of the kind Waterhouse sketched on the same journey; a similar example can be seen in the watercolour, *Scene at Pompeii* (cat. 6). Thus the painting demonstrates Waterhouse's careful research into the material culture of classical antiquity, as well as his technical dexterity at this point in his career: the depiction of bright sunlight, falling on the figure in a shadowy interior, is a particular tour de force.

More brilliant still is the smaller *Dolce Far Niente* (cat. 7, p. 81): the fluttering white feathers against the white marble wall and the abruptly foreshortened figure are feats of technical skill fit to vie with Alma-Tadema himself. By this date art critics routinely compared Waterhouse's work to that of Alma-Tadema, thirteen years older and still better known, but this work shows the younger artist developing novel ideas of his own. The interior is simpler and less cluttered with archaeological detail than similar scenes by Alma-Tadema. Despite the impeccable classicism of the Pompeian-style lamp at top right, or the cross-bands and clasped sleeves of the girl's drapery, the antiquarian note is muted, so that the painting appears fresh and modern. Indeed, the sunflower, emerging from a deep-blue glass vase, was a characteristic accessory of the contemporary Aesthetic Movement, used as a decorative motif in architectural sculpture and objects ranging from furniture to wallpaper, and the insouciant subject-matter reflects the Aesthetic Movement ideal of 'art for art's sake'. Waterhouse exhibited this work in 1879 at the Dudley Gallery, a less imposing venue than the Royal Academy, where he had been showing smaller works since 1873 (see for example cat. 2). However, his earlier Dudley exhibits had generally been modestly priced, around 25-35 guineas; *Dolce Far Niente* was offered at the much higher price of 80 guineas, despite its unpretentious subject and relatively small dimensions. This is a sign of Waterhouse's growing reputation; after 1881 he stopped exhibiting at the Dudley altogether. Perhaps the price also indicates the artist's esteem for the work, certainly one of his most engaging in its combination of technical flair and piquant subject-matter. **EP**

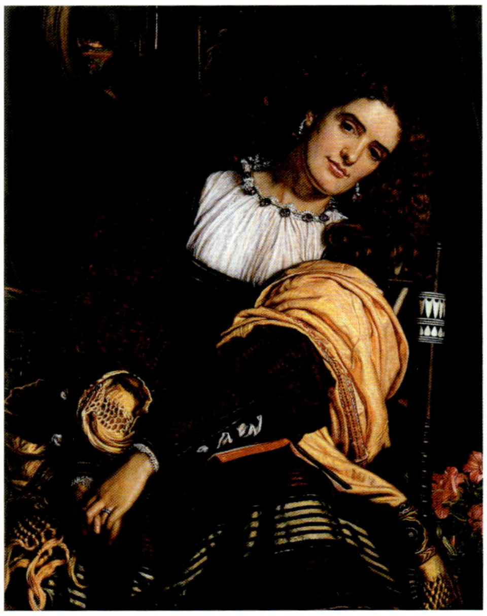

45. William Holman Hunt, *Il Dolce Far Niente*, c. 1859-1866, Retouched 1874-1875, Oil on canvas, 99 x 82.5 cm, Private collection

1 'The Royal Academy', *The Art Journal*, 1 July 1871, p. 176.
2 Painters cited were Albert Moore and his brother John Collingham Moore, Walter MacLaren, Thomas Armstrong, William Bright Morris, Edgar Barclay, William Blake Richmond, and George Heming Mason.

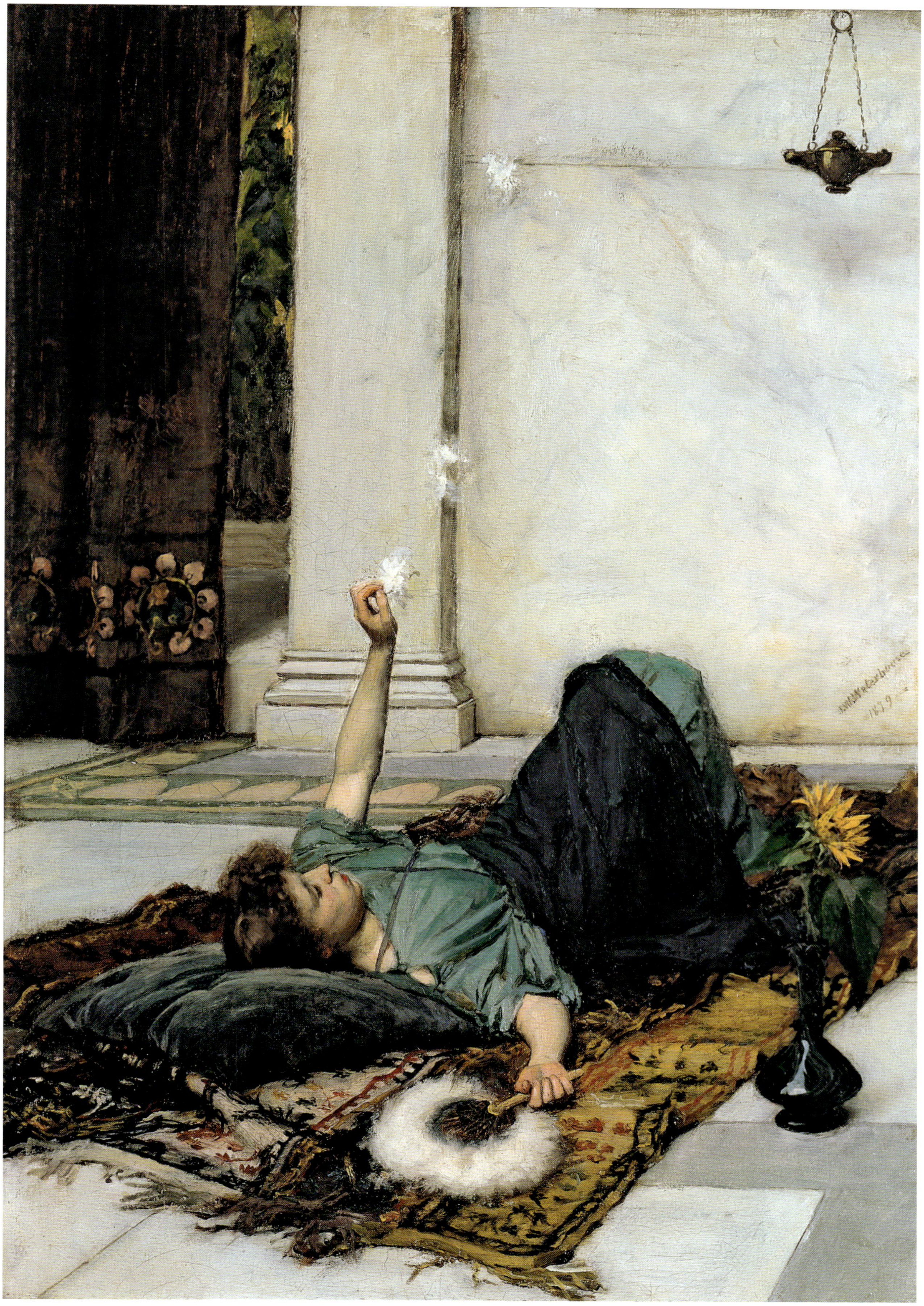

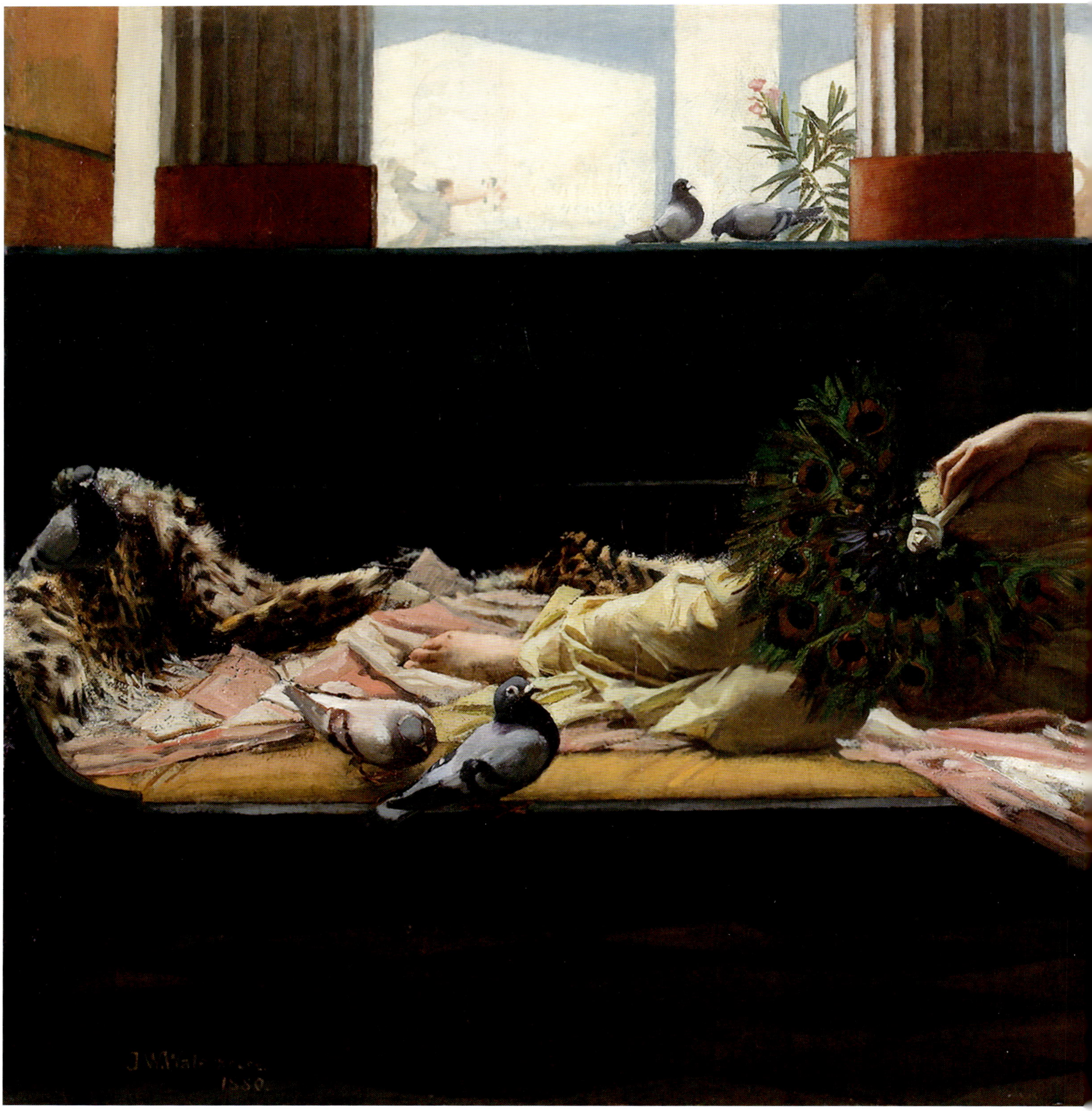

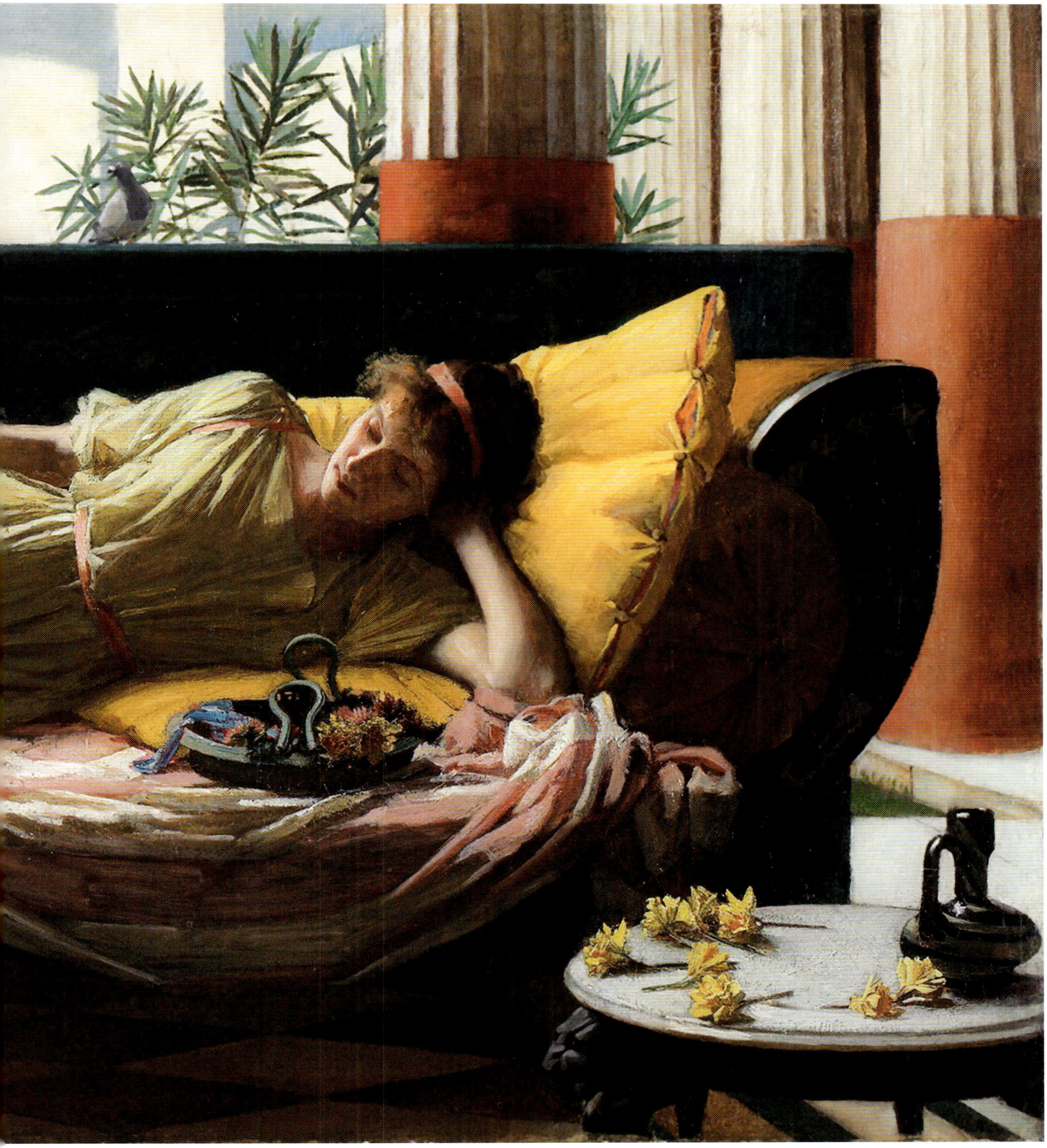

8. **Dolce Far Niente** 1880

OIL ON CANVAS, 50 X 95.5 CM - FIFE COUNCIL MUSEUMS, KIRKCALDY MUSEUM AND ART GALLERY, BEQUEST OF MRS. JOHN HARLY, 1927

9. The Household Gods 1880

OIL ON CANVAS, 102.6 X 74.3 CM - CHI MEI MUSEUM, TAINAN, TAIWAN - EXHIBITED ROYAL ACADEMY, 1880

This painting shows the *lararium*, deep within a Roman house, where images of the *Lares*, or household gods, were kept for daily worship. In an inner sanctum richly decorated with wall paintings, two young women offer flowers and wine before three bronze statuettes. The shallow square brazier, where a fire burns gently below the altar, resembles ancient examples such as one unearthed at the House of the Faun in Pompeii[1], more elaborately decorated but similar in size to the one Waterhouse depicts. The painting reflects contemporary interest in the domestic religious rites of the ancient Romans, described for example in Walter Pater's historical novel of 1885, *Marius the Epicurean*, and represented in a number of paintings by Waterhouse and Alma-Tadema. Interestingly, one of Alma-Tadema's patrons, the engineer John Aird (famous for relocating the Crystal Palace and later for building the Aswan Dam), bought this painting, which at a metre high is larger and more ambitious than most of Alma-Tadema's representations of domestic interiors. **EP**

1 Museo Archeologico Nazionale di Napoli, no. 72991.

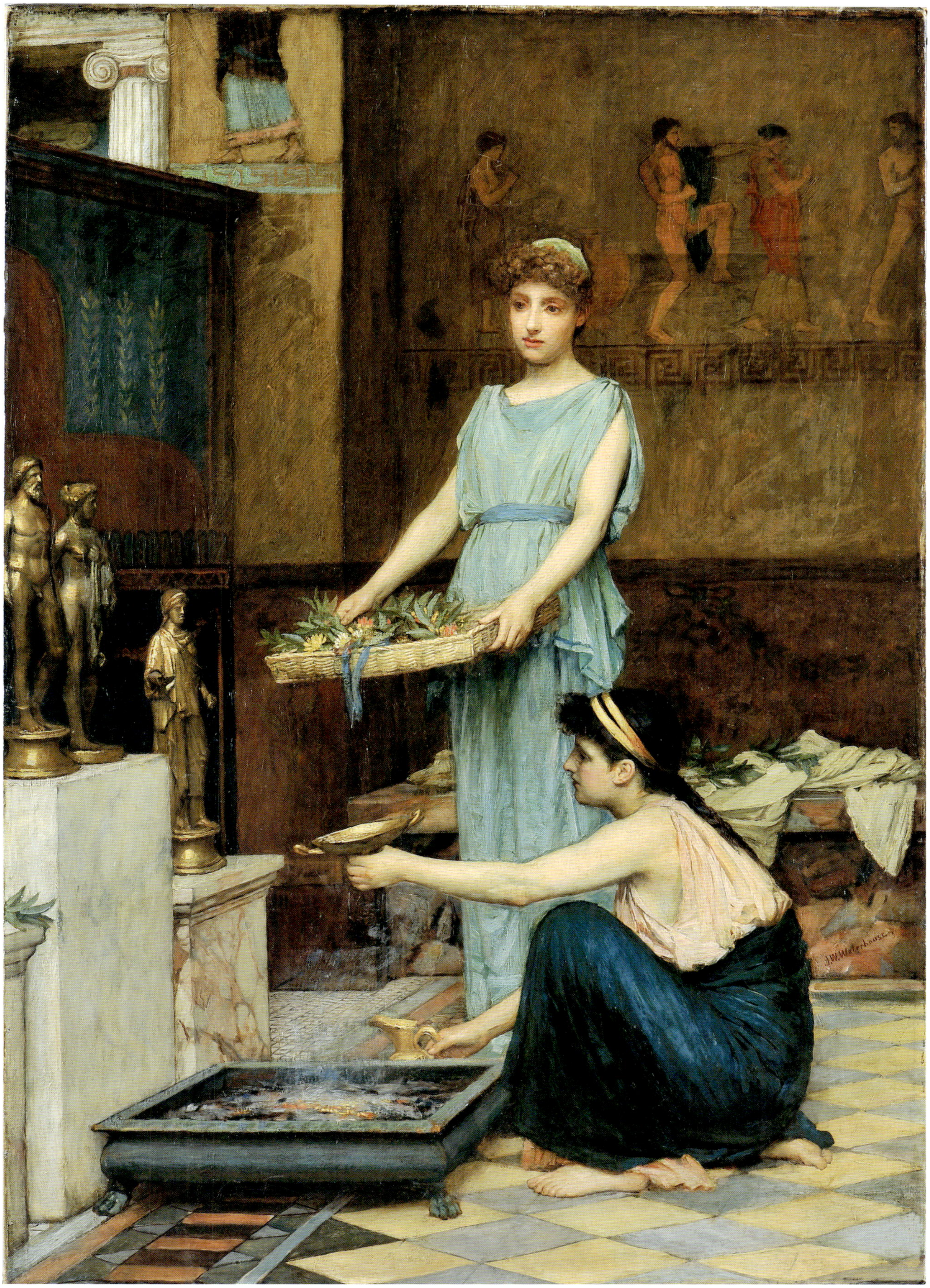

10. A Flower Stall 1880

OIL ON CANVAS, 57.8 X 79.3 CM - LAING ART GALLERY, TYNE AND WEAR MUSEUMS, NEWCASTLE UPON TYNE, BEQUEST OF JOHN LAMB, 1909
EXHIBITED DUDLEY GALLERY WINTER EXHIBITION, 1880

A Flower Stall appeared at the Dudley Gallery in 1880, while *The Household Gods* (cat. 9) and a painting entitled *A Pompeian Shop* (now lost) were at the Royal Academy. This was Waterhouse's most substantial group of paintings of ancient everyday life, and marked the culmination of this phase of his work; after 1880 his interests would shift to historical and finally to mythological subject-matter. Like the lost Royal Academy painting, *A Flower Stall* explores the commercial side of ancient life within a Pompeian environment, seen here in the characteristic paving stones and rectilinear street plan of the ancient town. The excavations at Pompeii had unearthed abundant evidence of everyday commercial activity, of special interest to nineteenth-century historians who increasingly studied the social and economic, as well as the political, history of the ancient world. Thus Pompeian shops and markets also featured in a number of Alma-Tadema's paintings, including *The Flower Market* of 1868 (fig. 8). In Waterhouse's painting, the sociological element is evident in the contrast between the heavily-draped flower-seller, her distaff at her feet, and her more elegant customers, higher in social class. The mundane commercial transaction is combined, however, with the aesthetic pleasure of an abundance of fragrant roses, a motif that would become more important in Waterhouse's later work (see cats 50, 51). **EP**

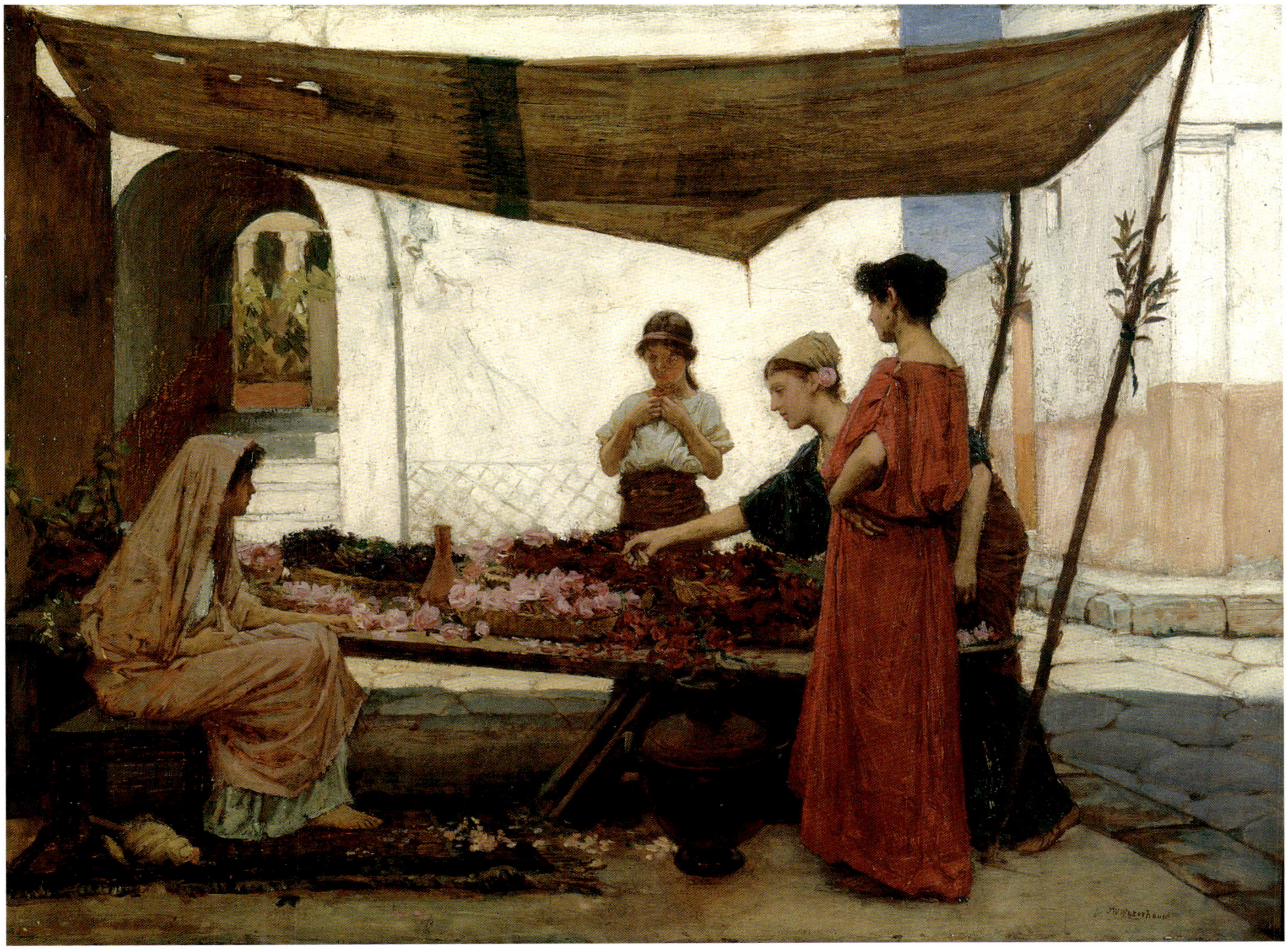

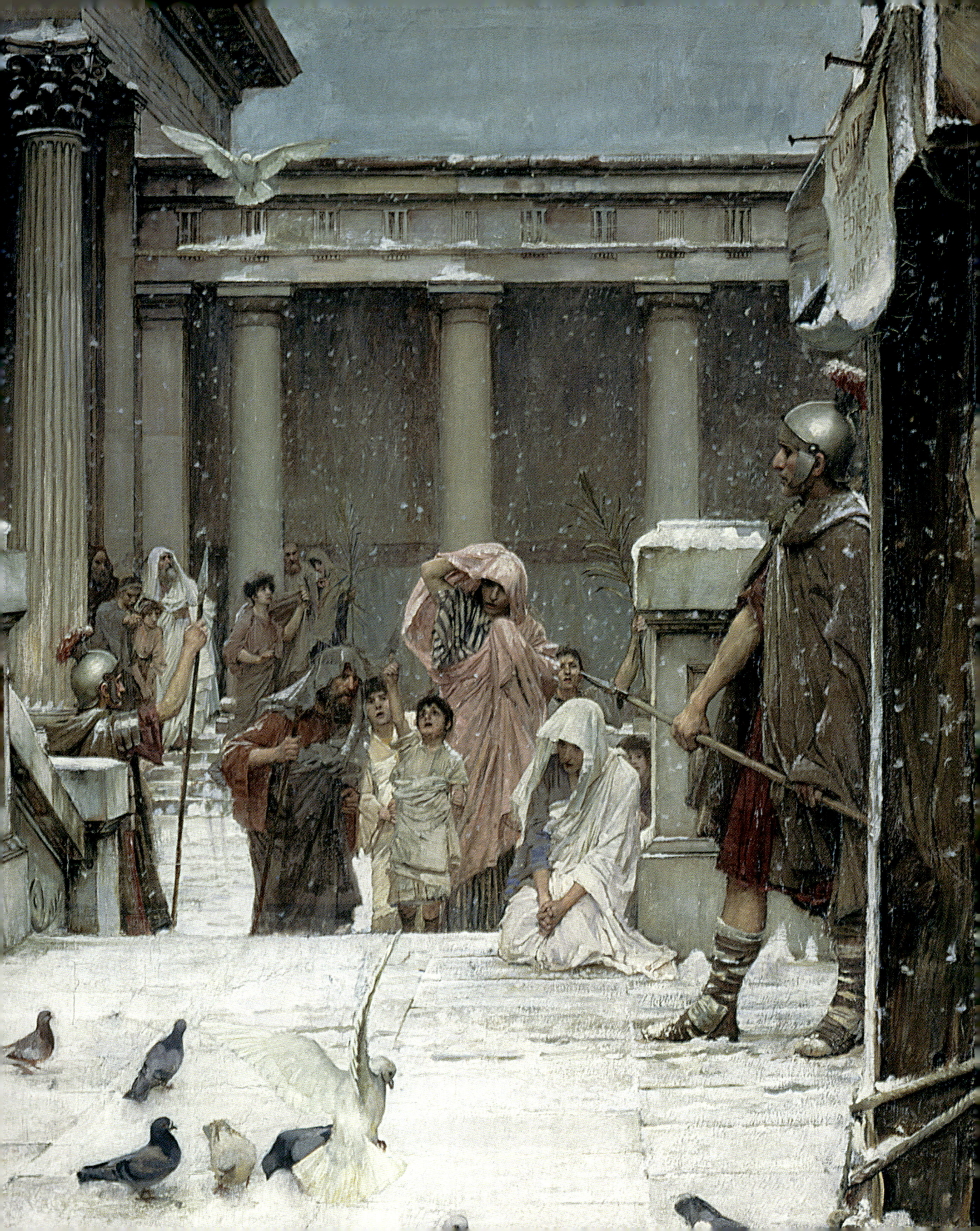

Building a Career

11. Diogenes 1882

OIL ON CANVAS, 208.3 X 134.6 CM - ART GALLERY OF NEW SOUTH WALES, SYDNEY, PURCHASED 1886 - EXHIBITED ROYAL ACADEMY, 1882

While there is a longstanding tradition, in Western art, for painting the philosophers of classical antiquity, Waterhouse gives this a new twist by juxtaposing the forbidding figure of Diogenes with a group of playful women. Nonetheless, he also contrives to refer to all of the traditional anecdotes about the philosopher of the fourth century BC, leader of the Cynics (the word means 'dog-like') – philosophers who espoused an extreme back-to-nature lifestyle, disdaining material possessions and the institutions of civil society. Barefoot, and dressed in a rough brown garment, Diogenes sits in the earthenware tub which famously served him as his only dwelling. Next to him is a lamp, which he reputedly used in his fruitless search for an honest man. According to another anecdote, Alexander the Great visited the philosopher in his tub, and respectfully asked him whether he could do him any service, to which Diogenes replied 'Get out of my sunshine'. Waterhouse transposes this legend to place an attractive blond woman, arrayed in pink, on the staircase where she casts a shadow over the philosopher, impervious to her charms. The painting thus demonstrates Waterhouse's growing skill in dramatising a great deal of narrative detail within a readily legible pictorial composition. Characteristically, too, the seemingly light-hearted scene asks the viewer to reflect on its possible moral implications. Should we admire the high-mindedness of the Cynic philosopher, who refuses to succumb to the delights either of feminine beauty or of the wealthy marble city around him? Or should we find his self-imposed squalor repellent, and side instead with the women who are prepared to enjoy life? The composition leaves the decision to the viewer.

This picture continues the series of historical subjects that had begun in 1878 with *The Remorse of Nero* (fig. 10). In 1886 it was acquired by the Art Gallery of New South Wales, thus becoming the second of Waterhouse's paintings to enter one of the new Australian public collections, following the Art Gallery of South Australia's purchase of *The Favourites of the Emperor Honorius* in 1883 (cat. 12). **EP**

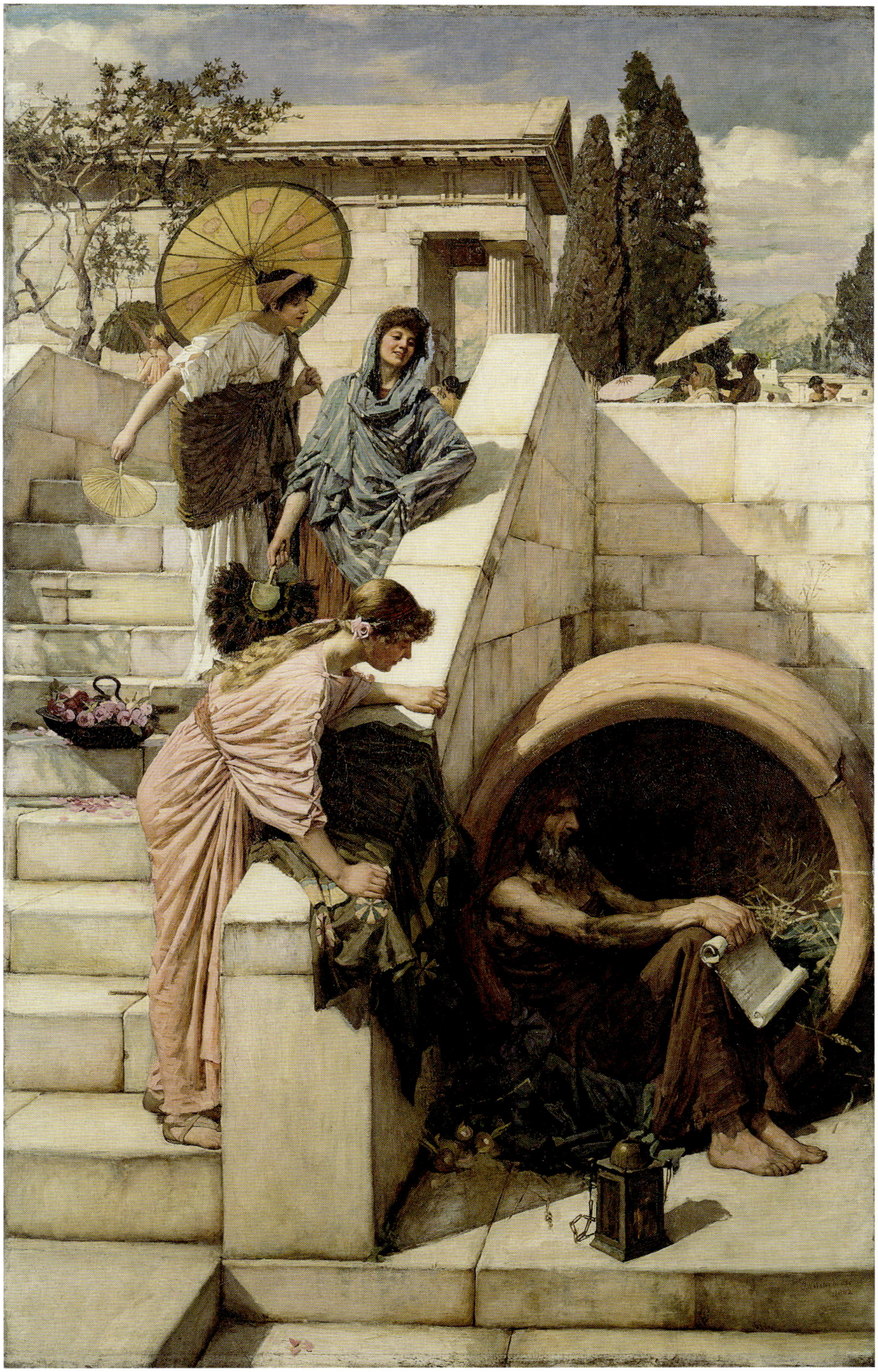

12. The Favourites of the Emperor Honorius 1883

OIL ON CANVAS, 119.3 X 205 CM - ART GALLERY OF SOUTH AUSTRALIA, ADELAIDE, PURCHASED 1883 - EXHIBITED ROYAL ACADEMY, 1883

As several art critics noted when this painting appeared at the Royal Academy exhibition of 1883, the youthful Roman Emperor Honorius (reigned 395-423 A.D.) featured in Edward Gibbon's magisterial work, *The History of the Decline and Fall of the Roman Empire* (1776-1788). However, the word 'favourites' in Waterhouse's title suggests that his immediate source was the novel of 1850 by Wilkie Collins (later famous as a writer of mystery novels), *Antonina; or, the Fall of Rome.* Collins introduces the reader to the figure of the youth before revealing his identity, to dramatic effect:

> Nothing could be more pitiably effeminate than the appearance of this young man.... An unmeaning smile dilated his thin, colourless lips; and as he looked down on his strange favourites, he occasionally whispered to them a few broken expressions of endearment, almost infantine in their simplicity. His whole soul seemed to be engrossed by the labour of distributing his grain, and he followed the different movements of the poultry with an earnestness of attention, which seemed almost idiotic in its ridiculous intensity. If it be asked, why a person so contemptible as this solitary youth has been introduced with so much care, and described with so much minuteness, it must be answered, that, though destined to form no important figure in this work, he played, from his position, a remarkable part in the great drama on which it is founded – for this feeder of chickens was no less a person than Honorius, Emperor of Rome.

Later in the novel, the word is repeated to chilling effect, when the besieged people of Rome (left unprotected while Honorius and his court reside in safety at Ravenna) are obliged to kill their 'favourites', that is their pets, for food (the word is twice repeated).[1] As this suggests, Waterhouse's scene does not simply represent an immature adolescent who is fond of birds. The young Emperor's neglect of his duty produces horrifying results, detailed with almost unbearable vividness in Collins's novel: the devastating invasion of Italy by the Gothic chieftain Alaric, the siege and eventually the sack of Rome in 410 A.D.. Perhaps the grimmest moral of the scene, though, is the courtiers' sycophantic acquiescence in Honorius's delinquency. As the critic for *The Times* wrote, with clear appreciation of the picture's ironies, the courtiers bring 'no tiresome news of Alaric's advance. With a truer sense of what should interest an Emperor they have brought, the one a book on ornithology, another a nosegay of flowers, a third some illuminated volume: but their master is as careless of their presence as if they had come to announce the sack of Rome'.[2]

In the scene from the novel, Honorius is standing up while he feeds the poultry; the two oil sketches here show Waterhouse gradually working out a composition of his own. These are of particular importance for showing how Waterhouse was developing his skills as a pictorial story-teller at this stage of his career. In the smaller sketch (cat. 13), presumably the earlier in the sequence, the courtiers are too distant to interact effectively with the figure of the Emperor; in the larger sketch (cat. 14) the mediating figure of the attendant or guard is developed, but threatens to assume too dominant a role. In the final painting (cat. 12) the attendant serves as a pivot between the two groups, centrally positioned but clearly subordinated behind a massive fluted pilaster, and the tension between Honorius and his court becomes a matter of psychological rather than merely physical distance. The statue, cut off at the knees in the sketches, is finally removed to the background but represented at full length, and identifiable as a version of the famous statue of the first Emperor, Augustus, which had been unearthed at Prima Porta, near Rome, in 1863. Thus the statue serves as a reminder of the early days of Roman Imperial power, its military stance in stark contrast to Honorius's slumping pose. The magnificent architecture of the palace interior demonstrates the luxury of the later Roman Empire, with accessories of appropriate date such as the lavish Byzantine throne. In all its details, as well as its principal narrative, the painting enacts the decline of the Roman Empire in which Honorius played such an ignominious part.

Despite Waterhouse's earlier successes at the Royal Academy, the *Times* critic still thought his name unfamiliar enough to remind readers that he should not be confused with the 'better known' architect and Royal Academician, Alfred Waterhouse (no relation).[3] Never again would such admonitions be necessary: *The Favourites of the Emperor Honorius*, with its balance between expansiveness of scale and sumptuous elaboration of detail, brought Waterhouse decisively to critical attention. The painting was immediately purchased by the Art Gallery of South Australia, the first of the artist's works to be acquired by a public gallery. **EP**

1 W. Wilkie Collins, *Antonina; or, The Fall of Rome: A Romance of the Fifth Century*, London: Richard Bentley, 1850, vol. I, pp. 48-49, vol. II, p. 199.
2 'The Royal Academy', *The Times*, 11 May 1883, p. 4.
3 *Ibid*, p. 4.

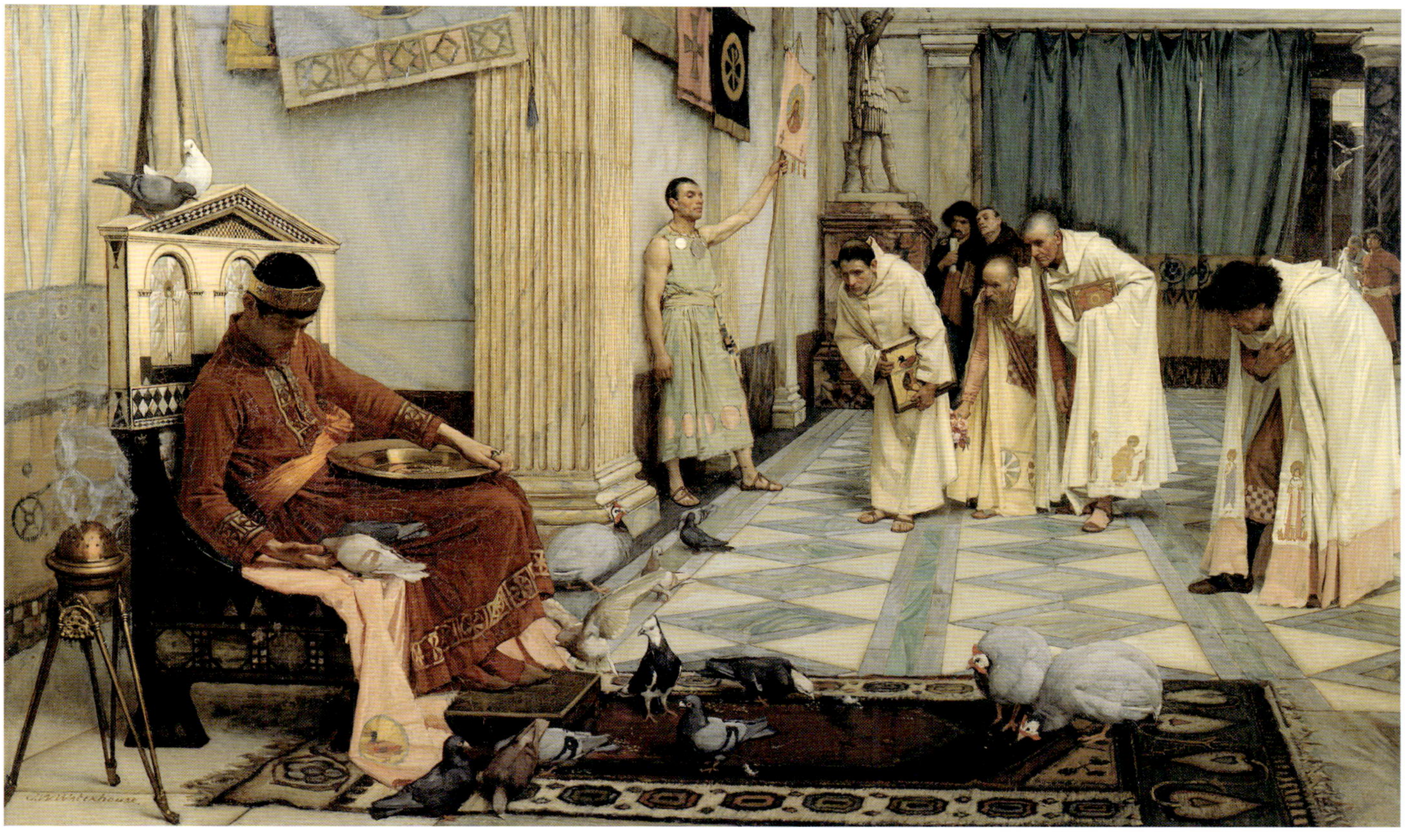

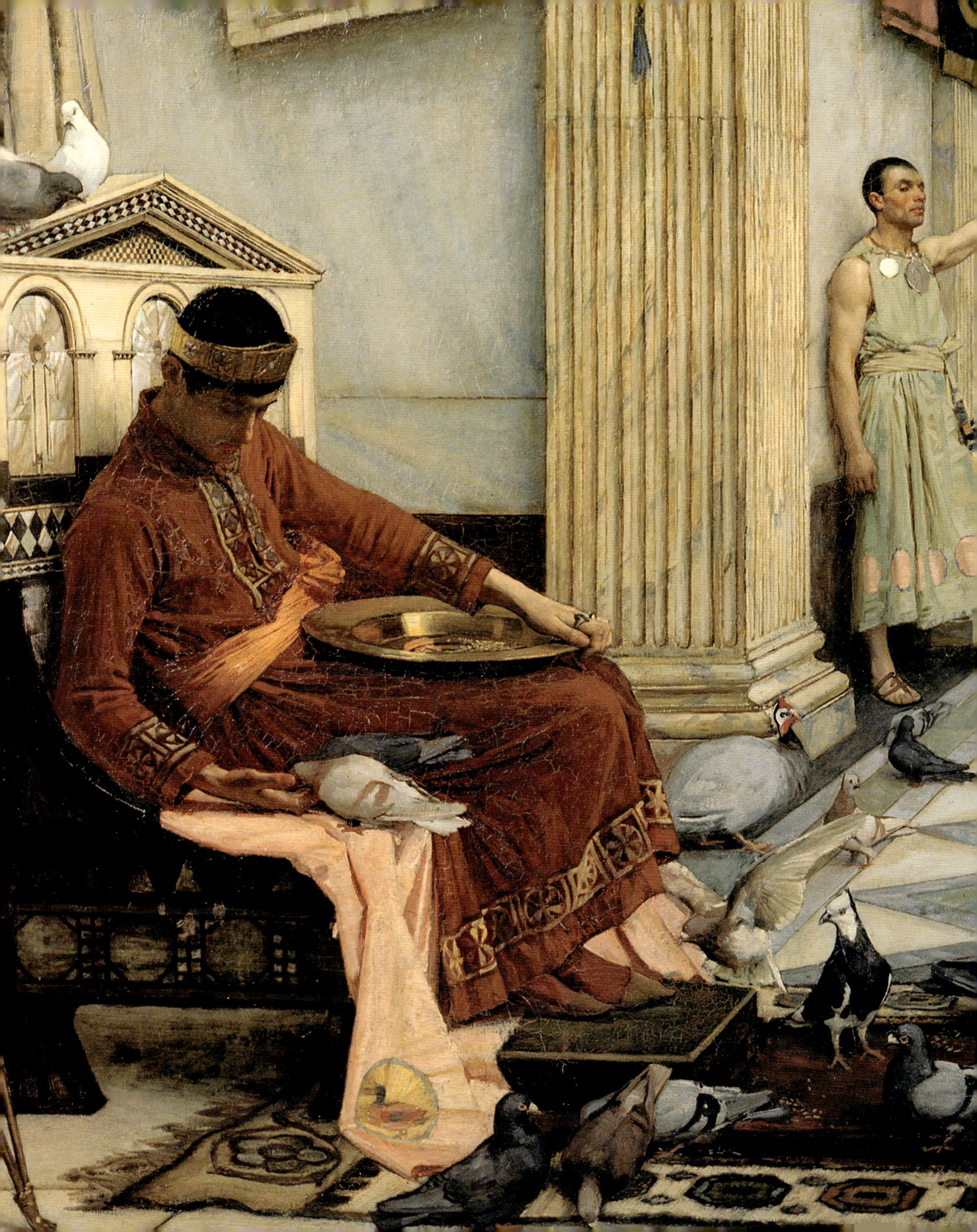

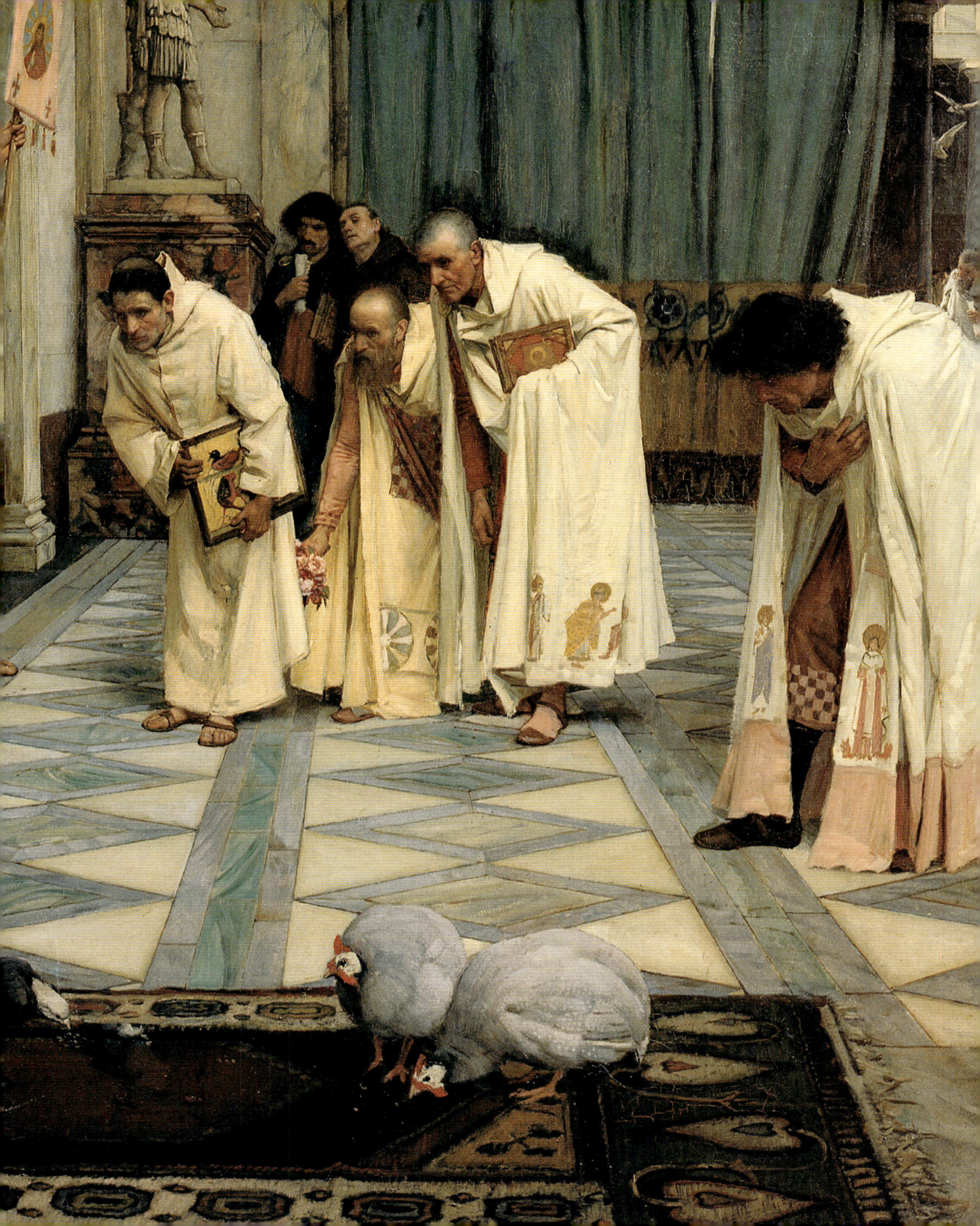

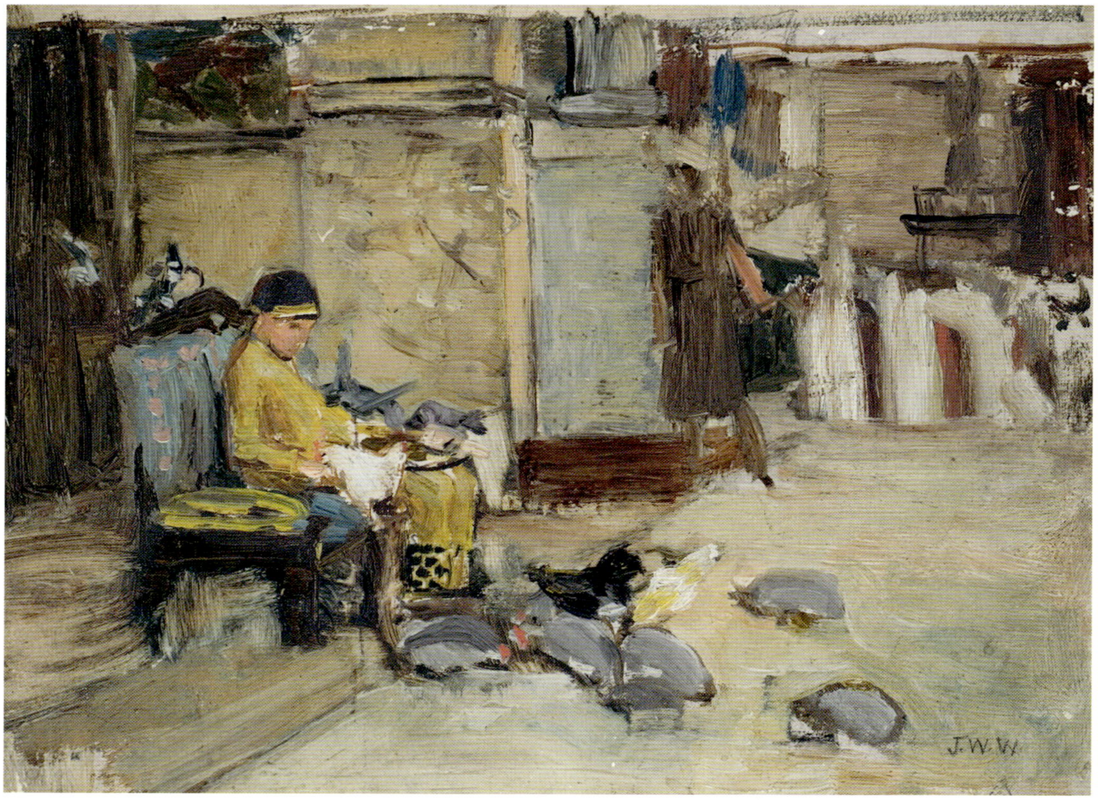

13. The Favourites of the Emperor Honorius c. 1882-1883

EARLIER SKETCH, OIL ON CANVAS, MOUNTED ON BOARD, 20 X 28 CM - COLLECTION JOHN PHYSICK

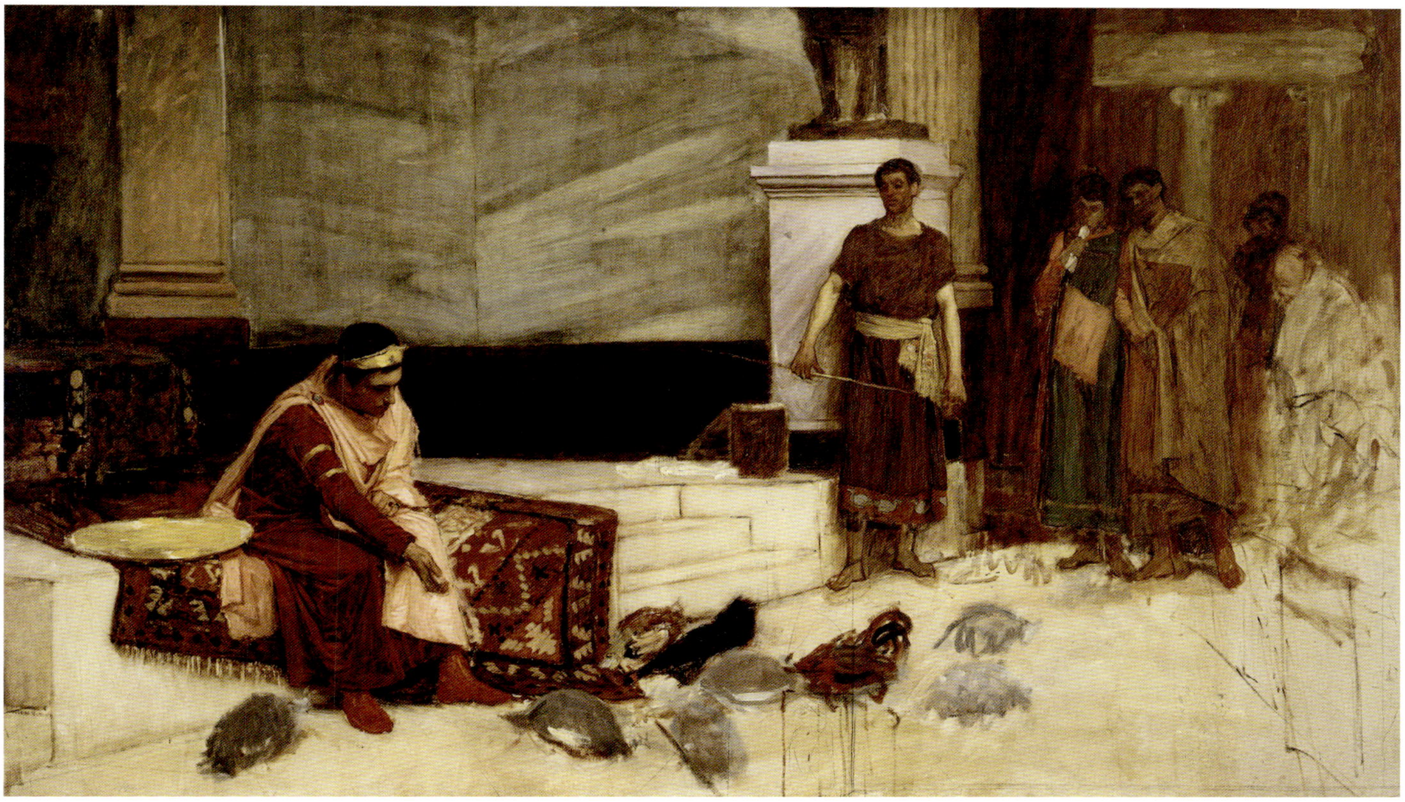

14. The Favourites of the Emperor Honorius c. 1882-1883

LATER SKETCH, OIL ON CANVAS, 94 X 166.5 CM - COLLECTION STEPHEN AND LINDA WATERHOUSE

15. Consulting the Oracle 1884

OIL ON CANVAS, 119.4 X 198.1 CM - TATE, GIFT OF SIR HENRY TATE, 1894 - EXHIBITED ROYAL ACADEMY, 1884

Principally an essay in exoticism and the occult, in *Consulting the Oracle* Waterhouse brought together a number of themes or leitmotifs that were to run throughout his work – the intense, hypnotic gaze of the main protagonist; an exotic female figure who arbitrates the world of mysticism; magical divination; and the disturbing effect of such experiences on the unconscious. When Waterhouse exhibited the painting at the Royal Academy in 1884, he added the following commentary:

> The Oracle or Teraph was a human head, cured with spices, which was fixed against the wall, and lamps being lit before it and other rites performed, the imagination of diviners was so excited that they supposed that they heard a low voice speaking future events.

It was an unusual and somewhat obscure subject. In ancient Judaic society Teraphim were generally simply household gods or idols. But according to the *Targum Pseudo-Jonathan*, Teraphim were originally human heads, taken from first born male adults who had been sacrificed. Shaved, salted, spiced, and with a golden plate bearing magic words placed under the tongue, it was believed Teraphic heads could talk and give guidance. In twentieth-century excavations of Jericho, evidence of human skulls having been used as cult objects was discovered, supporting the existence of this practice. It is possible that the worship of the heads originated first as a fetish representative of ancestors, but gradually they came to be considered oracular.

In Waterhouse's dramatic picture, the priestess holds out her hand for silence as she bends towards the head's lips to hear its words. Her rapt expression, and the pause before the prophecy is received, create an unbearable tension in her spectators, a mood passed on to viewers of the picture. The semi-circle of women all respond to this tension in different ways, their apprehension manifesting itself in gestures that indicate near hysteria or terror. Only the figure in red remains stoical and immune from this anxious atmosphere. Waterhouse was aware of artistic precedents for a group responding to a common source with a range of expressions. He was familiar with the works of Jean-Léon Gérôme, who used it a number of times, most notably in *Phryne before the Tribunal*, which had been exhibited in London in 1866. Interestingly, Waterhouse's combination of a curving group with a slightly separated single figure in *Consulting the Oracle* is a repetition of the overall composition of his own *Favourites of the Emperor Honorious* (cat. 12).

Waterhouse emphasises the evocative gloom of the interior with a glimpse of bright sunlight through an open window, an elegant device that also serves to offer a view of the world beyond this room and visually separates the priestess from her audience. Exotic scenes of Middle Eastern society continued to be popular in Victorian Britain. Their most famous exponent, John Frederick Lewis, had died in 1876, and Waterhouse's setting is reminiscent of those found in pictures by him. Frederic Leighton, President of the Royal Academy, also made occasional essays in the Middle Eastern genre such as *The Music Lesson* (1877), and famously decorated his Kensington house in Islamic style. However, Waterhouse had initially planned his picture to be an ancient Greek scene depicting the Pythian Sibyl at Delphi. This suggests it was the mystical dimension to the subject that primarily interested him rather than its precise historical or cultural origins.

Before *Consulting the Oracle* was exhibited, Waterhouse had already found a buyer. The sugar magnate and philanthropist Henry Tate paid the very considerable sum of £900 for this picture, the first of three major works he was to acquire. When it was shown at the Royal Academy in 1884, the *Illustrated London News* reproduced it across a double spread and commented favourably on it as 'a careful study of archaeology and history ... combined with bold drawing and rich colouring'. The critical reception elsewhere was generally good, although *The Art Journal* disliked what it termed the women's 'swollen features, glazed eyes and a certain ecstatic insincerity', and considered their open mouths unladylike.

A study for one of the heads in *Consulting the Oracle* survives (see cat. 69). Carefully drawn and shaded, it is closest to the impassive figure on the extreme right, although Waterhouse appears to have modified her features for the painting.
But there is also a resemblance to other figures among the priestess's spectators, and it appears that Waterhouse utilised and adapted the study again elsewhere in his composition.

Waterhouse's approach to his paintings was essentially an Academic one: he would make a number of preliminary figure drawings in black and white, and then make studies of drapery and other aspects of the composition. But on occasion he would also paint on his canvas directly from the model. For *Consulting the Oracle*, Waterhouse also made a watercolour study in grey and wash of the picture's overall composition, which is now in the Tate collection. **RU**

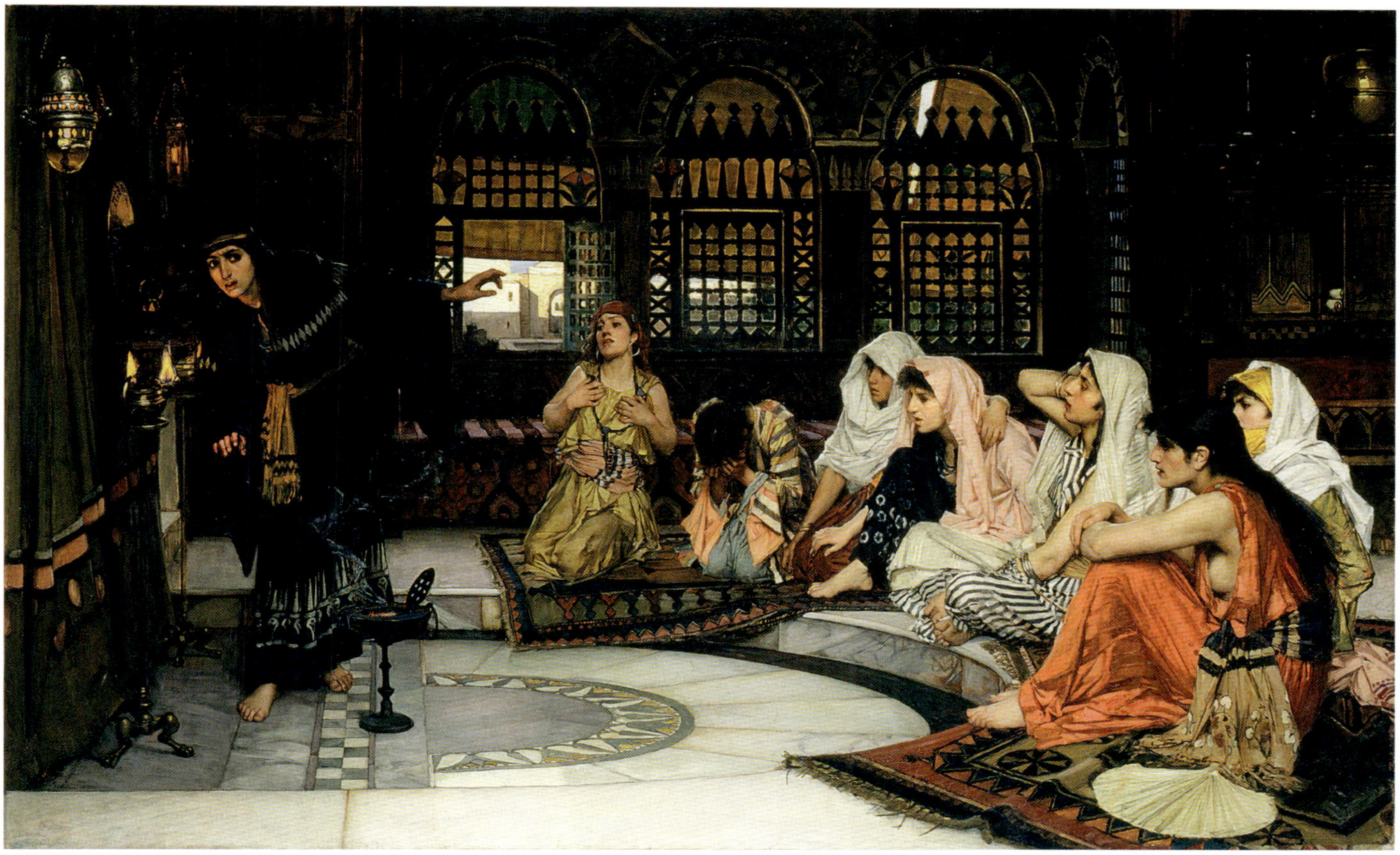

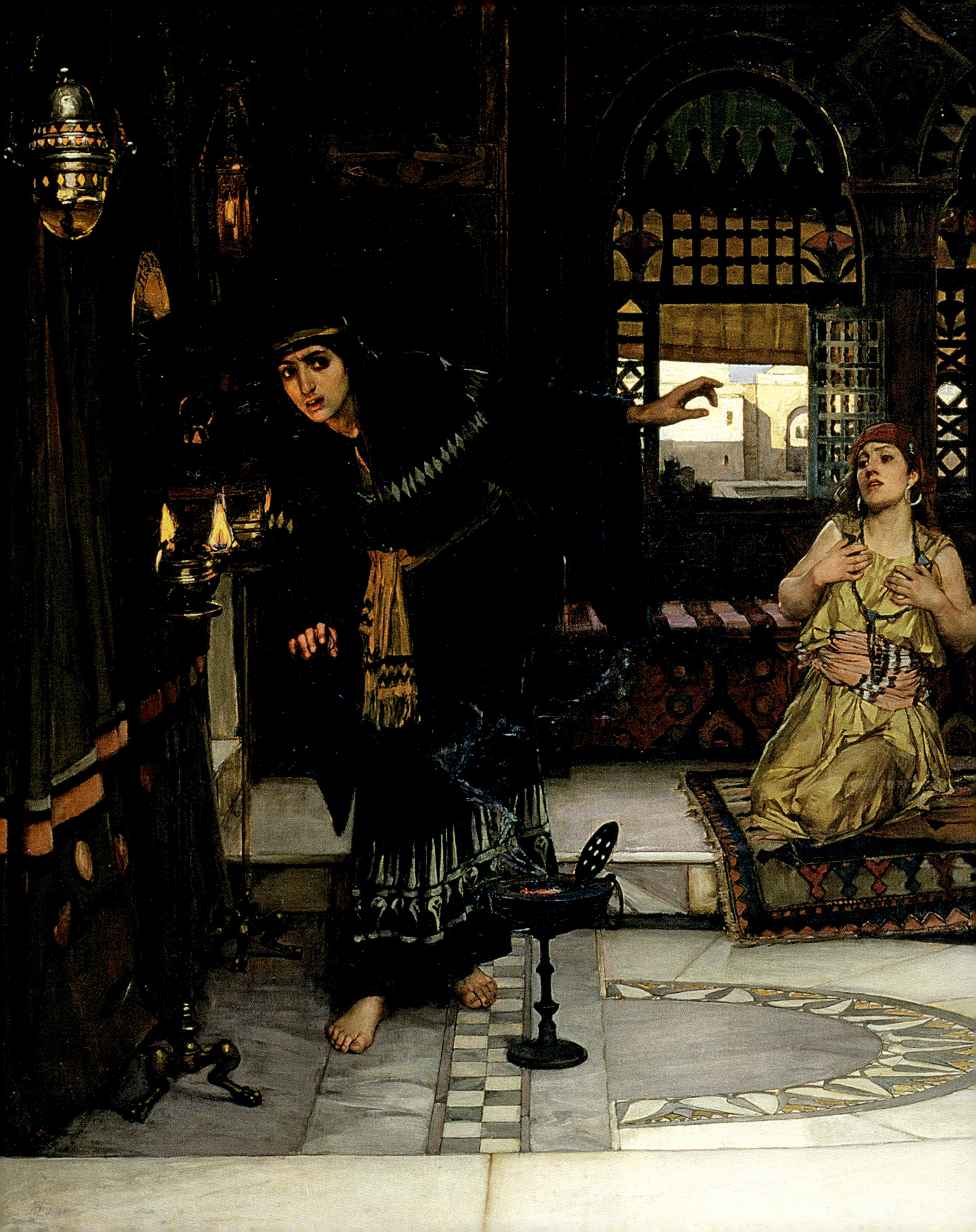

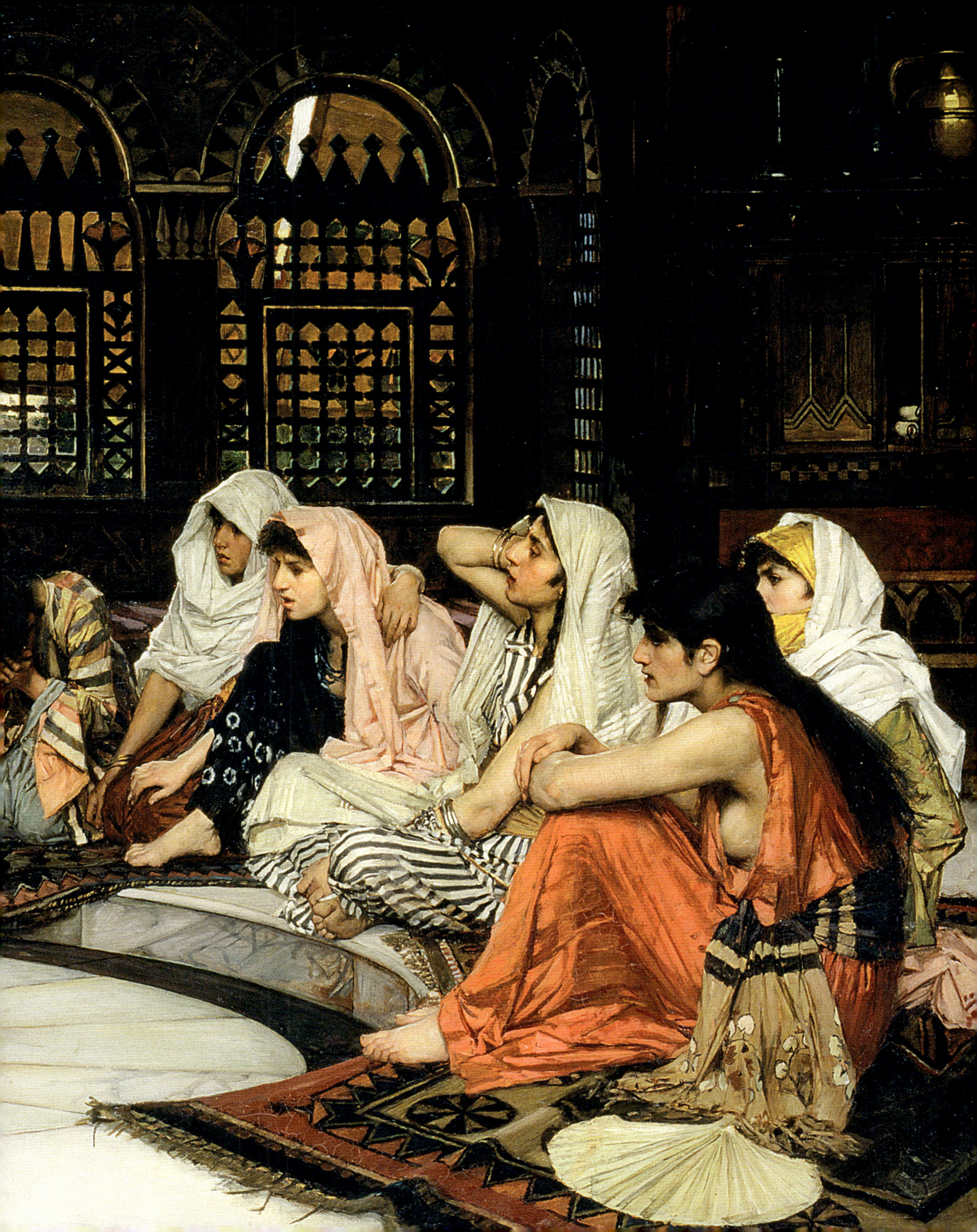

16. St Eulalia 1885

OIL ON CANVAS, 188.6 X 117.5 CM - TATE, GIFT OF SIR HENRY TATE, 1894 - EXHIBITED ROYAL ACADEMY, 1885

St Eulalia was martyred in 304 A.D., aged just twelve, for defying the orders of a magistrate to make sacrifices to the Roman gods. In a particularly gruesome punishment, two executioners tore her body with iron hooks, and held torches to her breasts and sides until finally she was suffocated by the smoke of her burning hair. In the Royal Academy exhibition catalogue, Waterhouse quoted the account given by Prudentius (348-after 405), the Christian Latin poet active in Spain: at the moment of Eulalia's death a white dove emerged from her mouth and a miraculous fall of snow extinguished the flames burning her body. In other accounts the snow fell over the field in which Eulalia's ashes were scattered.

It was a gory and disturbing subject for Waterhouse to choose, and not one that would be familiar to his public. Eulalia was not a particularly familiar martyr and perhaps Waterhouse was displaying his scholarship by selecting an incident taken from Prudentius. But Eulalia was the first of what became a series of paintings in which Waterhouse took as his subject a woman doomed to an unpleasant and unjust fate: *Mariamne* (cat. 18), *The Lady of Shalott* (cat. 20) and *Ophelia* (fig. 30) all followed *St Eulalia* in close succession. Evidently Waterhouse was attracted to Eulalia's story; in 1881 he exhibited a watercolour of the subject at the Dudley Gallery which *The Art Journal* described as 'a ghastly and unpleasant attempt at the foreshortening of a dead body' (1881, p.125).

This picture's composition is highly original and daring. Eulalia's figure is foreshortened dramatically and leads the eye only to a void of snow, emphasising her isolation. Her body lies still in the shape of the cross from which she has been taken down, transforming her into a Christ-like figure of suffering and veneration. The white doves hovering in mid air are those claimed to have issued from Eulalia's mouth, but they also become symbols of the Holy Spirit and the word of God. In the background a woman sits hunched in mourning, an equivalent to the Madonna, but hope is spelt by the excitement of the boy pointing to one of the doves and two women who hold palm fronds, symbols of peace and Christian victory.

There is a deliberate undercurrent of sensuality about Waterhouse's picture. The pure white snow contrasts sensuously with Eulalia's dead flesh and her hair spreads out around her like a nimbus. Like Dante Gabriel Rossetti and certain European Symbolist painters, Waterhouse was fascinated by women's hair as an object of – and metaphor for – male attraction, most famously represented in his art in *La Belle Dame Sans Merci* (cat. 28).

The picture was generally well received by the critics and it secured Waterhouse's election as an Associate of the Royal Academy in June 1885. Several reviewers noted Waterhouse's French style of painting in *St Eulalia*, and there were clear debts to a number of pictures of foreshortened figures by Jean-Léon Gérôme such as *The Death of Marshal Ney* (1868) that Waterhouse would have been able to see at the Royal Academy in 1870. But while connections to recent French art were clear, the critics, and no doubt the Academy, admired Waterhouse's English restraint in the way he treated Eulalia, leaving out the most unpleasant details of her fate and preserving the purity of her body. **RU**

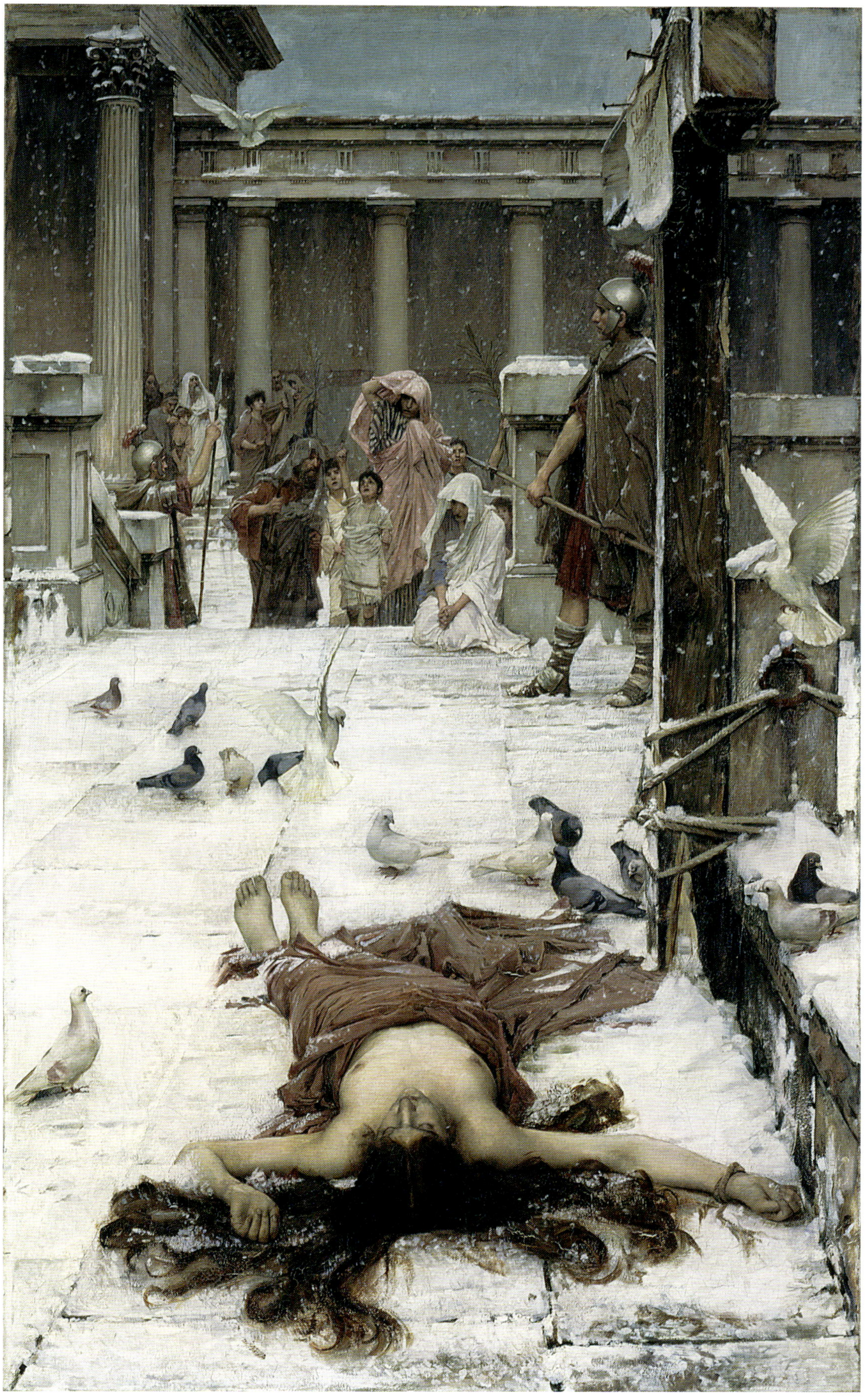

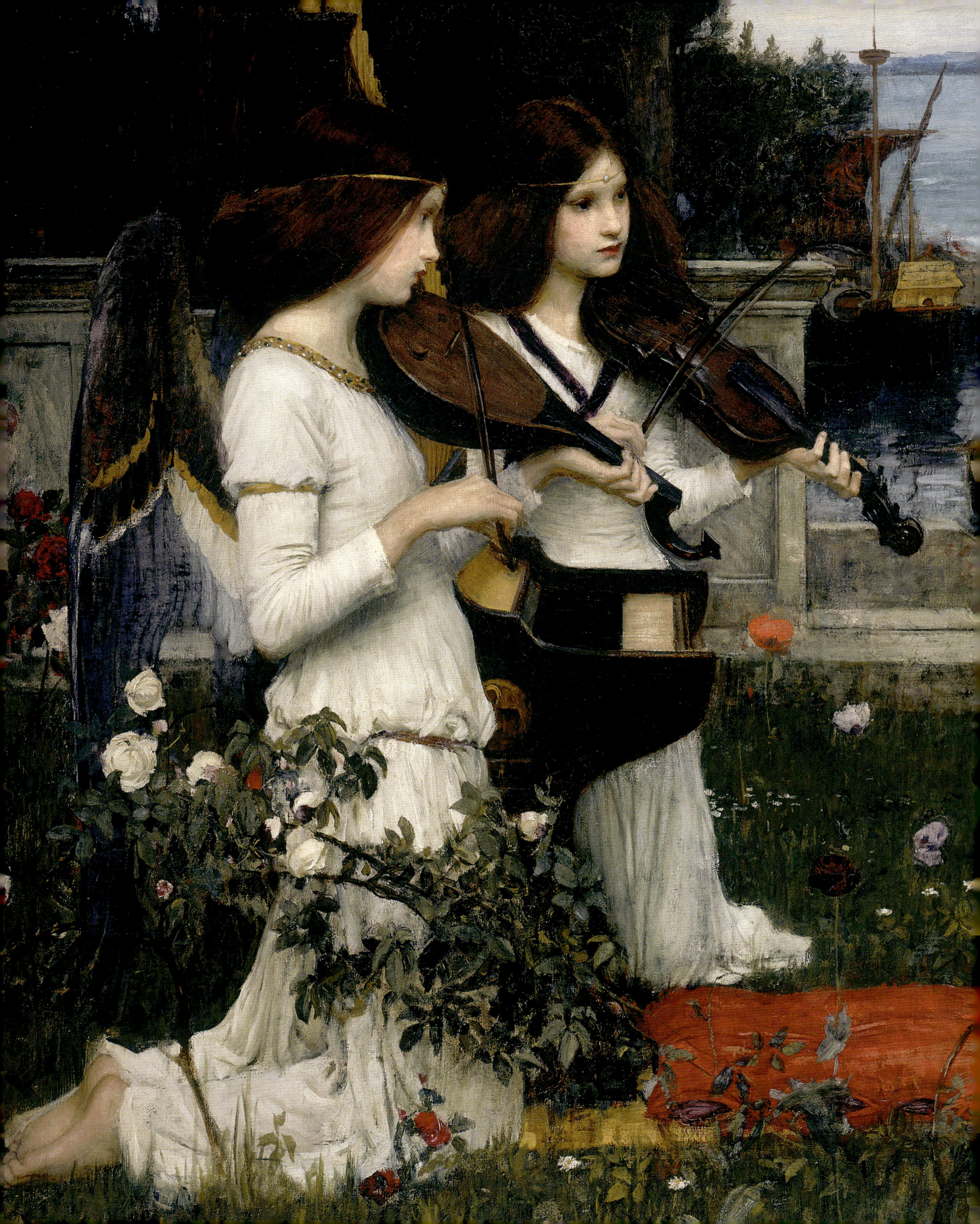

Associate of the Royal Academy

17. The Magic Circle 1886

OIL ON CANVAS, 182.9 X 127 CM - TATE, PURCHASED BY THE TRUSTEES OF THE CHANTREY BEQUEST, 1886 - EXHIBITED ROYAL ACADEMY, 1886

For *The Magic Circle,* his first picture submitted as an Associate of the Royal Academy, Waterhouse continued the theme of magic and occultism that he had started with *Consulting the Oracle* (cat. 15) in 1884. Indeed, the continuity of his interest in such material is confirmed by his contribution in 1881 to the Dudley Gallery of a sepia drawing of *The Magic Circle* (cat. 79). Waterhouse's large painted version is a dramatic tour de force: a dark haired sorceress chants incantations over a bubbling cauldron as she marks out in the ground the magic circle of the title. As her rod bites into the earth it brings forth smoke and the circle glows white. In her other hand the sorceress holds a druidical boline which was used to harvest magical herbs which can be seen tucked into her sash. She is surrounded by a sinister group of ravens which in pagan belief are omens and messengers of ill luck, infection, and most commonly, death. Waterhouse makes this connection explicit with the bird on the left, which perches on a human skull and caws at the sorceress. The precise interpretation of the witch's rite is ambiguous. In pagan ritual the drawing of a magic circle can be intended to protect the person contained within it. But conversely it can also be the area in which evil spirits summoned forth will gather. In Waterhouse's painting the ravens could symbolise evil which the sorceress is trying to banish, but the atmosphere suggests they are waiting for the malevolent spirits she is conjuring up. This reading seems more likely, as the birds on the right hold an attitude of anticipation and the rising fumes of the sorceress's bubbling pot seem poised to gather themselves into some tangible form. Indeed, there is a very strong resemblance to sensational contemporary photographs of ectoplasmic manifestation during séances, with which Waterhouse was evidently familiar.

Waterhouse was not alone in his fascination with such subjects. Interest in Celtic mythology, ceremony, and ritual enjoyed considerable revival in the 1880s in Britain. But although Waterhouse has given his sorceress a druid's boline, her dress is decorated with Greek warriors, and the architecture in the background appears to be Egyptian. This eclecticism appears deliberate, and Waterhouse may therefore be suggesting the continuity of hermetic knowledge through different cultures. This reading is strengthened by the Ouroboros that hangs around the sorceress's neck – a snake devouring its own tail. This is one of the oldest mystical symbols in the world, and appears in many cultures. But its earliest manifestation is in Egypt around 1600 BC. It represented the circle of life, creation out of destruction, and life out of death in an eternal cycle of renewal. In this respect it was closely related to the Egyptian legend of Isis and Osiris, whose conjunction and destruction make and remake the universe. Egyptian legend was a central topic in the revival of hermetic study and worship in Britain in the 1880s, and underpinned groups such as the Order of the Golden Dawn founded in 1887.

In the picture's formal qualities, Waterhouse is likely to have been partly inspired by two examples of later Pre-Raphaelite art of related occult subjects. Frederick Sandys's famous *Medea* (1866-1868) depicted the dark-haired sorceress chanting over a smouldering pot, her magic ingredients set out before her, and had caused a furore at the Academy in 1868 when it was rejected. The full-length format of Dante Gabriel Rossetti's *Astarte Syriaca* (1877) may have provided additional inspiration for Waterhouse.

The picture was a critical success when Waterhouse showed it at the Royal Academy and it was purchased by the Trustees of the Chantrey Bequest, an honour that went only to what was considered the best of that year's art and suitable for the national collection. But Waterhouse had painted *The Magic Circle* in an assimilated version of a French naturalist technique: the landscape elements show evidence of 'square brushing', a practice associated with painters such as Jules Bastien-Lepage that, using thin, liquid paint, covered the canvas quickly and gave it a sense of immediacy and vitality. The dull tones and almost misty quality of the landscape allowed full attention to fall on the figure. It was a technique much reviled by British art schools who prized precision of draughtsmanship over all else and were in any case xenophobically opposed to any foreign influence on the national style of painting. Waterhouse risked a negative response in adopting such techniques, but for *The Magic Circle* the critics chose not to emphasise this aspect of the painting, already too taken with the drama of its central incident. But the Chantrey Trustees voted only seven to three in favour of buying Waterhouse's canvas. Such formal dissent was unusual and gives some indication of the unease that French practices could provoke. However polarised the discussion, usually the votes recorded were unanimous, presenting a diplomatically united face. Voting for Waterhouse were Leighton, James Clark Hook, Philip Calderon, W.C. Marshall, William Pickersgill, James Sant and H.T. Wells; voting against were the arch Academic Poynter, George Dunlop Leslie, and the architect Alfred Waterhouse. **RU**

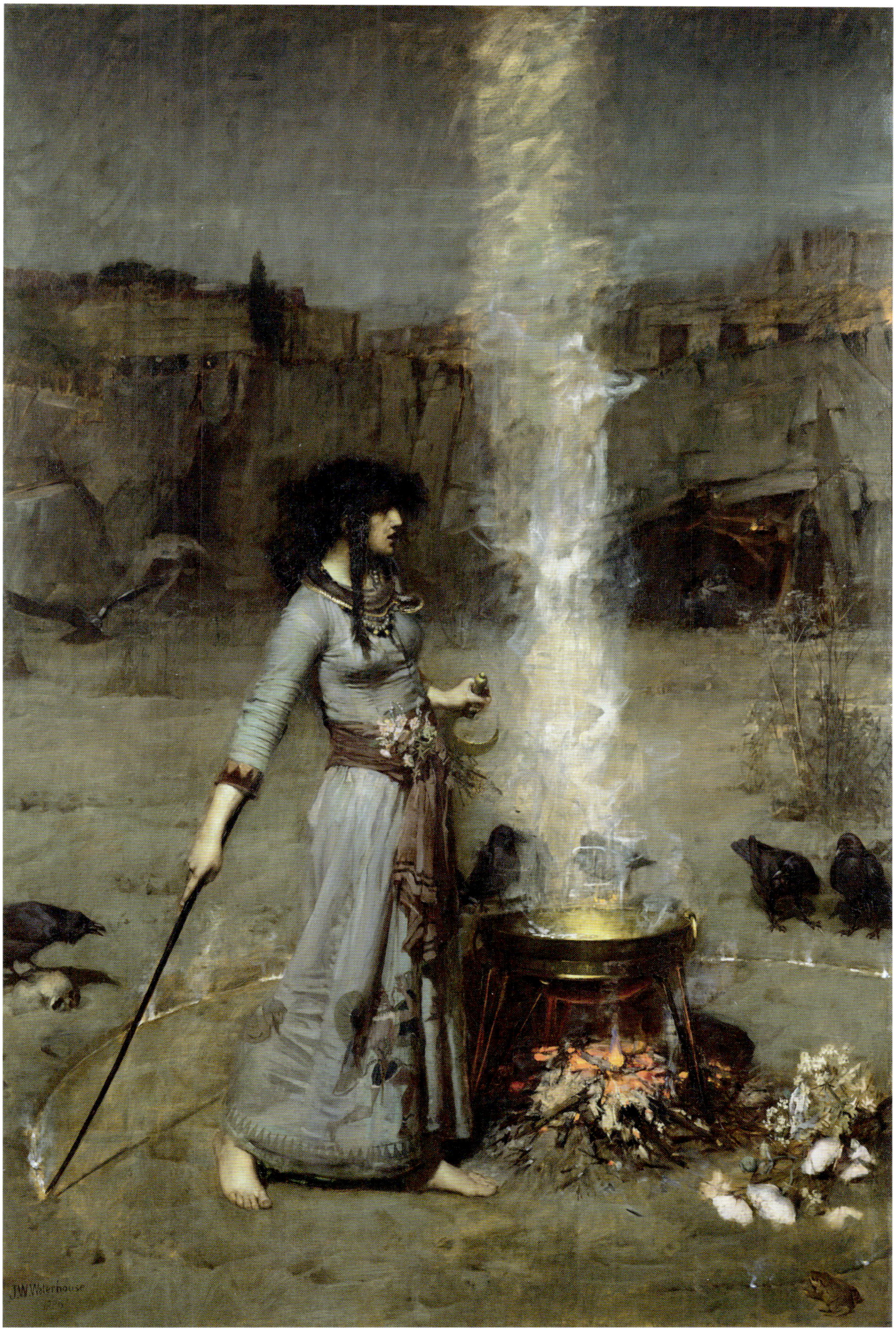
J.W. Waterhouse

18. Mariamne 1887

OIL ON CANVAS, 259 X 180 CM - PRIVATE COLLECTION COURTESY OF NEVILL KEATING PICTURES - EXHIBITED ROYAL ACADEMY, 1887

Mariamne is the largest painting Waterhouse ever made, and the culmination of the series of history paintings that had begun in 1878 with *The Remorse of Nero* (fig. 10). It is also a superb example of his skill in creating a pictorial narrative that is both intelligible at first glance and endlessly fascinating as its complexities unravel on further investigation. Its drama is apparent even to a viewer who knows nothing of Mariamne's story: we guess that the white-robed figure, descending a flight of steps in chains, has been condemned by the circle of old men lurking in the shadows behind her, while the male figure, cringing in his chair to the right, listens in evident horror to what must be the hostile whispering of the woman beside him. Little wonder that contemporary critics compared it to theatrical performance. Yet the details of Mariamne's intricate story add to the picture's impact, and show how Waterhouse could develop narrative complexity to a degree traditionally considered to be the province of literary, rather than pictorial, expression. Indeed, two very different versions of the story are found in the writings of the first-century Jewish historian Josephus, and perhaps the discrepancies are inevitable in a tale of multiplied double-dealing and deceit; in such a case, plain truth seems out of the question. Waterhouse's scene is loosely based on an episode that comes late in the longer of Josephus's two accounts (in his *Jewish Antiquities*, Book XV), where Herod the Great of Judaea convenes a trial to condemn his wife, Mariamne, to death for infidelity. Herod nonetheless remains in an agony of indecision, while his sister Salome urges him – successfully, in the event – to carry out the sentence. Mariamne is not guilty of the charge, but this is no simple story of a wronged heroine. Indeed the scene hinges on a basic paradox of the story: the one betrayal that does not, in fact, occur is the adultery for which Mariamne is put to death. Waterhouse hints at the duplicity of the judges, who in Josephus are swayed more by the vehement emotion of their powerful king than by the evidence, by relegating them to the shadowy background and showing them as decrepit grey-beards; the conflicting motives of Herod, and the ill-will of Salome, are evident. But the painting also captures the complexity of Mariamne's character. Josephus describes her as magnificently beautiful and dignified, yet also supremely arrogant and outspoken, and all of these aspects are expressed in her proud bearing, haughty backward glance, clenched fists, and above all in her way of holding centre stage.

The setting is intriguingly reminiscent of the interior of Alma-Tadema's studio at 17 Grove End Road, St John's Wood: the configuration of the apse, with its semicircular bench, and the decorated window to the right closely resemble photographs of the studio.[1] If Waterhouse modelled his interior on Alma-Tadema's studio, this would be fascinating evidence that the two artists were personally acquainted; Alma-Tadema moved to this studio-house in 1886, just the year before *Mariamne* was exhibited. The studio did not, however, have a flight of steps, so this must have been Waterhouse's invention, expertly calculated to enhance the drama of the scene. The marble lion, whose bared teeth contribute to the sense of menace, appears to be based on an Assyrian sculpture in the British Museum, discovered by the archaeologist Austen Henry Layard in 1849 and also used in Edward John Poynter's painting, *The Queen of Sheba's Visit to King Solomon* (1883-1890, Art Gallery of New South Wales).[2]

Mariamne was purchased by the prominent collector Cuthbert Quilter, who lent it to many of the major international exhibitions of the period; the painting won medals at the Exposition Universelle in Paris (1889), the World's Columbian Exhibition in Chicago (1893), and the Exposition Internationale in Brussels (1897). Thus the painting had made Waterhouse world-famous by the turn of the twentieth century. **EP**

1 For reproductions of contemporary photographs of Alma-Tadema's studio see Edwin Becker and others, eds, *Sir Lawrence Alma-Tadema*, exhibition catalogue, Amsterdam: Van Gogh Museum and Liverpool: Walker Art Gallery, 1996, pp. 126-127.

2 See Alison Inglis's catalogue entries on Poynter's painting and a related drawing, in St John Simpson, ed., *Queen of Sheba: Treasures from Ancient Yemen*, exhibition catalogue, London: British Museum Press, 2002, pp. 23-24.

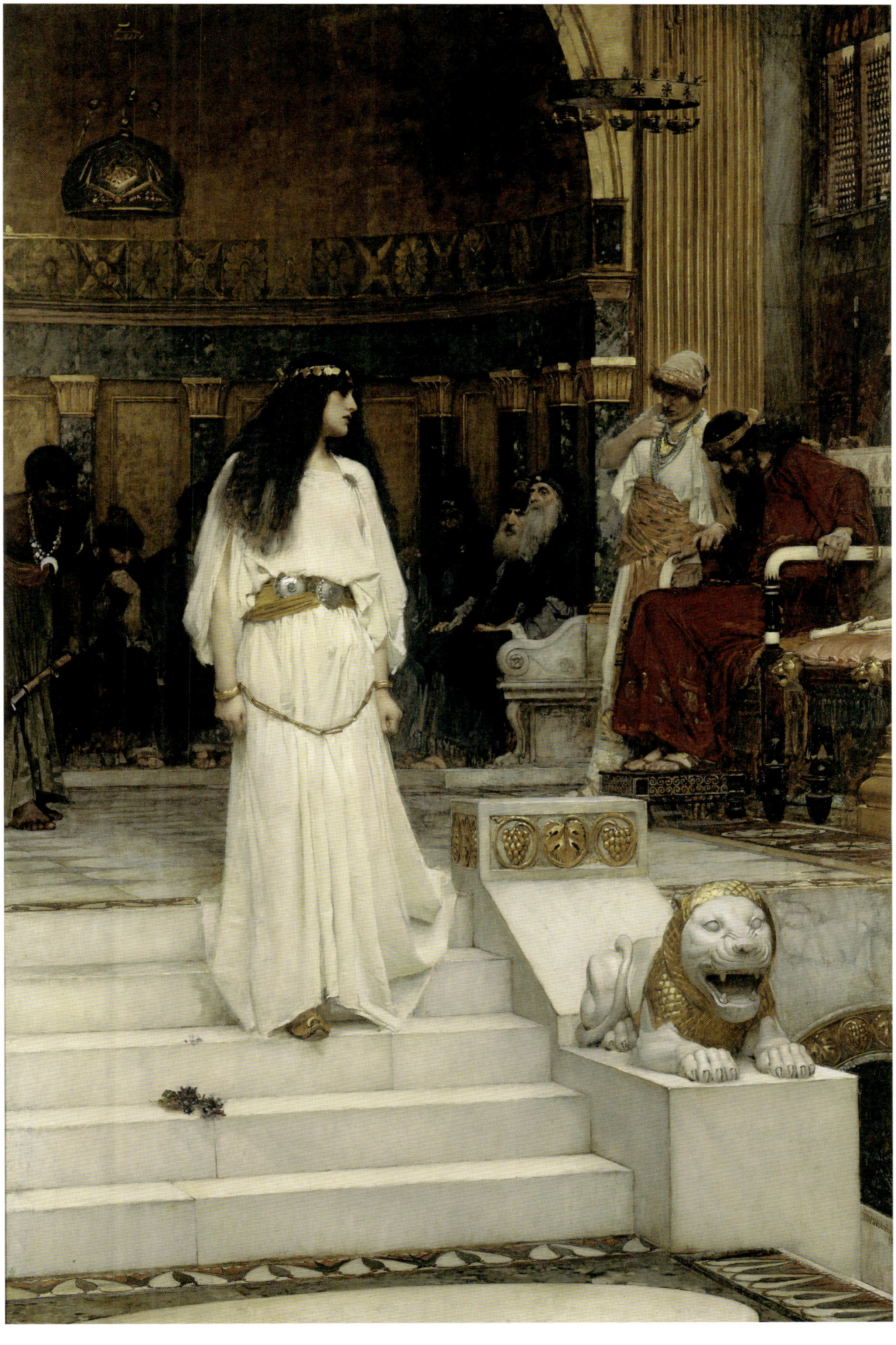

19. Cleopatra 1888

OIL ON CANVAS, 65.4 X 56.8 CM - PRIVATE COLLECTION COURTESY OF CHRISTIE'S - PUBLISHED IN *THE GRAPHIC* 1888, AND THEN EXHIBITED GRAPHIC GALLERY 1889

A sign of Waterhouse's growing prominence in the London art world was the invitation in 1887, alongside such artists as Alma-Tadema and Leighton, to contribute to the 'Gallery of Shakespearean Heroines', one of several series published by the *Graphic* magazine since its founding in 1869. The half-length representation of a single female figure of smouldering beauty was adapted to the format of the series, designed for reproduction in the magazine and in portfolio editions (the painting itself was also exhibited and subsequently auctioned at Christie's). The choice of Cleopatra, among the heroines of Shakespeare's plays, played to Waterhouse's reputation as a painter of classical antiquity, and the print was accompanied by a line from *Antony and Cleopatra*: 'Where's my serpent of old Nile? For so he calls me' (Act I, scene v, lines 25-26; Cleopatra refers here to her lover, the Roman general Antony). The painting, however, is a character study rather than a dramatic scene (and indeed Waterhouse's beauty appears younger than the aging queen of Shakespeare's play); perhaps the sinuous, foreshortened pose suggests something of the serpentine, in response to the quotation. The expertly painted white draperies link the figure to other heroines in contemporary works by Waterhouse, *The Lady of Shalott* (cat. 20) and *Mariamne* (cat. 18); the lion's head on the bench end also recalls the lion sculpture in the latter picture. Waterhouse had not chosen a Shakespearean subject since his early *Miranda* (cat. 3), but this commissioned picture points the way to later works such as the three versions of *Ophelia* (figs 18, 30, 39) and the late version of *Miranda* (cat. 62). **EP**

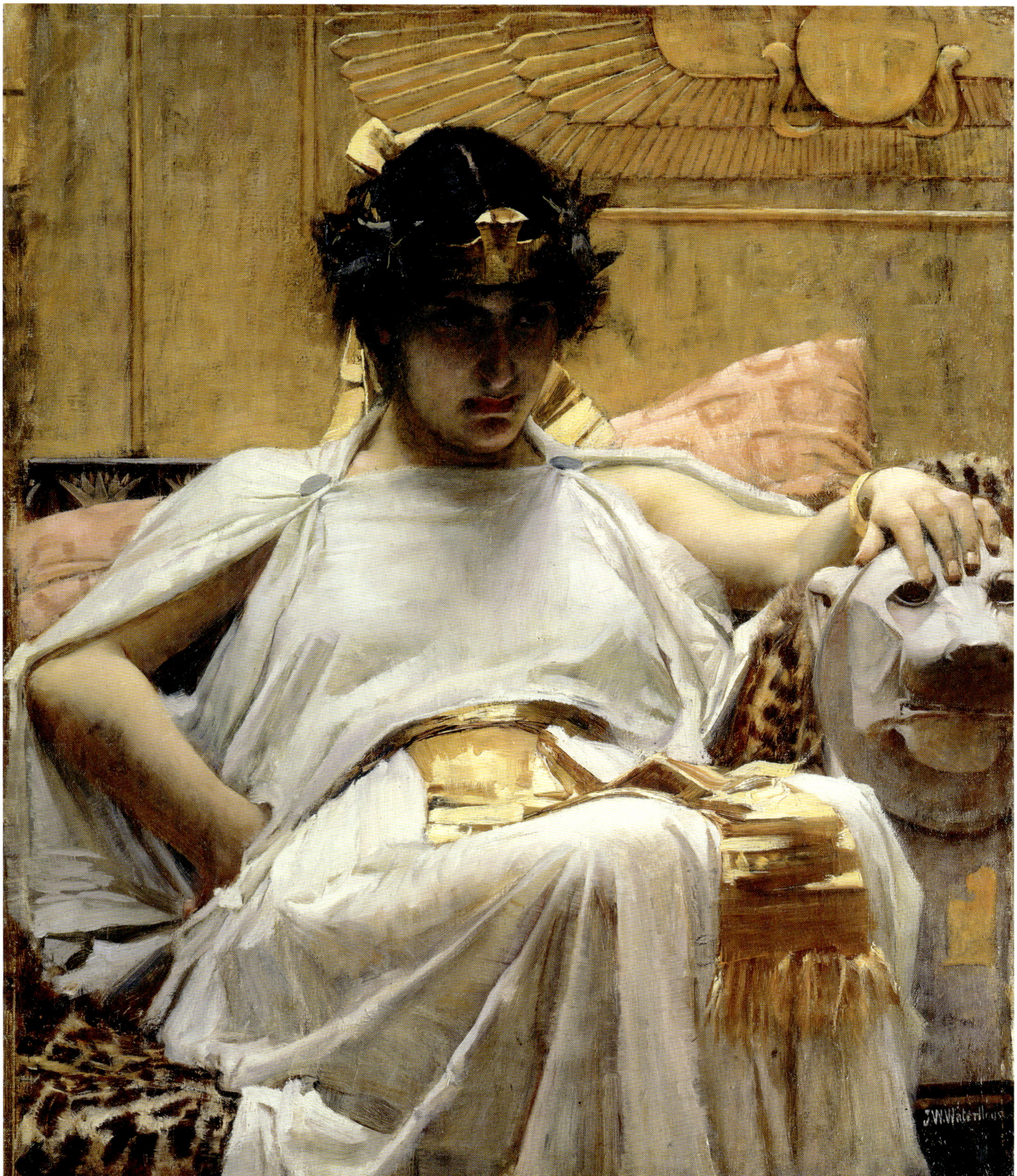

III

20. The Lady of Shalott 1888

OIL ON CANVAS, 153 X 200 CM - TATE, GIFT OF SIR HENRY TATE, 1894 - EXHIBITED ROYAL ACADEMY, 1888

Based on Tennyson's famous poem, *The Lady of Shalott* is the best known of all Waterhouse's works, a highly sophisticated piece of painting that evokes a magical world of dream-like romance. But the picture and its subject touch on a range of serious and troubling issues, ranging through female sexuality, gender politics, the relationship of the artist to society, and a ferocious contemporary aesthetic debate around naturalism and narrative.

Waterhouse followed closely Tennyson's poem, which enjoyed enormous popularity through the nineteenth century and into the twentieth. Tennyson himself enjoyed a sage-like status in Victorian Britain, a Poet Laureate able to combine the highest creative ideals with genuine mass-appeal, who seemed able to express all the certainties and doubts of the age in which he lived. His verse treatments of the legends of Arthur and the Knights of the Round Table were probably admired the most of all, and came to be seen as an allegory of all the seriousness of purpose, and frailties and failures, of the Victorian project. First published in 1832 and revised in 1842, Tennyson's 'Lady of Shalott' was one of his earliest excursions into Arthurian myth. It was inspired not by Thomas Malory's fifteenth-century *Morte d'Arthur*, but by *Donna di Scallotta*, an Italian fourteenth-century story. In 'The Lady of Shalott' a fairy woman is confined to a tower on an island up-river from Camelot. How she got there, or the nature of the curse which holds her prisoner, is never revealed:

> There she weaves by night and day
> A magic web with colours gay.
> She has heard a whisper say,
> A curse is on her if she stay
>   To look down to Camelot.
> She knows not what the curse may be

The curse forbids her to see the world other than reflected in a mirror, and she weaves 'the mirror's magic sights', and in the tapestry draped over the boat in Waterhouse's picture he depicts sights mentioned by Tennyson: 'An abbot on an ambling pad', 'knights ... riding two and two', and 'a funeral, with plumes and lights and music'. It is not until Lancelot rides by that passion is unleashed:

> His broad clear brow in sunlight glow'd;
> On burnish'd hooves his war-horse trode;
> From underneath his helmet flow'd
> His coal-black curls as on he rode,
> ...
> From the bank and from the river
> He flash'd into the crystal mirror,

Stricken with love and lust, the Lady turns and the curse is unleashed. She embarks on a voyage down the river, and dies, the curse fulfilled. In the Royal Academy catalogue Waterhouse quoted the passage which inspired his painting:

> And down the river's dim expanse,
> Like some bold seër in a trance,
> ...
> The broad stream bore her far away.

The story of the Lady of Shalott evidently held a deep fascination for Waterhouse and it formed the inspiration for a trilogy of paintings (see cats 30, 60). The taste for Arthurian subject-matter in the 1880s and 1890s can be related to social and political shifts in Victorian society, and Waterhouse was not alone in finding the Lady of Shalott's story attractive. It became a regular subject for British artists, particularly in the 1890s. This is now seen as connected with the shifting position of women in British society, and in particular, male concern about the growing economic and social independence of the 'New Woman'. The sexual and social dynamics of 'The Lady of Shalott' should not be underestimated. The story is an allegory of sexual longing, repression, fear, and punishment, and Tennyson's lyrical text adopts an overtly erotic rhythm. The poem's image of the Lady in a tower – its window glimpsed at the top left of Waterhouse's composition, and also portrayed in the tapestry – was a traditional symbol of chastity and containment. Its appearance in Tennyson's poem can be seen as a metaphor for the constraints of nineteenth-century home life. The Lady's story also parallels the decline and fall of Arthur's court, its sanctity broken by lust and inevitably leading to death and destruction. Indeed, the poem – and the painting – seem to fall on the side of warning of the consequences that acting on physical compulsion can bring, while also recognising the inevitability of giving in to such temptation.

Waterhouse's picture creates enormous tension by freezing the narrative, showing a moment where the Lady is poised between her previous life and the fulfilment of the curse. She holds the boat's chain, ready to let it slip. Her lips are parted, singing her fairy song, as the candles blow out one by one. This is not just the beginning of a journey towards death, but almost the last moment before expiring. The narrative chronology of Tennyson's poem is conflated, and Waterhouse took the image of expiration from Dante Gabriel Rossetti's picture *Beata Beatrix* (fig. 26). Here Rossetti had depicted the moment of revelation as, eyes shut, Elizabeth Siddall in the character of Dante's Beatrice passes from one world to the next. She is shown seemingly ecstatic, and Rossetti evidently suggests connections between orgasm, revelation, and extinction. **RU**

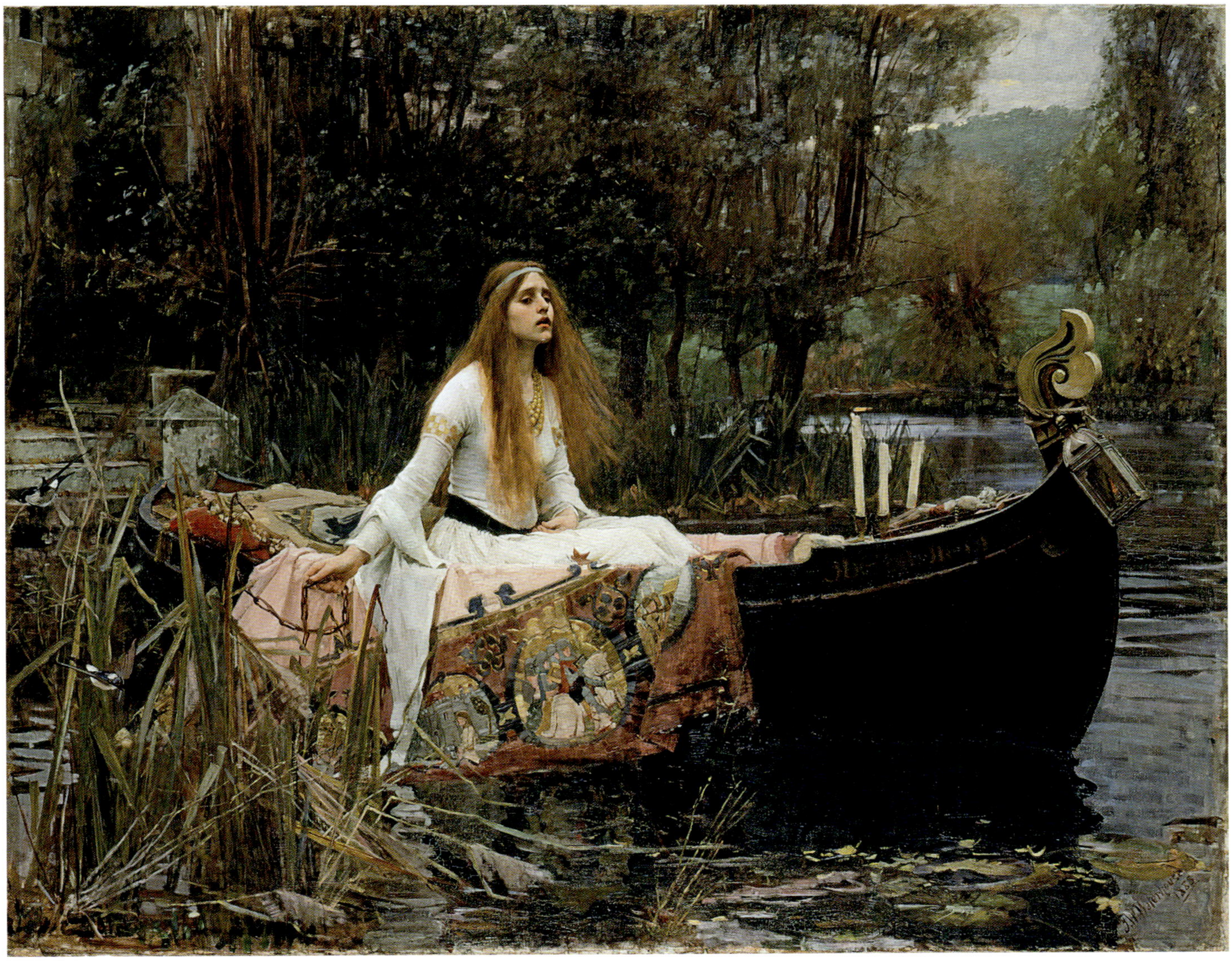

21. Circe Offering the Cup to Ulysses 1891

OIL ON CANVAS, 149 X 92 CM - GALLERY OLDHAM, GIFT OF MARJORY LEES, 1952 - EXHIBITED NEW GALLERY, 1891

In 1890, for the first time since his debut in 1874, Waterhouse did not exhibit at the annual Royal Academy exhibition. When he reappeared the next year, it was to make a dramatic new departure. Decisively, he abandoned the series of subjects from ancient history with which he had made his reputation, and secured his election as Associate of the Royal Academy; now he embarked on a new project, centred on the myths and legends of pagan antiquity, which would dominate the rest of his career. Like so much in Waterhouse's biography, the reasons for this sudden shift remain mysterious (see p. 28), but perhaps it is telling that his two major paintings of 1891 were both drawn from the story of the wanderings of Ulysses: while *Ulysses and the Sirens* was on view at the Royal Academy (cat. 22), *Circe Offering the Cup to Ulysses* appeared at the more progressive New Gallery. Like Ulysses himself, Waterhouse had embarked on a quest, and the two paintings represent episodes that frame Ulysses' journey to the mouth of the underworld in Book XI of Homer's *Odyssey*.

But it is the sorceress, Circe, who governs this sequence of events, something that is emphasised in this painting of Ulysses' first encounter with her. Both in *Odyssey* Book X and in Ovid's retelling of the same story (*Metamorphoses*, Book XIV), Ulysses immediately takes control of the situation, drawing his sword to overpower the sorceress; the phallic associations of the sword are obvious. But Waterhouse's painting instead dwells on the moment, fleeting in both ancient texts, when Circe raises her magic wand to threaten Ulysses; sketchbook drawings for the composition show that Waterhouse adjusted it repeatedly, each time making Circe more commanding (see cat. 95). While she dominates the picture space, towering above the viewer, Ulysses is glimpsed to the side, reflected in the mirror and in defensive posture; he reaches for his sword but does not yet brandish it. Thus Waterhouse offers a distinctive interpretation of the scene, one which centres on the magic powers of Circe rather than her eventual capitulation to Ulysses' masculine authority. The bright circular mirror behind her perhaps recalls a sun-disk, to allude to her descent from the sun-god Helios, which may also be a magic circle (see cat. 17 and p. 54). She sits regally enthroned, between two bronze lions baring their teeth (these lions resemble the one in *Mariamne*, cat. 18). Her enchantments have changed Ulysses' men into swine, two of which now loll soporifically around the throne in subservience (more are reflected in the mirror). Yet Circe dominates by subtle wiles, not physical force; the transparent blue gauze of her drapery reveals delicate limbs and slips from one breast, while she looks down at Ulysses (and the viewer, who shares Ulysses' view of her) with a wistful hauteur, perhaps tinged with pity or regret. She will seduce Ulysses, but she will also instruct him on how to proceed in his quest.

Some viewers have detected a resemblance between the bearded figure of Ulysses, in the two paintings of 1891, and contemporary photographs of Waterhouse himself. Certainly Waterhouse, like Ulysses, was fascinated by Circe, whom he represented again in 1892 (cat. 23) and to whom he returned toward the end of his life, in a series of drawings and oil sketches (cats 56, 57, 74), perhaps made in preparation for a painting never realised. **EP**

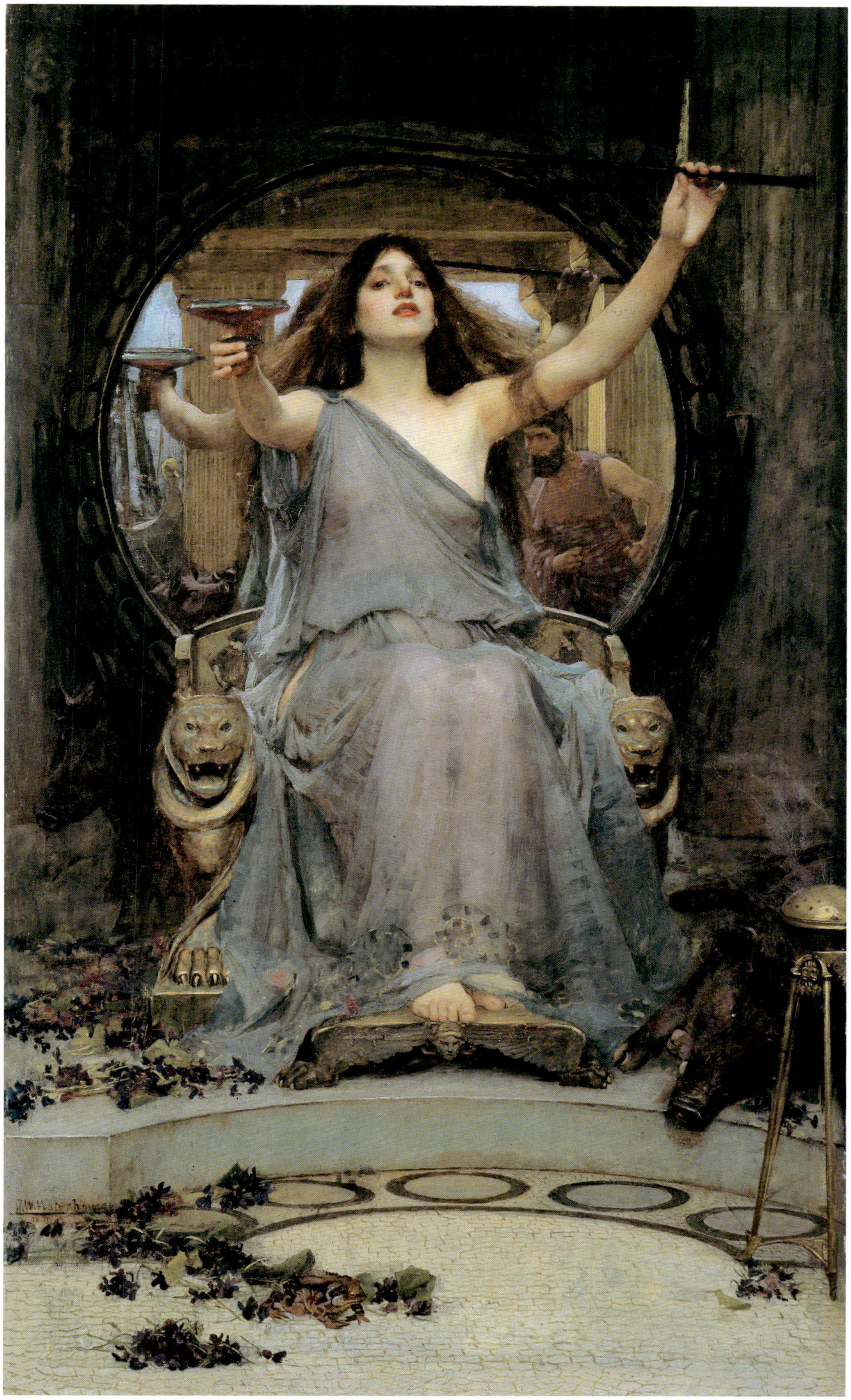

22. Ulysses and the Sirens 1891

OIL ON CANVAS, 100.6 X 201.7 CM - NATIONAL GALLERY OF VICTORIA, MELBOURNE, PURCHASED 1891 - EXHIBITED ROYAL ACADEMY, 1891

Exhibited at the Royal Academy while *Circe Offering the Cup to Ulysses* (cat. 21) was on view at the New Gallery, *Ulysses and the Sirens* represents a later event, from Book XII of Homer's *Odyssey*: after his journey to the underworld, Ulysses proceeds to encounter the Sirens, bird-women whose songs lure men to their deaths. Waterhouse took care to remind viewers of the link between this scene and the episode represented in the other painting: in the short text he appended to the picture's title in the Academy catalogue, scarcely necessary for so familiar a scene from ancient story, he notes that it was Circe who instructed Ulysses to resist the Sirens' baneful songs by stopping the ears of his men with wax, and having himself bound securely to the mast of his ship. Thus Waterhouse's first two mythological paintings are related not merely as successive episodes in the narrative of Ulysses' wanderings, but more rigorously as demonstrations of Circe's magic arts. This also introduces a subtle twist to the subject-matter: ostensibly the scene represents the male hero outwitting the bird-women, but ultimately it is Circe's wisdom that guides Ulysses and his ship to safety. Waterhouse also raises the stakes for his hero, by placing him in confrontation with seven Sirens, rather than the mere two mentioned in Homer; perhaps it is important that they make up the magic number seven.

At the time he designed this painting Waterhouse, like Ulysses, was travelling, perhaps seeking relief, or new inspiration, after the exertions of the 1880s and the death of his father in January 1890. One of his surviving sketchbooks (cat. 94) includes preliminary ideas for both *Ulysses and the Sirens* and *Circe Offering the Cup to Ulysses*, interspersed with scenes of landscape and architecture on the island of Capri, which he seems to have visited several times around 1888-1890. The forbidding rocks towards which Ulysses' ship is bound are reminiscent of the distinctive rock formations of the Marina Piccola (small harbour) below the town of Capri, one of which is traditionally known as the Rock of the Sirens. Waterhouse would often represent such rocks, including a rock arch similar to that of the Marina Piccola, in later pictures of mermaids and Sirens, including the one that became his Royal Academy diploma picture (cat. 35). The sketchbook also contains drawings of birds and bird-wings, some of which may also derive from Waterhouse's time on Capri, famous for its abundant bird-life; in a later letter, Waterhouse mentions drawing eagles in the London Zoological Gardens, as well as the inspiration of Capri.[1] Perhaps Waterhouse was searching for a visual form for the Sirens, who do not appear in the sketchbook drawings; in the final composition, he inserted figures of bird-women derived from a Greek vase in the British Museum (fig. 12). Nonetheless, the inspiration for Waterhouse's first mythological pictures seems to derive from his travels. If, on his visit of 1877, Waterhouse had imagined the streets of Pompeii repopulated with their ancient inhabitants, perhaps now, on his later journeys, he began to imagine the stories of ancient mythology coming to life in the dramatic and beautiful scenery of Capri and the Bay of Naples. **EP**

1 Letter from Waterhouse to his patron Julia Ellsworth Ford, dated 18 March (without a year, but probably 1903 or later), Beinecke Library, Yale University, Za//Ford (Julia Ellsworth)//Corresp/Mb-Z.

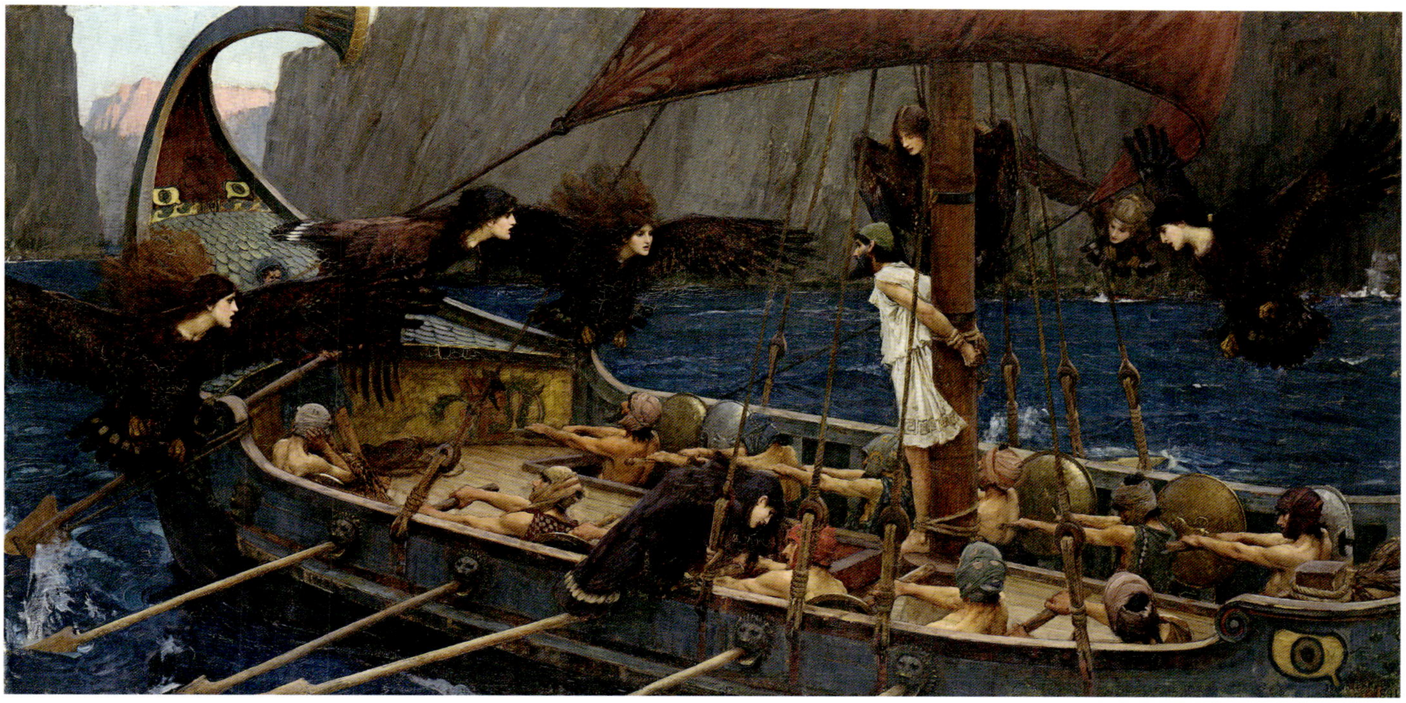

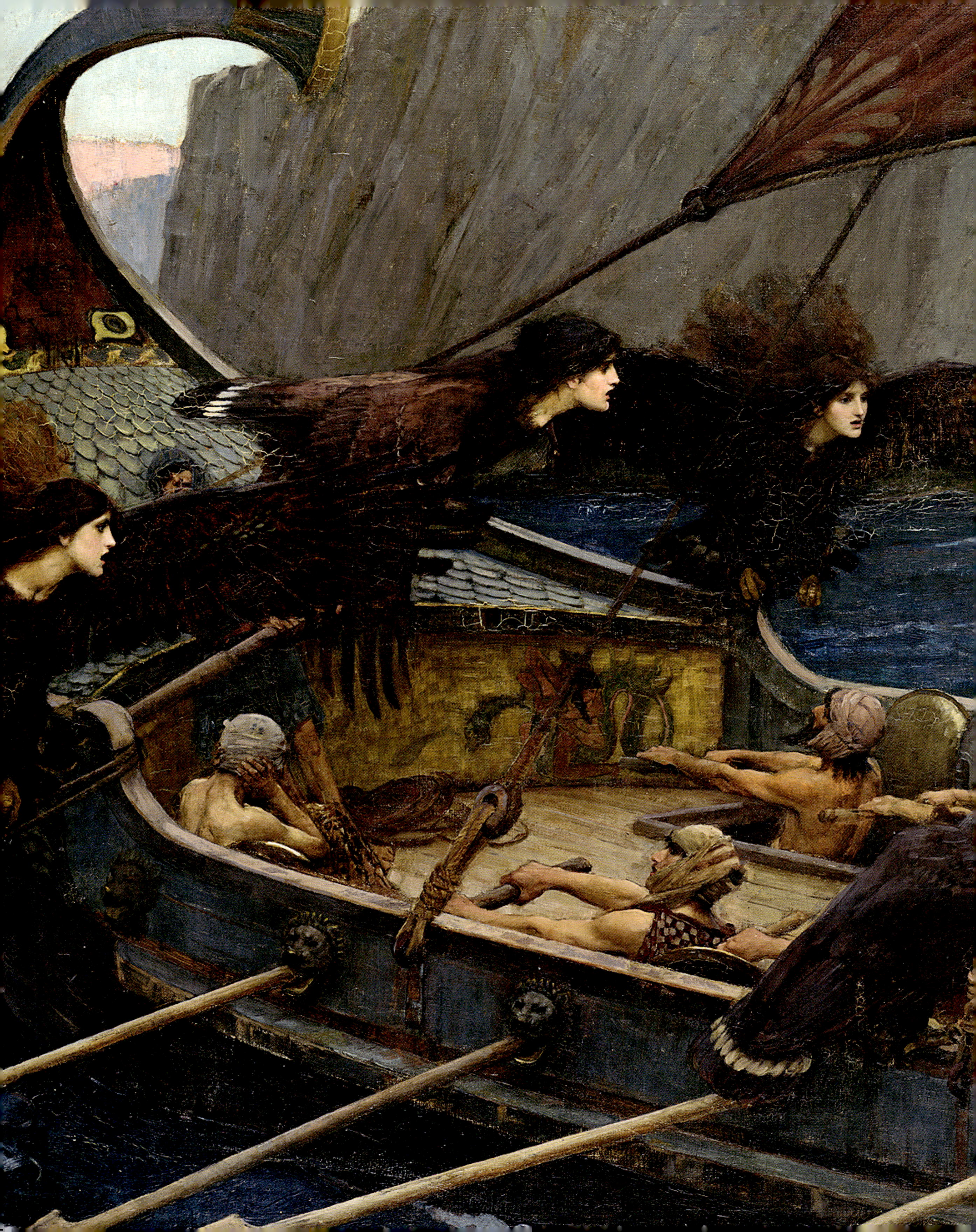

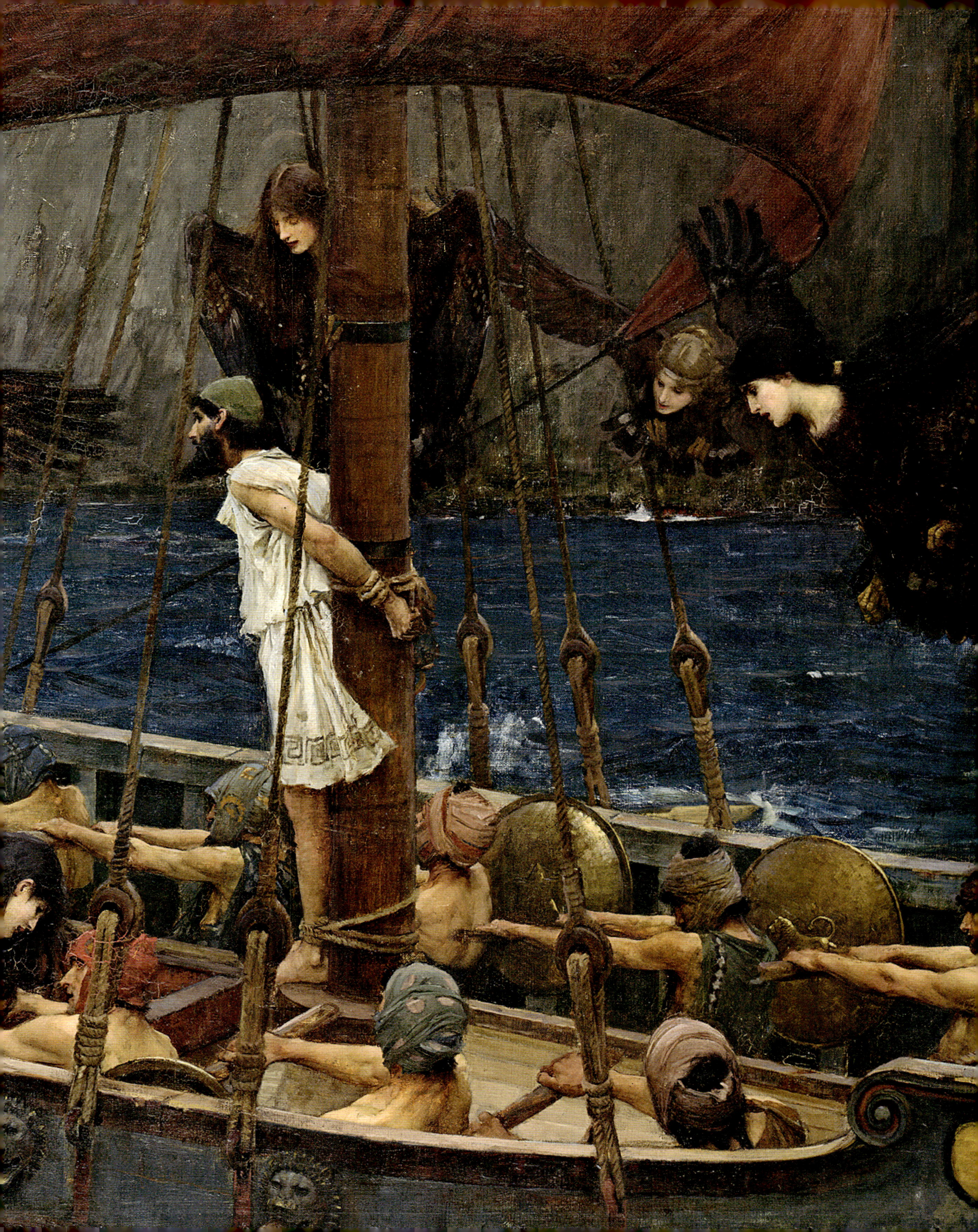

23. Circe Invidiosa: Circe Poisoning the Sea 1892

OIL ON CANVAS, 180.7 X 87.4 CM - ART GALLERY OF SOUTH AUSTRALIA, ADELAIDE, PURCHASED 1892 - EXHIBITED ROYAL ACADEMY, 1892

Waterhouse continues his fascination with the sorceress Circe in this dramatic painting, where the tall vertical format emphasises the sinister narrative: Circe, enraged by the refusal of the sea deity Glaucus to desert his beloved Scylla, pours a baneful green poison into the pool where Scylla has the habit of bathing. The scene is drawn from Ovid's *Metamorphoses*, Book XIV, with a fidelity unusual for Waterhouse, who ordinarily represented mythological stories in general terms, rather than closely following the indications of a specific text. Perhaps he even takes his cue, for the extraordinary colour-scheme of the picture, from Ovid's description of Circe putting on 'caerula velamina', robes the colour of the blue-green sea (line 45). Yet the luminous colouring, as well as the craggy surroundings, are also reminiscent of the caves, famous for their blue-green water and light effects, of Capri and the nearby Amalfi coast; Waterhouse characteristically combines an ancient literary reference with a powerful visual image drawn from his own experience. In Ovid's narrative, Scylla wades waist-deep into the poisoned water, which transforms the lower half of her body into barking dogs, and it has been suggested that the sea-monster on which Circe stands is Scylla herself, already transformed.[1] However, the monster displays fishlike and serpentine, rather than dog-headed forms, and a later letter from Waterhouse indicates that he meant the monster simply to demonstrate the evil effects of the poison.[2] **EP**

1 Angus Trumble, *Love and Death: Art in the Age of Queen Victoria*, exhibition catalogue, Adelaide: Art Gallery of South Australia, p. 102.

2 Letter from Waterhouse to his patron Julia Ellsworth Ford, dated 18 March (without a year, but probably 1903 or later), Beinecke Library, Yale University, Za//Ford (Julia Ellsworth)//Corresp/Mb-Z.

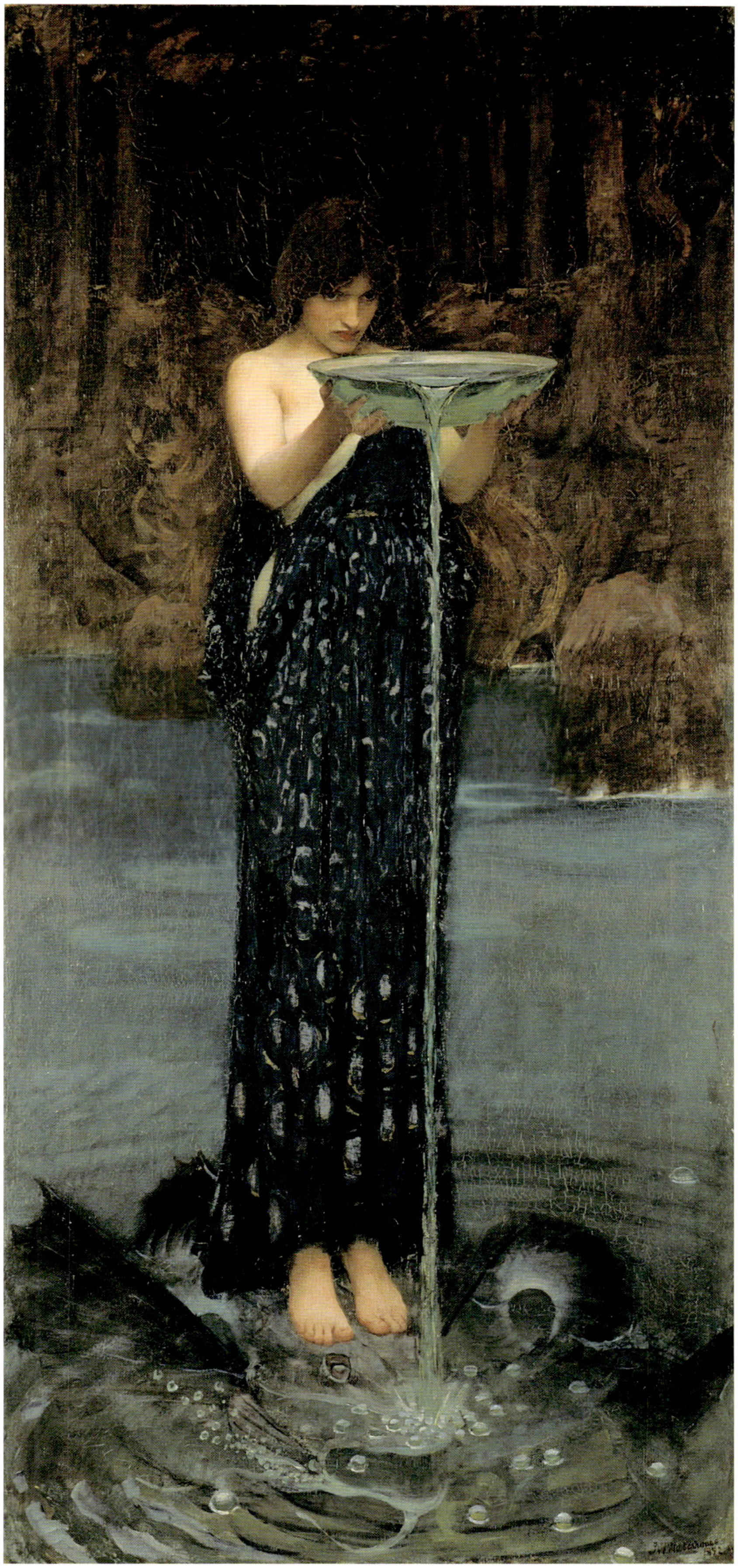

24. A Hamadryad 1893

OIL ON CANVAS, 159.8 X 62.1 CM - PLYMOUTH CITY MUSEUM & ART GALLERY, GIFT OF ALFRED DE PASS, 1926 - EXHIBITED ROYAL ACADEMY, 1893

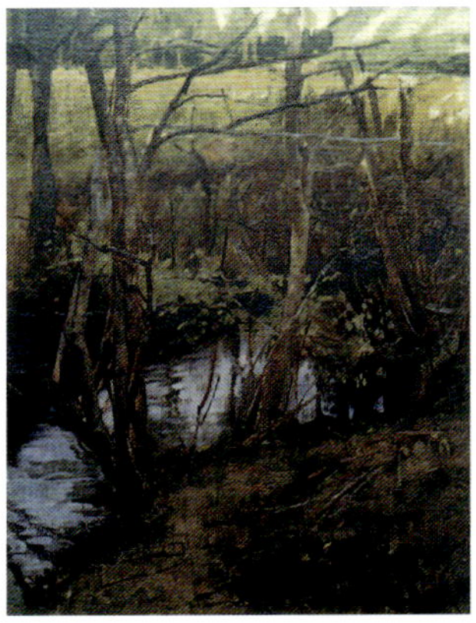

25. Landscape sketch for 'A Naiad' c. 1892-1893

OIL ON CANVAS, 44.5 X 34.3 CM - PRIVATE COLLECTION

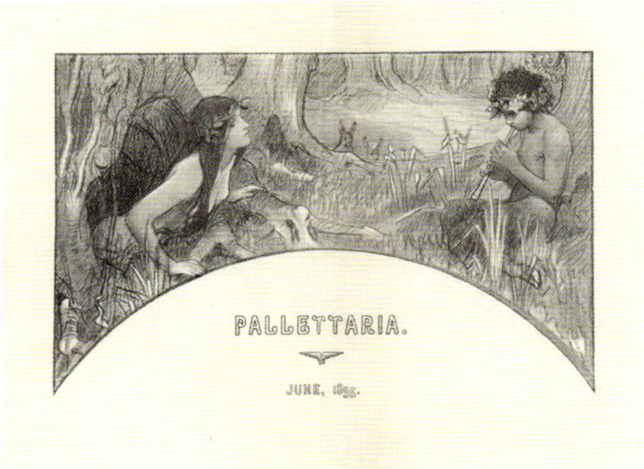

26. Unidentified artist, Programme cover for 'Pallettaria', June 1895

PEN AND INK ON PAPER, 23 X 29.3 CM - ROYAL ACADEMY OF ARTS, LONDON

In 1893, following two exhibition seasons in which he had introduced his major new project in ancient mythology (cats 21, 22, 23),[1] Waterhouse showed what may seem, at first thought, less important pictures showing minor deities of the pagan world: a tree-nymph with a child-satyr playing Pan-pipes (cat. 24, p. 123) and a water-nymph gazing at a boy (cat. 27, p. 125). Yet these paintings also adumbrate a significant new interest in nature mythology, which extends beyond the Mediterranean world of Ulysses and Circe to the English countryside; it may be telling that in the same year Waterhouse also turned to the English Romantic poet John Keats for another woodland scene, *La Belle Dame Sans Merci* (cat. 28). The landscape oil sketch (cat. 25, p. 122), unusual in Waterhouse's work, suggests the seriousness with which he approached this new interest, by making a careful study, from nature, of the rich but low-toned colouring of English woodland; the brilliant Mediterranean sunshine of the paintings exhibited in the previous two years has suddenly vanished. Yet the wooded landscape, however homely, becomes the habitat for a whole population of supernatural creatures, divinities that proliferate in every wood, stream, and field; with this comes a new range of pictorial ideas, in which human forms seem to grow organically from their natural environment. Thus the hamadryad's legs (cat. 24, p. 123) echo the roots of the tree-trunk, from which her upper body arises amidst a proliferation of flowers, while the naiad (cat. 27, p. 125) is sinuous as the winding stream, her arms slender as the saplings in which they twine. As the critic for the *Athenaeum* put it, the figure 'does not repeat the common error of painters' naiads, that of looking like a goddess or like a modern young lady without her clothes…; but, on the contrary, it is easy to see she can swim'.[2] In the later decades of the nineteenth century, there was much interest in pagan nature deities – followers of the goat-god Pan (whose name, cognate with the Greek word for 'all', could connote the universal presence of nature); such deities appear frequently in contemporary poetry.[3] Waterhouse's paintings of 1893, shown simultaneously at the Royal Academy and New Gallery, begin to experiment with imagining visual forms for the nymphs that would abound in later works; *A Naiad* presages the mythological painting of three years later, *Hylas and the Nymphs* (cat. 32). These creatures also quickly moved into the general visual culture of the period, as seen in the design, by an unknown artist, for the programme cover for a Royal Academy Schools' theatrical entertainment, *Pallettaria*, held in June 1895 (cat. 26, p. 122; the title refers piquantly to an artist's palette). The two little figures of nymph and Pan are overtly borrowed from Waterhouse's *A Naiad* and *A Hamadryad*. **EP**

1 At the Royal Academy in 1892 Waterhouse also exhibited an important painting of the mythological *Danaë*, untraced since it was stolen from the New York house of its owner, Julia Ellsworth Ford (1859-1950), in 1947.

2 *Athenaeum*, no. 3419, 6 May 1893, p. 577.

3 See Patricia Merivale, *Pan the Goat-God: His Myth in Modern Times*, Cambridge, Mass.: Harvard University Press, 1969.

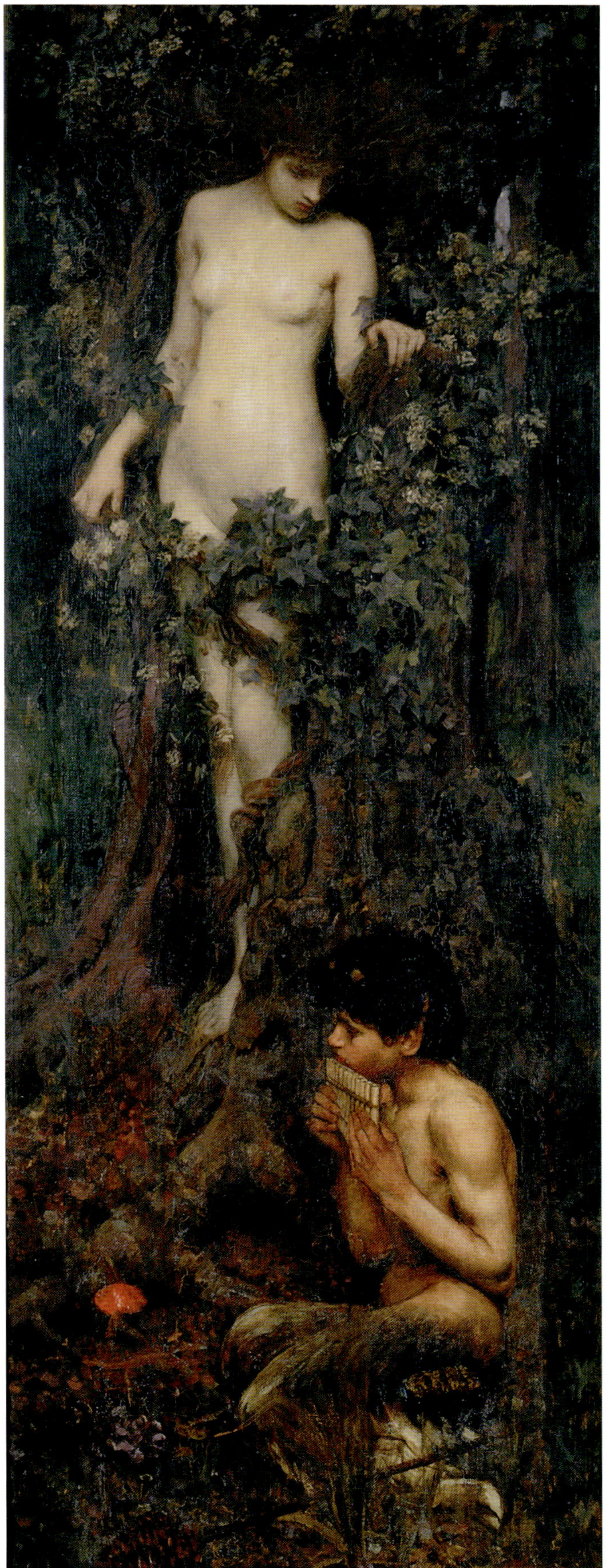

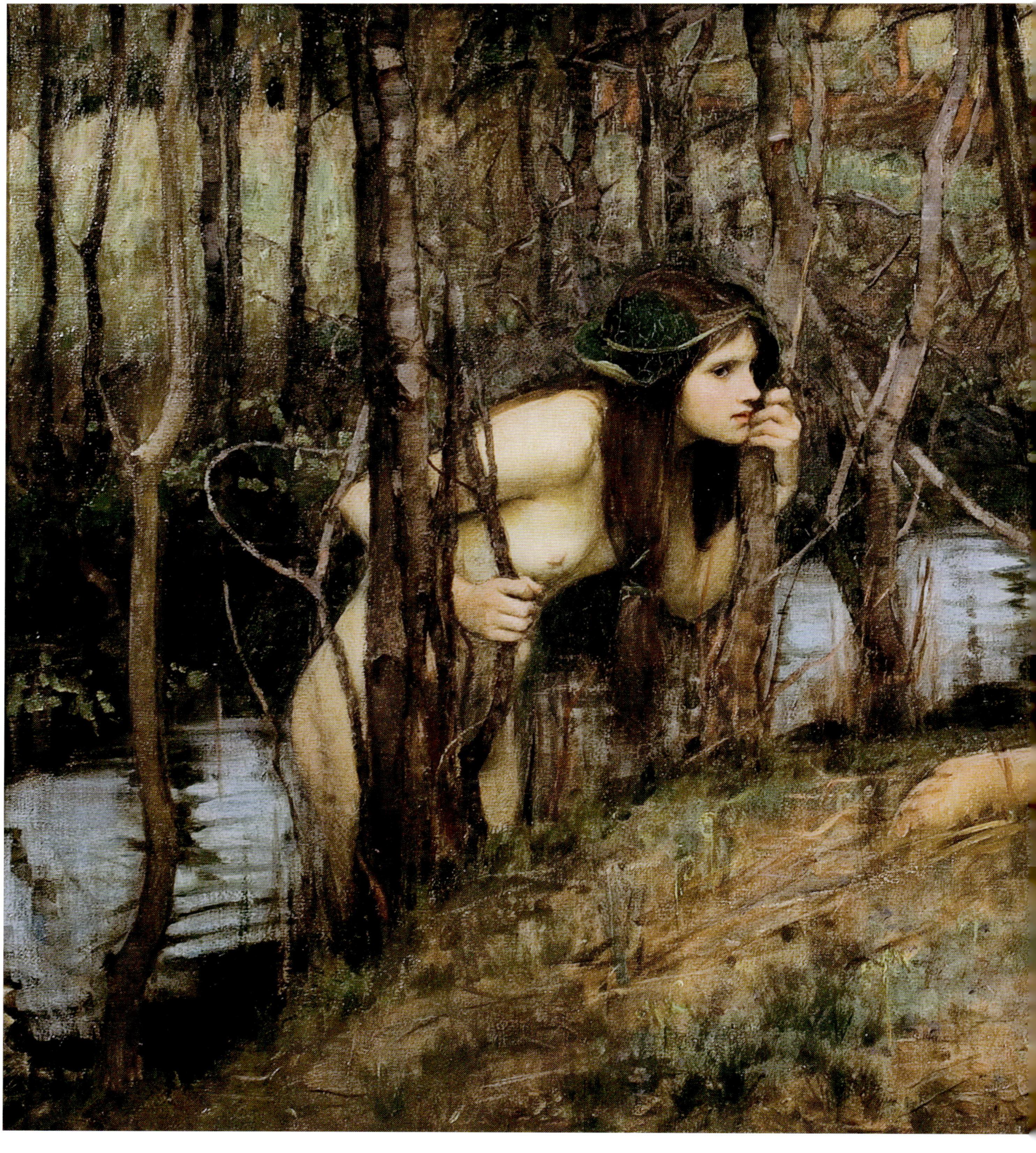

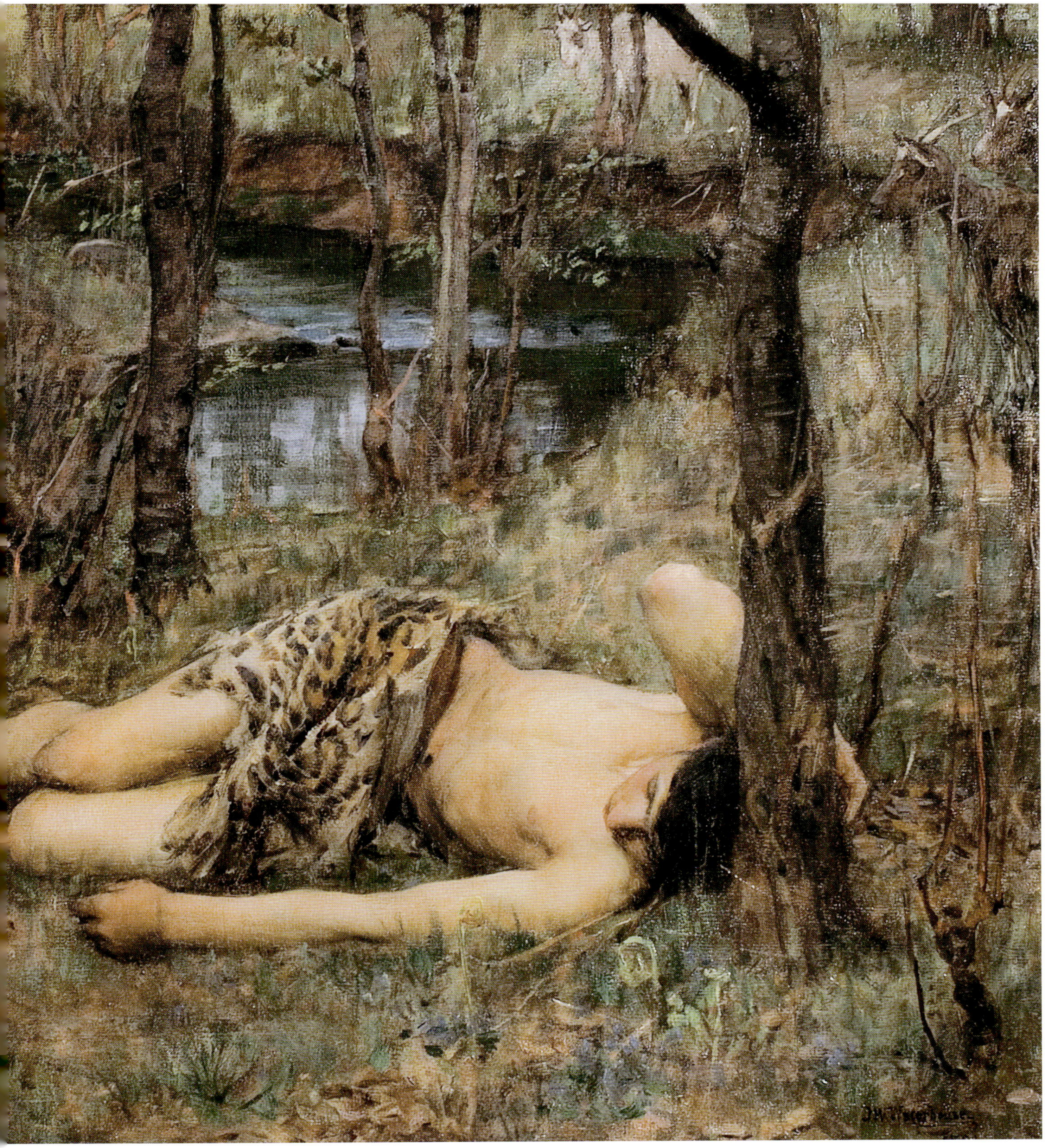

27. A Naiad 1893

OIL ON CANVAS, 66 X 127 CM - COLLECTION SIR TIM RICE - EXHIBITED NEW GALLERY, 1893

28. La Belle Dame Sans Merci 1893

OIL ON CANVAS, 110.6 X 81 CM - HESSISCHES LANDESMUSEUM, DARMSTADT, PURCHASED 1964 - EXHIBITED ROYAL ACADEMY, 1893

In *La Belle Dame Sans Merci*, Waterhouse took as his subject the poem of the same title of 1820 by John Keats. A knight encounters a beautiful enchantress:

I met a lady in the meads,
Full beautiful—a faery's child,
Her hair was long, her foot was light,
And her eyes were wild.

But the woman is not all that she seems. As with the mermaid (cat. 35) or Lady of Shalott (cat. 20), a terrible price will be paid for congress with this other-worldly being that lives under the curse of solitude. As the knight dreams he is warned away by others who have fallen victim to her charms:

She took me to her elfin grot,
And there she wept, and sigh'd full sore,
And there I shut her wild wild eyes
With kisses four.

And there she lulled me asleep,
And there I dream'd - Ah! woe betide!
The latest dream I ever dream'd
On the cold hill's side.

I saw pale kings and princes too,
Pale warriors, death-pale were they all;
They cried – 'La Belle Dame sans Merci
Hath thee in thrall!'

When he awakes he is alone, and wanders heartbroken with longing for his fairy love.

Waterhouse's painting is sexually charged and highly symbolic. The knight bends down, fascinated, towards the upturned face of the fairy. On her sleeve she wears a heart, and encoils him like a serpent with her long hair. The knight is completely powerless; his eyes meet hers in rapt fascination as if he is hypnotised, and his lance drops to his side in a neat double metaphor of both defencelessness in the face of temptation, and of masculine virility. The knight's closely fitting armour protects and encloses him, making him invulnerable to physical contact, like an all-surrounding chastity belt. The scene takes place in a dense wood, a further symbol of entanglement and moral disorientation. Waterhouse creates enormous tension by the proximity of the two figures' faces. From our own experience, we recognise this as the romantic time-stopping moment before they kiss, full of erotic tension. But in Waterhouse's painting we also know that once their lips meet the knight will be lost. The fairy has already circled him with her hair, pulling him down towards her, and she is in the process of tying a knot. What should be a lovers' knot, eternally weaving together their souls, will in fact prove fatal. As in other pictures, Waterhouse plays on male fears of vulnerability; in the face of overwhelming attraction and compulsion there is a psychological anxiety about helplessness. The title too – 'The Beautiful Woman without Mercy' – spells out the characterisation of woman as unremitting in her demand to be loved. These were all themes much treated in European Symbolist pictures from this time, and it is important to consider Waterhouse within this pan-European context (see pp. 51-61). Waterhouse's intention of seeing the fairy as destructive is emphasised by the oil sketch of a mermaid he was developing at this time (cat. 36). **RU**

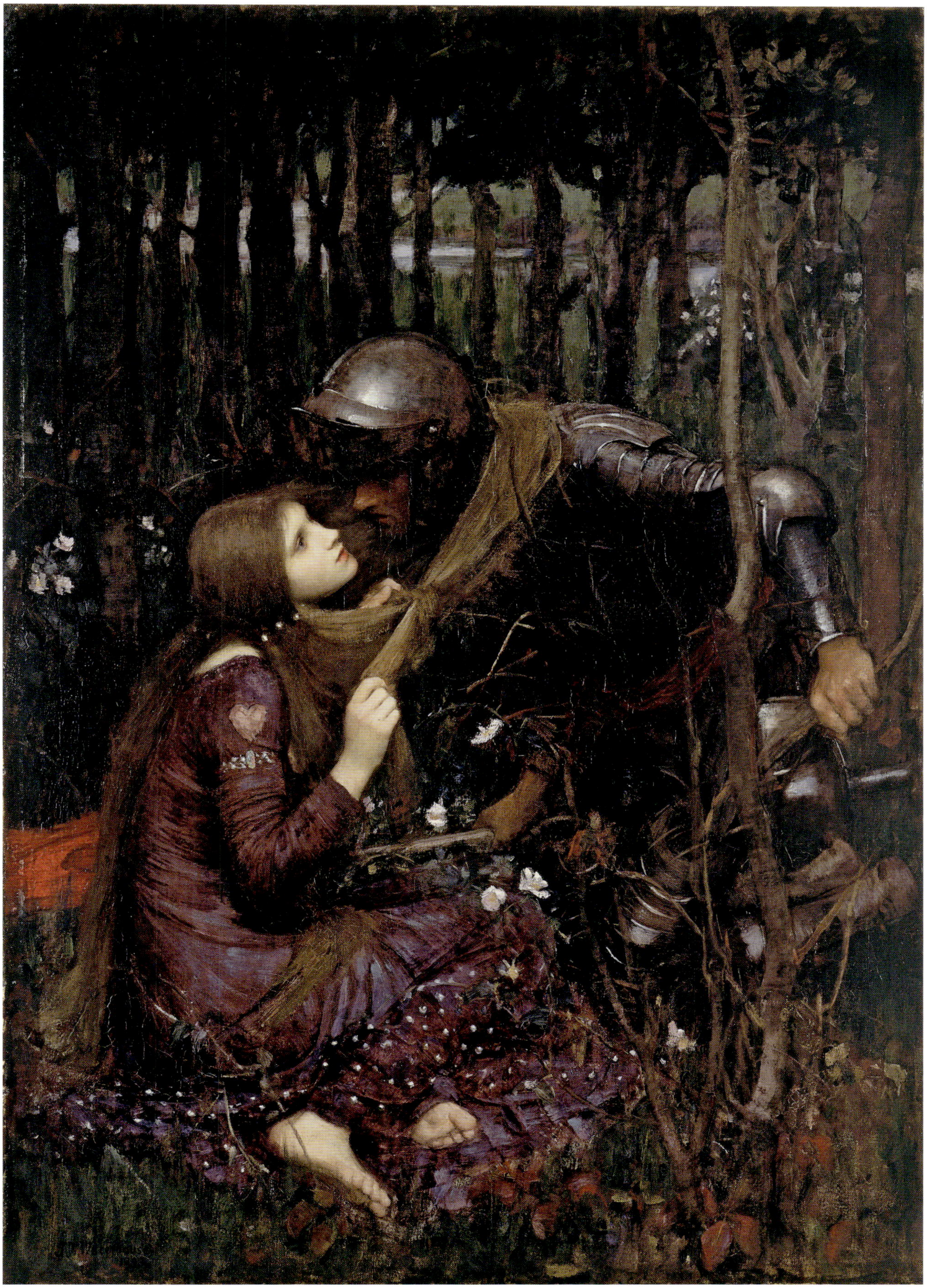

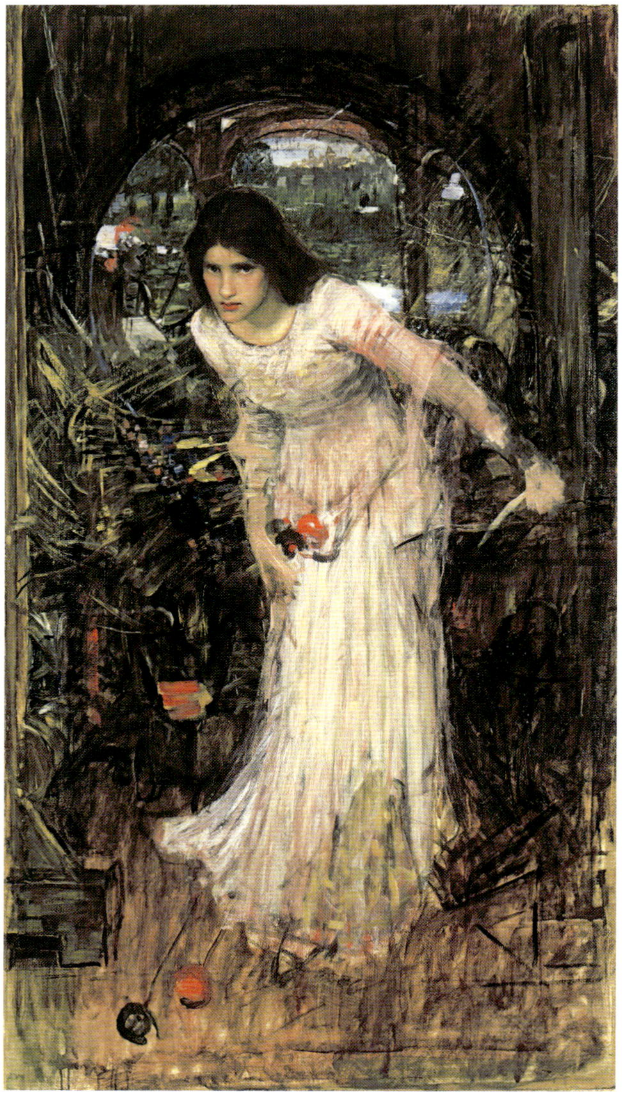

29. The Lady of Shalott 1891-1893

SKETCH - OIL ON CANVAS, 120.5 X 68.3 CM - FALMOUTH ART GALLERY, GIFT OF ALFRED DE PASS, C. 1939

Waterhouse illustrates the climactic moment in Tennyson's poem when the Lady of Shalott, unable to contain her desire for Lancelot any longer, or bear her isolation, turns to gaze upon the world:

> She left the web, she left the loom,
> She made three paces thro' the room,
> She saw the water lily bloom,
> She saw the helmet and the plume,
>   She looked down to Camelot.
> Out flew the web and floated wide,
> The mirror crack'd from side to side
> 'The curse is come upon me', cried
>   The Lady of Shalott.

Waterhouse brilliantly captures the drama of the moment, freezing her movement as the Lady turns and rises from her chair, hesitating before the sight of Lancelot as the curse begins to take effect and the mirror cracks. Her intense, piercing gaze creates enormous tension, and her expression is one that subtly combines fear with desire, and a longing for freedom and involvement in the world. Psychologically convincing, these same emotions characterise the passage from innocence to sexual revelation which is the theme underlying Tennyson's allegorical story. The golden threads of the Lady of Shalott's tapestry wind around her, and she erupts from these restraints as if emerging from a cocoon, a metaphor for sexual awakening. In the mirror, Lancelot is seen reflected as he rides past, his lance pointing up towards the spreading

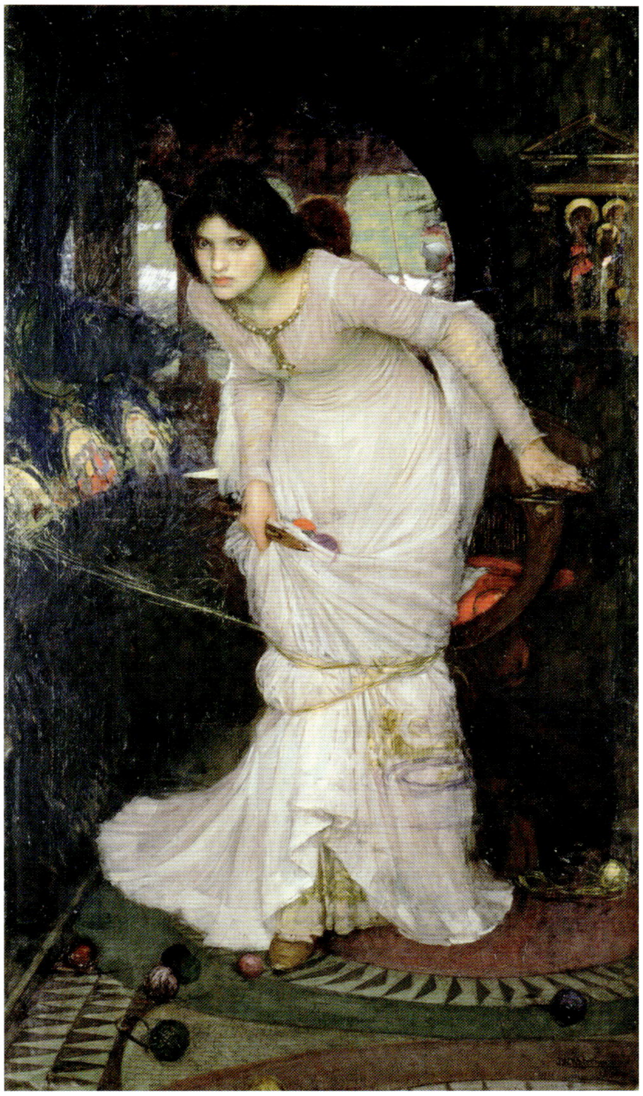

30. The Lady of Shalott 1894

OIL ON CANVAS, 142.2 X 86.3 CM - LEEDS ART GALLERY, PURCHASED 1895 - EXHIBITED ROYAL ACADEMY, 1894

crack; the Lady tightly grasps her tapestry shuttle. Tapestry and embroidery were considered suitable and seemly activities for Victorian women, but ones that were also restrictive and tied to the home. The Lady of Shalott has been making images of Lancelot in tapestry, but turns away from this activity in an act of defiance that asserts her right to life and freedom. At far right is an altar to the Virgin, which now she metaphorically turns her back on; the candles blowing out symbolise both her fading life, and an end to her Madonna-like purity. Waterhouse borrowed this altar motif from Millais's *Mariana* (1850-1851), a picture whose subject was another imprisoned woman wracked with longing.

Waterhouse planned this follow-up to his 1888 *Lady of Shalott* success extremely carefully. He made a large number of sketchbook studies which experimented with several different schemes for the pose and setting of the Lady. In addition he made the almost full-size oil sketch which is shown here (cat. 29). There were a number of Pre-Raphaelite sources from which Waterhouse evidently took inspiration. Holman Hunt had designed the illustration for Moxon's edition of Tennyson for the same moment in the poem (fig. 37), later developing it into oil versions. From Hunt Waterhouse took the imagery of the Lady's entanglement in her weaving threads. But a further close source was Hunt's *The Awakening Conscience*, in which the natural world is reflected in a mirror behind the errant courtesan. Indeed, the subjects of female desire and moral capitulation are closely allied. **RU**

31. St Cecilia 1895

OIL ON CANVAS, 123.2 X 200.7 CM - PRIVATE COLLECTION - EXHIBITED ROYAL ACADEMY, 1895

Waterhouse was at the height of his career when he painted *St Cecilia*, and following its exhibition at the Royal Academy he was elected a full Academician. He took the subject from 'The Palace of Art' by Tennyson, a poet he revered:

> … in a clear wall'd city on the sea,
> Near gilded organ pipes, her hair
> Wound with white roses, slept St Cecily;
> An angel look'd at her.

Waterhouse filled the margins of his copy of Tennyson (cat. 100) with composition sketches inspired by the poems. The volume inspired four of his major canvases, notably *The Lady of Shalott* and *St Cecilia*. 'The Palace of Art' is about the struggle to preserve art and beauty, and Waterhouse's portrayal of St Cecilia stays very close to Tennyson's brief description. Because she is the patron saint of music, Waterhouse suitably has the angels playing softly to Cecilia, either side of the organ mentioned by Tennyson. (By tradition, Cecilia is credited with the invention of the organ.) Waterhouse would have been familiar with Dante Gabriel Rossetti's illustration for the Moxon edition of Tennyson, which shows St Cecilia herself playing the organ and swooning back into the arms of a lover. In certain accounts of the Saint's life, as Rossetti acknowledges, Cecilia's beautiful playing of music leads an angel to fall in love with her. Cecilia's husband glimpses them together and brings to both a heavenly crown of martyrdom. The story expresses the idea of the connection between musical expression and physical love. In Waterhouse's picture the angels are not simply serenading the patron saint of music; they have fallen in love with her and together they are surrounded by roses, the emblems of love. Cecilia was also blind, and the patron saint of the blind. Waterhouse's picture is full of references to the experience of the different human senses: the sound of the angel's music and the trickle of water from the fountain; smell from the poppies and roses; touch from the beautiful embroidery of Cecilia's gown and her fingers upon the rose and book; and sight from the beauty gathered before us. These sensory elements are also a recapitulation of the connections between art and music that were the mainstay of 1860s Aestheticism, and the sleeping woman recalls the paintings of Albert Moore. However transcendent the picture is on the surface, it also contains a warning. Poppies are symbols of sleep, fitting the subject of the picture. But more darkly they are also emblems of death, indicating the eventual martyrdom that will come from love between temporal and heavenly beings. This theme of the irreconcilability of two worlds or creatures was one Waterhouse treated elsewhere in pictures such as *A Mermaid* (cat. 35) and *La Belle Dame Sans Merci* (cat. 28).

There are a number of influences in the picture; the architectural setting recalls Alma-Tadema, for instance. But the most notable inspiration was evidently Burne-Jones's *Briar Rose* series, which Waterhouse had seen at the Agnew's Gallery in 1890, which featured a sleeping princess and which had been acquired by Waterhouse's client, Alexander Henderson (later first Baron Faringdon). Despite the Pre-Raphaelite character of *St Cecilia*, Waterhouse adopted a modern technique for its execution. The broad brushing of the foreground and landscape elements, and the fall of Cecilia's dress, create a semi-abstract paint effect that is concerned with the sensation of viewing as much with communicating detail. The picture was an immediate success at the Academy, with *The Times* describing it as 'One of the most brilliant and essentially modern performances of this eclectic age'. It was bought by George McCulloch, who had made a fortune prospecting in Australia, and formed a notable art collection. Shortly afterwards he also purchased Burne-Jones's *Sleeping Princess* (1870-1895), a variation of the central panel of *The Briar Rose* series on which Waterhouse had partly based *St Cecilia*. **RU**

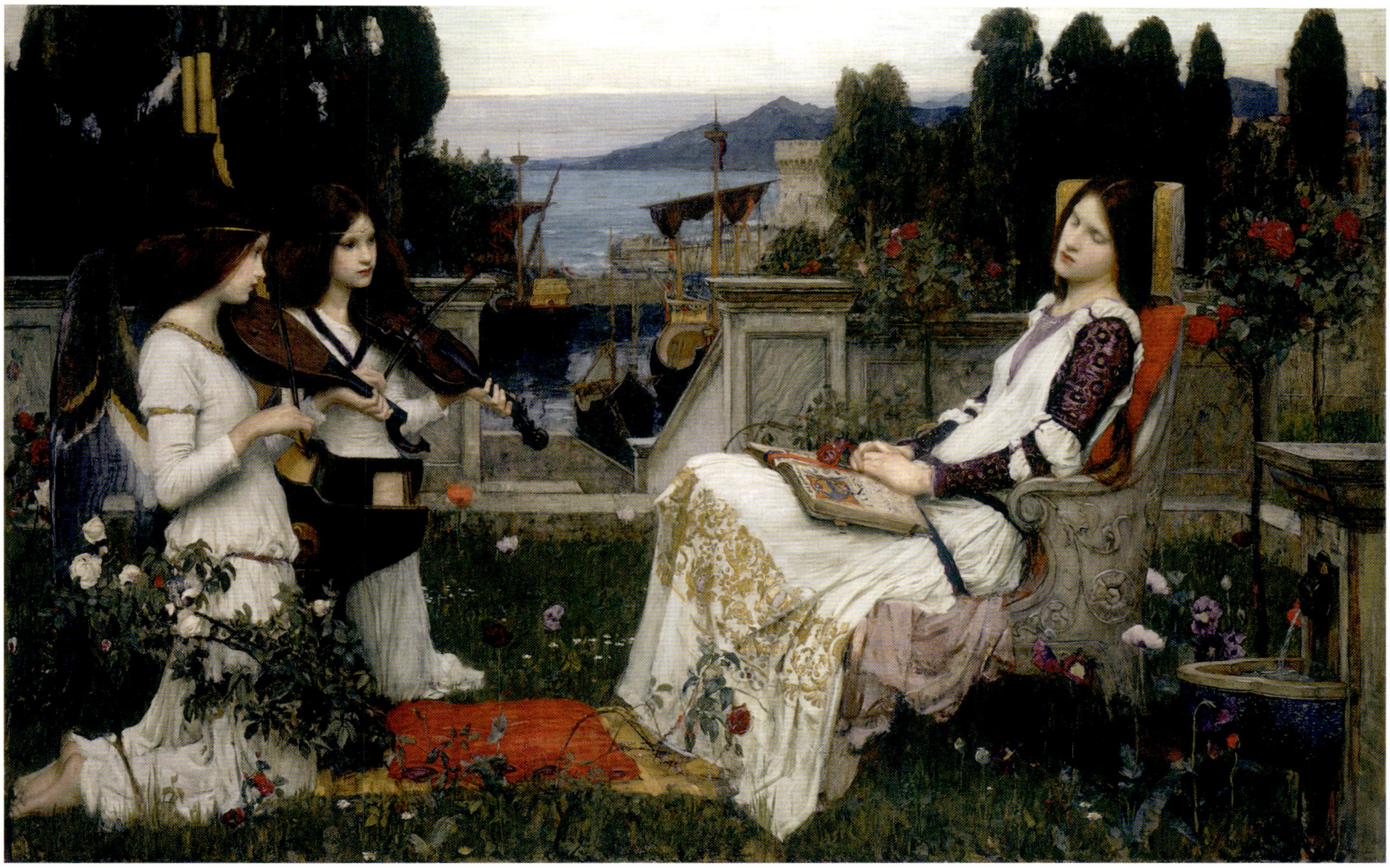

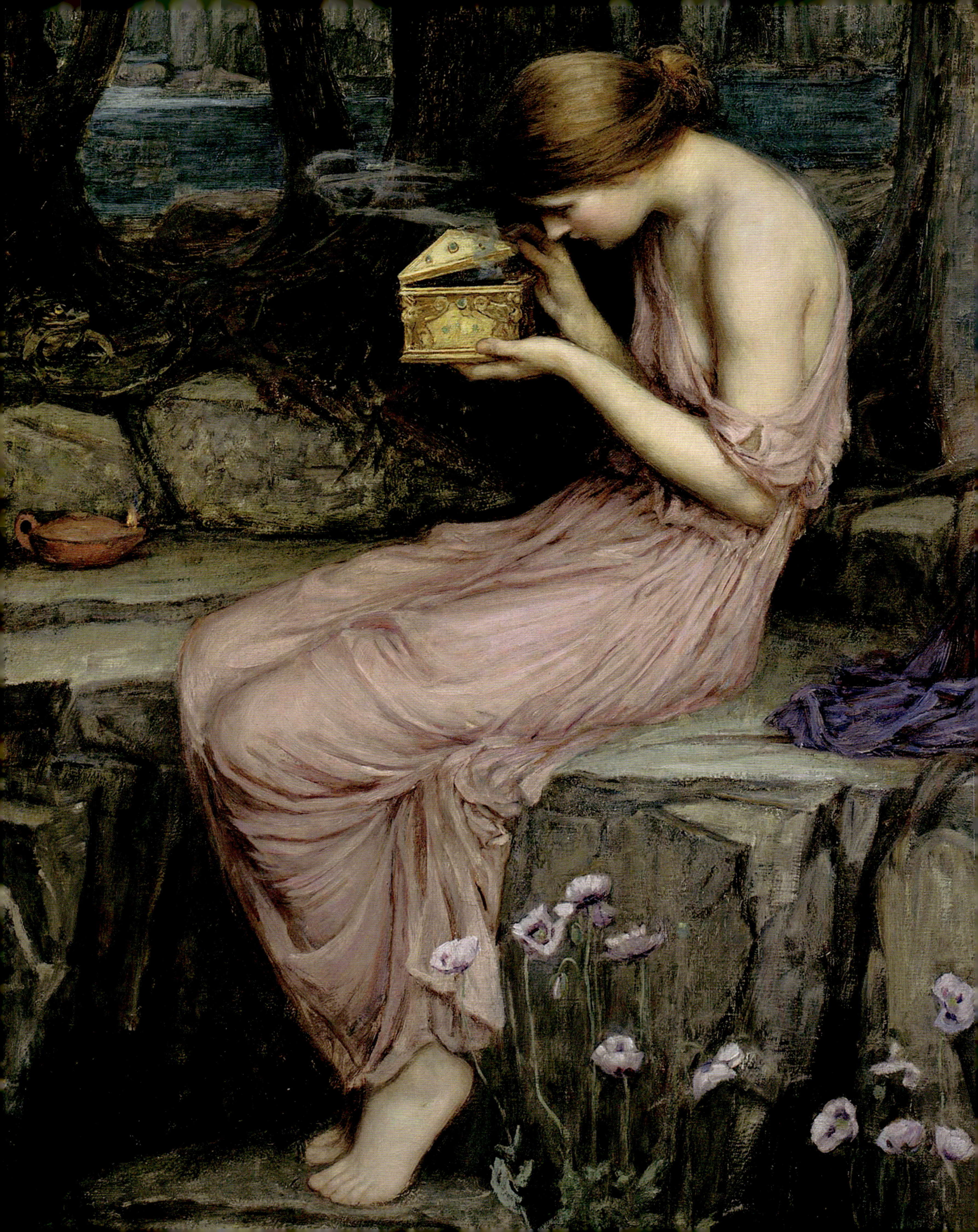

Royal Academician

32. **Hylas and the Nymphs** 1896

OIL ON CANVAS, 98.2 X 163.3 CM - MANCHESTER CITY GALLERIES, PURCHASED 1896 - EXHIBITED MANCHESTER AUTUMN EXHIBITION, 1896

Like the landscape of Millais's *Ophelia* (fig. 23), of which it is strongly reminiscent, the setting of this painting is deep within an overgrown woodland; indeed, the clump of reeds at bottom left is virtually a quotation from Millais's painting, which suggests a deliberate association between the watery deaths of Hylas and Ophelia. With no glimpse of sky or meadow, there is no escape for the beautiful youth, except down through the murky pool to the underworld. The myth of Hylas, the beloved companion of Hercules on the voyage of Jason and the Argonauts (see cat. 48), is often referenced in ancient literature, and poignantly recounted in the thirteenth *Idyll* of the Greek poet Theocritus. As in Theocritus, Hylas has brought a vessel in search of water to quench the Argonauts' thirst, and finds a pool thick with vegetation; the nymphs of the spring, again as in the Greek poem, cling to his hand, enraptured by his beauty. As in *La Belle Dame Sans Merci* (cat. 28) and the later *Lamia* (cat. 46), he is mesmerised by the gaze of one of the nymphs, and his leaning pose unmistakably suggests the dénouement, his fall into the pool. The fallen woman was a frequent theme in Victorian painting; here Waterhouse powerfully imagines the fallen man. In some ancient tellings Hylas was entrapped by just one nymph; Theocritus does not specify the number, but Waterhouse multiplies his nymphs to the magic number seven, the number of Sirens in *Ulysses and the Sirens* (cat. 22) and later of daughters of Danaus in *The Danaïdes* (cat. 47). Some critics complained that the nymphs looked too much alike, as if they were all drawn from one model.[1] Drawings, and close scrutiny of the faces, suggest that Waterhouse may have used at least two models,[2] but the uncanny resemblance among the faces is crucial to the hypnotic power of the scene, and its supernatural resonances.

Hylas and the Nymphs quickly and enduringly became a popular icon, frequently reproduced and instantly recognisable to audiences worldwide. Partly this was due to its acquisition by the public gallery of the city of Manchester, also a sign of Waterhouse's prominence in the later Victorian art world; unusually, because the artist could not finish it in time for the Royal Academy exhibition of 1896, it appeared first at the Manchester Autumn Exhibition of that year and was already the property of the Manchester Corporation when it was finally displayed at the Academy in 1897. The gallery also lent it to many of the major international exhibitions of succeeding years, including the great Exposition Universelle of 1900 in Paris. However, the painting's lasting fame, like that of *The Lady of Shalott* (cat. 20) and *Echo and Narcissus* (cat. 43), is due above all to the visual power with which it realises its haunting story. **EP**

1 See for example 'The Royal Academy', *The Times*, 1 May 1897, p. 10.
2 Three drawings reproduced in a contemporary article are evidently from one model, and relate to the two central, forward-facing figures behind the one who grasps Hylas's arm ('Mr. J.W. Waterhouse's Painting, "Hylas and the Nymphs"', *Studio*, vol. X, 15 May 1897, pp. 243-247); a drawing of two figures now in the Ashmolean Museum, Oxford, appears to show a different model and relates loosely to the two figures at the right. However, it is dangerous to speculate on the models for Waterhouse's figures; not only did he generalise and idealise the features of his models, so that the resulting figures conform to a small number of types, but he may also have used his well-trained visual memory to import reminiscences of favourite types into drawings made from other models. On Waterhouse's memory training see A. Lys Baldry, 'J.W. Waterhouse and his Work', *Studio*, vol. IV, January 1895, pp. 103-104; R.E.D. Sketchley, *The Art of J.W. Waterhouse, R.A.*, Christmas Number of *The Art Journal*, 1909, p. 7.

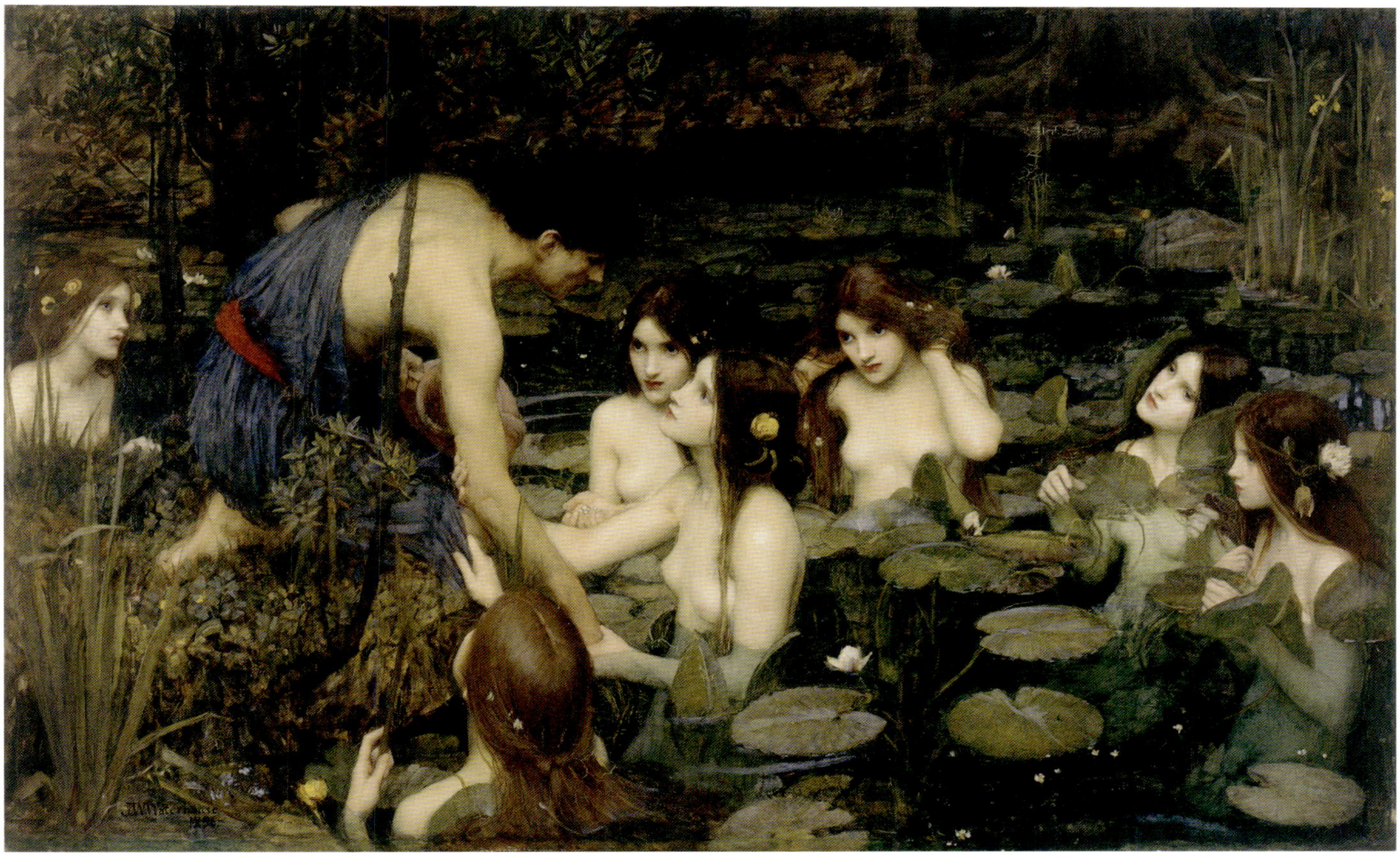

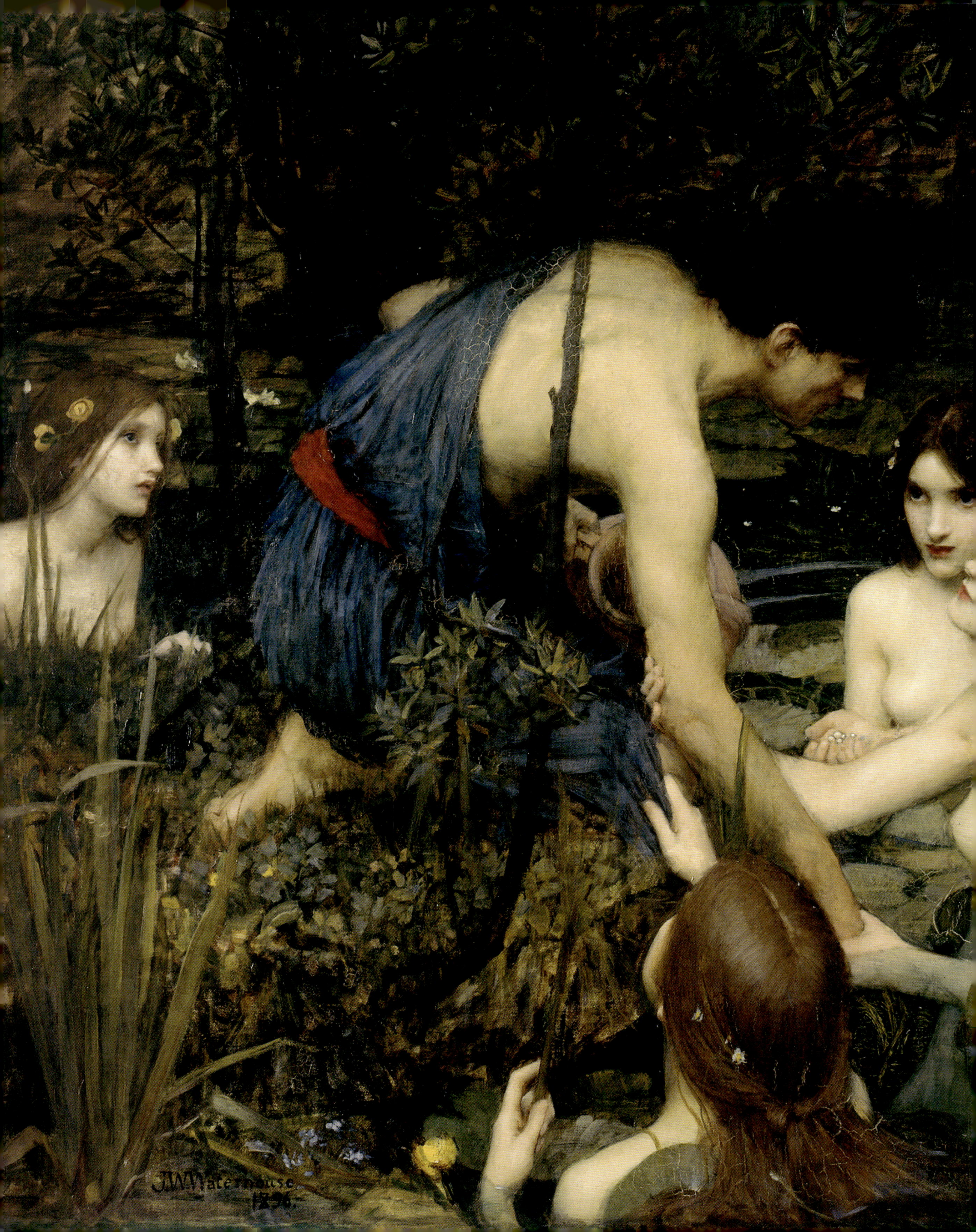
JWWaterhouse
1896.

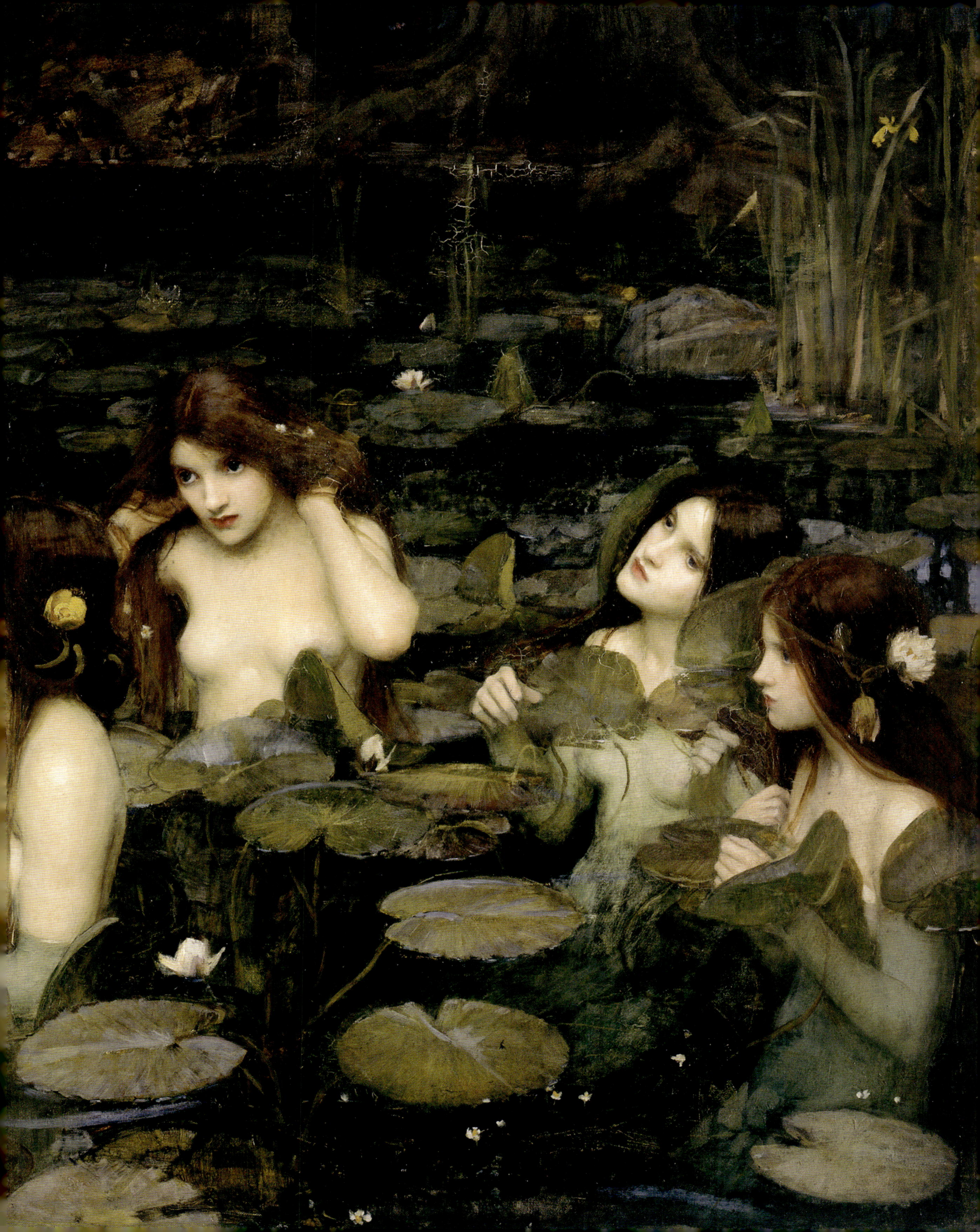

33. Mariana in the South 1897

OIL ON CANVAS, 114.4 X 72.4 CM - PRIVATE COLLECTION COURTESY OF PETER NAHUM AT THE LEICESTER GALLERIES, LONDON - EXHIBITED NEW GALLERY, 1897

In Shakespeare's *Measure for Measure*, Mariana is abandoned for five years in a moated grange by her fiancé Angelo because her dowry was lost at sea. Mariana still loves Angelo and her enclosed condition becomes a metaphor for unfulfilled sexual longing. Waterhouse took his title from a poem by Tennyson, which dwells in depth on Mariana's spiralling feelings of loneliness and yearning. Tennyson's sensuous language and imagery, and rhythmic meter, all combine to suggest an atmosphere of fevered sexual desire. Waterhouse based his picture closely on two of Tennyson's stanzas:

> Low on her knees herself she cast,
> Before Our Lady murmur'd she;
> Complaining, 'Mother, give me grace
> To help me of my weary load.'
> And on the liquid mirror glow'd
> The clear perfection of her face.
> 'Is this the form,' she made her moan,
> 'That won his praises night and morn?'
> And 'Ah,' she said, 'but I wake alone,
> I sleep forgotten, I wake forlorn.'
> ...
>
> And, rising, from her bosom drew
> Old letters, breathing of her worth,
> For 'Love,' they said, 'must needs be true,
> To what is loveliest upon earth.'
> An image seem'd to pass the door,
> To look at her with slight, and say
> 'But now thy beauty flows away,
> So be alone for evermore.'
> 'O cruel heart,' she changed her tone,
> 'And cruel love, whose end is scorn,
> Is this the end to be left alone,
> To live forgotten, and die forlorn?'

Kneeling before the glass, contemplating her beauty, Mariana loosens her flowing hair. She is a prisoner, condemned to serve a sentence of chastity. Her beauty remains unappreciated and unfulfilled and, yearning for physical love to make her whole, she suffers the cruellest punishment of all. In this she is like the Lady of Shalott, whose story so fascinated Waterhouse. Indeed, the round chiffonier mirror recalls Holman Hunt's illustration to 'The Lady of Shalott' in Moxon's Tennyson (fig. 37), which Waterhouse had quoted previously in his own painting of the subject in 1894 (cat. 30). But Waterhouse's composition is startlingly original and perfectly conceived. The angled reflection in the oval glass would challenge any painter's skills, but Waterhouse achieves both accuracy and poetry. The black and white tiles stretching off to the door give a sense of the echoing emptiness of the moated grange and cleverly emphasise Mariana's solitude. In the top left corner we glimpse the altar to the Madonna at which she has been praying. As in Tennyson's poem, this neatly connects Mariana's enforced purity with the purity of the Virgin.

In Mariana's long white dress and reflection in the mirror there is some distant invocation of Whistler's *Little White Girl: Symphony in White No. 2* (1864). But the principal sources are Pre-Raphaelite. Images of women narcissistically contemplating themselves in mirrors appear in a number of Pre-Raphaelite pictures with which Waterhouse is likely to have been familiar. Rossetti's *Fazio's Mistress* (1863) and *Lady Lilith* (1864-1868) both gaze at themselves. But the closest source was Millais's famous painting of *Mariana* (1850-1851), where she stretches in a similar side view after working on her embroidery, staring at a stained glass window. This was a picture Waterhouse had seen at the Grosvenor Gallery in 1886 and he may have seen it more recently when it was exhibited in Birmingham in 1891. For the double view of Mariana, Waterhouse is likely to have been inspired by Rossetti's employment of the device in his illustration to 'Mariana in the South' in Moxon's edition of Tennyson. **RU**

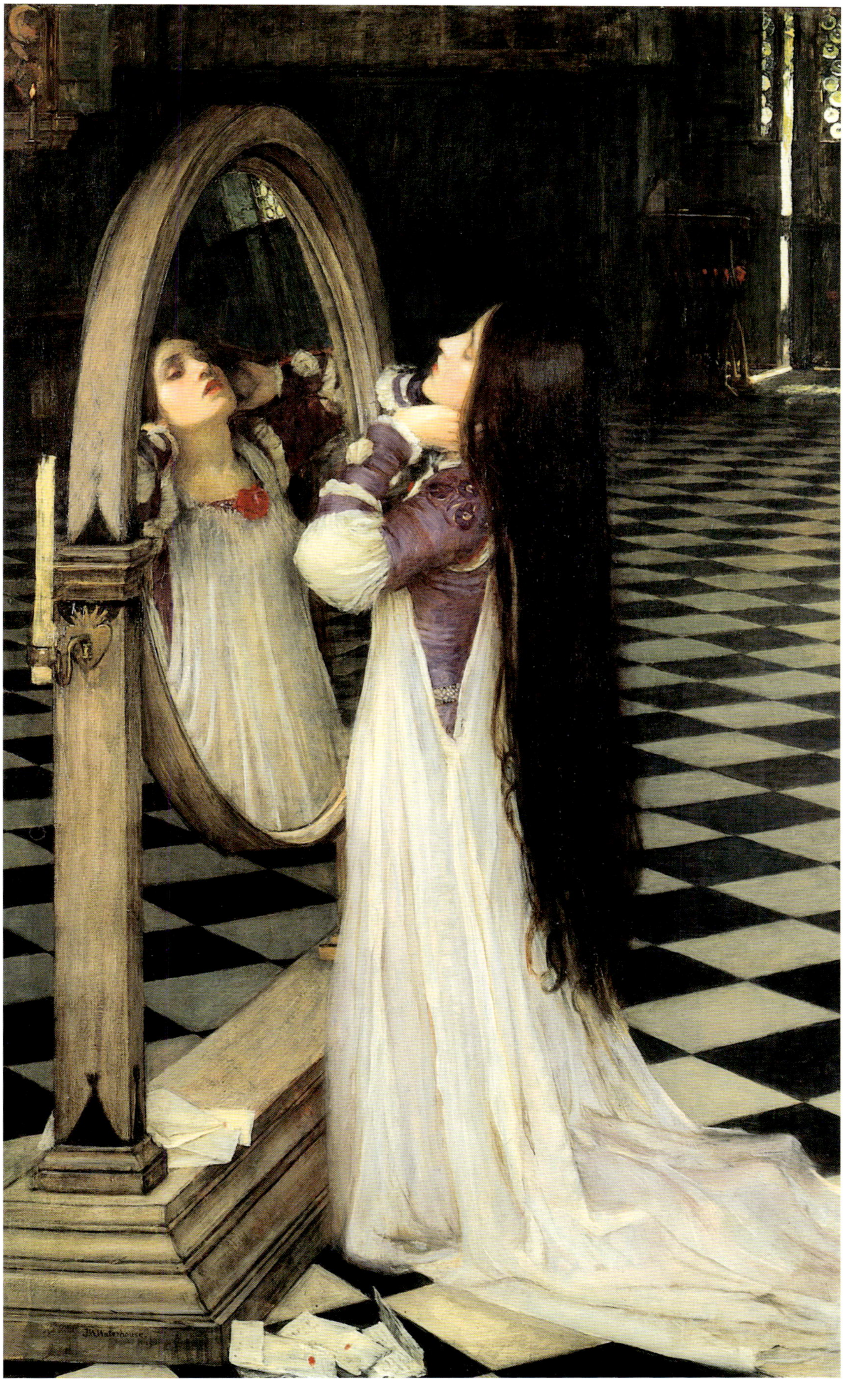

34. **Ariadne** 1898

OIL ON CANVAS, 91 X 151 CM - PRIVATE COLLECTION - EXHIBITED ROYAL ACADEMY, 1898

Waterhouse takes his cue from the opening lines of the tenth of Ovid's *Heroides*, poems in the forms of letters from mythological heroines to their absent lovers: Ariadne, writing to her faithless lover Theseus, begins by remembering how she slept while he stole from her side, abandoning her on the island of Naxos. Theseus's departing ship appears at the mouth of the harbour behind the sleeping figure, bound for the azure sea and the distant rocks of Mediterranean islands, just tinged with the morning light (the seascape harks back to earlier scenes inspired by Capri, such as *Ulysses and the Sirens*, cat. 22). The painting does not, however, follow the course of Ovid's narrative, or the equally celebrated version of the story in Catullus's poem 64, both of which represent the distraught and raging Ariadne, upbraiding her betrayer. Instead it presents Ariadne's last poignant moment of innocence, just before she wakes. To do so it draws on a visual source, the ancient marble sculpture of the Vatican Museum, known since the Renaissance as *Cleopatra* but plausibly identified at the end of the eighteenth century as a representation of Ariadne, the daughter of King Minos of Crete.[1] Like the sculpture, Waterhouse's painting shows the heroine reclining with one arm thrown over her head, a pose frequently used in ancient and later art for sleeping figures, often maenads or bacchantes, exhausted after revelry (compare Alma-Tadema's *After the Dance*, fig. 44). The association of the pose with Bacchic imagery may be significant, for in some versions of the myth the god Bacchus comes to rescue Ariadne in her desolation; in the painting, the spotted panthers, animals sacred to Bacchus, clearly allude to this version of the story. Perhaps, too, there are subtle hints of the famous Latin poems, which complicate the tranquillity of the slumbering figure. The billowing sails of the departing ship recall Ariadne's anguish, in *Heroides* 10, at seeing Theseus's sails filling with the south wind as she strains to catch her last glimpse. And the drapery, slipping from the youthful figure's tender breast, brings to mind Catullus's description of Ariadne, careless of the drapery that flies from her bosom as she paces the windblown shore; in this passage, too, the poet compares Ariadne to the marble figure of a bacchante. Waterhouse has translated the histrionic drama of the poems into an image of slumber; but the lolling panthers, and the hint of awakening sensuality in the exposed breast, suggest that more of the story is yet to come. **EP**

1 See Francis Haskell and Nicholas Penny, *Taste and the Antique: The Lure of Classical Sculpture 1500-1900*, New Haven and London: Yale University Press, 1982, cat. no. 24, pp. 184-187.

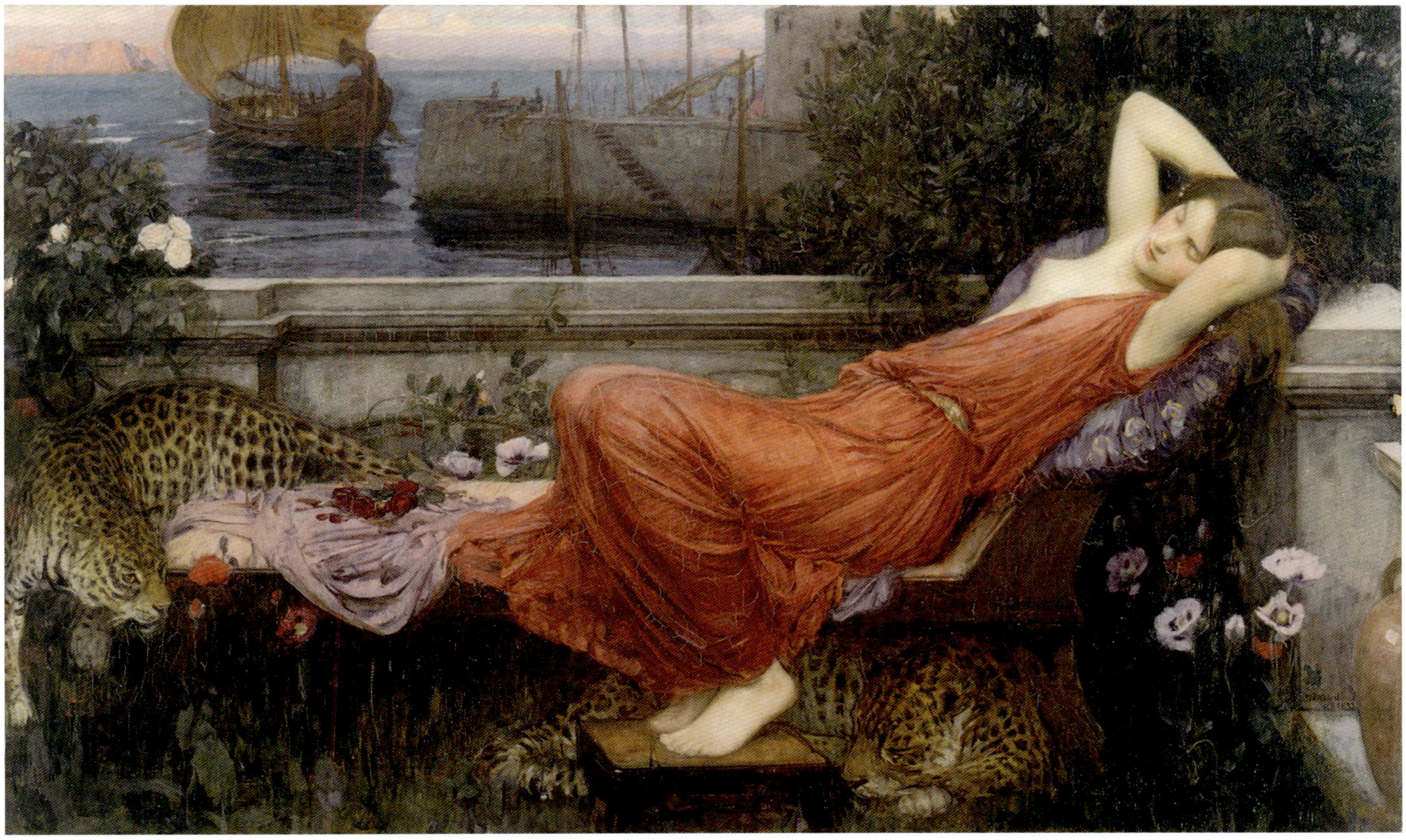

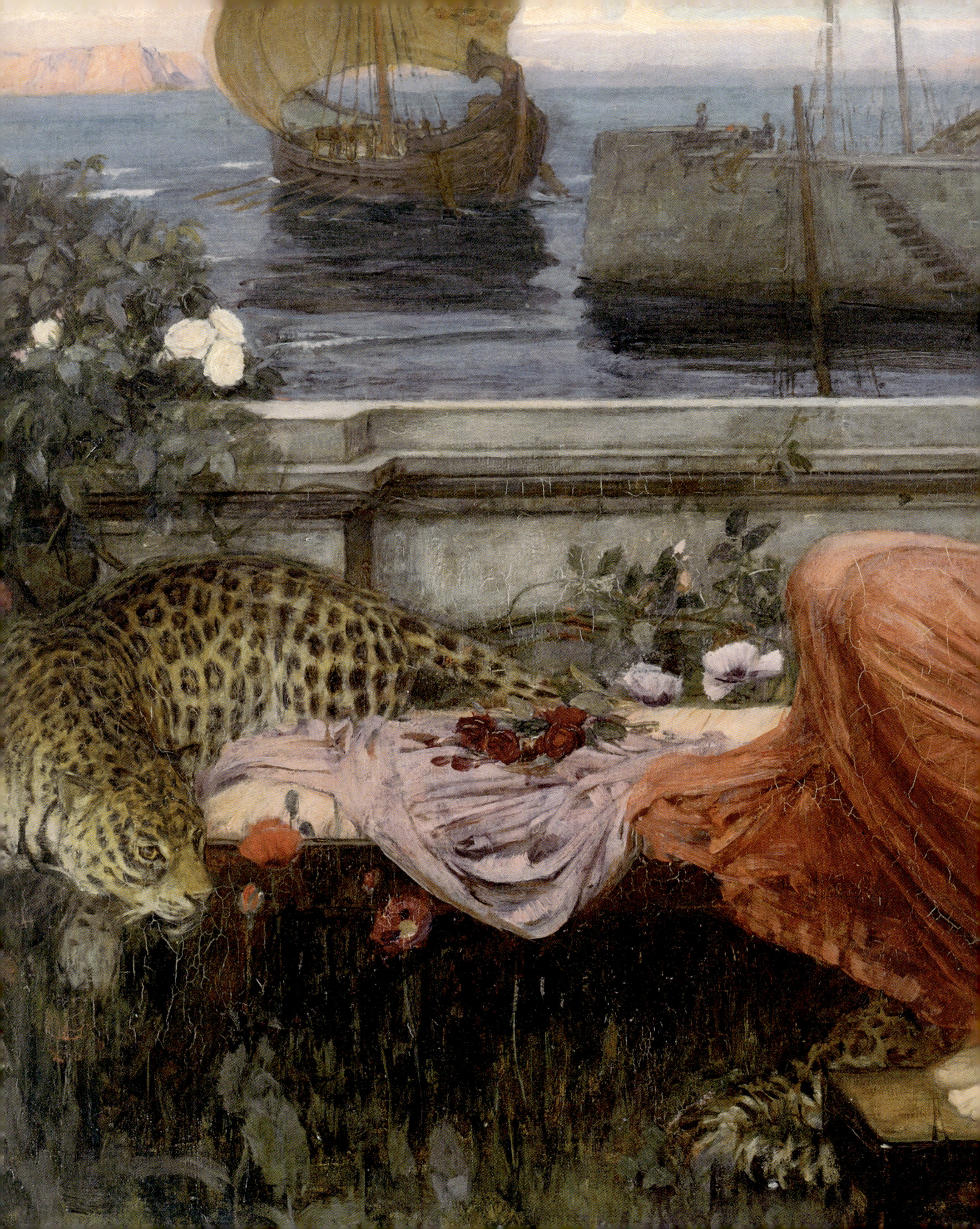

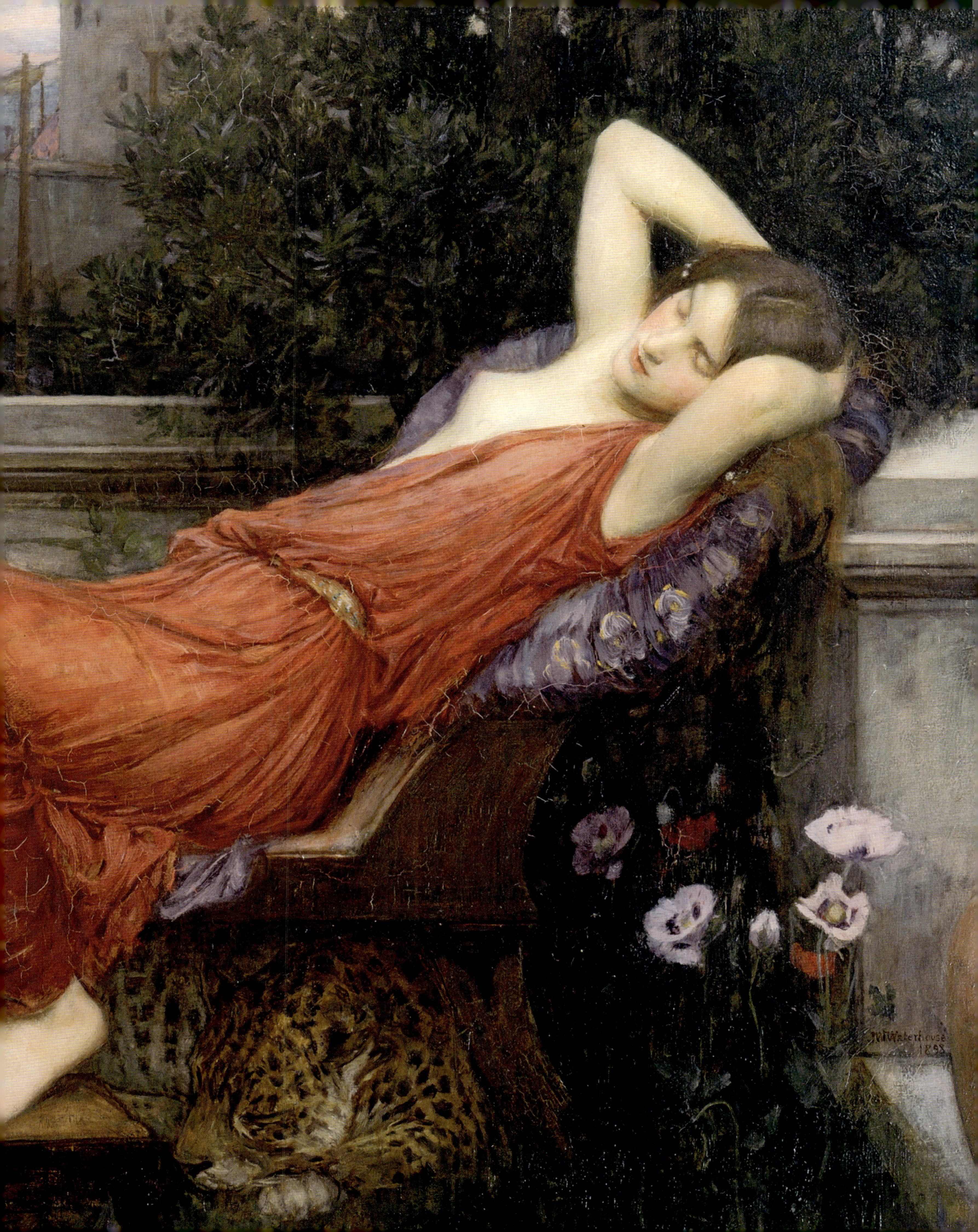

35. A Mermaid 1900

OIL ON CANVAS, 96.5 X 66.6 CM - ROYAL ACADEMY OF ARTS, LONDON, DIPLOMA WORK PRESENTED BY THE ARTIST 1900 - EXHIBITED ROYAL ACADEMY, 1901

The mermaid was the traditional folklore siren, luring sailors to their doom with her beguiling song. Half fish, half human, the mermaid longed only for the company of a man. But the inability of either to inhabit the environment of the other could lead only to tragedy and death. For Waterhouse the subject again presented a mystical, ethereal temptress whose attractiveness for men would prove lethal. For the mermaid herself, the inability to form a union with humankind spelled a kind of curse, and doomed her always to be unfulfilled. The mermaid represented a very clear archetype of male anxiety in the face of an enchanting woman to whom capitulation could prove disastrous. In this, Waterhouse's subjects held great similarity to images of female temptresses by European Symbolist painters such as Franz von Stuck, Gustav Klimt, and others. There are similarities too in the strategy of using traditional mythology as a way of articulating new concerns and anxieties. With the questioning of gender roles and calls for women to be socially and politically independent, alongside a demand for proper sexual fulfilment, the 1890s saw throughout Europe an almost millennial male anxiety about their status and appropriate role.

In Waterhouse's picture the mermaid combs out her long red hair, singing her mesmerising song, and therefore Waterhouse links feminine narcissism with masculine vulnerability to beauty. In front of her is a large shell containing pearls, which traditionally were said to be formed from the tears of dead sailors. Snake-like, the mermaid's tail coils around her, as if she is embracing herself. Indeed, if she kills all who come to her, this will be the only embrace she will experience. It is possible Waterhouse was partly inspired by Tennyson's poem 'The Mermaid' (1830), which includes the lines:

> Who would be a
> A mermaid fair,
> Singing alone,
> Combing her hair …

In choosing to paint a bizarrely hybrid creature – half fish, half human – Waterhouse's canvas recalls the paintings of the Symbolist painter Arnold Böcklin. Böcklin painted several pictures of mermaids, and others of similarly cross-bred creatures such as centaurs who have undercurrents of melancholy from their hybrid status. It is tempting to speculate whether Waterhouse might ever have seen Böcklin's work at any of the international or secessionist European exhibitions, where it achieved considerable notice. Around 1892 Waterhouse made a companion study, never realised as a full-scale painting, which depicts a merman wallowing in the shallows. He supports his head on his hand in an attitude of melancholy that is so highly reminiscent of Böcklin that it must suggest some familiarity with his work. **RU**

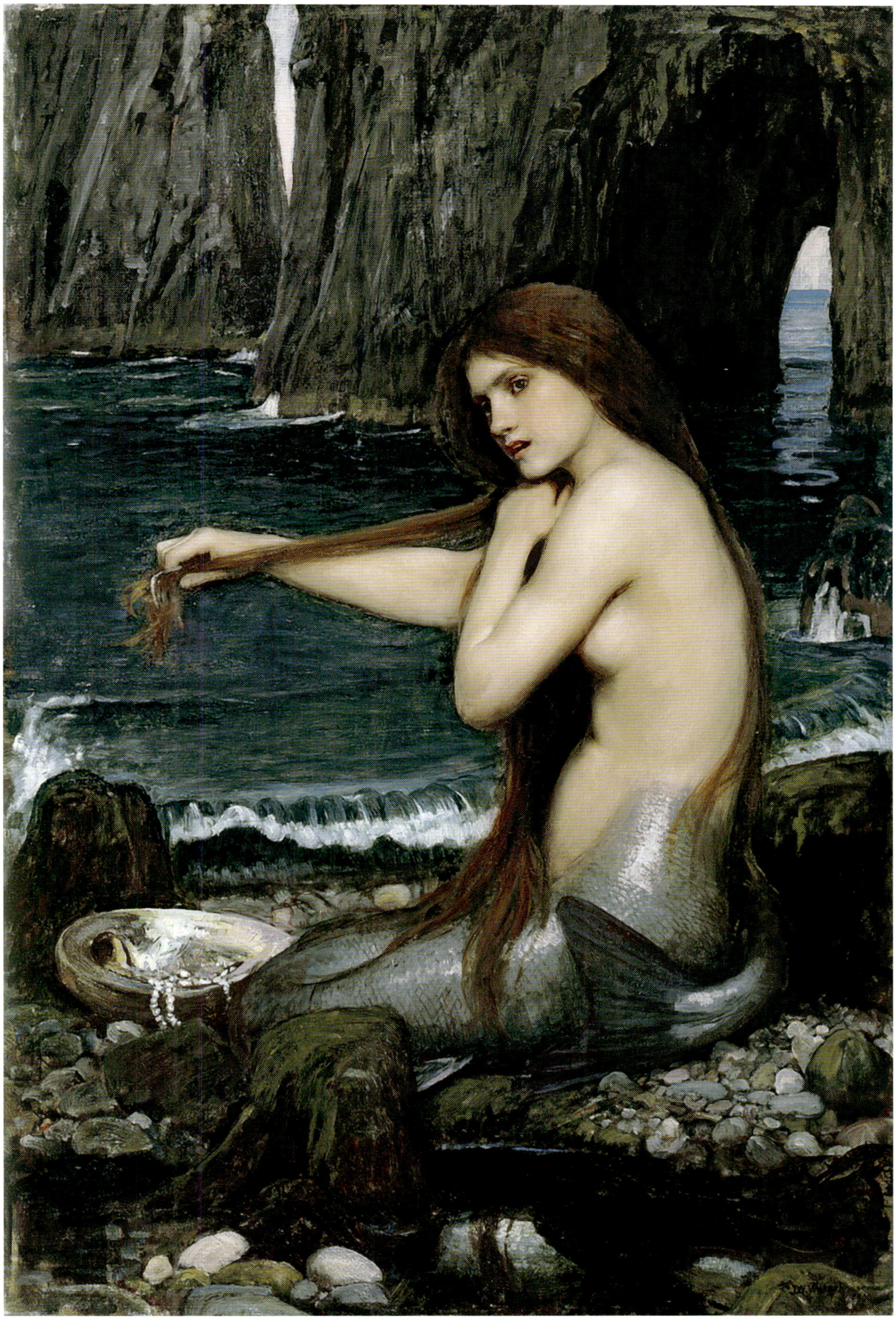

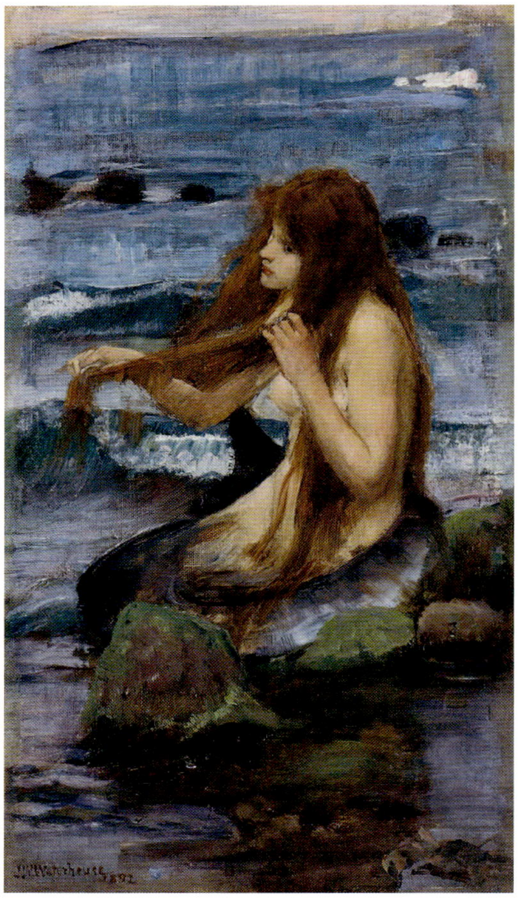

36. **A Mermaid** 1892

SKETCH - OIL ON CANVAS, 33.5 X 19.5 CM
PRIVATE COLLECTION, NEW YORK

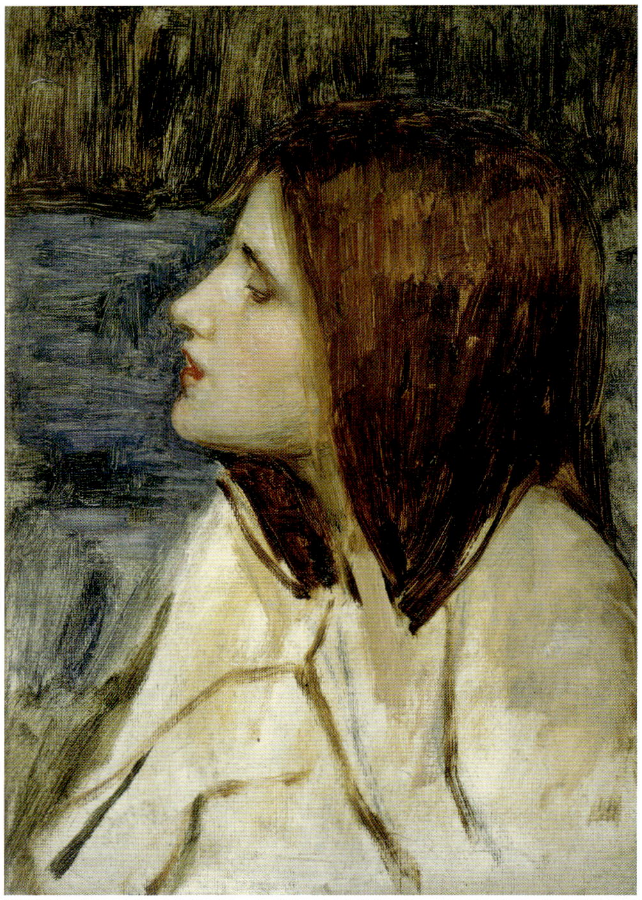

37. **Head of a Girl** c. 1892-1900

SKETCH - OIL ON CANVAS MOUNTED ON BOARD,
34.3 X 24.1 CM - PRIVATE COLLECTION, NEW YORK

In 1892 Waterhouse signed and dated a small oil sketch of a mermaid combing her hair (cat. 36). Its date confirms that this motif fascinated him for at least eight years, as it was only in 1900 that he finally completed the larger *A Mermaid* (cat. 35) as his long-overdue Diploma Work for the Royal Academy's collection. Cats 37 and 38 show Waterhouse experimenting further with the motif of a girl arranging her hair, which also informed his *La Belle Dame Sans Merci* of 1893 (cat. 28), *Ophelia* of 1894 (fig. 39), and *Hylas and the Nymphs* of 1896 (cat. 32). Indeed, the symbolic interconnections of Waterhouse's nature-women become evermore compelling as one compares their formal and compositional similarities. **PT**

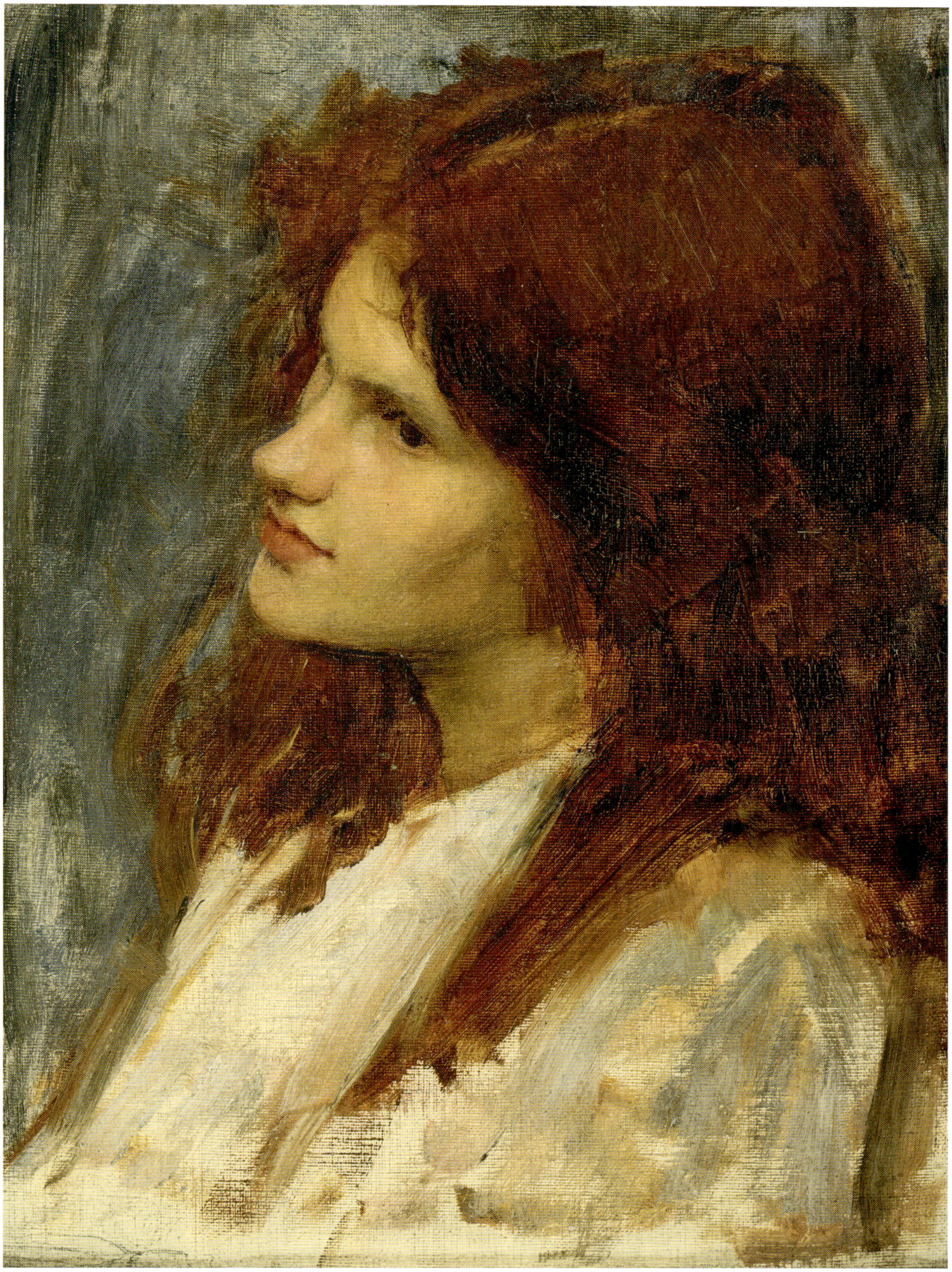

38. **Head of a Girl** c. 1892-1900

SKETCH - OIL ON CANVAS ON BOARD, 35.6 X 25.4 CM - KELLEY GALLERY, PASADENA, CALIFORNIA

39. **The Siren** c. 1900

OIL ON CANVAS, 81 X 53 CM - PRIVATE COLLECTION COURTESY OF SOTHEBY'S - SOLD BY AGNEW'S FOR THE ARTIST TO J. GRESHAM, 14 FEBRUARY 1901

Waterhouse began composing *A Mermaid* (cat. 35) as early as 1892, but did not complete that Diploma Picture until 1900, five years after it was due at the Academy. As soon as he had mastered that aesthetic challenge, he probably produced or completed *The Siren* for quick commercial sale. The mermaid has been transferred to a rock, and her bowl-like shell adapted into a lyre. Waterhouse employs the same exquisitely painted blue-green water and dark rocks to accent the girl's unearthly complexion.

Like *Ulysses and the Sirens, Circe Invidiosa*, and other major works of the 1890s, *A Mermaid* and *The Siren* reflect Waterhouse's continuing linkage of sex, death, water, and music. Yet *The Siren* differs from *A Mermaid* by actually showing – rather than suggesting – the enchanting deadliness of a hybrid fish-woman. Fish-tailed temptresses luring sailors onto rocks were common enough in his era, but Waterhouse's canvas contains several illogical features. The sailor's musculature is masculine, yet his pleading face, flowing hair, and earring convey femininity. Although the mast bobbing in the waves suggests that a ship has just sunk, the sea appears fairly calm. Finally, the Siren's mouth appears closed, inferring that her gaze has become as lethal as her song. **PT**

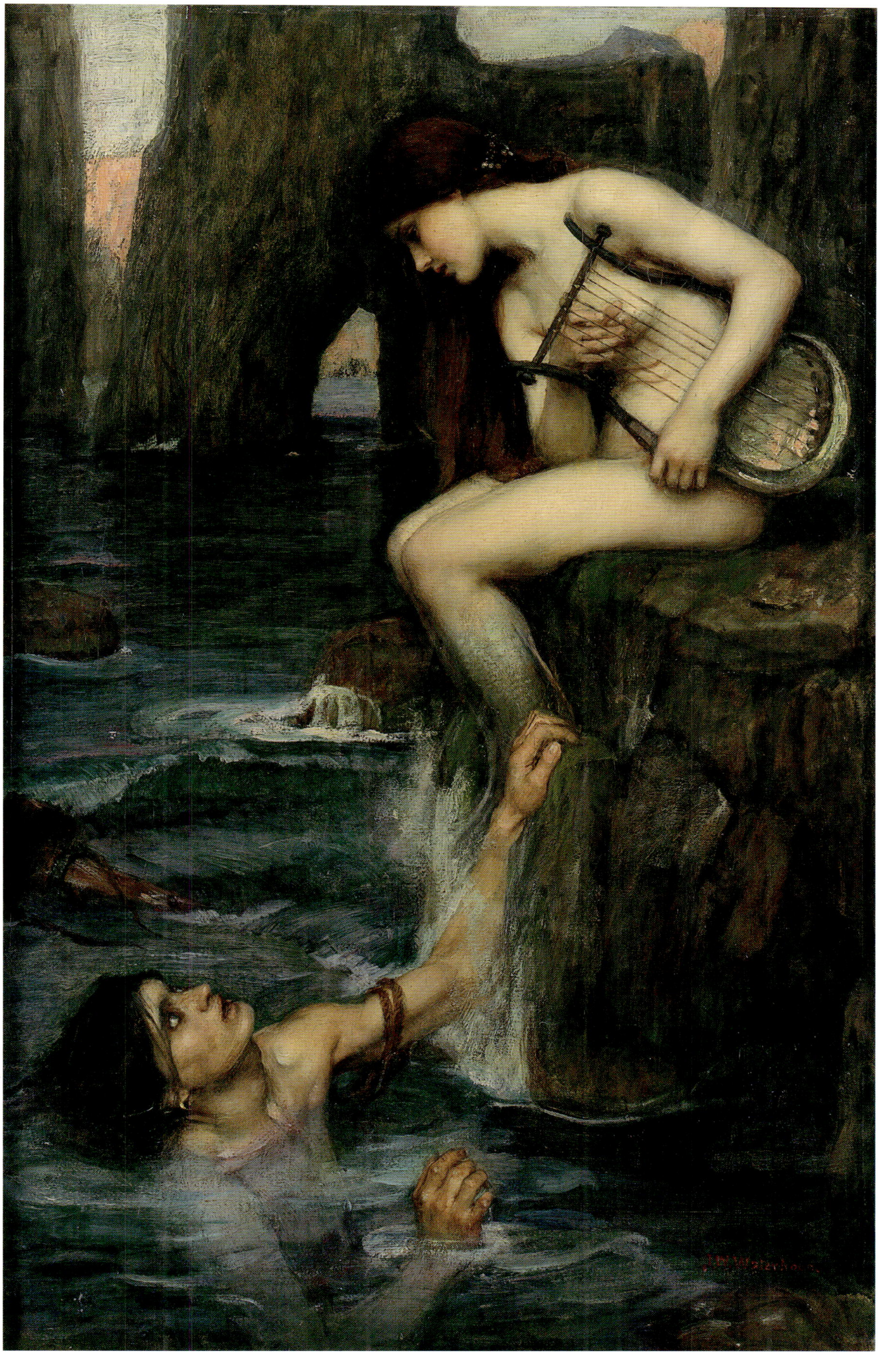

40. **Destiny** 1900

OIL ON CANVAS, 68.5 X 54.6 CM - TOWNELEY HALL, BURNLEY BOROUGH COUNCIL, PURCHASED 1906 - FIRST DONATED BY THE ARTIST TO THE EXHIBITION OF ARTISTS' WAR FUND PICTURES, 1900

Beyond its beauty, this painting demonstrates Waterhouse's prominence in England's art establishment. In 1899, Britain blundered into the Boer War against a comparatively small force of rebels in South Africa. Appalling losses generated an outburst of patriotism among British artists, and the *Magazine of Art* reported that Waterhouse himself inaugurated the Artists' War Fund to benefit the injured and widowed: 'within a very short time nearly every artist of considerable importance in the kingdom [had] associated himself with the scheme.'[1]

Ultimately, 339 painters and sculptors donated works. Waterhouse left it to his friends E.J. Poynter (President of the Royal Academy) and M.H. Spielmann (a prominent critic) – as president and honorary secretary of this initiative – to secure the patronage of Queen Victoria, whose sculptor-daughter Princess Louise opened the Exhibition of Artists' War Fund Pictures at London's Guildhall Art Gallery in January 1900. The artworks were then auctioned by Christie's, realizing more than £12,000. Waterhouse's contribution, *Destiny,* was purchased by his sometime-dealer Agnew's and sold promptly to John F. Haworth of Burnley, Lancashire, who bought at least two more Waterhouse pictures in 1903.[2]

Destiny reprises Waterhouse's favoured motif of the circular mirror, which here reveals departing ships, towards which the maiden raises her cup in valediction. The artist has cleverly compressed columns, a battlement, a stream, the sea, and a tessellated floor into a grid in which the figure seems enmeshed. Watching sailors undertake adventure, this woman stays behind, alone and girdled like the Lady of Shalott (cats. 30, 60). Waterhouse probably intended the gold paint decorating the globe and galleons' flags to endow a historicist effect and remind viewers of South Africa's gold mines. The red gown and blue cup mimic the Union Jack, suggesting that Waterhouse intended the lady to personify Britain, if not the very notion of Destiny. Other attributes of Britain include the globe it dominated in 1900, what seems to be a Bible, and galleons evoking those that defeated the Spanish Armada in 1588.

Given Waterhouse's relative invisibility in his colleagues' written correspondence, it is intriguing that he took such a leadership role in the Artists' War Fund. Moreover, at exactly the same time, he volunteered to design one of twelve *tableaux vivants* for *A Dream of Fair Women,* an elaborate entertainment directed by the renowned actor-manager Herbert Beerbohm Tree at Her Majesty's Theatre. Presented there on 13 February 1900 in aid of those who had lost family members in the war, this 'masque of war and peace' featured music conducted by Arthur Sullivan and also enjoyed Queen Victoria's patronage.[3]

There is further evidence that Waterhouse supported Britain's proactive role in the world. In 1911 his best friend, the poet-landscapist Peregrine M. Feeney (1837-1913), published a volume that contains panegyrics to various conservative heroes, including Thomas Carlyle, the explorer David Livingstone and journalist Henry Stanley, and British forces in the infamous 'Rorke's Drift' battle in South Africa (1879). Feeney's volume also includes 'A Call to Arms: The Election, December 1910', which urges readers to rise for 'King and Constitution' against the Liberal government.[4] Waterhouse's friendship with Feeney suggests that he may have shared such right-wing views, as did his artist-friends Frank Bramley and George Frampton.

All of these associations further encourage the reading of *Destiny* as an imperialist image, albeit a very beautiful one. **PT**

1 *Magazine of Art,* vol. 23, Feb 1900, p. 188, and Guildhall Library, Pamphlet 5343, 'The Artists' War Fund, 1900, Catalogue of the Exhibition'.

2 Haworth also bought *Zephyrs* (Hobson 1980 checklist no. 122) and *March Winds* (145). His daughter Mary married the 2nd Lord Hayter; they owned *Mariana in the South, Juliet* (1898), and the 1894 *Ophelia.*

3 Advertisement in *The Times,* 3 Feb 1900, p. 10. Other tableaux were arranged by G.H. Boughton, Ernest Crofts, Edward Onslow Ford, Frederick Goodall, Solomon J. Solomon, J.J. Shannon, and J.M. Swan. Unfortunately, the commemorative programme contains no scenic design drawings or photographs.

4 P.M. Feeney, *Verses in Various Moods* (London: T. Fisher Unwin for private circulation only, April 1911).

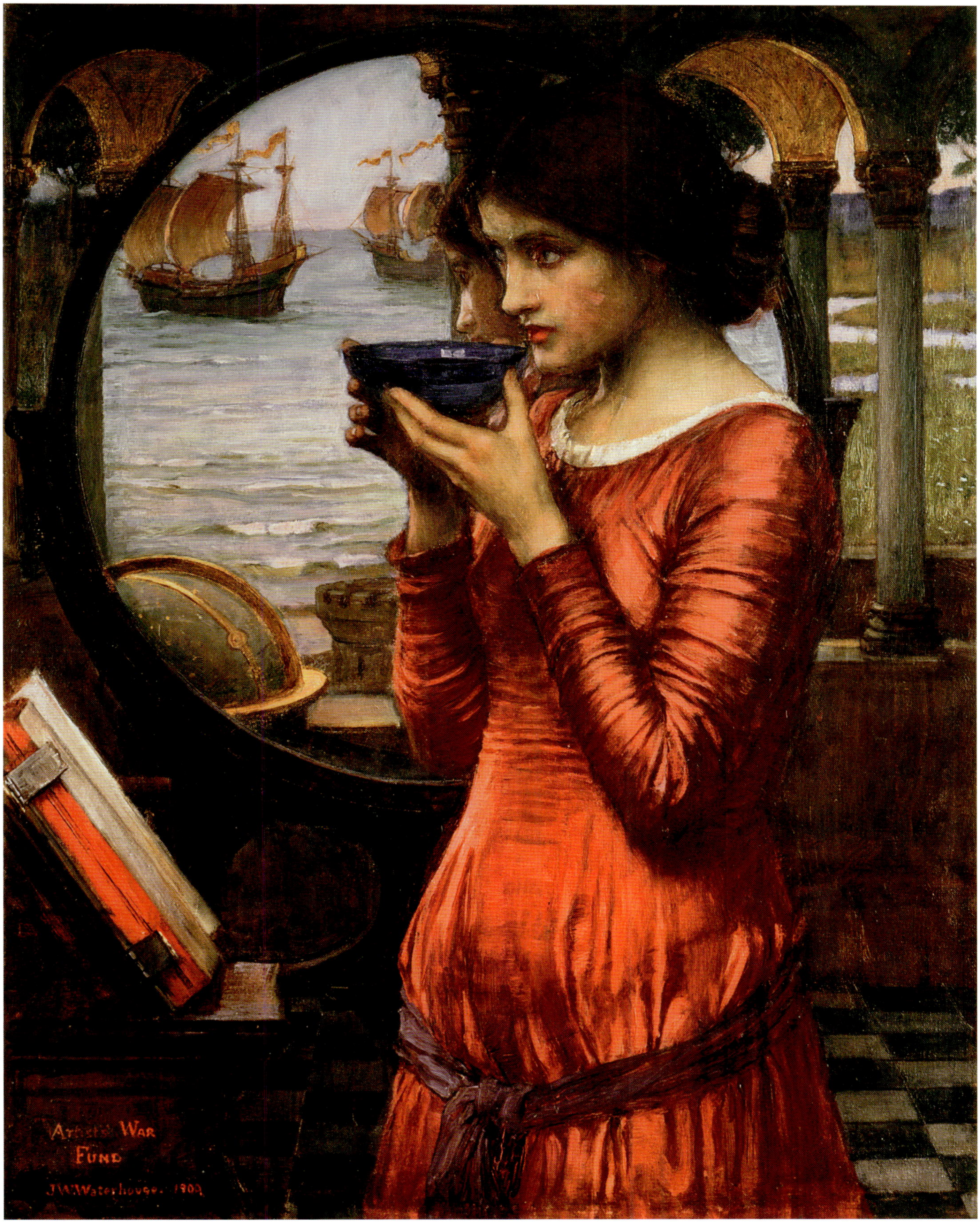
Artists' War
Fund

41. Nymphs Finding the Head of Orpheus 1900

OIL ON CANVAS, 149 X 99 CM - COLLECTION SIR TIM RICE - EXHIBITED ROYAL ACADEMY, 1901

The musician Orpheus is the quintessential hero of the mythological tradition for epitomising both the power and the tragedy of creative art. His song is victorious over the Sirens, beasts, stones, and even mortality; when he plays to Pluto and Proserpina they release his dead wife, Eurydice, from the underworld. But Eurydice is lost again, when he cannot resist the temptation to look back at her, and Orpheus himself is finally dismembered by maenads, maddened in their Bacchanalian rites. Even then, his severed head and his lyre continue to make music as they float downriver to the sea. Little wonder that the figure of Orpheus has been a favourite with artists, writers, and composers throughout the Western tradition. Artists of the Symbolist generation in the later nineteenth century took up the story's suggestion of the misunderstood artist or *poète maudit*, and in particular the image of Orpheus's severed head and lyre, which appears in haunting works by such artists as Gustave Moreau (fig. 42), Odilon Redon (fig. 43), and Gustav Klimt. Orpheus's journey to the underworld and the magic power of his song are also central elements in the occult tradition, and the Orphic mystery religions were a special focus of Jane Harrison's scholarship, explored at length in her *Prolegomena to the Study of Greek Religion* of 1903. Waterhouse draws on the final stages of Orpheus's story, as told in Ovid's *Metamorphoses*, Book XI, but invents his own ending: the head and lyre, floating in deep green water, are discovered by two of the naiads who inhabit the forests of Waterhouse's own later work. The pool of water perhaps represents a route to the underworld, and the head is livid in death, yet also feminine in its delicate features and long red hair, waving in the water and twining with the strings of the lyre. The nymphs' wondering glances suggest innocence, but viewers familiar with the *Metamorphoses* might be reminded, chillingly, of the maenads who have torn him limb from limb. **EP**

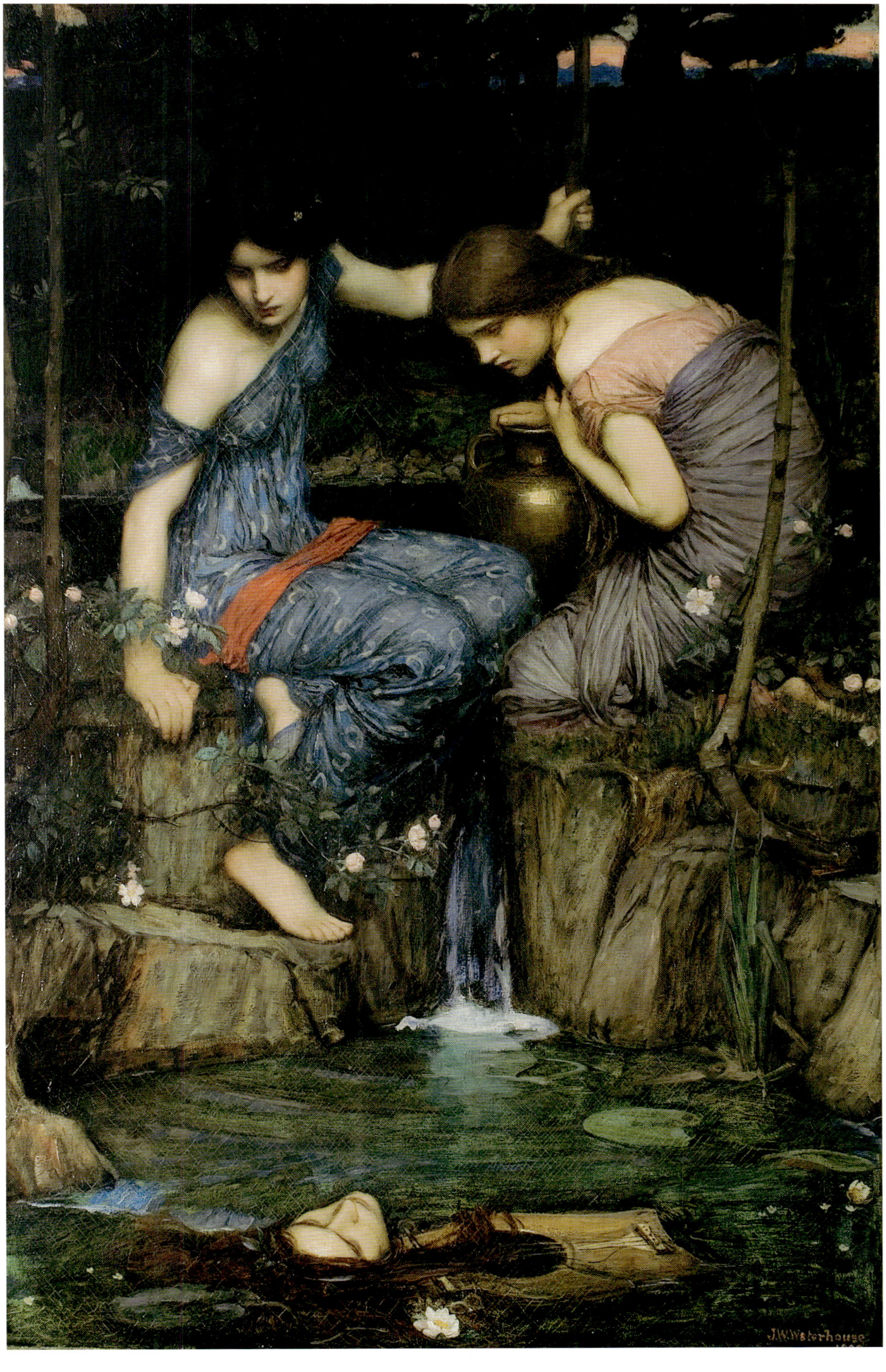
J.W. Waterhouse

42. Windflowers 1902

OIL ON CANVAS, 114 X 79 CM - PRIVATE COLLECTION - EXHIBITED ROYAL ACADEMY, 1903

Like many works of Waterhouse's later years, *Windflowers* has no overt mythological subject; the title refers simply to the anemones that the figure has been gathering. However, the painting continues the interest in nature imagery that had begun in the 1890s, now, as in a number of paintings of the early twentieth century, developed to show the effects of the winds on flowery landscapes and intricately folded draperies. The title of a contemporary work, *Boreas* of 1903 (private collection), refers to the mythological god of the north wind, not seen in the painting except by implication, as the wind that disturbs the draperies of the female figure, who closely resembles the figure in the present painting. Perhaps the omission of a mythological reference, in the title *Windflowers*, is meant to generalise and universalise the theme; the full-length figure with her billowing draperies and flying hair is one of Waterhouse's most striking inventions. But the painting may also include a secret, or at least oblique, reference to the myth of Proserpina, which according to Rose Sketchley's article of 1909 held special significance for the artist. The anemones are spring flowers, one of the kinds that bloomed in the vale of Enna when Proserpina was swept to the underworld; according to Sketchley, the 'blended hues' of the anemone, in the legend, 'show an origin in spiritual and mortal earth'.[1] The figure may, then, be one of the numerous surrogates for Proserpina that appear throughout Waterhouse's later work (see p. 32). **EP**

1 R.E.D. Sketchley, *The Art of J.W. Waterhouse, R.A.*, Christmas Number of *The Art Journal*, 1909, p. 23.

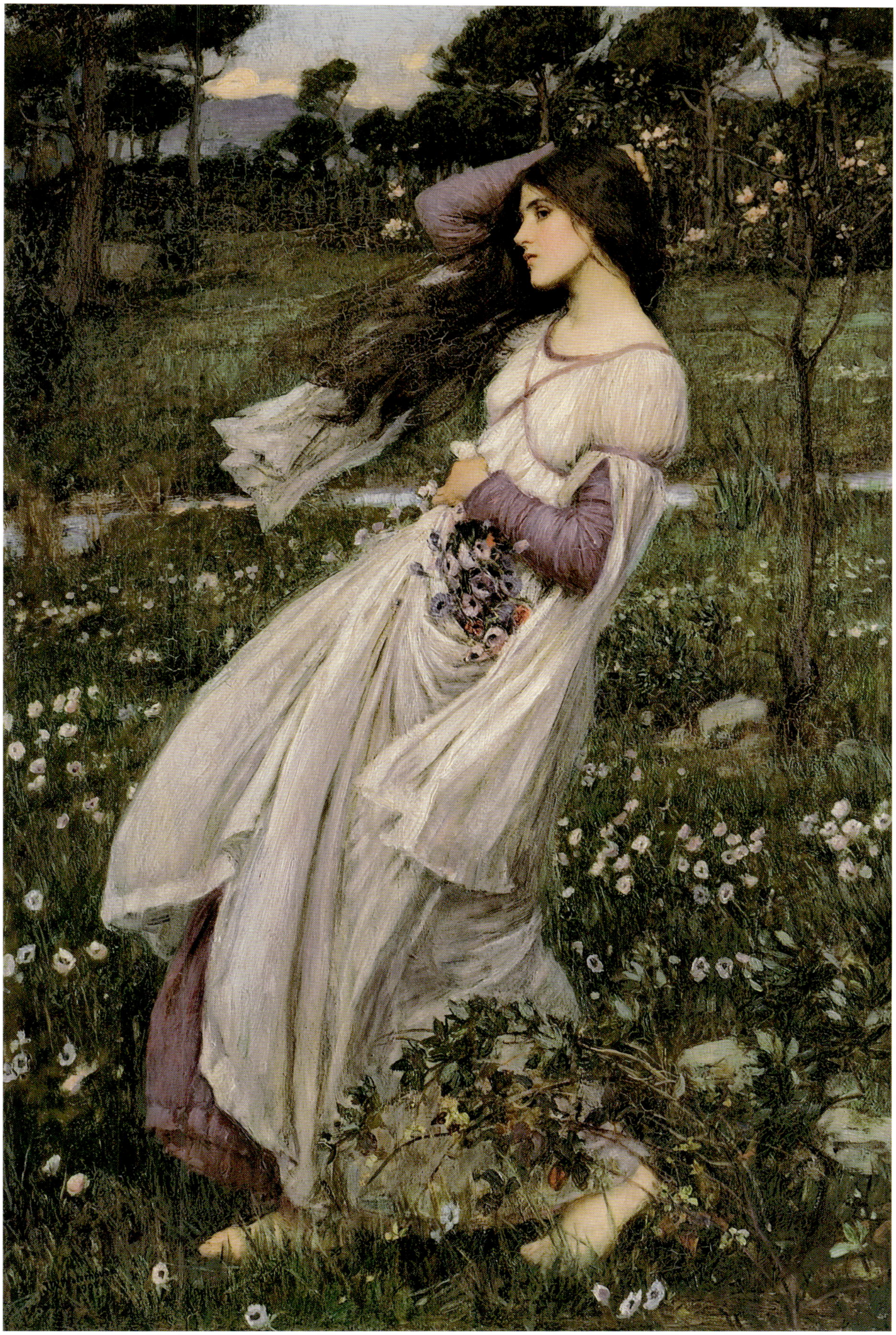

43. Echo and Narcissus 1903

OIL ON CANVAS, 109.2 X 189.2 CM - WALKER ART GALLERY, NATIONAL MUSEUMS LIVERPOOL, PURCHASED 1903 - EXHIBITED ROYAL ACADEMY, 1903

The myth of Narcissus, the beautiful youth who falls in love with his own reflection in a pool of water, has been a favourite with artists since antiquity. Narcissus's reflection can serve as a metaphor for representational art, demonstrating the powerful attraction of mimetic images; the Greek writer Philostratus even called Narcissus the inventor of the art of painting. In the primary ancient telling of the myth, Ovid's *Metamorphoses*, Book III, Narcissus becomes like a marble statue, transfixed as he gazes at his reflection. Waterhouse follows Ovid by introducing the related myth of Echo, the nymph who loves Narcissus in vain. The composition is one of the artist's deceptively simple inventions: we grasp the entire narrative in a glimpse, yet its ramifications unfold as we reflect on the scene. The prostrate, foreshortened pose of Narcissus gives us a clear view both of the whole of his lithe body and of the reflection of his head, shoulders, and hands in the pool (for a sketchbook drawing in which Waterhouse explores this pose, see cat. 96). Echo sits nearby, yet fails to make contact; Waterhouse was a master of this kind of compositional relationship, seen for example in *The Favourites of the Emperor Honorius* (cat. 12), where figures are physically contiguous yet psychologically distant. This emphasises the poignancy of the story of double unattainable loves: Echo can never attract Narcissus's attention, just as Narcissus can never achieve union with his beloved reflection. Moreover, the myth has further resonances. Narcissus, pining for his unrealisable love, is transformed into the flower that bears his name, which appears on the right edge of the canvas, next to the youth's bare foot. This flower is also associated with the myth of Proserpina, which according to Rose Sketchley's article of 1909 was particularly important to the artist (see p. 32); the deep, dark pool into which Narcissus gazes is, like the pool in *Hylas and the Nymphs* (cat. 32) and the flowery vale of the story of Proserpina, a route into the underworld. The landscape, as in other paintings of this period, is an English woodland, with a prominent oak and a stream winding into the distance. Thus the composition, straightforward as it appears on first glance, draws together many of Waterhouse's special concerns in the later phase of his career. Just a few years later, in his essay of 1910 on Leonardo da Vinci and in 'On Narcissism' of 1914, Sigmund Freud would develop his psychoanalytic interpretation of the myth of Narcissus. Already, though, in Waterhouse's painting of 1903 the complexities of unsatisfied desire are vividly imagined, for example in the futile gesture of Narcissus's right hand, unable to touch the beloved image, or the unease of Echo's pose, precariously balanced on the rocky ledge, and forever separated from her beloved across the dark pool. **EP**

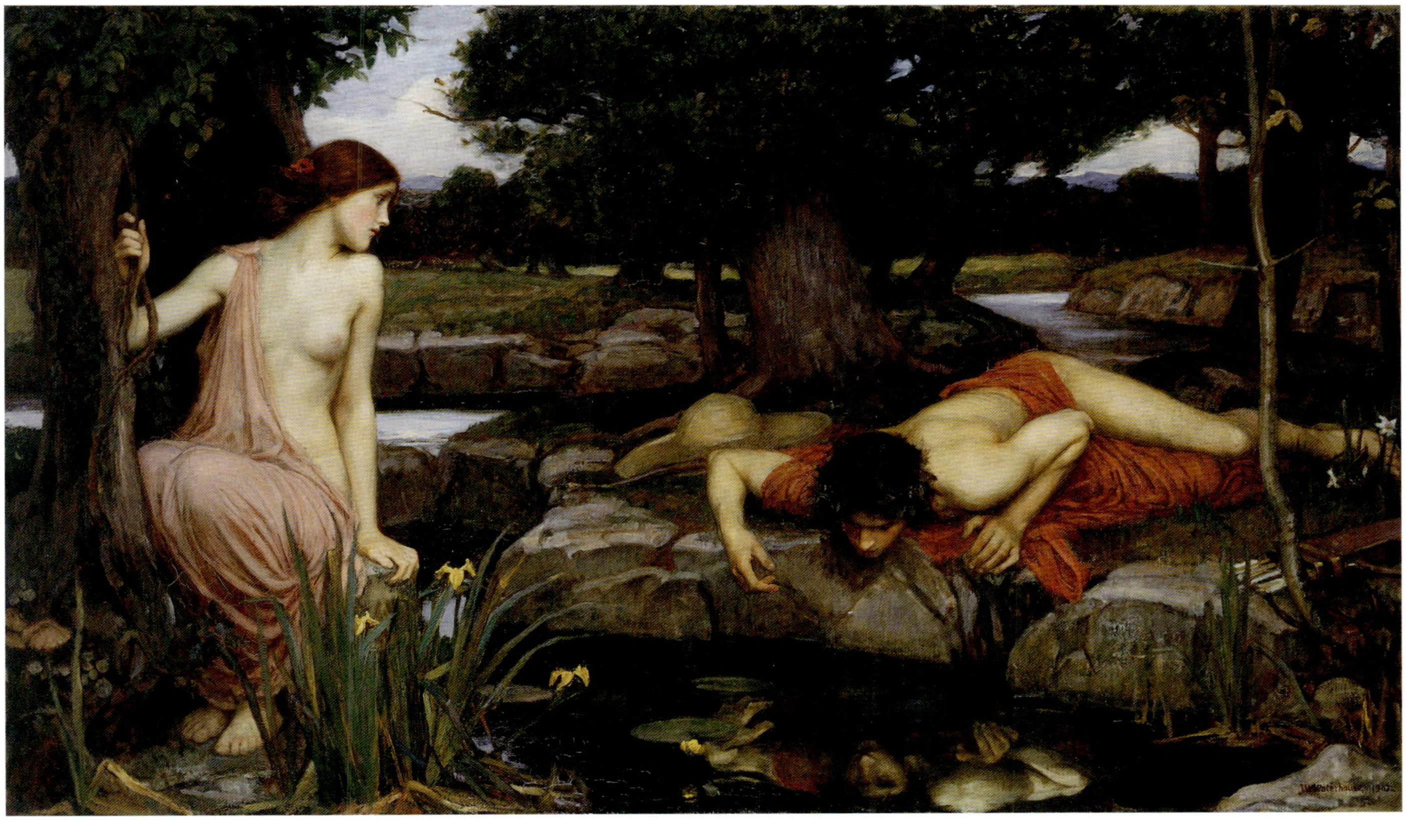

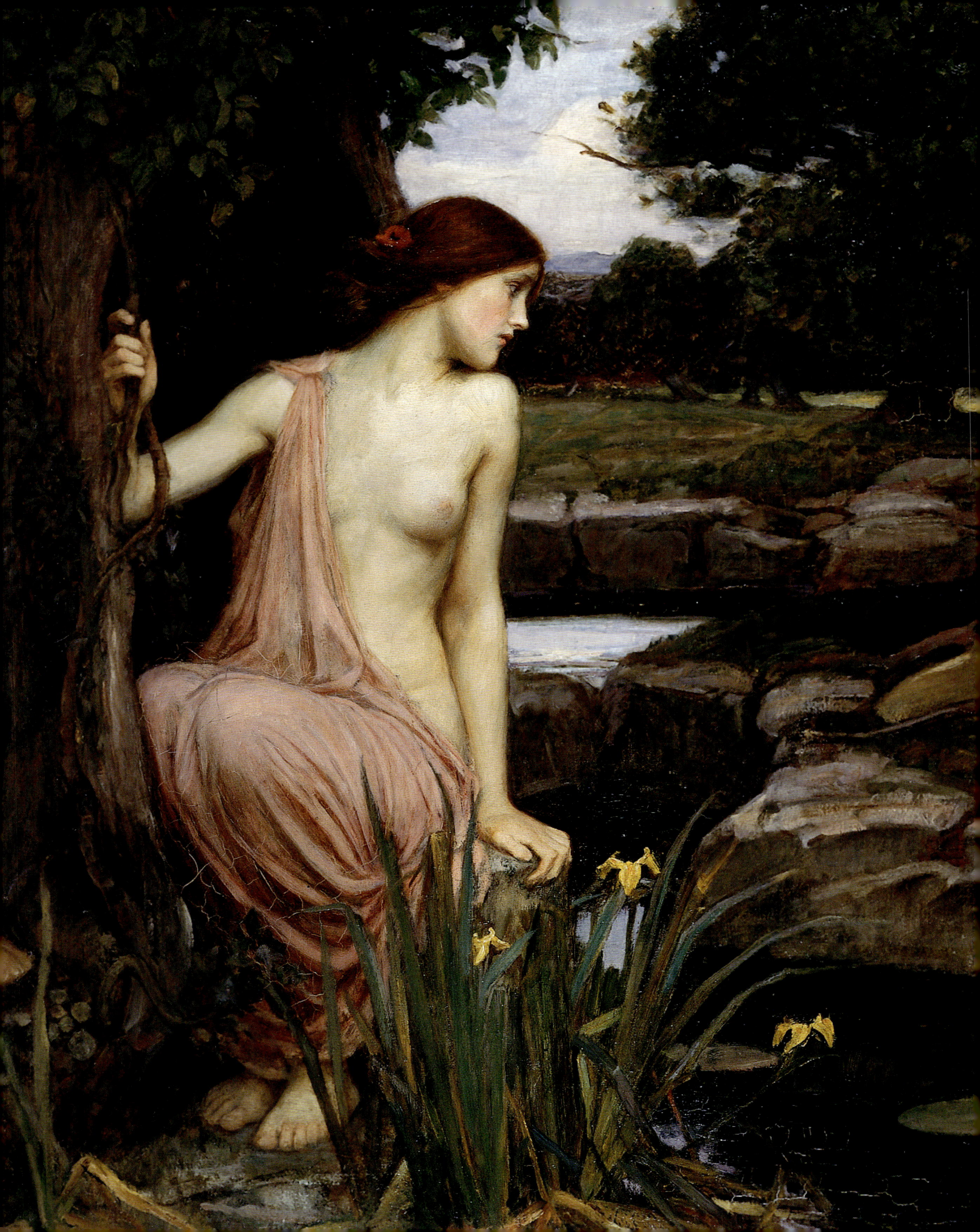

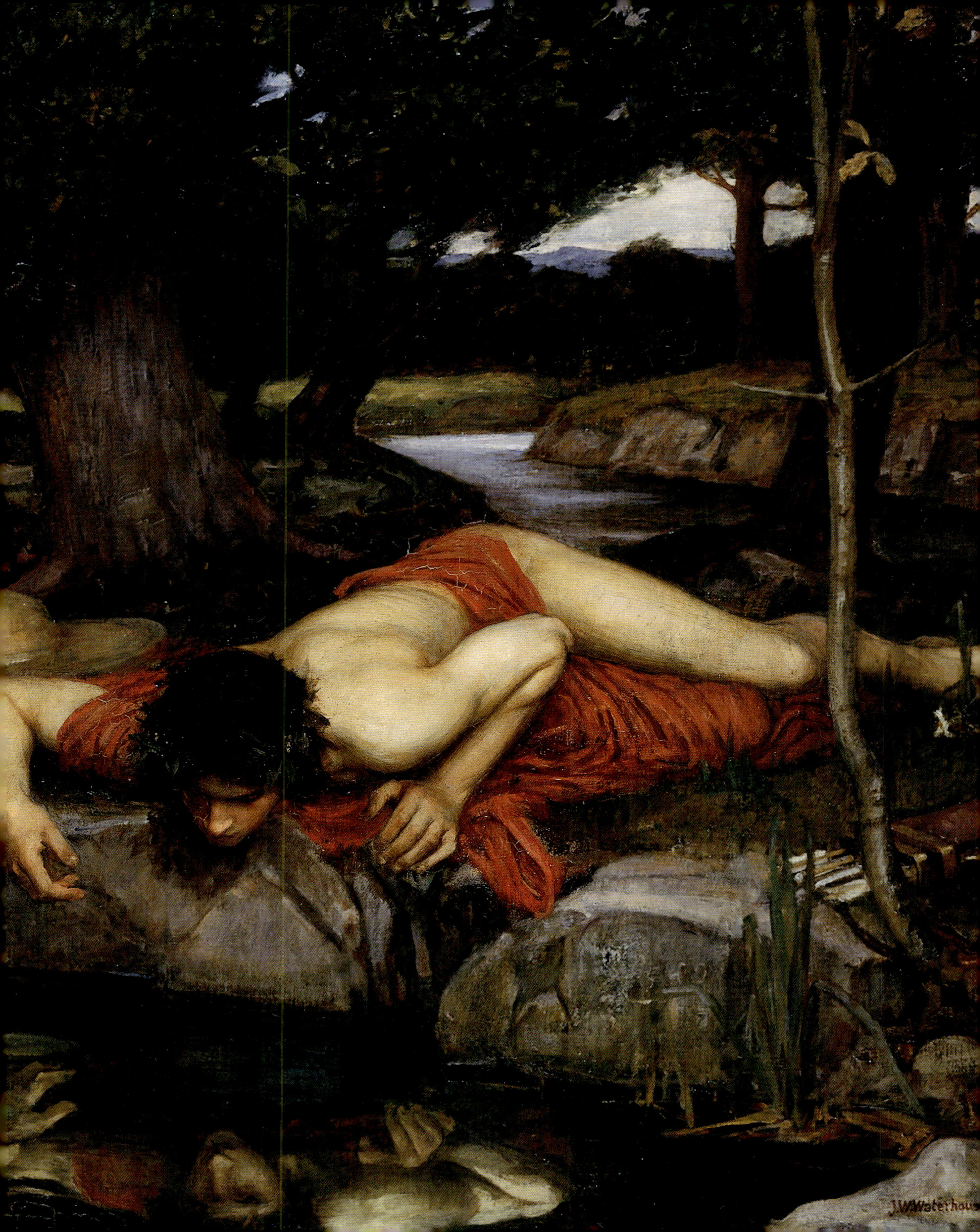
J.W.Waterhous

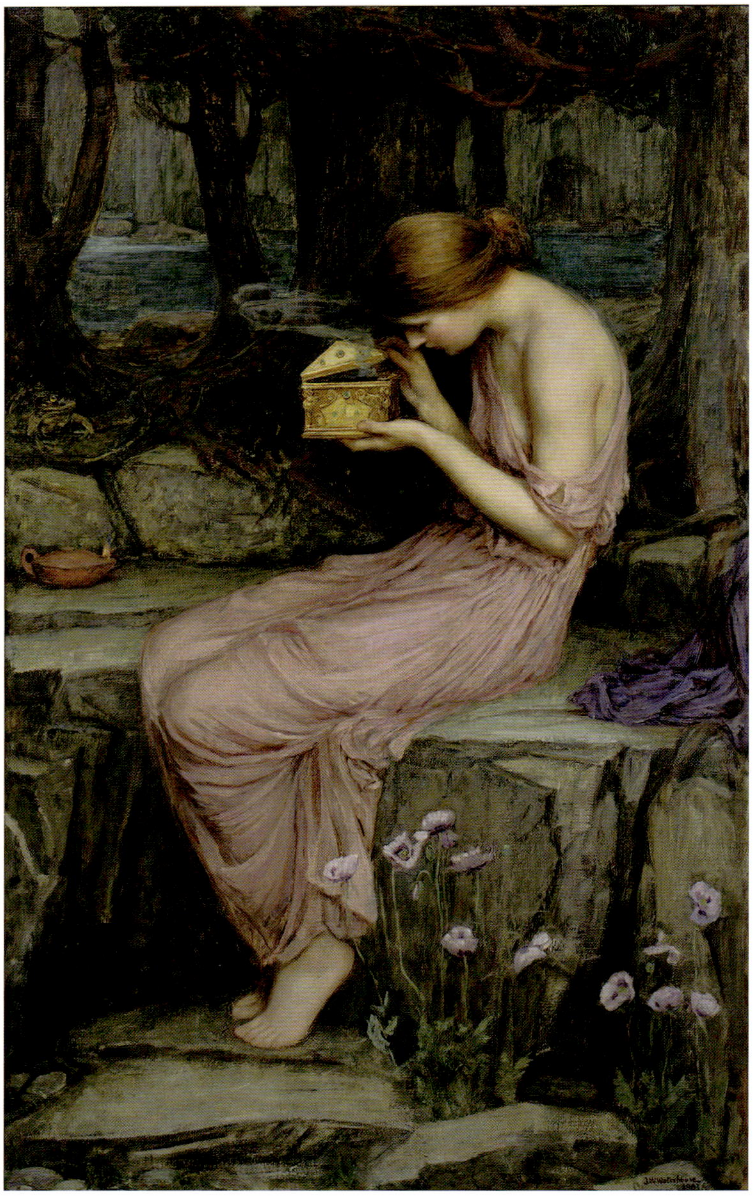

44. Psyche Opening the Golden Box 1903

OIL ON CANVAS, 117 X 74 CM - PRIVATE COLLECTION COURTESY OF CHRISTIE'S - EXHIBITED ROYAL ACADEMY, 1903

Psyche's quest to gain the love of Cupid, recounted in the *Metamorphoses* (or *Golden Ass*), a novel of the second century A.D. by the Latin author Apuleius, had already attracted the attention of William Morris, who included it among the narrative poems of his *Earthly Paradise* of 1868-1870; Edward Burne-Jones, who made a number of paintings based on Morris's narrative; and Walter Pater, who incorporated a translation of Apuleius's Latin text into his novel of 1885, *Marius the Epicurean*. Waterhouse's paintings are fascinating examples of his reworkings of earlier Pre-Raphaelite imagery in the later phase of his career, but he develops his own distinctive interpretation of the myth. His two paintings, exhibited in successive Royal Academy exhibitions, show parallel scenes from different stages of the narrative, both of which emphasise Psyche's discoveries of the unknown as she pursues her quest. The painting exhibited a year later, *Psyche Opening the Door into Cupid's Garden* (cat. 45), in fact shows the earlier episode from the narrative. Psyche, doomed to marry a terrifying monster, has been spirited away by Zephyr, the god of the west wind; she wakes to find herself (although she does not yet know it) at the entrance to Cupid's domain and, with

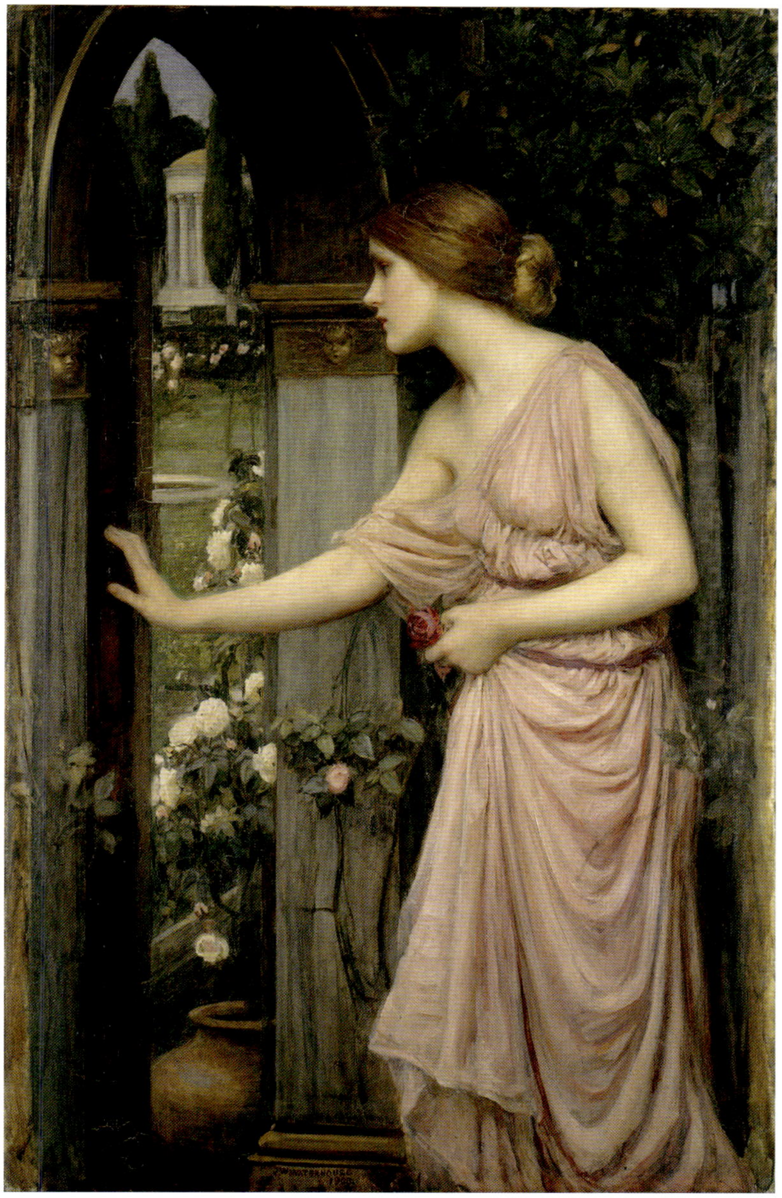

45. Psyche Opening the Door into Cupid's Garden 1903

OIL ON CANVAS, 109.5 X 72 CM - HARRIS MUSEUM AND ART GALLERY, PRESTON, PURCHASED 1908 - EXHIBITED ROYAL ACADEMY, 1904

curiosity overcoming trepidation, pushes open the door. The painting gives a tantalising glimpse into an enchanted world beyond the door, a classical garden abounding in the roses of love; at the very end of his life Waterhouse would paint another enchanted garden, this time drawn from a story by Boccaccio (cat. 66). *Psyche Opening the Golden Box* (cat. 44) shows a scene near the end of the narrative. After many vicissitudes, Psyche has been commanded to journey to the underworld with a golden casket, which Proserpina fills with a secret charm for eternal beauty; Psyche is forbidden to open the casket, but cannot resist the temptation. Thus the story involves familiar themes in Waterhouse's work, and in the occult tradition: the journey to the underworld, an encounter with Proserpina, and defiance of the gods. The story parallels that of Orpheus, unable to resist the temptation of looking back at Eurydice, but this time there is a happy ending: after opening the box, Psyche will fall into a deathly slumber, but Cupid will rescue her. *Psyche Opening the Golden Box* is also a parallel subject to *Pandora* (which Waterhouse painted in 1896, fig. 14): both women defy the instructions of the gods, to open boxes that contain secrets forbidden to mortals. **EP**

46. Lamia 1905

OIL ON CANVAS, 146 X 90.2 CM - PRIVATE COLLECTION - EXHIBITED ROYAL ACADEMY, 1905

Waterhouse was clearly fascinated by the thrilling dangers of love and beauty, epitomised by the singing *femmes fatales* of John Keats. In 1893, he exhibited his vision of Keats's *La Belle Dame Sans Merci* (cat. 28), and this Romantic poet surfaced again in 1905, when Waterhouse sent to the Royal Academy this first *Lamia*. Here a different armoured knight in a darkened wood, Lycius, gazes down into the eyes of a slightly older red-haired temptress.

In Greek myth, after Lamia's children were killed by the goddess Hera, she sought vengeance by sucking the blood of men she seduced and devouring children; her name means 'she who swallows up'. In his 1819 retelling, Keats describes how the god Hermes facilitates the metamorphosis of an iridescent snake, with a 'Circean' head of glinting eyes and teeth, into a beautiful woman who remains coldblooded. Waterhouse's *Lamia* entrances with her gaze, touch, and 'song of love, too sweet for earthly lyres'.

Keats never explicitly brands this animal-woman as evil, celebrating instead her beauty and the sensual exhilaration she offers. Ultimately, Lamia is defeated by the stare of Lycius's wise old tutor; his interference epitomises the triumph of science over beauty and imagination, regretted by Keats and other Romantics, and surely by Waterhouse. Lycius's armoured foot reads as the tail of Lamia, whose coiling drapery, patterned like the brilliantly hued scales she has shed, contrasts with her pale advancing arms. Keats set his story in classical Corinth, but Waterhouse transposed it to the Middle Ages so that he could show the armour signifying male containment.

In his long career, Waterhouse painted multiple treatments of only six themes: The Lady of Shalott, Ophelia, Circe, Psyche, Miranda, and Lamia. It is telling that all are women whose stories feature passionate transitions from one state of being to another. Waterhouse seems to have made three additional versions of this *Lamia,* all measuring between 142 and 146 cm high – quite large within his oeuvre. He may have felt encouraged to do so given the prestige of this picture's first owner – Sir Alexander Henderson (later first Baron Faringdon, 1850-1934), who acquired it during its inaugural appearance at the Academy, and whose extended family were Waterhouse's most enthusiastic patrons.

The collapse of Waterhouse's reputation within 25 years of his death is underscored by the fact that this painting was sold unrecognized at Christie's on 18 September 1942. As lot 110, it was described merely as 'A maiden kneeling before a knight in armour in a wood'. **PT**

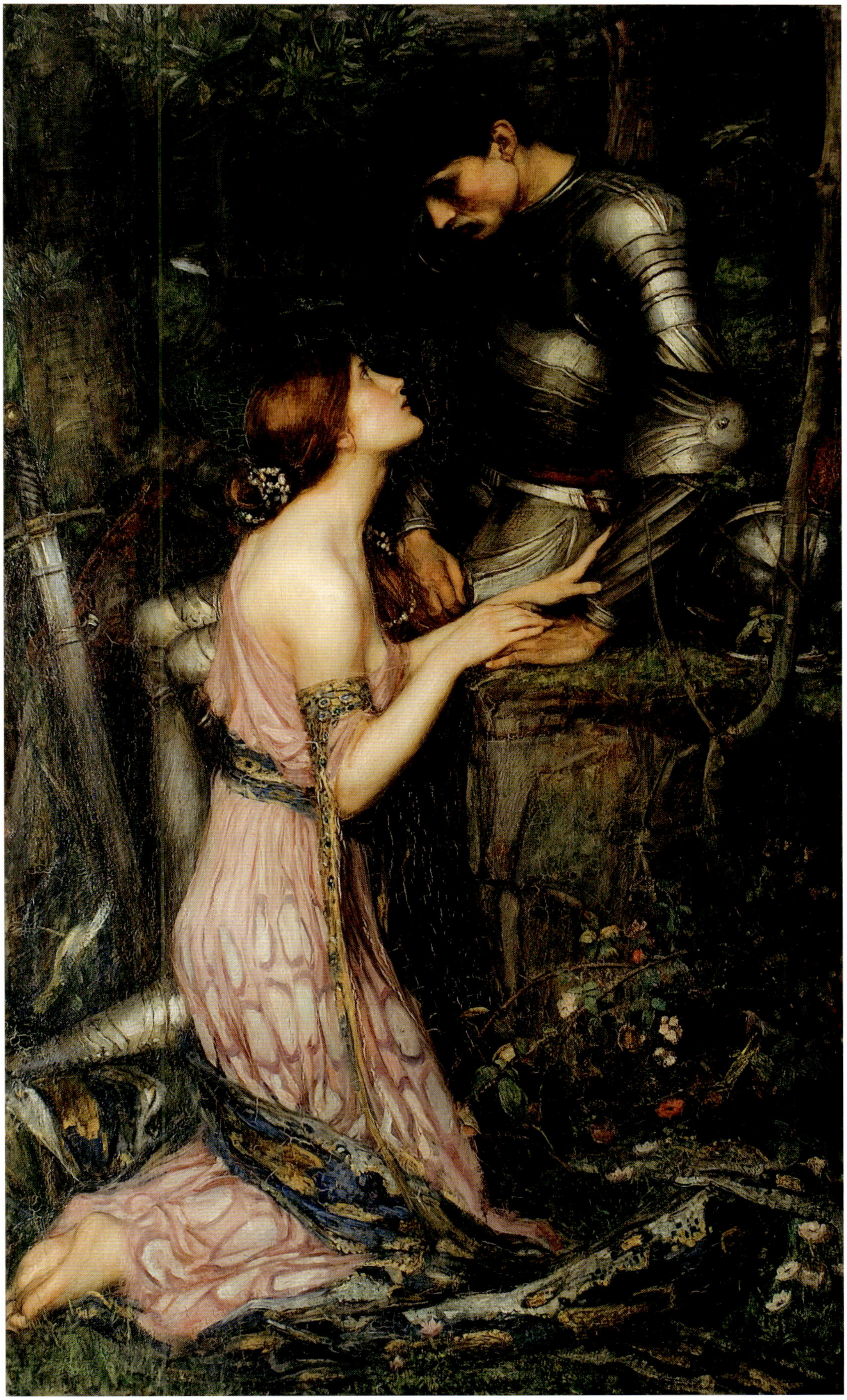

47. The Danaïdes 1906

OIL ON CANVAS, 163.3 X 128 CM - ABERDEEN ART GALLERY AND MUSEUMS, PURCHASED 1927 - EXHIBITED ROYAL ACADEMY, 1906

Many of Waterhouse's mythological paintings refer obliquely to the underworld, or represent figures who journeyed there and back (Ulysses, Orpheus, Psyche, Dante). Here he takes his viewers on a journey to the underworld itself, a barren, rocky landscape, where we see figures often glimpsed by travellers to the underworld in Latin texts: the daughters of Danaus, or Danaïdes. Their earthly crime had been to murder each of their husbands on their collective wedding night; thus they are doomed, for all eternity, to pour water into a perpetually leaking vessel. The punishment of the Danaïdes may have been a late addition to their myth, something explored in considerable detail in Jane Harrison's discussion, part of her treatment of Orphic mysteries in her major work, *Prolegomena to the Study of Greek Religion*, published in 1903, shortly before Waterhouse's painting.[1] In ancient texts the Danaïdes number 50; Waterhouse represents seven of them, the same magic number as his Sirens (cat. 22) and nymphs (cat. 32), in a circling procession that suggests the endlessness of their task. The sombre tones of the draperies and the earthy hues of the barren rocks provide a subdued backdrop for the pearly skin-tones of the women, and their burnished vases. Indeed the vases, one for each figure, bring to mind the severed heads of their husbands; in *Nymphs Finding the Head of Orpheus* of 1900 (cat. 41), a similar burnished vase corresponds to the single severed head. **EP**

1 Jane Ellen Harrison, *Prolegomena to the Study of Greek Religion*, Cambridge University Press, 1903, pp. 614-624. A slightly smaller version of the subject, with only five figures, is dated 1904, but seems not to have been exhibited (Collection Lord Lloyd Webber).

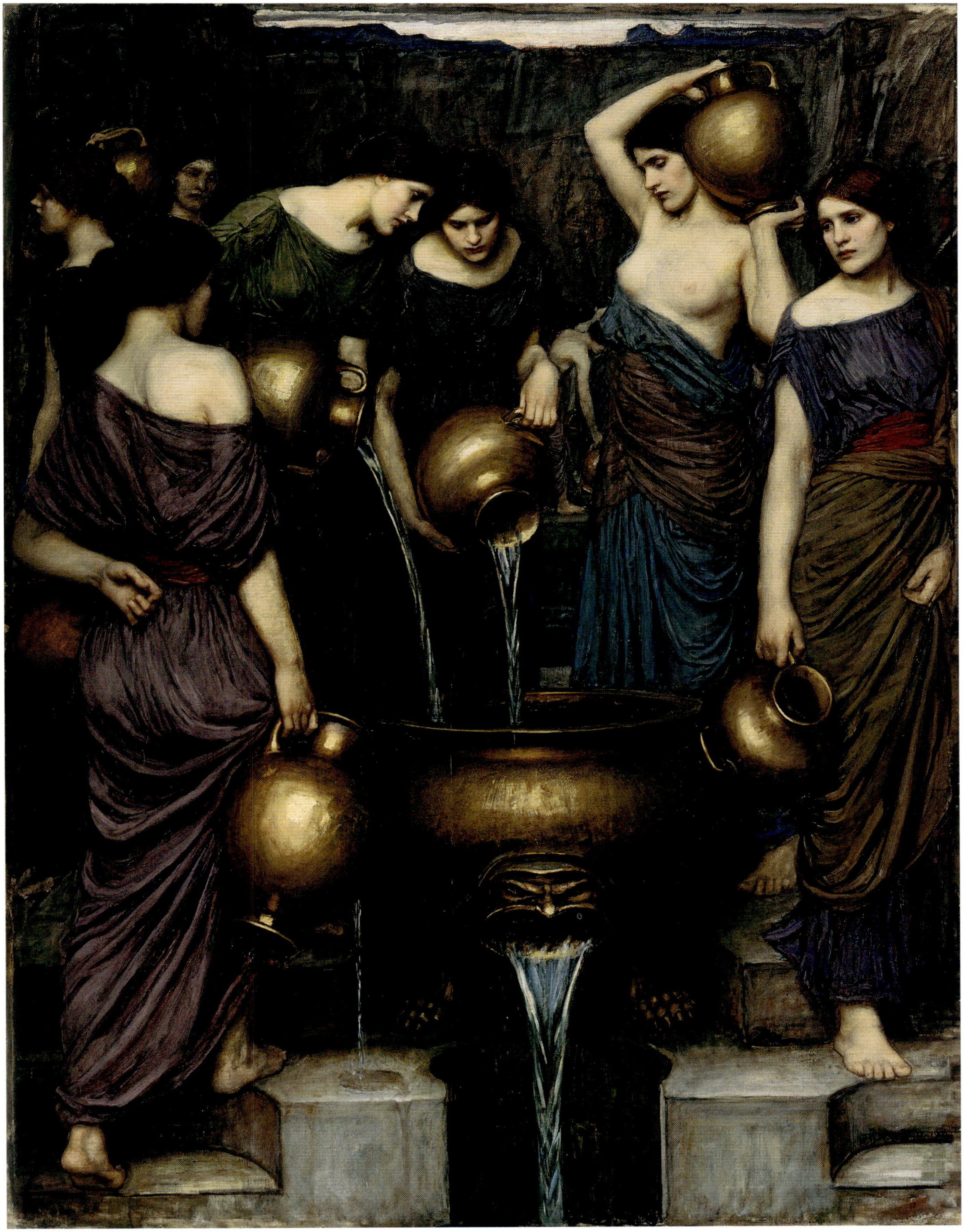

48. Jason and Medea 1907

OIL ON CANVAS, 134 X 107 CM - THE ROB DICKINS COLLECTION COURTESY OF CHRISTIE'S - EXHIBITED ROYAL ACADEMY, 1907

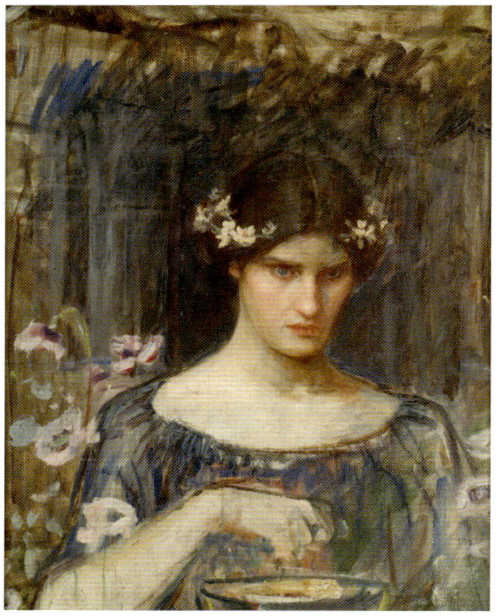

49. **Medea** c. 1906-1907

SKETCH - OIL ON CANVAS, 61 X 53 CM - COLLECTION STEPHEN AND LINDA WATERHOUSE

Medea is a common subject in Western art, often portrayed in the sensational act of murdering her children in revenge for Jason's infidelity, the event around which the Greek tragedy of Euripides is centred. Waterhouse portrays her, instead, in her character as wise sorceress, the niece of Circe who, like her aunt, may offer instruction to a man she favours. Here she is seen mixing a potion for Jason, leader of the Argonauts, charged with retrieving the Golden Fleece from Colchis, where Medea's father reigns. As so often in Waterhouse's work, the scene does not correspond precisely to one in an ancient literary source, but it conflates elements of the story as it is found in Ovid's *Metamorphoses*, Book VII, and the Greek epic *Argonautica* by Apollonius of Rhodes; William Morris's long narrative poem of 1867, *The Life and Death of Jason*, retells the story in English. In these sources, Medea goes alone, deep into the forest, to mix a potion which she then brings to Jason's bedchamber; the potion will anoint him against the fire-breathing bulls and earth-born army, which he must overcome in his quest for the Golden Fleece. By combining the two episodes, Waterhouse devises one of his typically effective pictorial narratives, legible at a glance yet psychologically complex. This is the first significant encounter between Jason and Medea, a parallel scene to *Circe Offering the Cup to Ulysses* (cat. 21), and sketchbook drawings show that he experimented with different alternatives for grouping the two figures. Waterhouse also made a full-scale oil sketch for the upper body of Medea (cat. 49), different in colouring from the final painting; the gesture and the surrounding foliage are roughly indicated, and the artist seems to have used the sketch to study the expression of Medea's face, absorbed in her task yet with a troubled stare. Already at this juncture, in the literary sources, she fears that Jason will betray her. Jason's complex pose, grasping his spear with both hands as he gazes intently at Medea, suggests his dependence on her magic powers at this point in the narrative. Despite their proximity, the two figures are not quite in accord, and their eyes fail to meet, perhaps a warning of the tragic dénouement of their love. **EP**

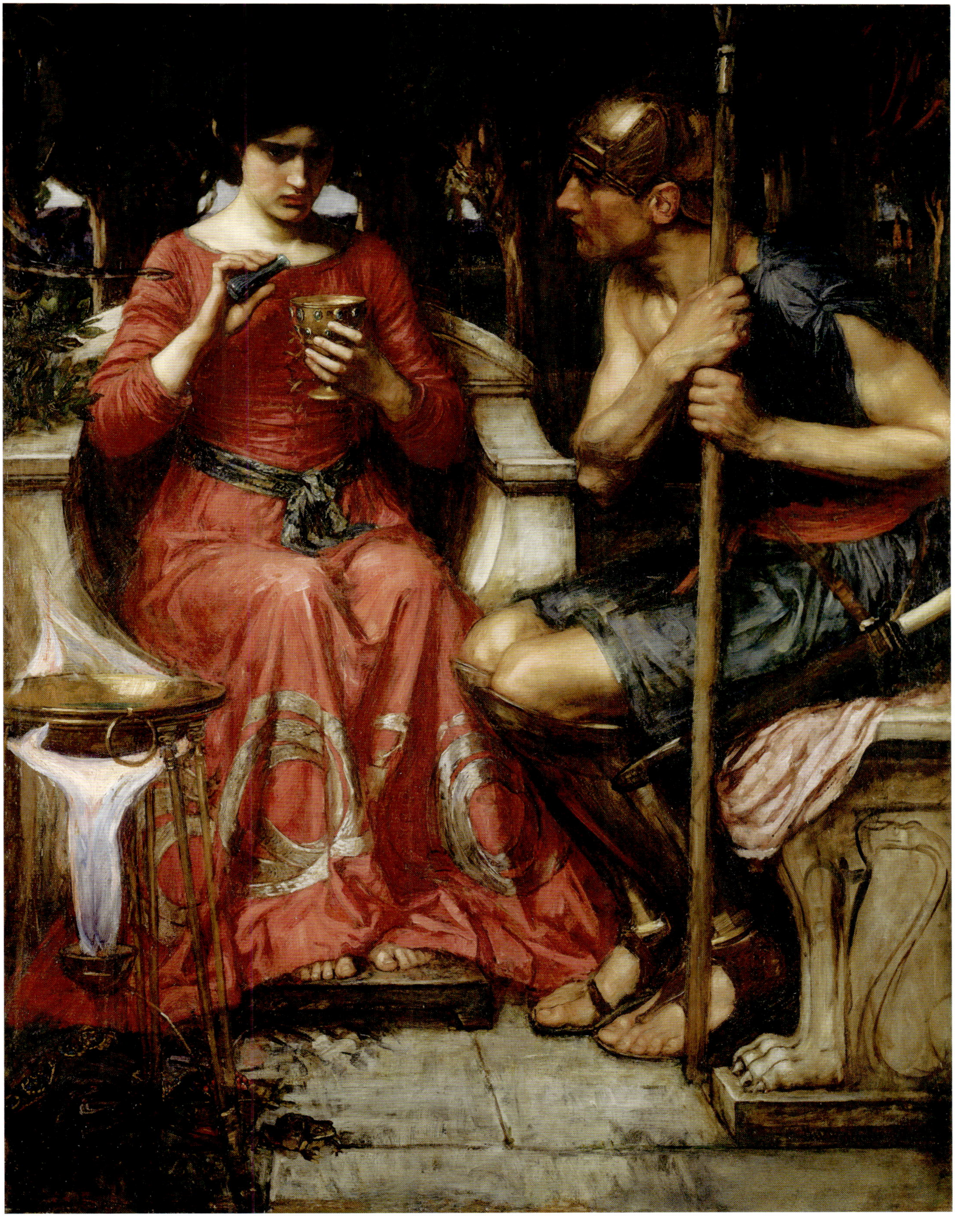

50. The Soul of the Rose 1908

OIL ON CANVAS, 88.3 X 59.1 CM - PRIVATE COLLECTION COURTESY OF CHRISTIE'S - EXHIBITED ROYAL ACADEMY, 1908

In an Italianate walled garden, a woman breathes deeply of the scent of a rose. In traditional theories of the senses, smell is the lowest, most material, or even bestial of the five; yet the title of this work links the image of smelling the rose, instead, with the 'soul'. The phrase is drawn from a line in Tennyson's long poem of 1855, *Maud* ('And the soul of the rose went into my blood', Part I, XXII, stanza VI) but the painting does not illustrate the narrative of the poem; the quotation serves rather to establish a poetic mood. The implied mingling of the material and spiritual is much in keeping with the symbolic system of Waterhouse's later works. As the art historian Christina Bradstreet has suggested, the woman's pose, and her absorption in the rose, hint that the powerful scent has conjured a dream or memory of her beloved; her cheek is flushed to match the colour of the rose.[1] But the scent of the rose may be a path to spiritual transcendence, as well as sensual or erotic delight. Waterhouse's critic and biographer Rose Sketchley mentioned this painting, along with *Windflowers* (cat. 42) and several other late paintings without specific subject-matter, as her final examples: 'art such as this has a ministry that reaches beyond sense, endows sensation itself with a more assured capacity of final fulfilment beyond – say, rather, through – the visible ends of the world'.[2] **EP**

1 Christina Bradstreet, '"Wicked with Roses": Floral Femininity and the Erotics of Scent', *Nineteenth-Century Art Worldwide*, spring 2007, at http://19thc-artworldwide.org.

2 R.E.D. Sketchley, *The Art of J.W. Waterhouse, R.A.*, Christmas Number of *The Art Journal*, 1909, p. 25.

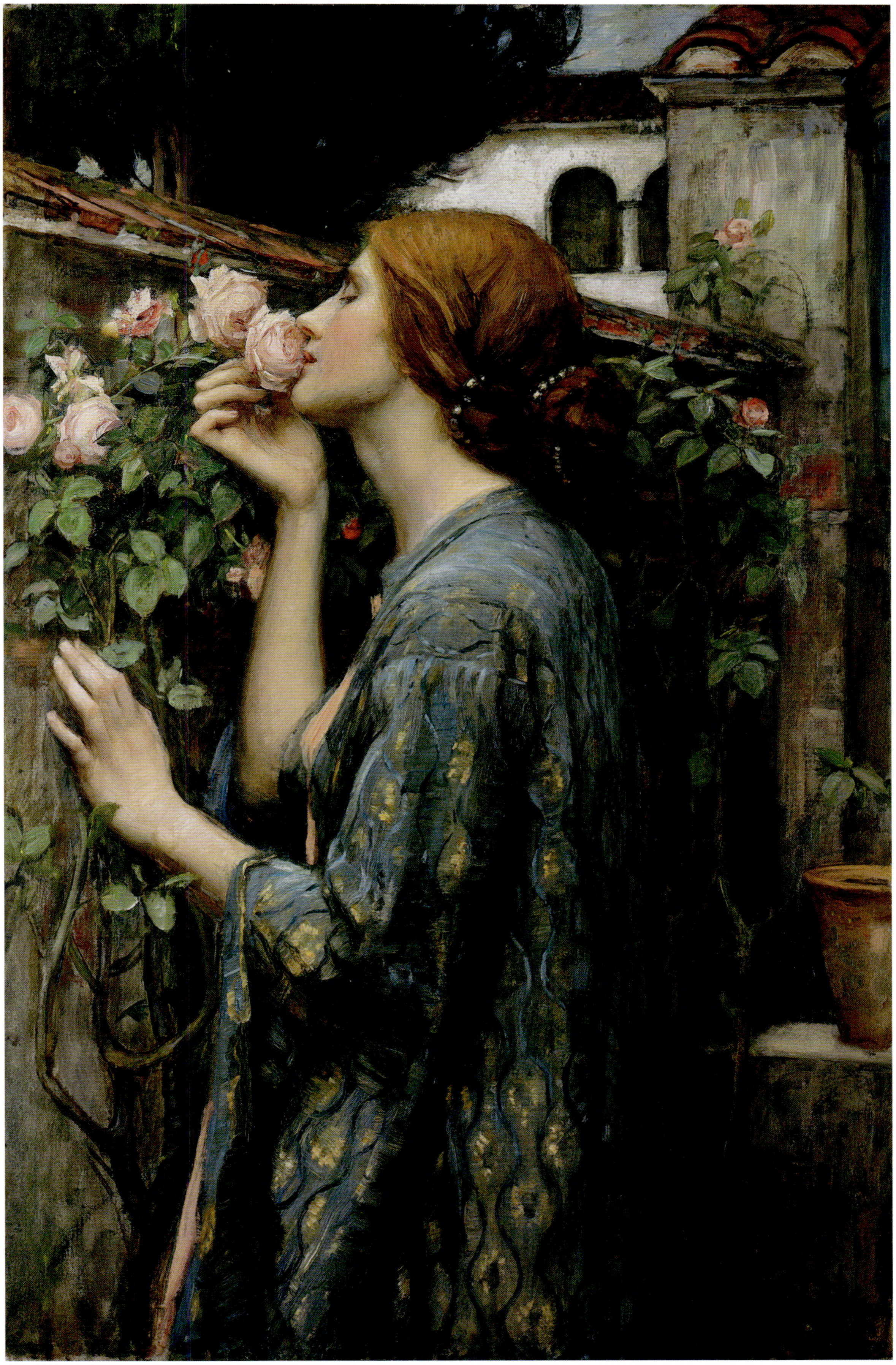

51. 'Gather Ye Rosebuds While Ye May' 1908

OIL ON CANVAS - 61.6 X 45.7 CM - PRIVATE COLLECTION COURTESY OF CHRISTIE'S - EXHIBITED ROYAL ACADEMY, 1908

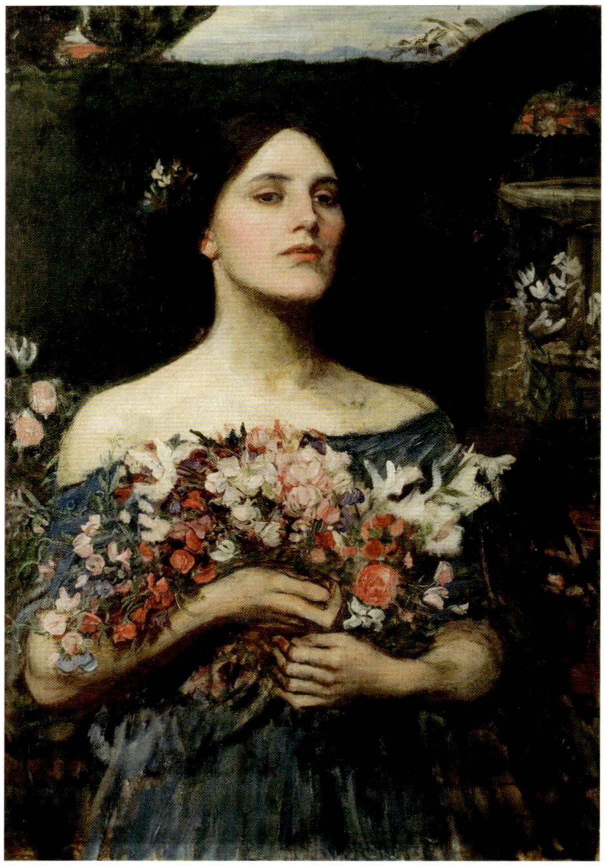

52. **'Gather Ye Rosebuds While Ye May'** c. 1908

OIL ON CANVAS, 79 X 57 CM - PRIVATE COLLECTION

Throughout his career, Waterhouse closely associated women with the beauty, simplicity, and decay of flowers, while valuing both as vessels of the seeds of new growth. From 1908 through 1914, flower-women assumed added significance for him, initially through a series of plotless images. In 1908 he sent to the Academy this *'Gather Ye Rosebuds While Ye May'*, which shows a red-haired woman presenting a bowl of flowers, her head reflected in a rectangular mirror behind. Unfinished and unsigned, cat. 52 is a variation set in a Renaissance garden with a brunette maiden who has just picked her flowers. For both versions, and also for a multi-figure painting he sent to the Academy a year later, Waterhouse drew his title from the well-known poem by Robert Herrick (1591-1674), 'To the Virgins, to Make Much of Time', which warns that the 'flower that smiles to-day,/To-morrow will be dying'. **PT**

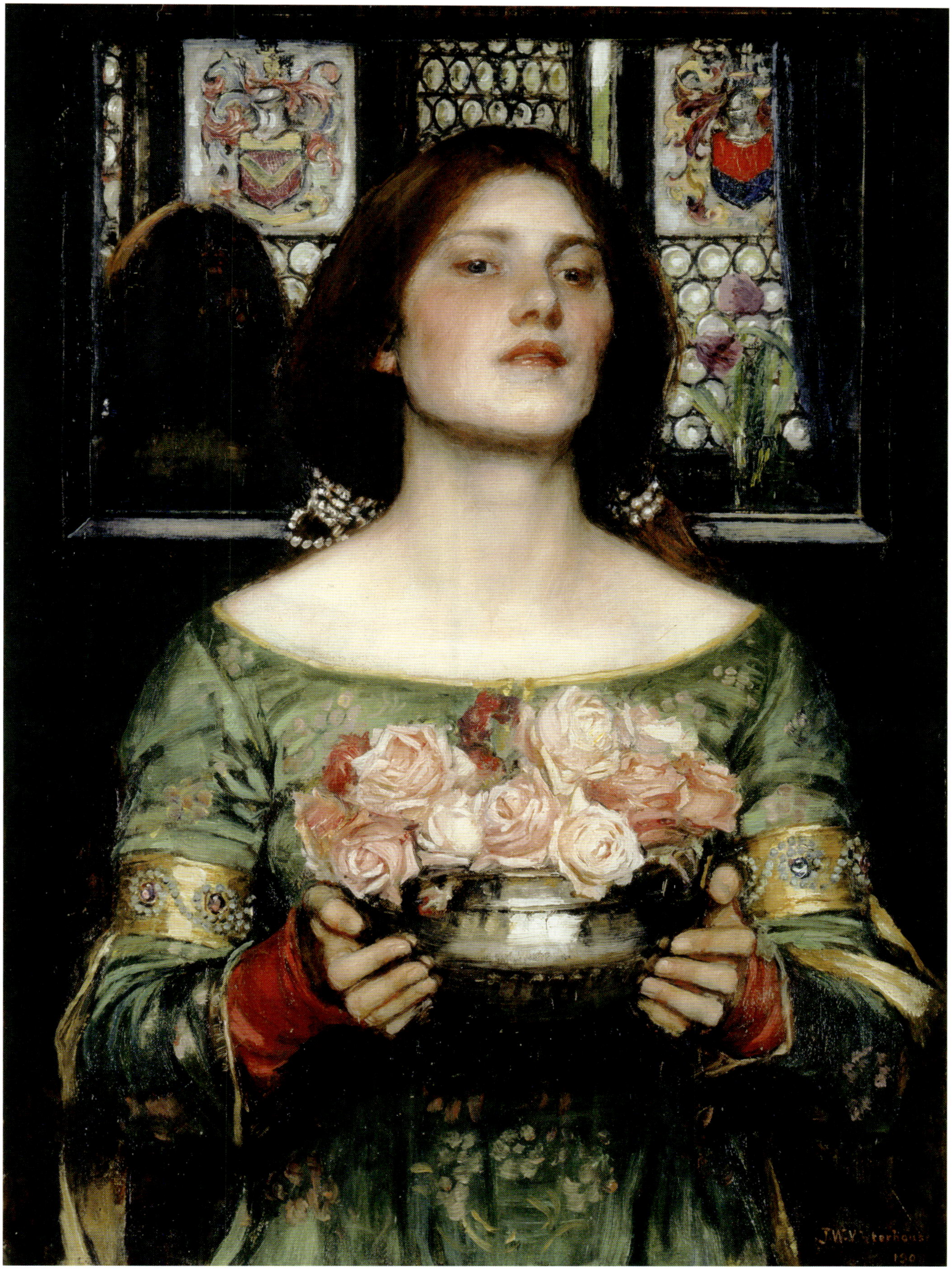

53. Lamia 1909

OIL ON CANVAS, 92.5 X 57.5 CM - PRIVATE COLLECTION COURTESY OF CHRISTIE'S

Having exhibited a *Lamia* in 1905 (cat. 46) and made three additional treatments of that two-figure composition, Waterhouse sent to the Academy's 1909 Summer Exhibition a one-figure picture bearing the same title. In it the same girl – still attired in pink with a glittering coil – arranges her hair alone while admiring herself in the water's reflection. Waterhouse had occasionally shown women with one or both breasts exposed, most notably in *Echo and Narcissus* (cat. 43). Here we glimpse a particularly sensual and intimate moment: the arms are raised to accentuate the unusually ample breasts, and the hair bound tightly in 1905 now cascades over both shoulders.

This work includes such characteristic details as the bluish twilit mountains in the distance; the ominous thicket of trees inspired by Renaissance prototypes; the closely studied, nearly writhing trunks growing from the bank at left; the gauzy, translucent gown with its folds conveyed by slashes of pink and lake paint; the Pre-Raphaelite aquatic plants Waterhouse had been inserting into foregrounds since the 1888 *Lady of Shalott* (cat. 20)*;* and the murky yet reflective water below. Several details differ in an even larger variation of this picture, seen on Waterhouse's easel in a now-lost photograph of c. 1908-1909.[1]

Waterhouse was hardly unique in depicting Lamia alone. In 1909, the same year as this picture, his former student Herbert Draper painted her with a rather bird-like face in profile. More importantly, George Frampton RA (whose works were collected by Waterhouse) had exhibited at the Academy in 1900 his haunting sculpture of Lamia with eyes closed, her ghostly flesh made of ivory set off by bronze and opals. **PT**

1 This photograph is the frontispiece in Anthony Hobson, *The Art and Life of J.W. Waterhouse RA 1849-1917* (London, 1980).

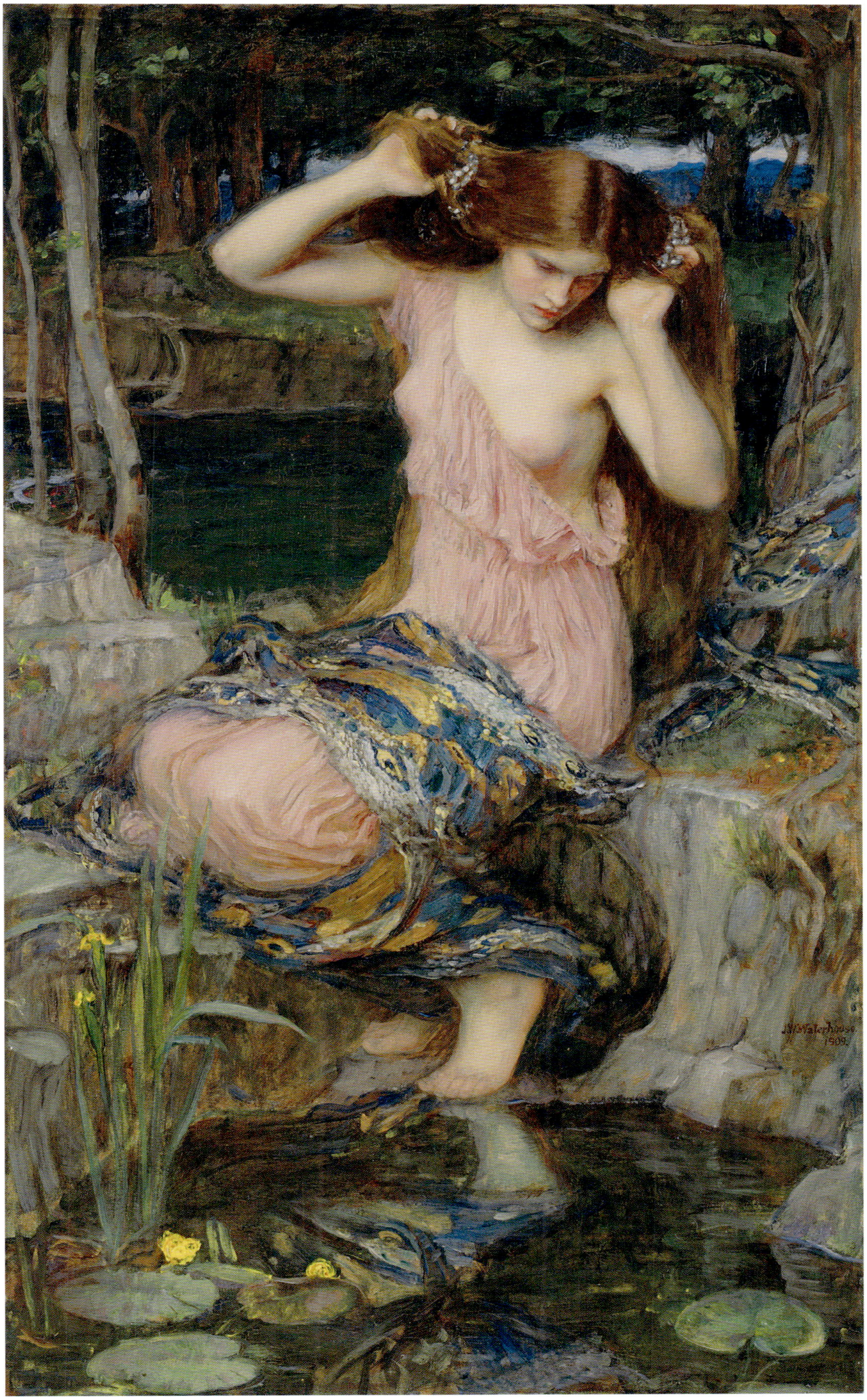
J.W.Waterhouse
1909

54. **Vanity** c. 1908-1910

OIL ON CANVAS, 66 X 68.6 CM - PRIVATE COLLECTION COURTESY OF PETER NAHUM AT THE LEICESTER GALLERIES, LONDON

This is one of two undated paintings by Waterhouse, both entitled *Vanity,* which present the traditional motif of a woman gazing into a mirror, adorning herself with flowers and jewellery. The artist surely drew inspiration from the preening redheads celebrated by Dante Gabriel Rossetti; we can be confident he saw, at the Academy in 1906, that Pre-Raphaelite forerunner's pivotal foray in this terrain, *Bocca Baciata* ('the mouth that has been kissed', 1859). Also pertinent is Rossetti's *Lady Lilith* (1864-1868). **PT**

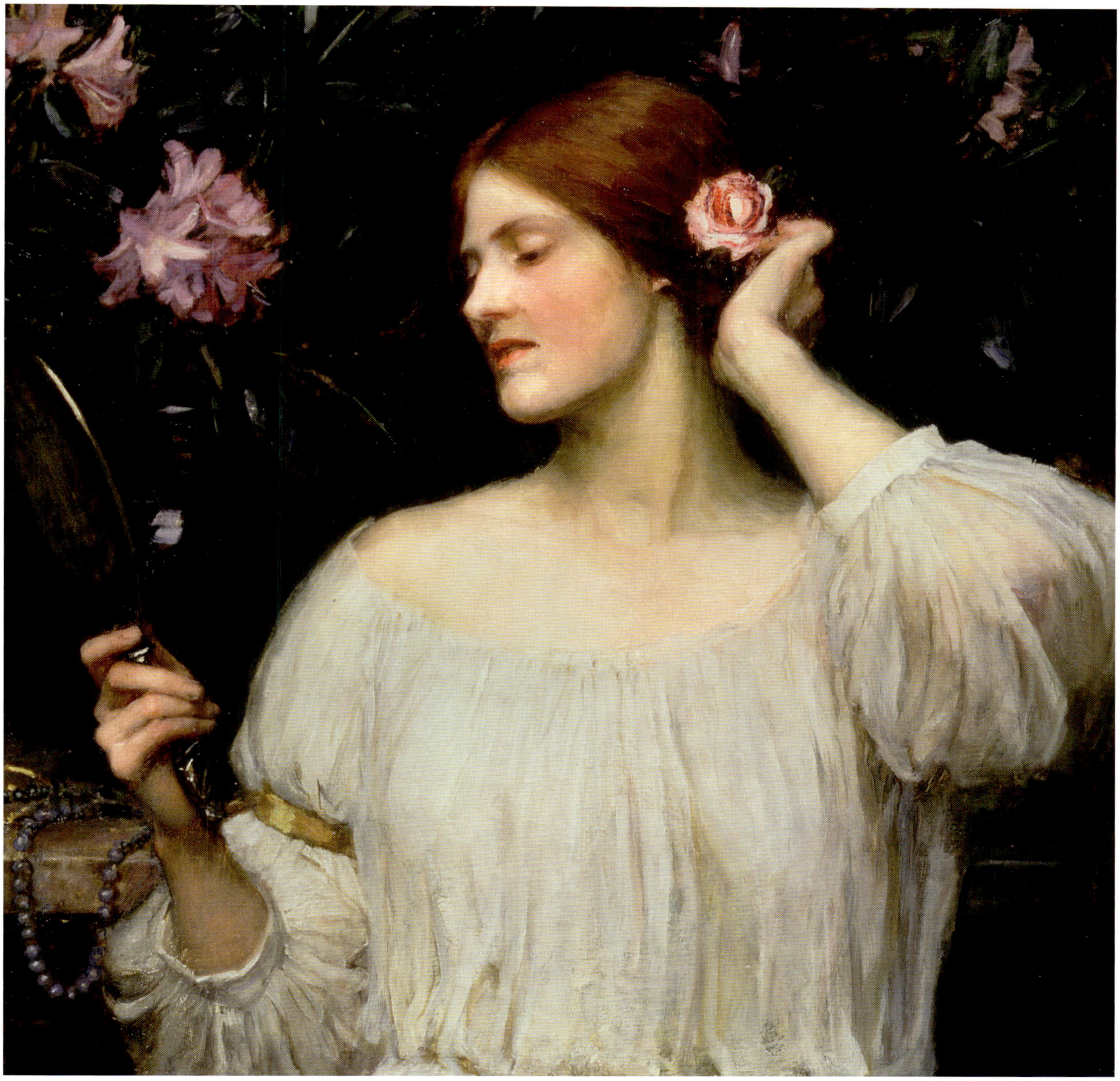

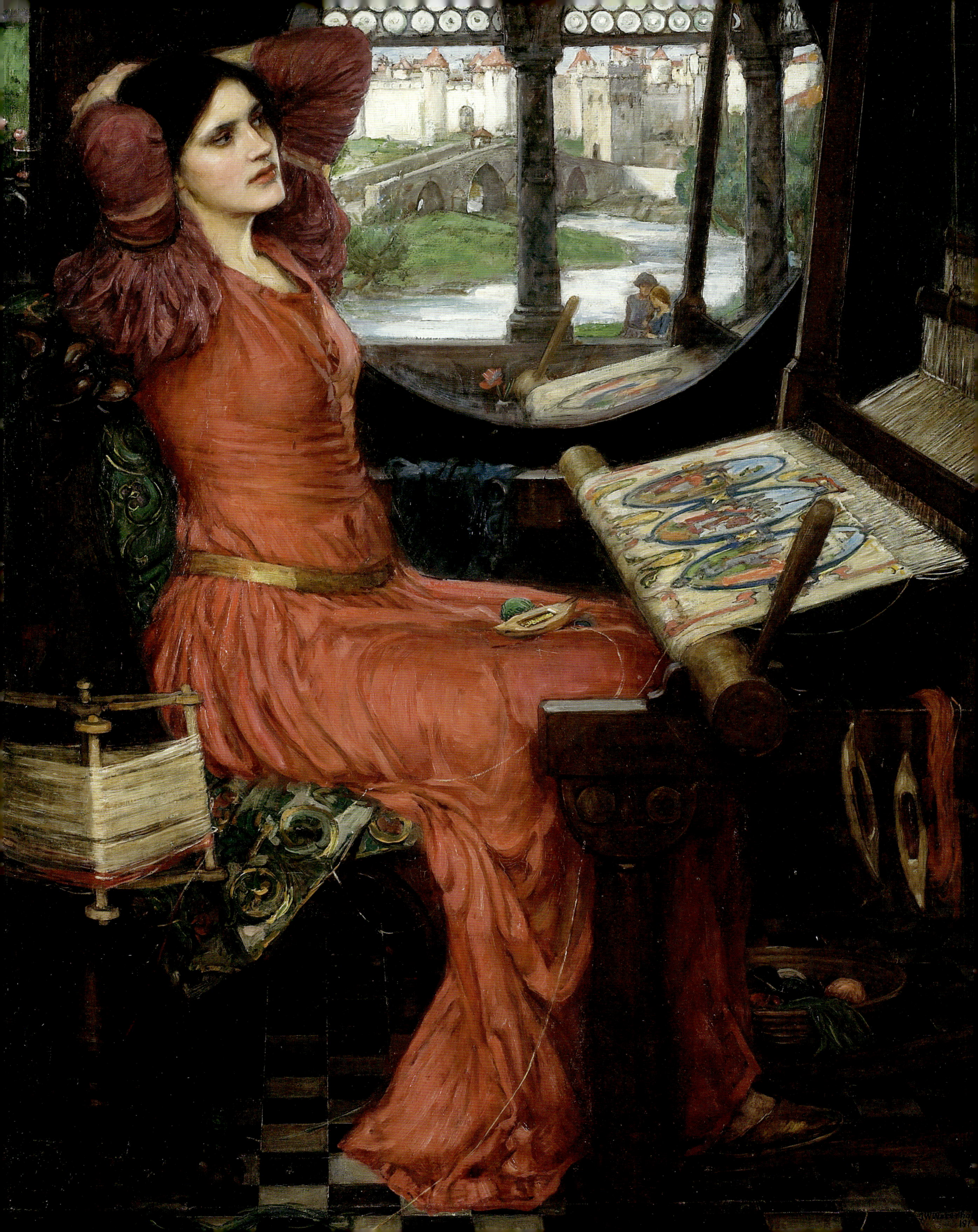

The Final Years

55. 'Listening to my Sweet Pipings' 1911

OIL ON CANVAS, 57.8 X 102.2 CM - COLLECTION ANNA SUI - EXHIBITED ROYAL ACADEMY, 1911

Waterhouse took the title and subject for this picture from Shelley's poem 'Hymn to Pan' (1820). In the poem Pan relates how his piping expresses the music of desire and brings the world to sleep. But his craving for Syrinx ends in sadness, as rather than submit to his desire she chooses to metamorphose into a reed. In Waterhouse's painting Pan has become an unthreatening small boy rather than a lustful faun and, while he has the beginnings of horns, he has an otherwise wholly human form. In Greek mythology Pan was the god of pastures and forests, the universal deity who expressed the fecundity of nature, and Waterhouse suggests this oneness with nature in the beautiful river meadow setting. The woman – who from her lack of alarm does not appear intended to be Syrinx – listens to Pan's music contemplatively, but also with a certain troubled melancholy. She is perhaps most likely to represent nature itself, brought to life with Pan's music in an allegory of the natural world's fertility. But the ambiguity of the conjunction, suppression of any narrative, and links between music and contemplative states look back almost half a century to Aesthetic paintings of the 1860s. It is also reminiscent of the rural idylls in a similar format made by so-called Etruscan painters such as George Heming Mason and Nino Costa. But there is most resonance with the famous sequence of pictures of somnambulant women painted by Leighton such as *Idyll* (c. 1880-1881), which features two reclining women listening to a man playing a shepherd's pipe, *Cymon and Iphigenia* (1884) and, less similar in format, *The Garden of the Hesperides* (c. 1892) and *Flaming June* (c. 1895). Leighton was long dead and in a world that was turning to modernism to express its spirit, it is as if Waterhouse were expressing his belief in the eternal subjects of nature, myth, and creation. His closest source of inspiration for the picture came from a particularly venerable source. Piero del Cosimo's *Satyr mourning over a Nymph* (c. 1495) had been acquired by the National Gallery in 1862. Waterhouse adopted Cosimo's wide format, reclining figure, and high horizon for his own picture and, in a pencil study for the painting (cat. 81), Waterhouse initially contemplated having an additional figure kneeling at the woman's head as in Cosimo's composition. Compositionally, if not also in subject, there is close similarity between '*Listening to my Sweet Pipings*' and Waterhouse's own *A Naiad* (cat. 27), although there the recumbent figure is male. **RU**

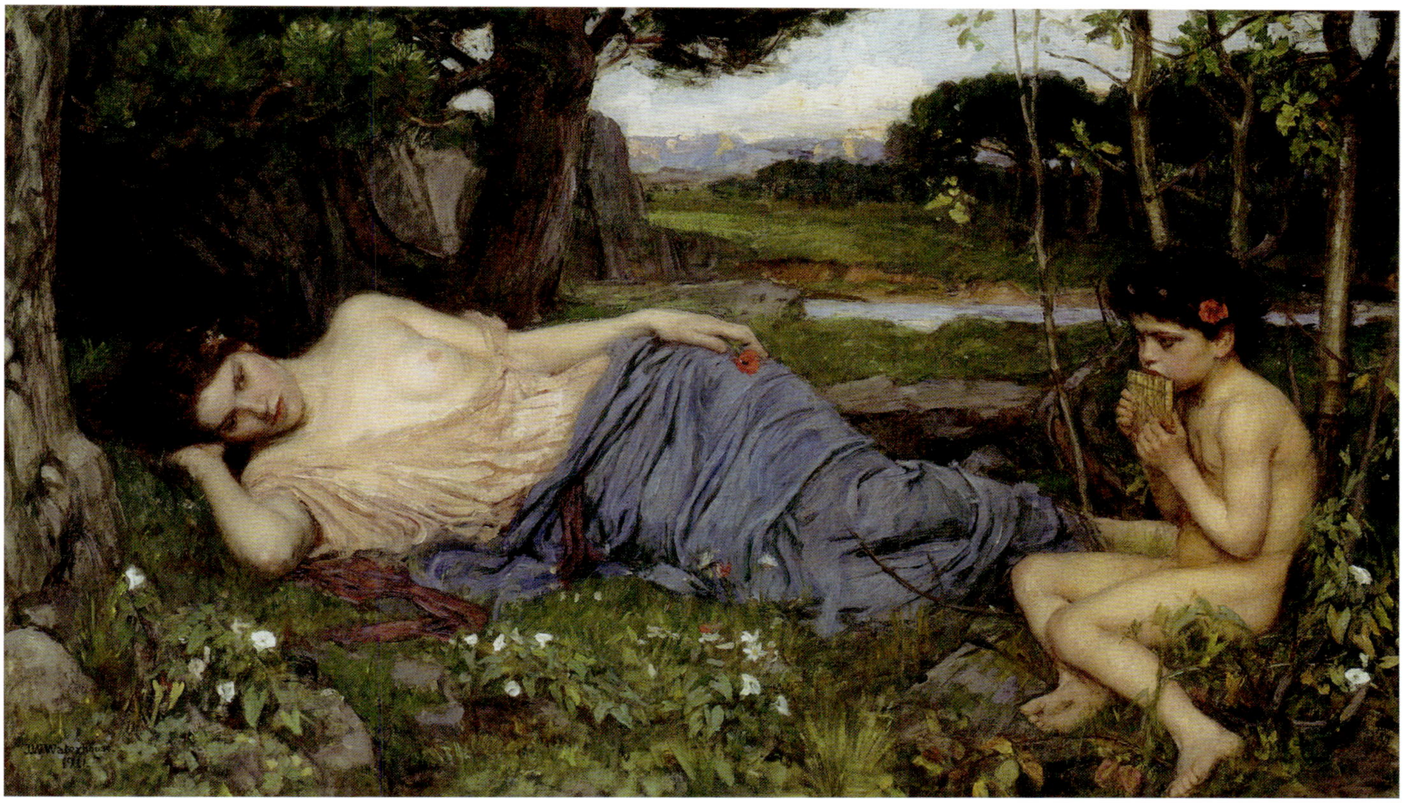

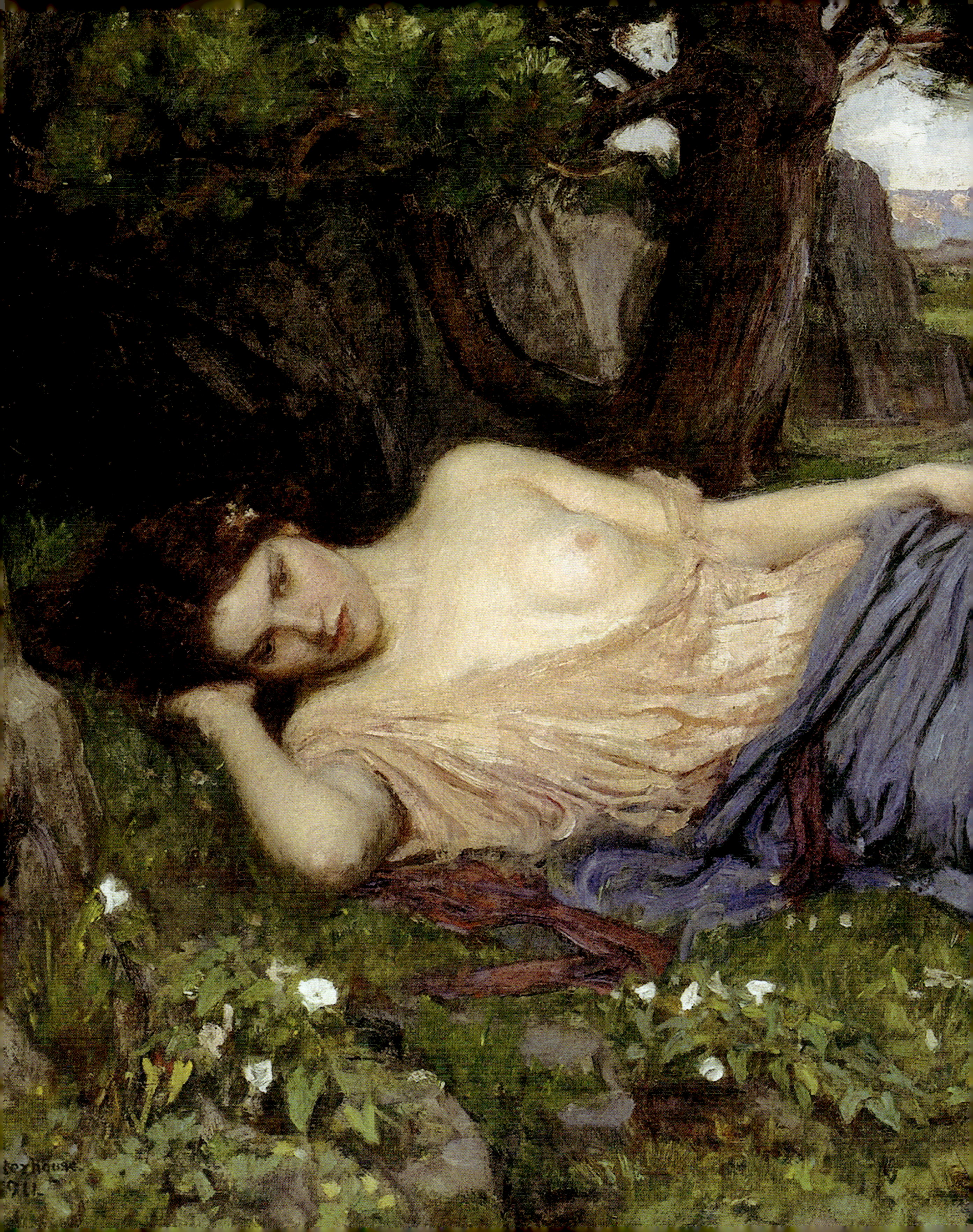

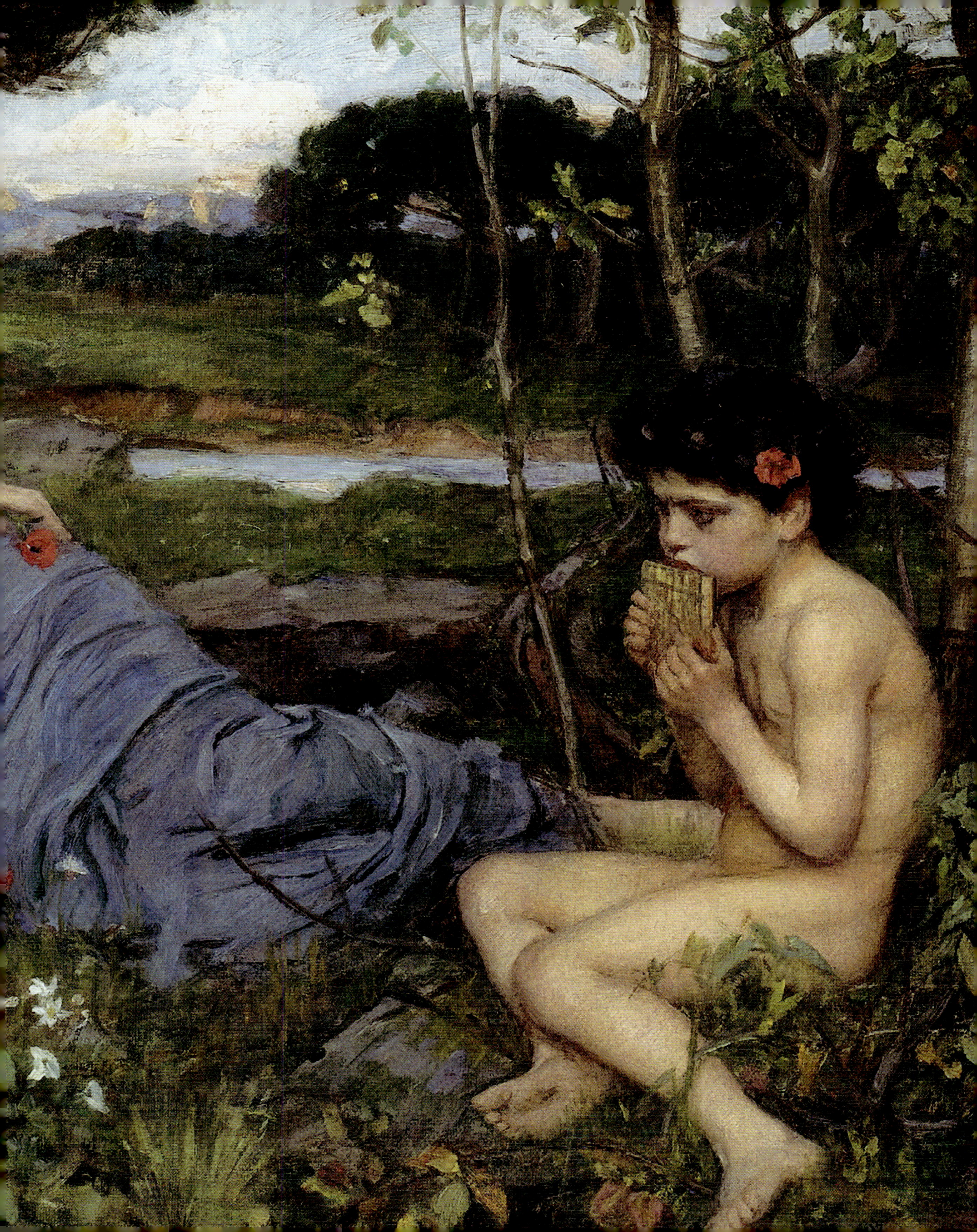

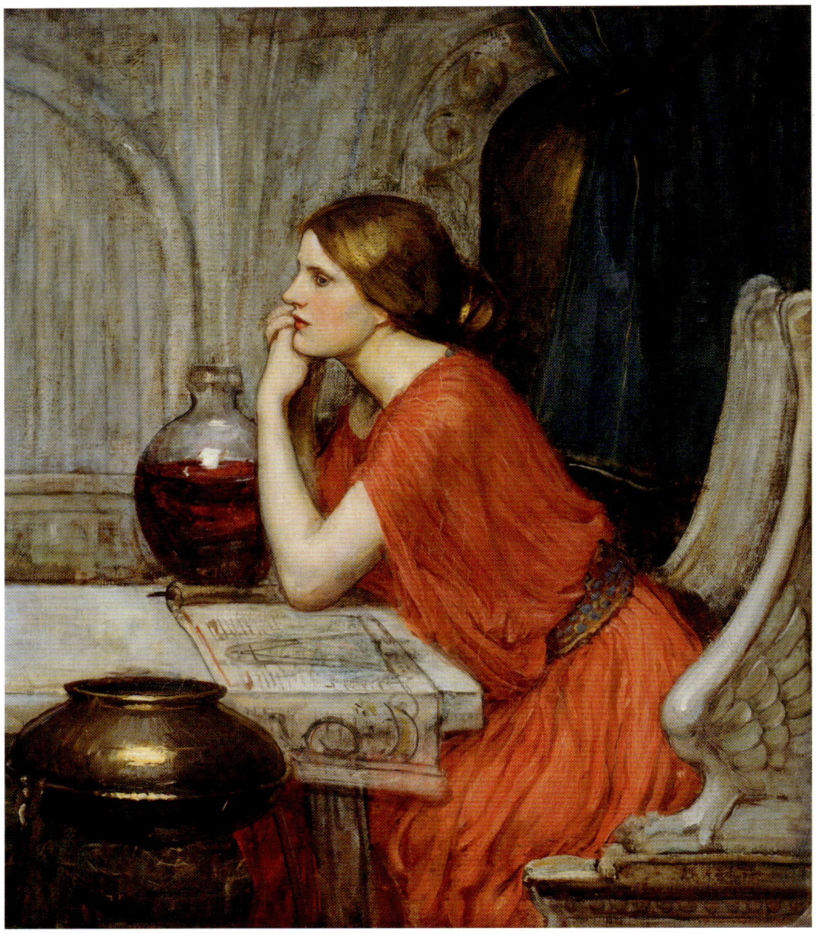

56. **Circe** c. 1911-1914

SKETCH - OIL ON CANVAS, 86.3 X 77.2 CM - PRIVATE COLLECTION

In the final years of his career, Waterhouse returned to the figure who had fascinated him when he first took up mythological subject-matter around 1890: the sorceress Circe. In the years after 1910 he designed a new composition, with Circe seated at a marble table, lost in contemplation amidst the paraphernalia of her magic arts. The composition is explored in two oil sketches of substantial size (cats 56, 57), with varying details but similar in the presentation of the figure herself, who also has affinities with the figure of Penelope in the contemporary painting, *Penelope and the Suitors* (cat. 58). A delicate pencil and chalk drawing (cat. 74) represents a head in profile, closest perhaps to the head of Circe in the narrower oil sketch (cat. 56). However, the profile and the arrangement of the hair, swept back into a simple bun, resemble the figures of both Circe (in both oil sketches) and Penelope. In the drawing, the head is upright on the neck, which suggests it is a study from the model which might have been part of the preliminary work for either composition, or both. Both painted compositions alter the pose of the drawing

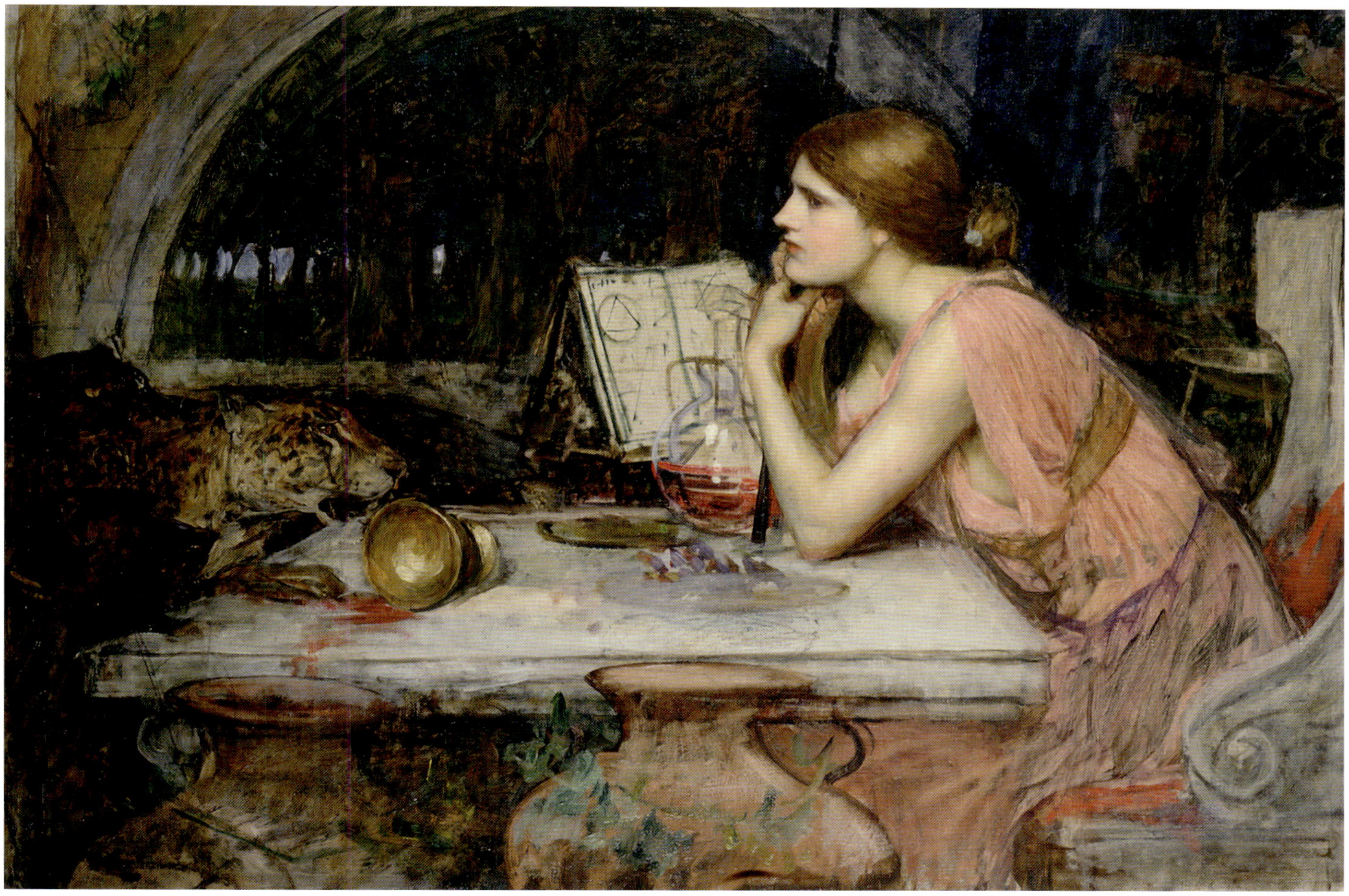

57. Circe c. 1911-1914

SKETCH - OIL ON CANVAS, 76 X 110.5 CM - PRIVATE COLLECTION COURTESY OF PETER NAHUM AT THE LEICESTER GALLERIES, LONDON

to give a pronounced forwards inclination to the neck for narrative purposes, as Penelope bites off a thread and Circe meditatively leans her chin on her hands (in one of the oil sketches, cat. 57, the hands also clasp her magic wand). Thus Ulysses' faithful wife and his sorceress-lover come to resemble one another, and in the larger of the two oil sketches (cat. 57) Circe, like Penelope, has woven a tapestry; it depicts the scene of Ulysses encountering the Sirens, as in Waterhouse's painting of 1891 (cat. 22). Moreover, the blood-red colour of Circe's potion and the brazen tripods, in both oil sketches, hark back to *Circe Offering the Cup to Ulysses* (cat. 21). The new composition, then, makes explicit the crucial role of Circe in directing Ulysses' voyages, as well as creating a new link between the learned sorceress and the 'wise Penelope' (see cat. 58). At the same time it sets up a web of interconnections, woven together as intricately as a tapestry, between Waterhouse's first mythological paintings of 1891 and those of his final years. **EP**

58. **Penelope and the Suitors** 1912

OIL ON CANVAS, 129.8 X 188 CM - ABERDEEN ART GALLERY AND MUSEUMS - COMMISSIONED BY ABERDEEN ART GALLERY AND EXHIBITED THERE 1912, THEN ROYAL ACADEMY 1912

Waterhouse's first subjects from classical mythology were drawn from the wanderings of the Greek hero Ulysses, as recounted in Homer's *Odyssey* (cats 21, 22). Fittingly, the artist returned to the last stages of Ulysses' story for the last of the mythological subjects he showed at the Royal Academy, based on the scene in Book XIX of the *Odyssey* where Penelope tells Ulysses (now home, but still in disguise) of the ruses she has used to avoid yielding to her numerous suitors: 'So then in the daytime I would weave the mighty web, and in the night unravel the same'.[1] The painting elaborates Penelope's tale, to show her working at the loom while suitors importune her, trying to beguile her with the lyre or offering flowers and gifts. The cue for the composition may have been a fresco by the Renaissance artist Pintoricchio, acquired by the National Gallery in 1874, which shows the suitors bursting into a chamber with wide-open windows, through which other scenes from the *Odyssey* are glimpsed (fig. 46). Waterhouse borrows the idea of the open-windowed room, but reorients the composition to powerful dramatic purpose, causing Penelope to turn her back in defiance of the suitors, who lean aggressively through the windows. He also draws on the recent excavations of Heinrich Schliemann, at Mycenae and Troy, to imagine the architecture of the Homeric age: massive white buildings are seen through the windows, and the interior is adorned with burnished metalwork and archaising wall-paintings. At first thought, Penelope, the faithful wife, appears an anomalous subject, amidst the many *femmes fatales* of Waterhouse's later career. Yet the loom links Penelope to the Lady of Shalott (and particularly to Waterhouse's last version of the subject, cat. 60), and Penelope's profile pose recalls that of Waterhouse's late oil sketches of Circe (cats 56, 57). Conventionally speaking, Penelope and Circe would be rivals for Ulysses' love, and moral opposites, as loyal wife and seductress respectively. But Penelope's epithet, constantly repeated in the prose translation of the *Odyssey* by S.H. Butcher and Andrew Lang that Waterhouse may have consulted, is 'wise'.[2] Thus she may take her place among the many women, in Waterhouse's work, who have the gift of secret knowledge or special insight. **EP**

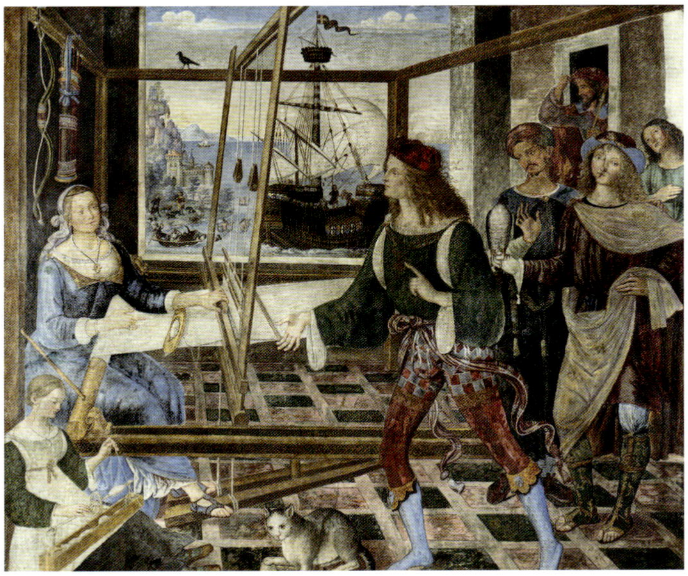

46. Bernardino Pintoricchio, *Penelope with the Suitors*, c. 1509, Fresco, detached and mounted on canvas, 125.5 x 152 cm, National Gallery, London

1 S.H. Butcher and Andrew Lang, *The Odyssey of Homer: Done into English Prose*, 4th ed., London: Macmillan, 1883, p. 315.

2 The phrase 'wise Penelope' occurs throughout S.H. Butcher and Andrew Lang, *The Odyssey of Homer: Done into English Prose*, 4th ed., London: Macmillan, 1883. Waterhouse may have used this translation, first published in 1879, to which he refers in a letter of 1891 apropos of *Circe Offering the Cup to Ulysses*; see Peter Trippi, *J.W. Waterhouse*, London: Phaidon, 2002, note 30 on p. 238. Andrew Lang was an influential writer on anthropology, folklore, and religion; his major work, *Myth, Ritual and Religion*, appeared in 1897. He is still best known for his collections of fairy tales (starting with *The Blue Fairy Book*, 1889).

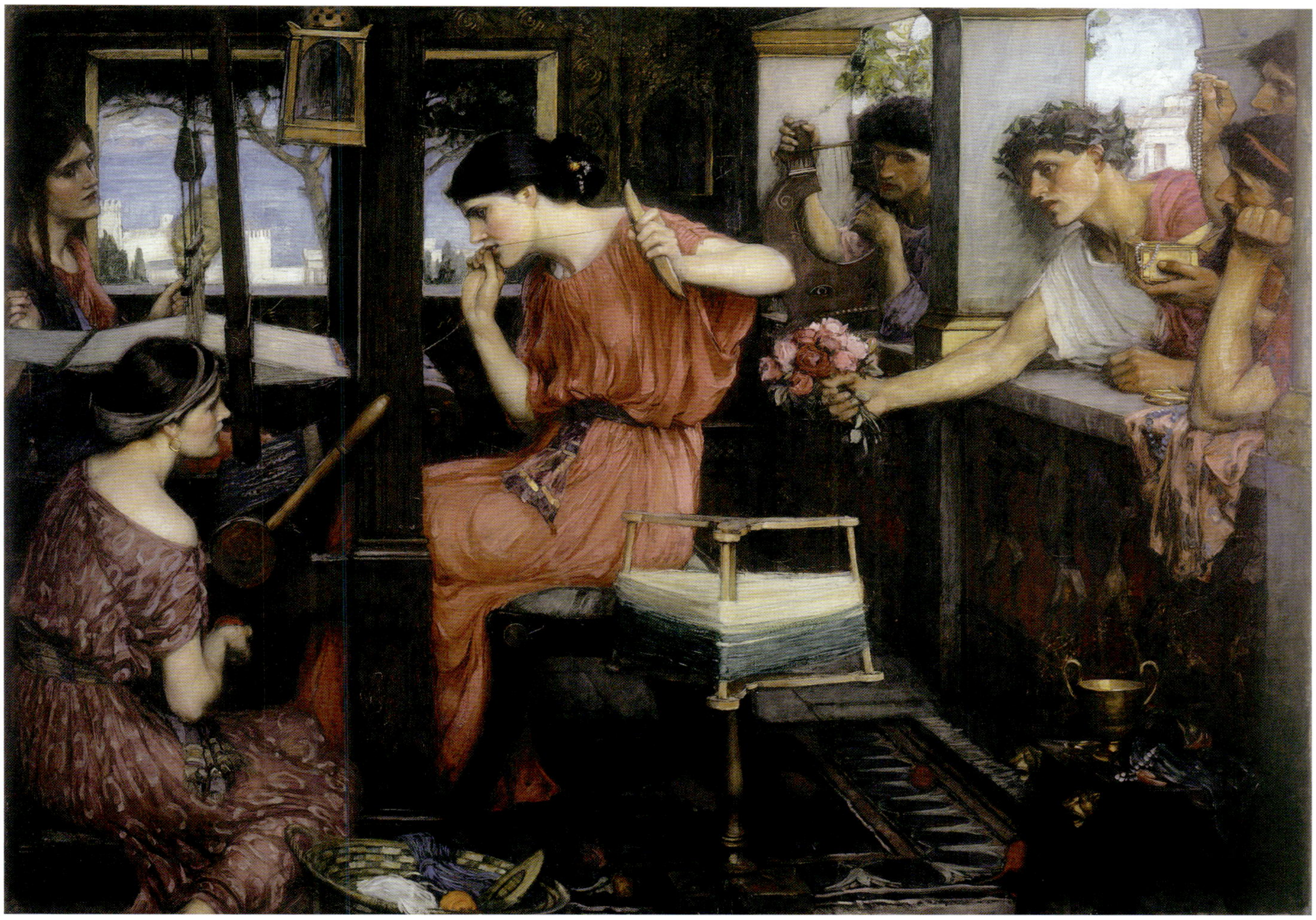

59. The Love Philtre c. 1913-1914

SKETCH - OIL ON CANVAS, 58.4 X 45.7 CM - KELLEY GALLERY, PASADENA, CALIFORNIA

Waterhouse never lost interest in the connections of women with magical liquids. In the second decade of the twentieth century, we can trace this trajectory from the unfinished Circe canvases c. 1911-1914 (cats 56, 57) through to *Tristram and Isolde* of 1916 (cat. 63). In 1914, he exhibited at the Academy the now-unlocated *Love Philtre,* which shows a brunette, standing in profile in a vaguely 'Jacobethan' interior, pouring a potion into a cup. The present unsigned sketch is related in spirit and theme, though by having this girl look directly at the viewer, Waterhouse reprises his more malevolent Medea pictures seven years earlier (cats 48, 49).

As in Waterhouse's other unfinished oil sketches, we can savour here his lively brushwork and witness how he elaborates the model's face and hair before pursuing costume, props, and backgrounds. **PT**

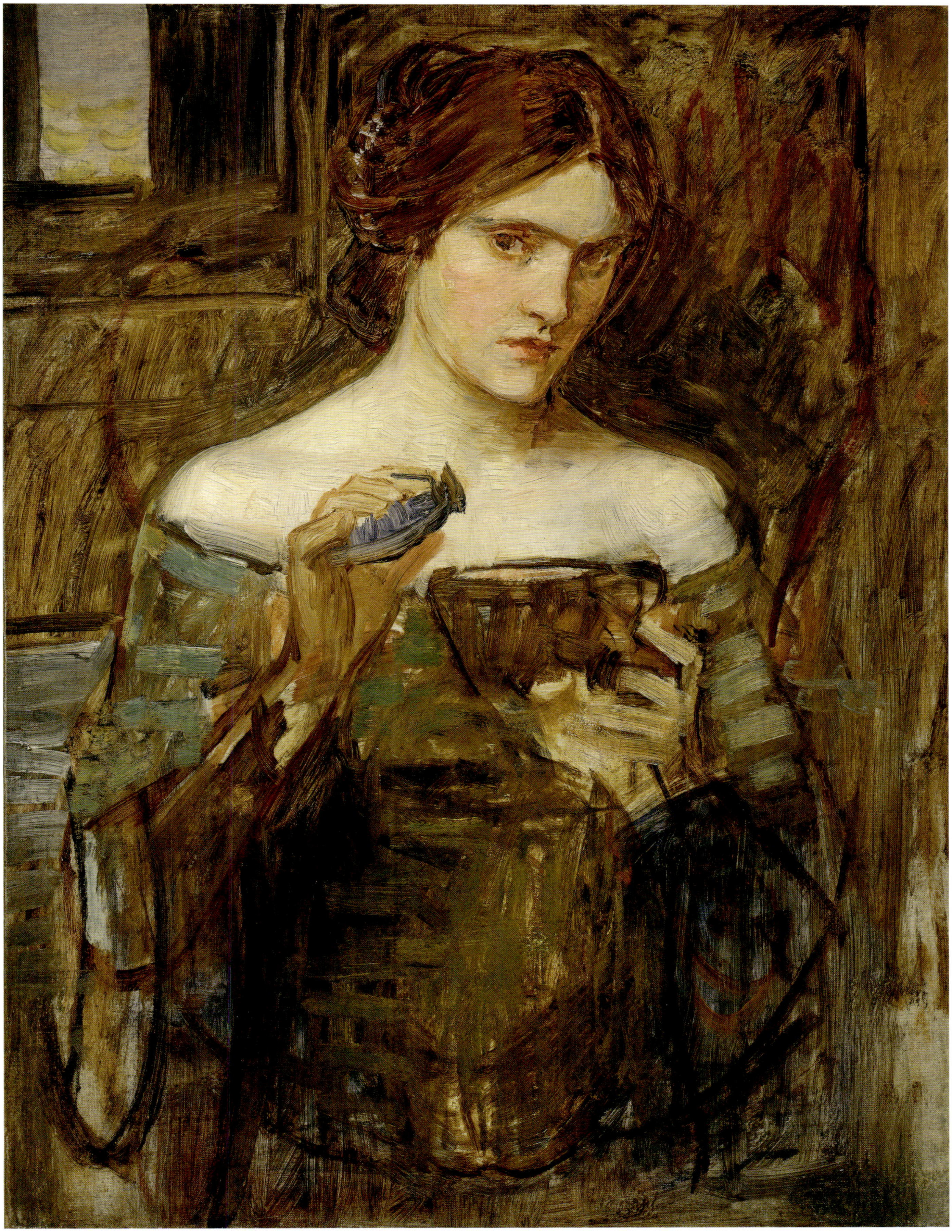

60. 'I am Half Sick of Shadows', said the Lady of Shalott 1915

OIL ON CANVAS, 100 X 74 CM - ART GALLERY OF ONTARIO, TORONTO, GIFT OF MRS PHILLIP B. JACKSON, 1971 - EXHIBITED ROYAL ACADEMY, 1916

This was the last in Waterhouse's sequence of paintings based on Tennyson's 'The Lady of Shalott', although it treats the earliest incident in the narrative – the beginning of her frustration. Isolated in her tower, the Lady only experiences life glimpsed in a mirror. Although she is initially content weaving her magic cloth, after seeing a funeral pass by and then 'two young lovers lately wed', dissatisfaction begins to take hold. The connections between these two images – of true love and life's short span – are plain, and she too wants to experience physical passion. Yearning for a meaningful, fulfilled life, the Lady of Shalott declares: 'I am half sick of shadows'. This is the unhappy and bored state that Waterhouse depicts, just before the sight of Lancelot riding past will bring unbearable temptation, and ultimate tragedy:

> His broad clear brow in sunlight glow'd;
> On burnish'd hooves his war-horse trode;
> From underneath his helmet flow'd
> His coal-black curls as on he rode,
> As he rode down to Camelot.
> From the bank and from the river
> He flash'd into the crystal mirror,
> 'Tirra lira,' by the river
> Sang Sir Lancelot.

Waterhouse deftly suggests different stages of the narrative in the mirror's reflection: the two lovers passing by that prompt this state of dissatisfaction; Camelot, where Lancelot rides to and from; and the river that will ultimately carry her dead body. Reflecting the arches of the tower's window, the mirror contains a heart shape, emblematic of the love the Lady craves. In a watercolour study for the composition[1], Waterhouse originally showed the Lady slumped back in her chair, a hand held up to her face in frustration. But for the finished oil he adopted a much more sensual pose with the lady stretching upwards hands behind head. This made reference to Millais's *Mariana*, another subject with a heroine plagued by sexual longing. It was a picture Waterhouse had first seen in 1886 and to which he referred repeatedly in his own works (cats 30, 33). Made towards the end of Waterhouse's life, *'I am Half Sick of Shadows' ...* was his last essay on a story that had evidently fascinated him over thirty years and which in some intangible way seemed to allude to his own creative imagination. **RU**

1 Victoria and Albert Museum, Sketchbook E.2-1949, p. 23 (cat. 97).

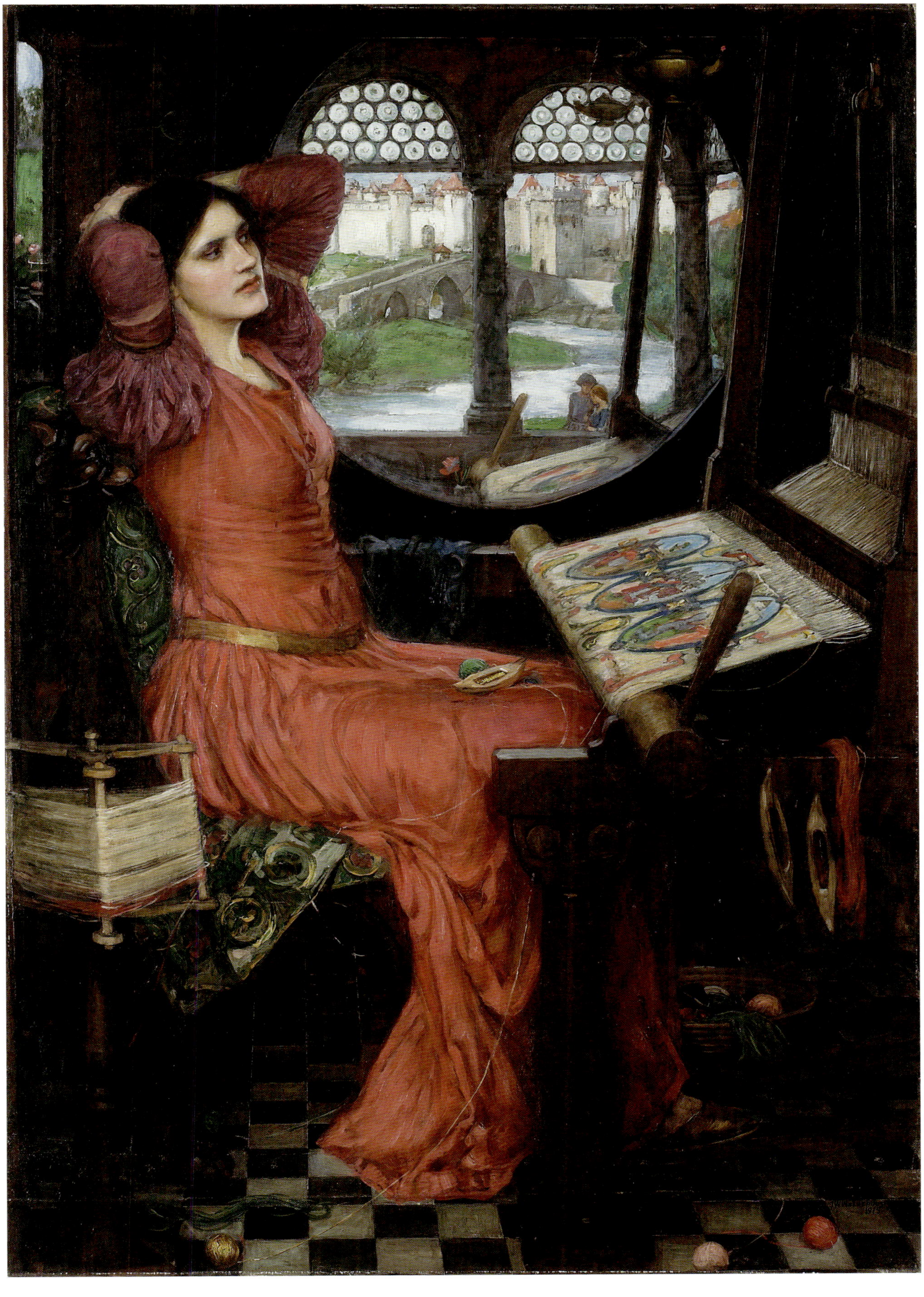

61. Fair Rosamund c. 1916

SKETCH - OIL ON CANVAS, 60.6 X 48 CM - AMGUEDDFA CYMRU/NATIONAL MUSEUM WALES, CARDIFF, GIFT OF SIR WILLIAM GOSCOMBE JOHN RA, 1940

Very late in life, Waterhouse treated various Romantic narratives that had fascinated the early Pre-Raphaelites, including two tragedies set in the Middle Ages. In contrast to the legendary origins of *Tristram and Isolde* (cat. 63), *Fair Rosamund* draws upon some verifiable facts. Henry II, who ruled England 1154-1189, kept his mistress, Rosamund Clifford, in a mansion surrounded by a maze, which Queen Eleanor negotiated with silk thread in order to murder her rival. Celebrated by Chaucer, Tennyson, and Swinburne, this legend's eroticism and violence also appealed to such late Pre-Raphaelites as Eleanor Fortescue-Brickdale and Evelyn De Morgan.

Like the Lady of Shalott, Rosamund is a confined artist weaving an image of knights riding. Here she pauses to watch for her lover, unaware that her life will soon be cut like the thread that betrays her. Her namesake flowers appear near the window, symbolizing the love that offends the queen, who is glimpsed through the curtains ominously decorated with sword-brandishing riders. The threat that Rosamund poses to Eleanor is reinforced by her little crown. Although a concubine, Rosamund takes the kneeling position and clasped hands of sainthood, converting this scene into a morbid variant of the Annunciation, a scene of which Waterhouse had exhibited in 1914. Indeed, Rosamund was buried at a nunnery and venerated as a martyr to Eleanor's hatred.

The present picture is an unfinished though well developed oil sketch for the larger version that Waterhouse signed and dated 1916, and which was exhibited at the Academy shortly after his death in 1917. On the verso appears a quick pencil sketch of the head and arching upper body seen in 1915's *'I am Half Sick of Shadows', said the Lady of Shalott* (cat. 60): Waterhouse could simply not stop drawing, nor inter-associating the predicaments of the Lady and Rosamund.

This canvas was acquired at some point by the 'New Sculptor' William Goscombe John RA (1860-1952).[1] Waterhouse collected works by at least one New Sculptor, George Frampton, and his funeral was attended by at least four others, so it is possible that Goscombe John bought this work as a memento of friendship. **PT**

1 The painting's curatorial file reveals nothing about when Goscombe John acquired it. Thanks to Dr. Anne Pritchard, Assistant Curator of Historic Art, National Museum Wales.

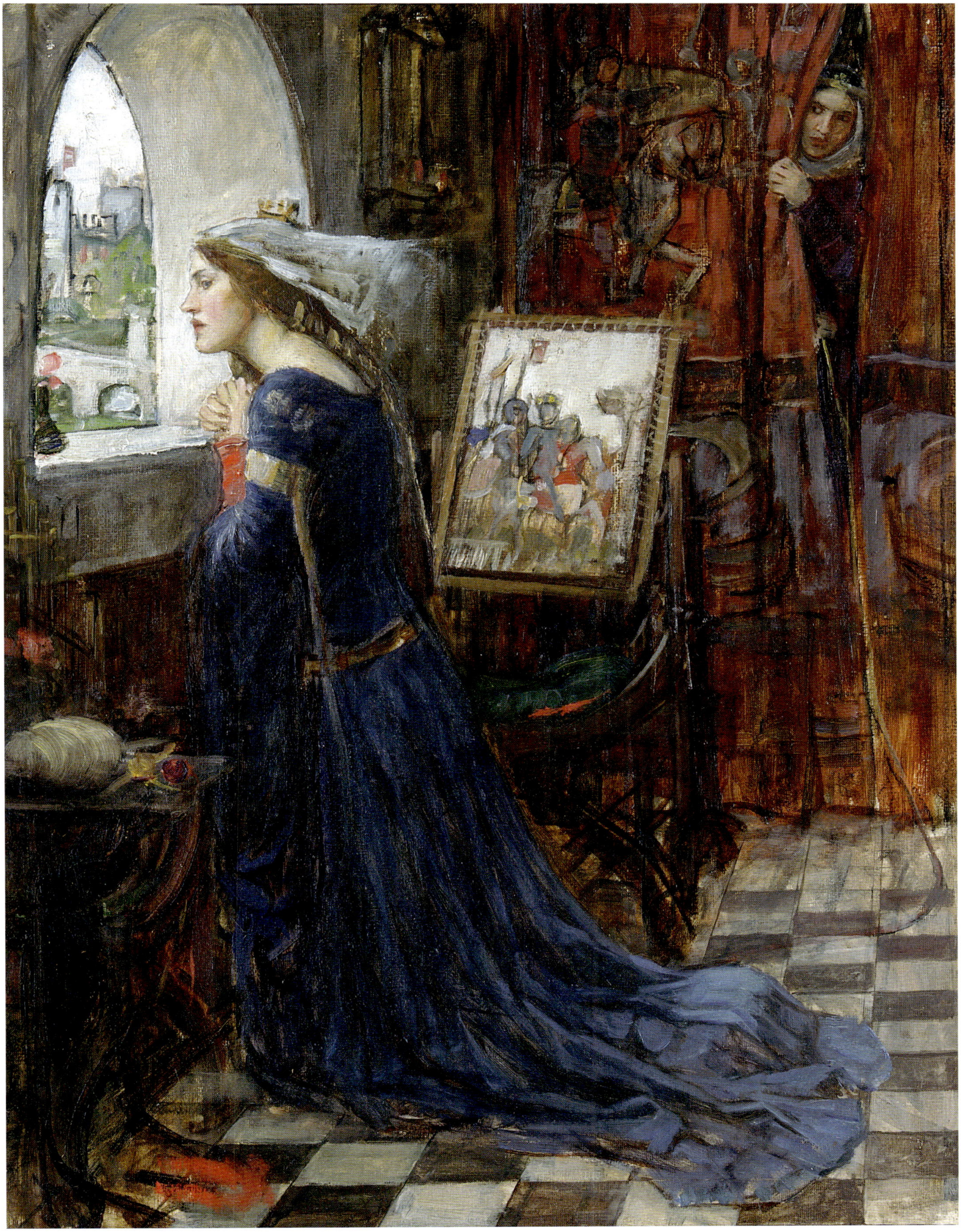

62. **Miranda** 1916

OIL ON CANVAS, LAID ON BOARD, 47.5 X 60 CM - COLLECTION NICKY AND ROMA RYAN COURTESY OF THE MAAS GALLERY - EXHIBITED ROYAL ACADEMY, 1917

At the very end of his life Waterhouse returned to a subject he had first essayed at the very beginning of his career, Miranda from Shakespeare's play *The Tempest* (see cat. 3). Indeed the later composition repeats the earlier one in basic outline, and the artist repeated it on two canvases, one shown at the last Royal Academy exhibition of his lifetime (1916; private collection), and the present work, a close repetition at smaller scale, exhibited at the Academy in 1917, the year of his death. However, the basic compositional similarity makes the differences from the earlier *Miranda* all the more striking. Where the earlier painting shows the storm just beginning to brew, in the later work it rages: the boat, larger and closer to the shore, tosses in the foaming waves and the wind whips through Miranda's hair and draperies, now of Renaissance design rather than the restrained classicism of the earlier costume. This costume is more appropriate to the date of Shakespeare's play, but perhaps more importantly its heavy folds and deep colouring reinforce the increased drama of the later composition. Both figures turn away from the viewer, in three-quarter lost profile, but the later Miranda, with her loosened hair and vivid colouring, is far bolder than her wistful counterpart of 1875. This Miranda is the Shakespearean sister of the windblown female figures in many of Waterhouse's later works, for example that of *Windflowers* (cat. 42). **EP**

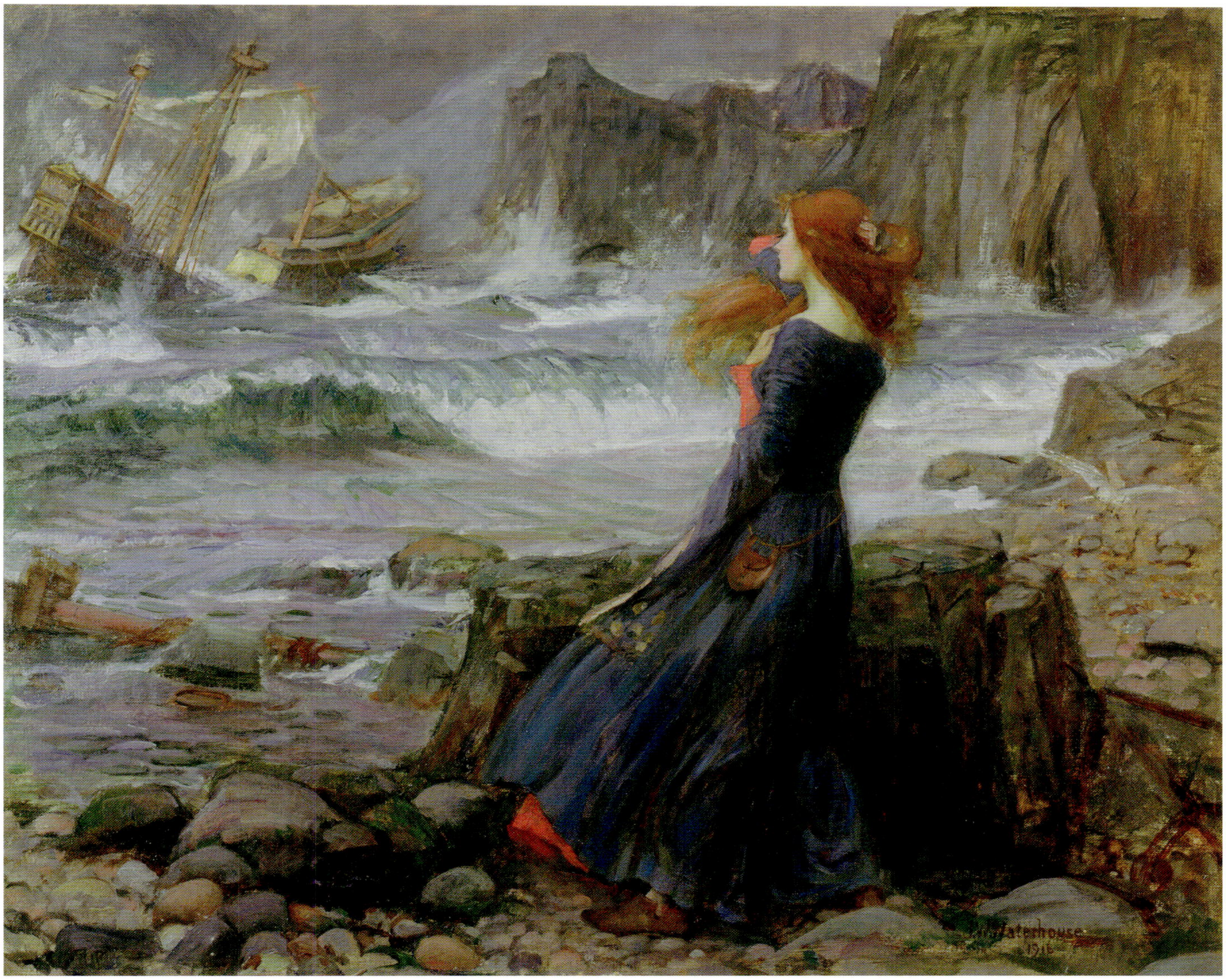

63. Tristram and Isolde 1916

OIL ON CANVAS, 107.5 X 81.5 CM - PRIVATE COLLECTION, NEW YORK - EXHIBITED ROYAL WEST OF ENGLAND ACADEMY, BRISTOL, 1916

In Celtic myth, the wounded Tristram is healed by Isolde – or Iseult – daughter of the King of Ireland. Telling his uncle King Mark of Isolde's beauty on his return, Tristram is sent to secure her marriage to the king. Unknown to both of them, on the journey back to England they take a potion which makes them fall madly in love with each other. Despite her love for Tristram, Isolde fulfils her duty to marry King Mark. But she continues an adulterous liaison with her lover which the king eventually discovers. Tristram flees to Brittany where he is wounded and sends for Isolde to come and heal him. The vessel in which she travels is ordered to fly a white flag if she is on board and a black one if she refused to come. In jealousy, Tristram's own wife tells him it is black, and in despair and longing he dies. When Isolde arrives, overcome with grief for her true love, she also expires. The story was retold by Malory in the *Morte d'Arthur*, with Tristram as one of the Knights of the Round Table. The triangular relationship between Tristram, Mark, and Isolde anticipates the adultery of Guinevere with Lancelot, betraying Arthur and bringing about the collapse of Camelot's sanctity. Waterhouse shows the key moment when the ill-fated pair drink the potion that will bring about tragedy. The flask, half empty, rests behind the couple. Isolde looks at Tristram as if in a trance and with rising yearning, indicating she is already beginning to come under the power of the love potion. The chalice passes between them as if they are receiving the Eucharist, suggesting the sacramental nature of love, their faces flushed with passion. Isolde wears a green cloak decorated with Celtic motifs, and a small crown, that refer to her Irish royal origins. The legend of Tristram and Isolde had become famous through Richard Wagner's opera (1865), and their story came to represent doomed love and the perils of adultery.

In his profile treatment of the pair of figures, and the way the length of their bodies fill the height of the picture space, it is possible Waterhouse took inspiration from Burne-Jones's wood engraving *Sigurd the Crusader* (1862), which shows the Norse hero stepping from a ship to embrace his love Hinda. **RU**

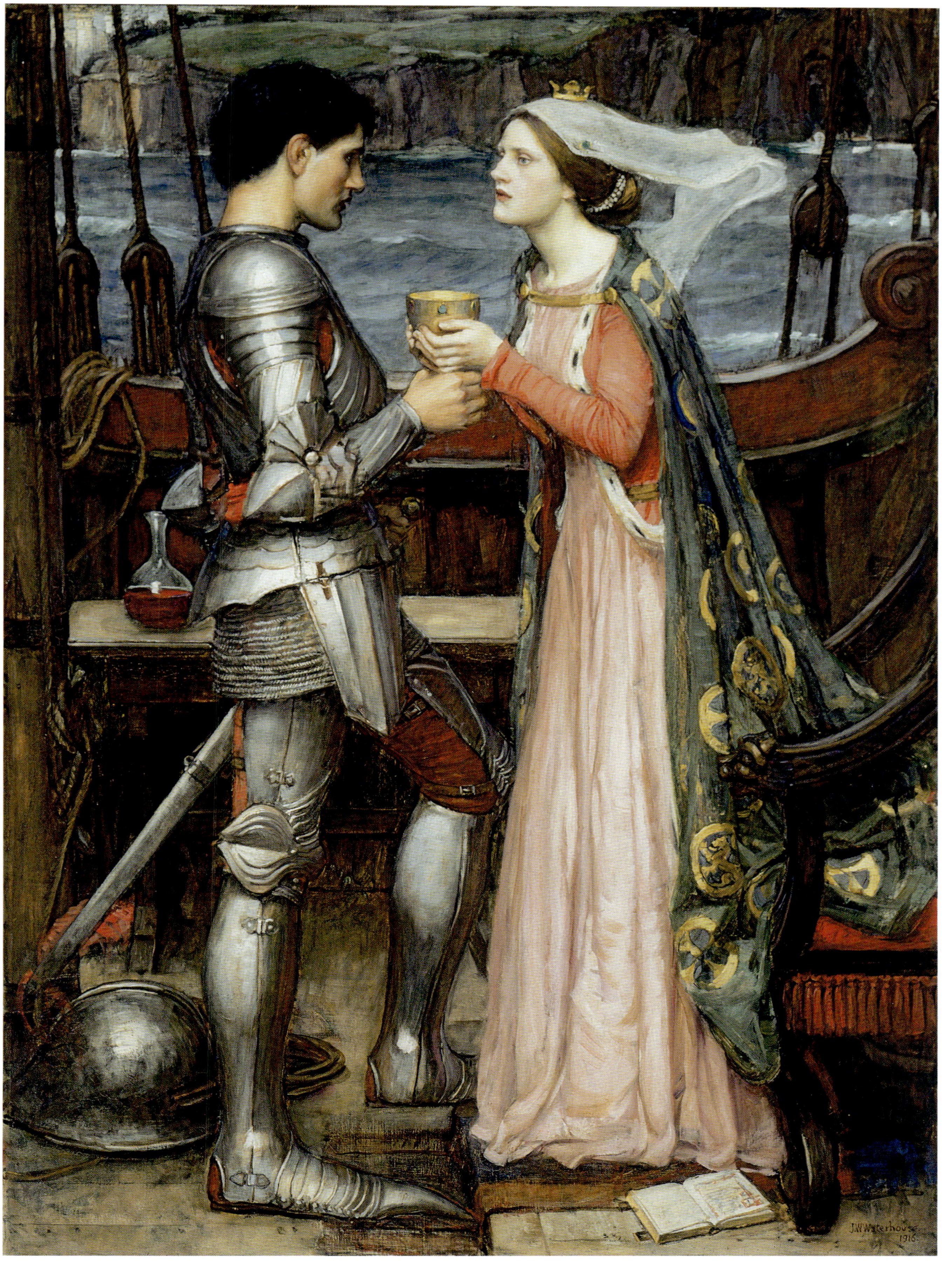

64. Dante and Matilda c. 1916-1917

(FORMERLY KNOWN AS *DANTE AND BEATRICE*)
OIL ON CANVAS, MOUNTED ON WOOD, 49.5 X 62.2 CM - DAHESH MUSEUM OF ART, NEW YORK, PURCHASED 1997

This oil sketch, together with another representing the female figure and flowering tree on the left,[1] were left in the artist's studio at the time of his death, and sold in the posthumous studio sale of 1926. The headdress of the kneeling male figure to the right is immediately recognisable as that of Dante, with lappets over the ears, seen for example in the many representations of the Italian poet by his namesake, Dante Gabriel Rossetti. Accordingly, the sketch became known as *Dante and Beatrice*, with reference to one of the greatest love stories of the Western tradition. On closer examination, though, the scene, sketchy as it is, can be identified as a faithful representation of Dante's *Purgatorio*, Canto XXVIII. Dante has reached the Earthly Paradise, at the top of the mountain of Purgatory, and kneels beside the river Lethe; the two sketchy figures behind him must be his guides on his quest, the poets Virgil and Statius (on their heads, barely sketched, are what appear to be laurel wreaths, traditional attributes of poets). Across the river, on the opposite bank, is Matilda – a counterpoise to Beatrice who represents the active life, as Beatrice the contemplative. Dante has not yet, then, achieved the goal of his quest, his reunion with his beloved Beatrice. But the encounter with Matilda is significant, not merely as a stage on the journey: Matilda, like so many of the female figures in Waterhouse's later paintings, is gathering flowers. Moreover, when Dante addresses Matilda he makes explicit reference to the story of Proserpina:

> Thou puttest me in remembrance of what thing Proserpine was,
> and where, when by mischance
> Her mother lost her, and she lost the spring.[2]

Dante's journey to the underworld and subsequent ascent through Purgatory to Paradise, recounted in the three books of his *Divine Comedy*, made him an exemplary figure for the occult tradition. A crucial source for connecting Dante to the secret tradition was the writings of Gabriele Rossetti, Italian patriot and exile, Dante scholar, and father of the painter Dante Gabriel Rossetti.[3] This oil sketch therefore unites several of the key concerns of Waterhouse's final years: the return to the subject-matter and imagery of early Pre-Raphaelite days, his new interest in the Italian Renaissance (also seen in the Boccaccio subjects, cats 65, 66), and his fascination with myths and stories that relate to the occult tradition. Dante's journey through hell makes him a counterpart to Ulysses and Orpheus. However, as in so many of Waterhouse's works since *Circe Offering the Cup to Ulysses* (cat. 21), the focus is on the female figure, in this case Matilda, who will take over from the male poets, Virgil and Statius, as Dante's spiritual guide, showing him the way, finally, to Beatrice and Paradise. **EP**

1 The sketch has recently appeared at auction (Christie's, London, 5 June 2008, lot 54).
2 Dante, *Purgatorio*, Canto XXVIII, lines 49-51, trans. Laurence Binyon, in Paolo Milano, ed., *The Portable Dante*, Harmondsworth: Penguin, 1977, p. 334.
3 See Leon Surette, *The Birth of Modernism: Ezra Pound, T.S. Eliot, W.B. Yeats, and the Occult*, Montreal and Kingston, London, and Buffalo: McGill-Queen's University Press, 1993, pp. 108-122 and *passim*.

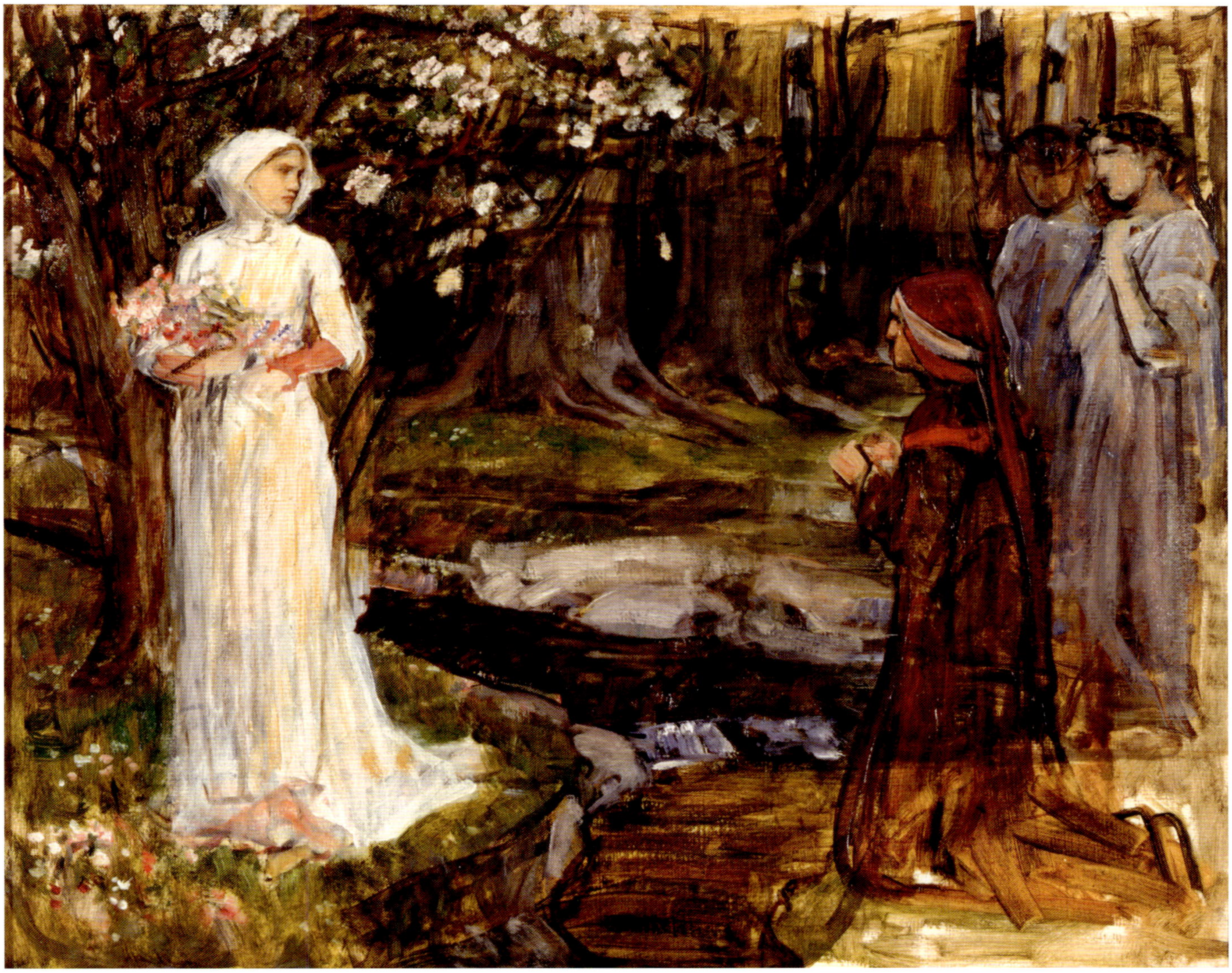

65. The Decameron 1916

OIL ON CANVAS, 101 X 159 CM - LADY LEVER ART GALLERY, NATIONAL MUSEUMS LIVERPOOL, PURCHASED 1916 - EXHIBITED ROYAL ACADEMY, 1916

In Giovanni Boccaccio's *Decameron*, seven maidens and three youths flee from the horrors of the Florentine plague of 1348, vividly described in the introduction to the novel, to a series of beautiful country retreats, where they pass the time by telling stories to one another. It is easy to see how this scenario might appeal to the artist in the midst of World War I, a catastrophe more terrible even than the Florentine plague. This painting, shown at the last Royal Academy exhibition of Waterhouse's lifetime and the second of the war period, shows the storytellers themselves, assembled in a beautiful garden. The setting recalls the garden described in the introduction to the third day of Boccaccio's novel, where the figures gather next to an elaborately decorated fountain, but Waterhouse, never inclined to slavish illustration of his literary sources, shows a simpler garden with a plain marble urn. In the novel, one of the characters acts as king or queen each day, and wears a laurel crown; Waterhouse instead gives a gold crown, easier to relieve against the green foliage, to one of the women. The storytellers of the foreground group make up the magic number seven, but the painting shows only nine figures in all, one short of Boccaccio's complement; moreover, the reduction disturbs Boccaccio's original symbolism of 7 + 3 to make up the perfect number ten.[1] It is difficult to believe that this was an oversight, given Waterhouse's obvious interest in number symbolism. Did he simply run out of time or energy to paint the last figure (he was by now in his sixties, and ailing)?[2] Or can we read the absence of one young man as a poignant allusion to the losses of the war? **EP**

1 Some viewers read the rightmost figure as male, but the hairstyle and the design of the sleeve are closer to female figures in Waterhouse's work of this date. The figure may be not quite finished, and the features read as androgynous to twenty-first-century eyes (as do many of Waterhouse's figures of both sexes, particularly in this later period). If the figure is male, then Waterhouse has left out one of Boccaccio's seven women, which seems improbable given his addiction to groups of seven (see cats 15, 22, 32, 47).

2 A memorandum preserved at the Lady Lever Art Gallery indicates that, while Waterhouse was still at work on the painting, the dealer Arthur Tooth (handling the painting's purchase by the soap magnate W.H. Lever, later Lord Leverhulme) expected it to have ten figures on completion, although it is unclear whether this represents the artist's plan or simply Tooth's assumption. Waterhouse later wrote to Lever (31 March 1916) warning him that the painting might not be ready for that year's Royal Academy since a model had defected to the country; it is possible that Waterhouse simply decided to make do with nine figures, in the absence of the model, after he wrote the letter. The painting did, in fact, appear at the Royal Academy in 1916. I am grateful to Edward Morris for searching the Lady Lever archive for this correspondence.

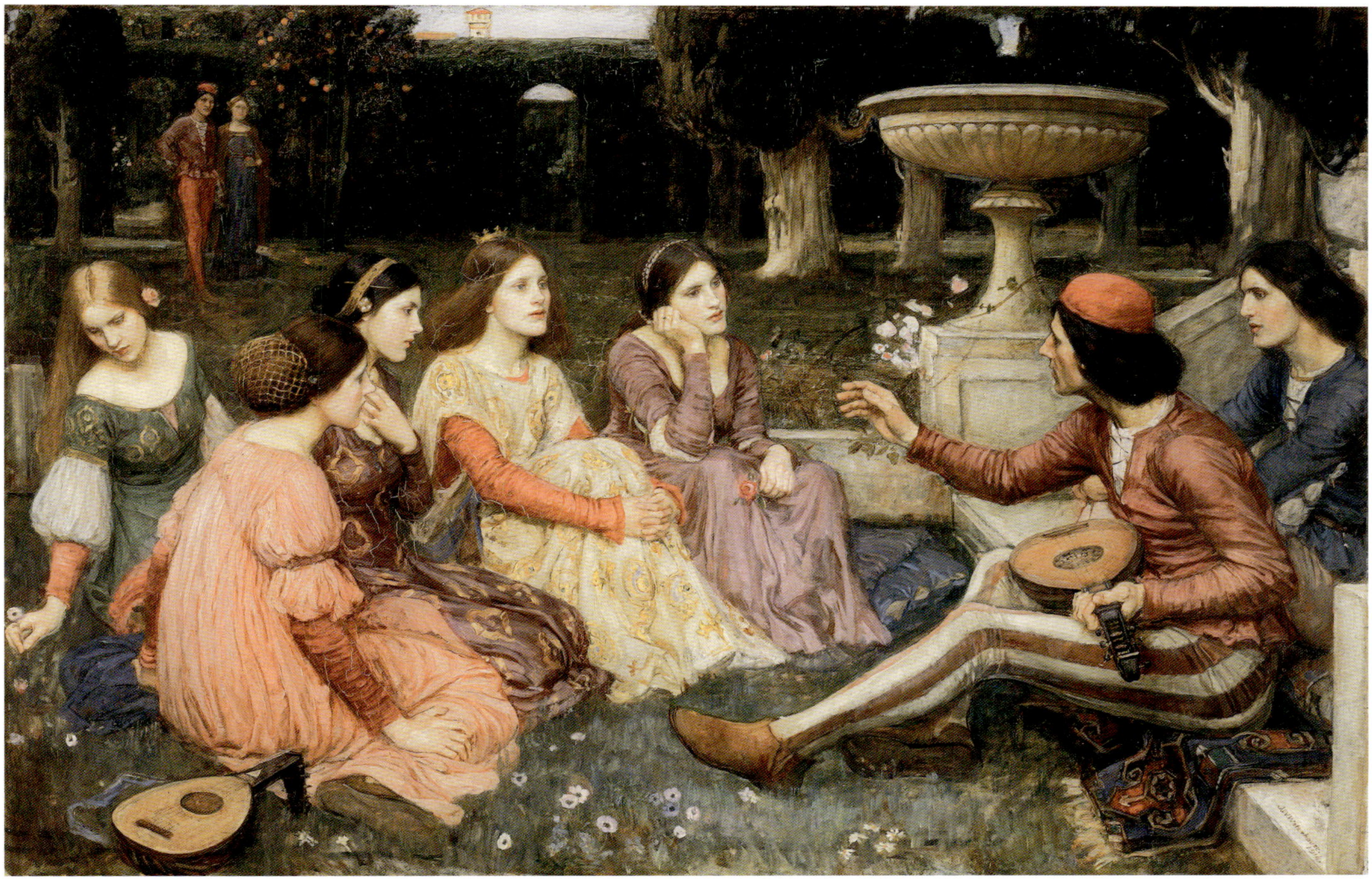

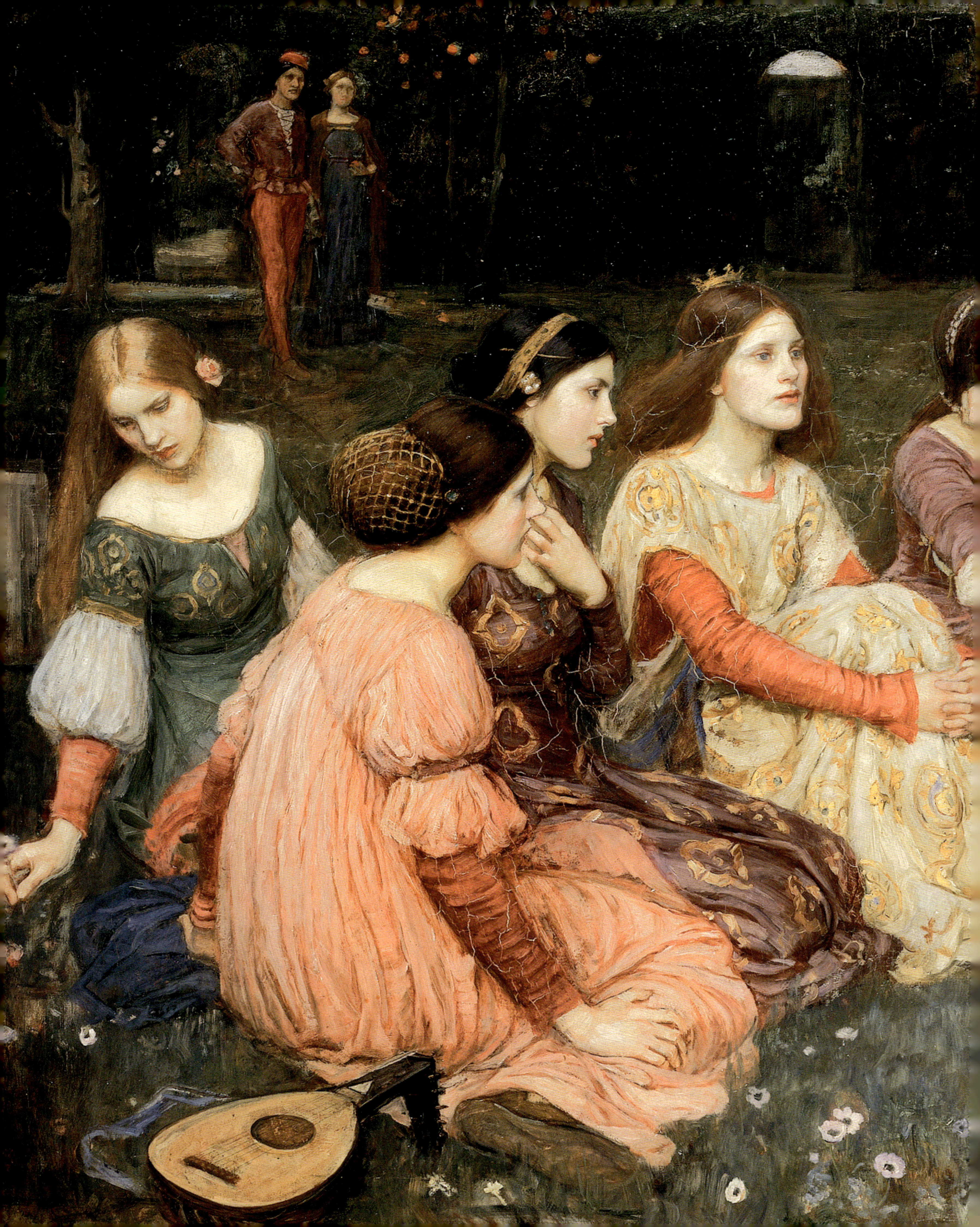

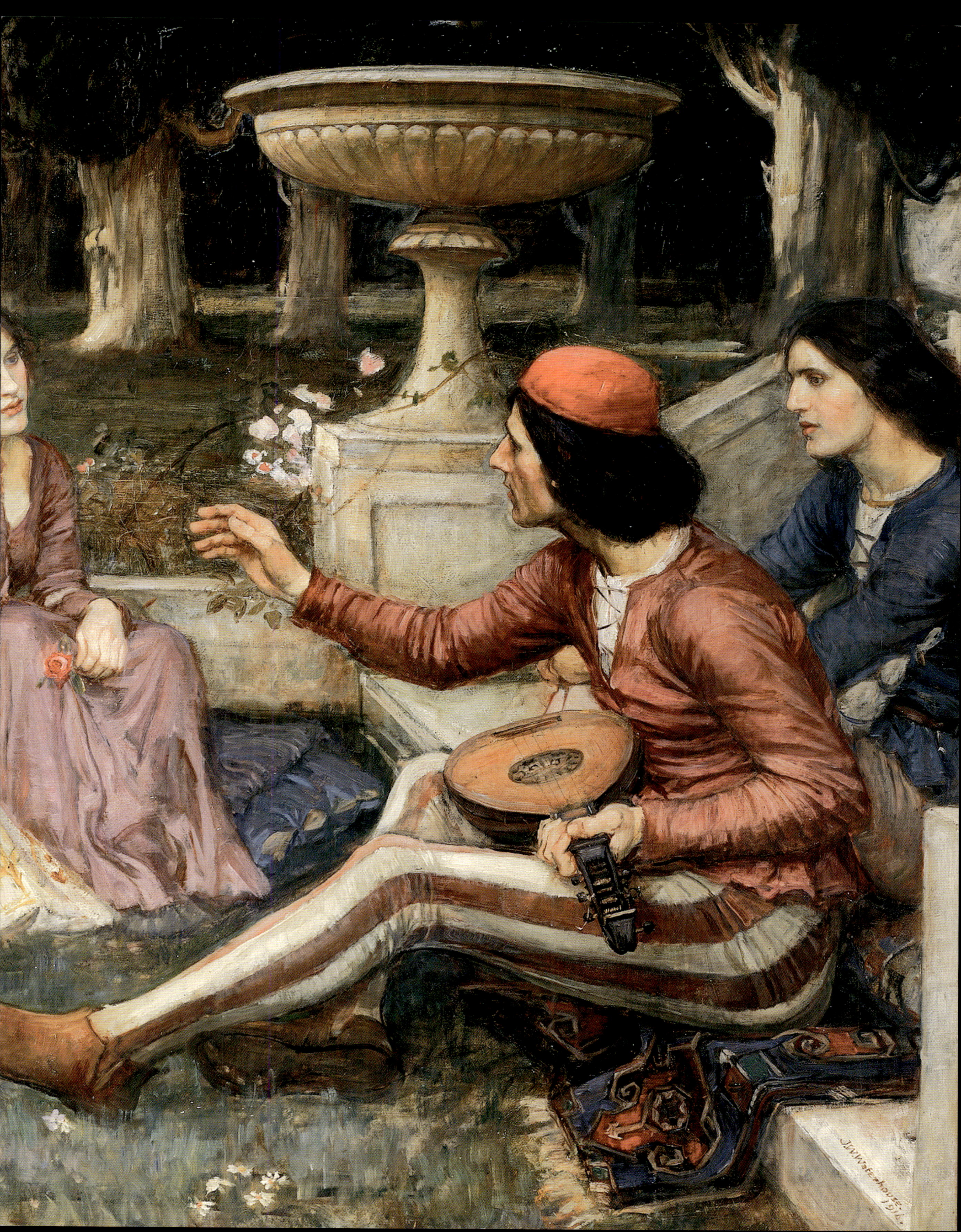
J.W.Waterhouse

66. The Enchanted Garden: from Boccaccio's Tales c. 1916-1917

OIL ON CANVAS, 115.5 X 160 CM - LADY LEVER ART GALLERY, NATIONAL MUSEUMS LIVERPOOL, PURCHASED 1922 - EXHIBITED ROYAL ACADEMY, 1917

This unfinished painting, shown at the Royal Academy of 1917 just after the artist's death in February of that year, shows a garden within a garden: a tale about a magic garden, recounted in the garden retreat as the fifth tale on the tenth and last day of the *Decameron*. The faithful wife Dianora has tried to evade the unwanted attentions of Messer Ansaldo, by promising to yield only if he can give her a garden that blooms in January. Ansaldo, with the help of a magician (probably the shadowy figure with a wand, at extreme left), makes the garden appear; in the event, he releases Dianora from her rash promise. Perhaps Waterhouse intended the note of hope to come as a welcome relief, in the grimmest year of the war. Ironically, or tragically, he died before he could finish it. Nonetheless, the composition, organised with the artist's usual flair for pictorial storytelling, and the vibrant colours of the lush garden make their point, recalling the earlier enchanted garden, in *Psyche Opening the Door into Cupid's Garden* (cat. 45). In the earlier picture, though, the curious Psyche – and the viewer – remain outside. In *The Enchanted Garden*, the figures and the viewer are admitted to the magic realm, while the snowy winter is kept at bay, just glimpsed outside the doorway on the left. **EP**

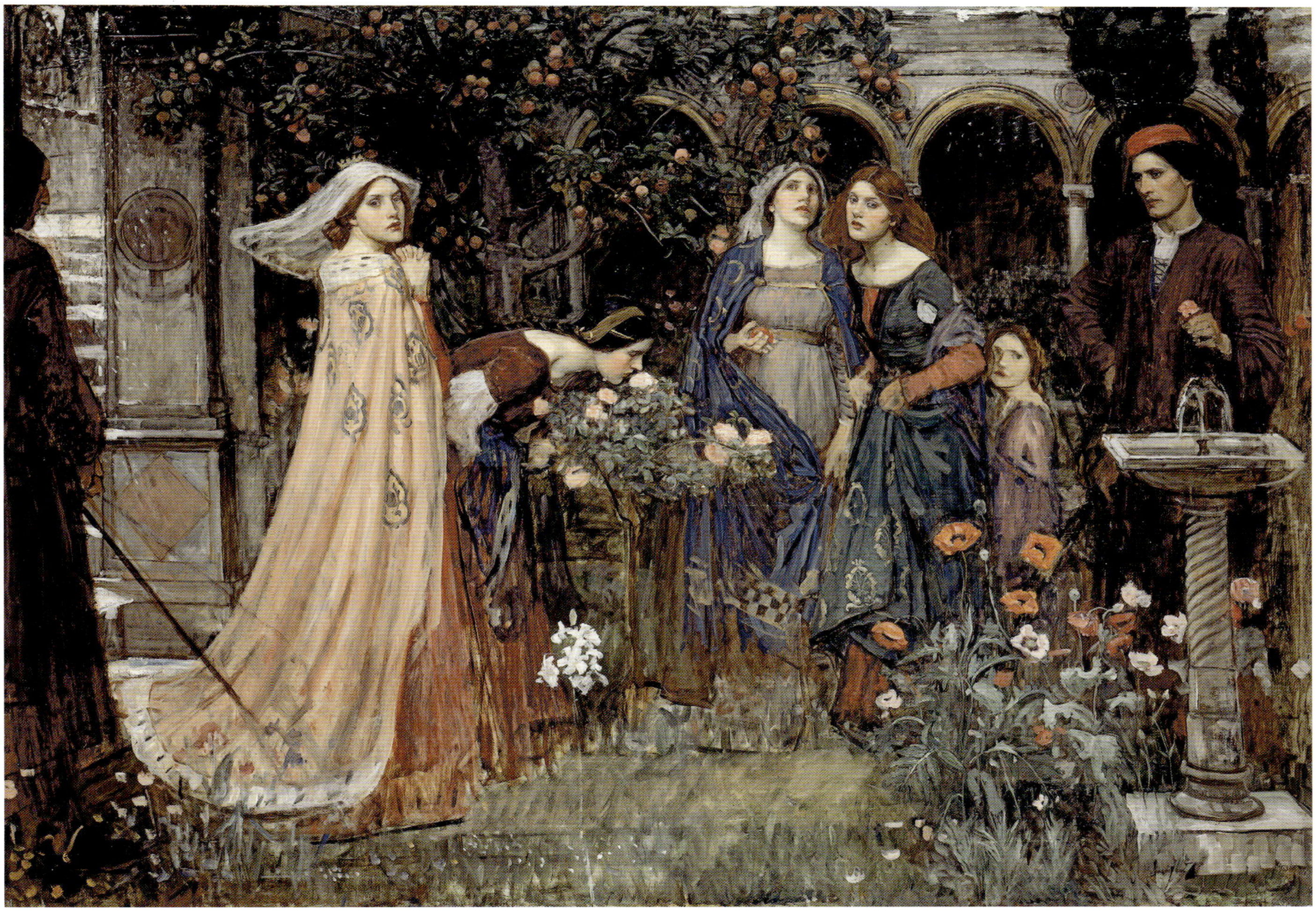

67. The Decameron c. 1915-1916

SKETCH - OIL ON CANVAS, 53 X 89.5 CM - COLLECTION STEPHEN AND LINDA WATERHOUSE

This large oil sketch for one of Waterhouse's last pictures, *The Decameron* of 1916 (cat. 65), is of particular interest for demonstrating how the artist refined his composition. The basic design is one that Waterhouse had used throughout his career, based on a semicircle of figures facing, and attending to, a single figure opposite them; earlier examples include *The Favourites of the Emperor Honorius* (cat. 12), *Consulting the Oracle* (cat. 15), and *Hylas and the Nymphs* (cat. 32). That design is perfectly suited to the subject-matter from Boccaccio's *Decameron*, in which a group of young men and women, fleeing the plague, retire to a series of garden retreats and tell stories to one another. In the oil sketch, Waterhouse has already established the composition, but there are differences in detail. The male figure on the right is playing his lute, rather than making the dramatic gesture with his hand that appears in the finished painting. The group of five female figures, to the left, is similar to that of the finished painting, except for minor details (for example, the crowned figure, representing the member of the group who is taking charge of proceedings for the day, wears a white veil which gives emphasis to the crown, but which disappears in the finished painting). However, there is a sixth female figure in this group, reclining and leaning her head on the seated figure to the right of the group; interestingly, this is the sketchiest figure, an indication that the artist was still unsure about how to position it. Perhaps Waterhouse decided that the arrangement failed to make a clear separation between the groups; in the final painting, he moves the figure to a position behind the lute-playing man, opens up the space between the groups, and introduces the man's hand gesture to link the two groups. A particularly interesting feature of the oil sketch is the suggestion, in the right background, of an elaborate fountain. While this would be replaced, in the final painting, by the simpler urn, it is closer to the fanciful garden ornaments that Boccaccio describes, in exuberant detail. Although the handling of the oil sketch is much freer and more spontaneous, the colour scheme is as rich and verdant as that of the final painting, with just a few changes of hue. The work suggests that Waterhouse used the process of making an oil sketch, at reasonably large scale, to help him in the design of both composition and colour scheme. **EP**

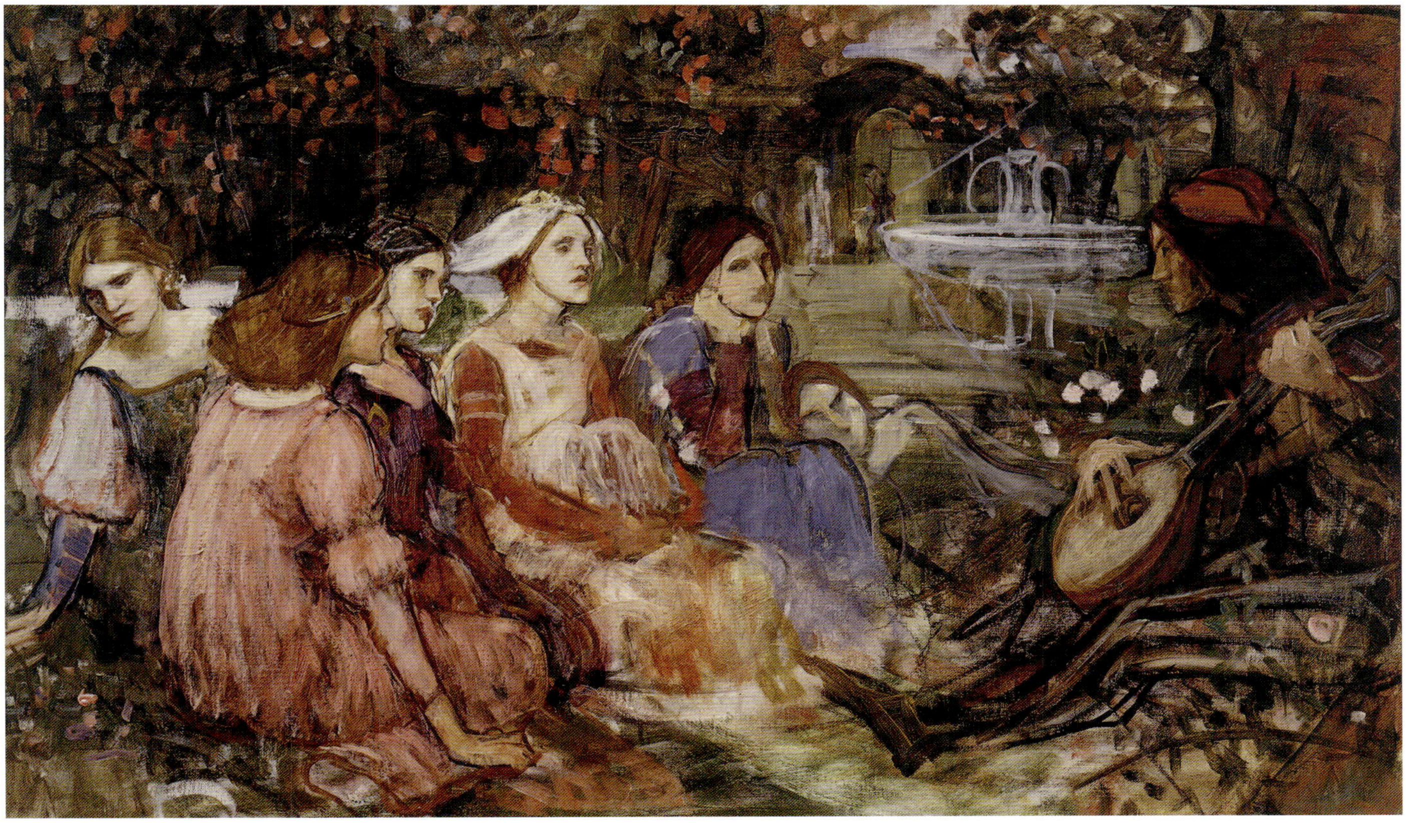

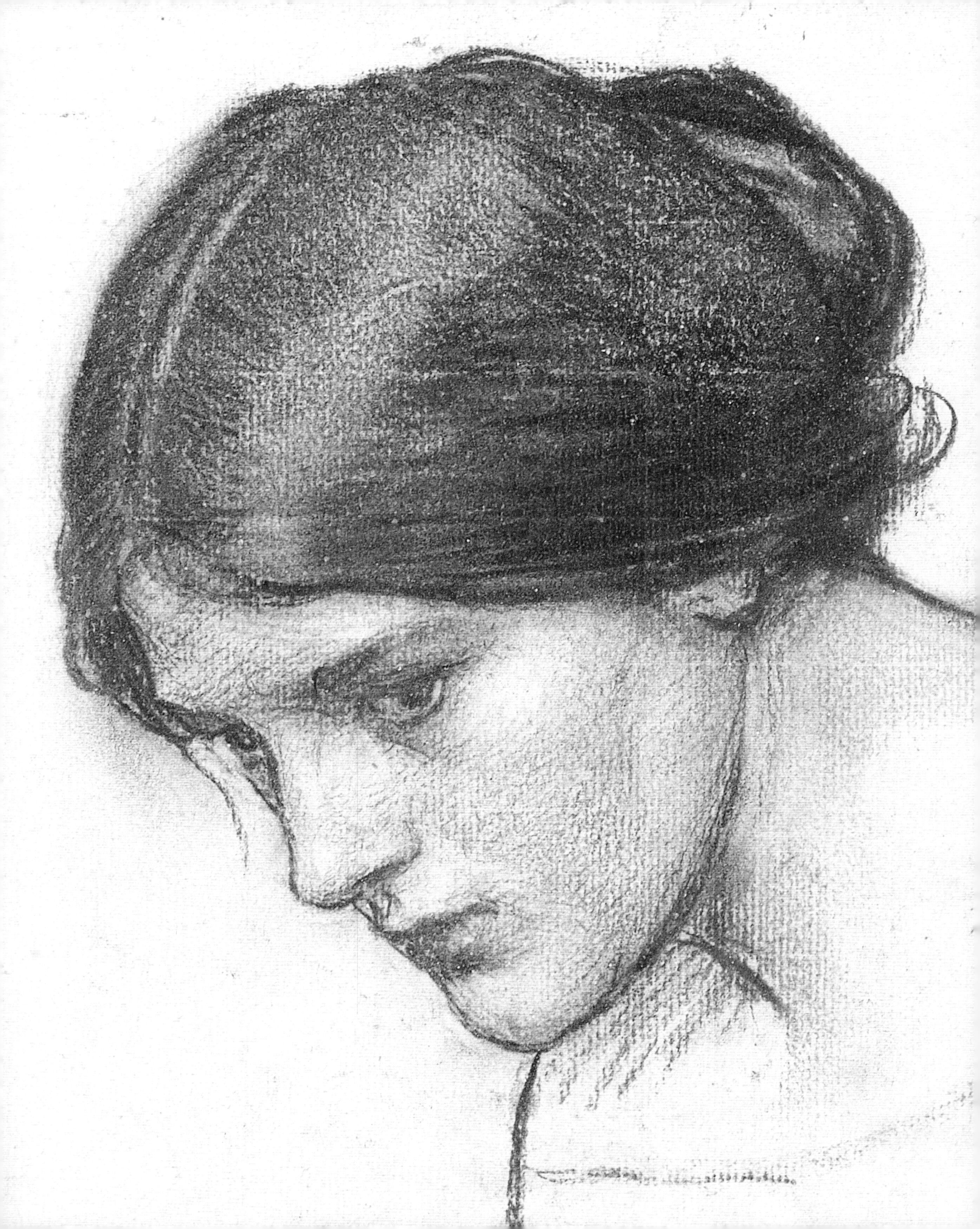

Drawings and Sketchbooks

DRAWINGS OF YOUNG WOMEN

Only thirteen of Waterhouse's sketchbooks are known to have survived intact, but hundreds of loose sheets emerged from his studio at various times, especially during the studio sale held at Christie's on 23 July 1926. During that 100-lot auction instigated by Esther Waterhouse, large quantities of drawings were bundled into portfolios and sold as single lots. Ostensibly, all of these carry the distinctive round seal stamped and then hand-numbered by Christie's. (See, for example, cat. 75.)

Like Dante Gabriel Rossetti, Edward Burne-Jones, and Albert Moore – to name just a few peers – Waterhouse transcended female models' particularities to create his own idealised, instantly recognizable type, varied primarily by hair colour. By 1898, however, even his friend M.H. Spielmann had joined a list of commentators who regretted Waterhouse's 'single type of feminine beauty [which] should occasionally be varied.'[1] An interesting case is presented by the virtuosic *Study for the Portrait of the Marchioness of Downshire* (cat. 78), made in preparation for the commissioned oil portrait exhibited at the Royal Academy in 1914. Although the sitter was real, she essentially becomes a 'Waterhouse girl', barely distinguishable from his idealised women.

The other drawings of women's heads gathered here were surely consulted by Waterhouse over the years, constituting a veritable archive of gazes and poses that he could orchestrate into new compositions. Unfortunately, drawings made at Primrose Hill Studios (1878-1900) are rare today; many may have been discarded when the Waterhouses moved to St John's Wood in autumn 1900. (A fortunate survivor is cat. 69.)

Setting aside the notion of type, one specific female model appears in many Waterhouse paintings made from 1889 until his death in 1917. The search for her name has pivoted on the drawing of her head (cat. 75), which was most likely made c. 1904-1905 in preparation for the oil painting of 1905, *Lamia* (cat. 46). Its inscription ('Miss Muriel Foster/ Buxton Rd/Chingford') is problematic because 1904-1905 seems late in their relationship for Waterhouse to record his favourite model's name and address, as if she were a newcomer. Although it is possible he jotted her details for another artist's reference, this seems unlikely because the 1926 sale stamp on this sheet confirms that it remained in Waterhouse's possession until his death. The inclusion here of another, very similar drawing of Lamia's head (cat. 76) underscores how thoroughly Waterhouse prepared for compositions important to him.

If *the* Waterhouse girl was indeed Muriel Foster, then the most promising candidate is a Muriel Foster who lived 1878-1969. Her second cousin was the architect Alfred Waterhouse RA, who could have introduced her to his fellow Academician, with whom he shared a surname but no blood ties. Despite this connection, though, it would have been highly unusual for Quakers – as the Foster family members were – to let their eleven-year-old daughter model in 1889. Thus the search remains open.[2]

Regardless, viewers today admire the simultaneous beauty, delicacy, and erotic allure of the Waterhouse girl, whose resemblance in physique and colouring to several supermodels on catwalks today is uncanny. Like Waterhouse's nymphs, these modern models 'read' as both quintessentially English and universally fashionable; thin but not sickly, fit but not muscular. **PT**

1 *Magazine of Art*, 1898, p. 465.
2 James K. Baker and Cathy L. Baker, 'Miss Muriel Foster: The John William Waterhouse Model', *Journal of Pre-Raphaelite Studies* 8, autumn 1999, pp. 70-82; and 'The Lamia in the Art of J.W. Waterhouse', *British Art Journal*, vol. V, no. 2 (Autumn 2004), pp. 15-22.

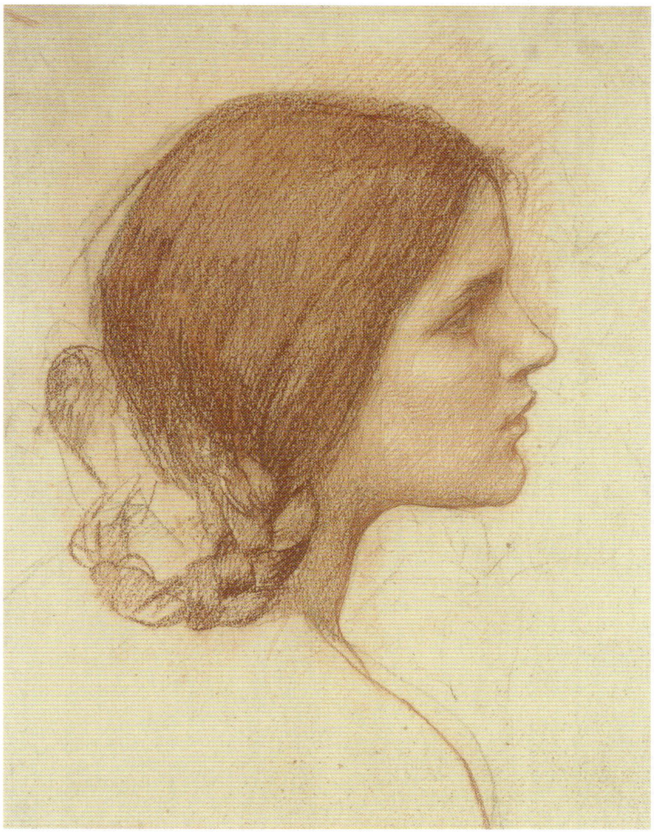

68. **Head of a Girl** c. 1905

RED AND BLACK CHALK ON PAPER, 37.5 X 31.1 CM
PRIVATE COLLECTION COURTESY OF CHRISTIE'S

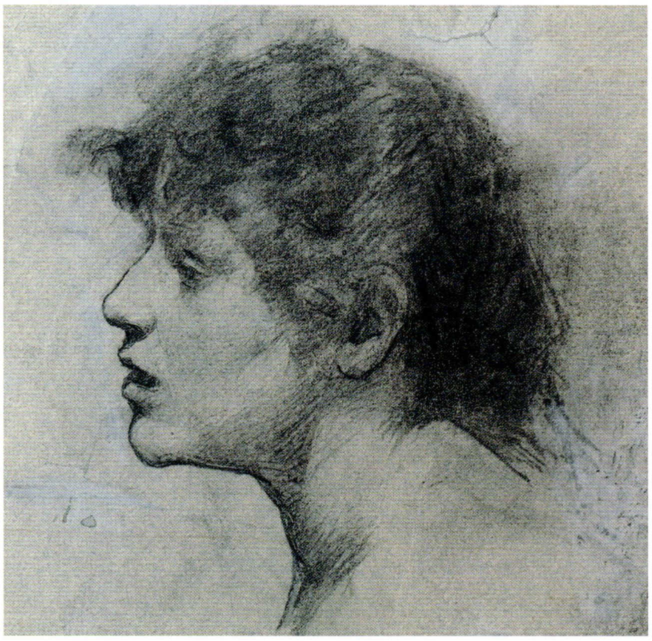

69. **Head of a Woman** c. 1883-1884

BLACK CHALK HEIGHTENED WITH WHITE ON BLUE PAPER,
21 X 21.5 CM - PRIVATE COLLECTION

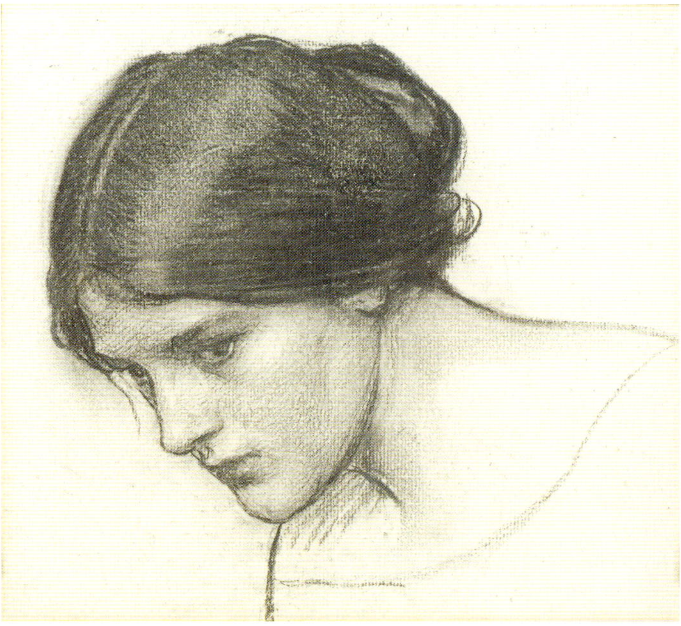

70. **Head of a Girl** c. 1903

BLACK CHALK HEIGHTENED WITH WHITE ON PAPER,
23.5 X 26 CM - PRIVATE COLLECTION

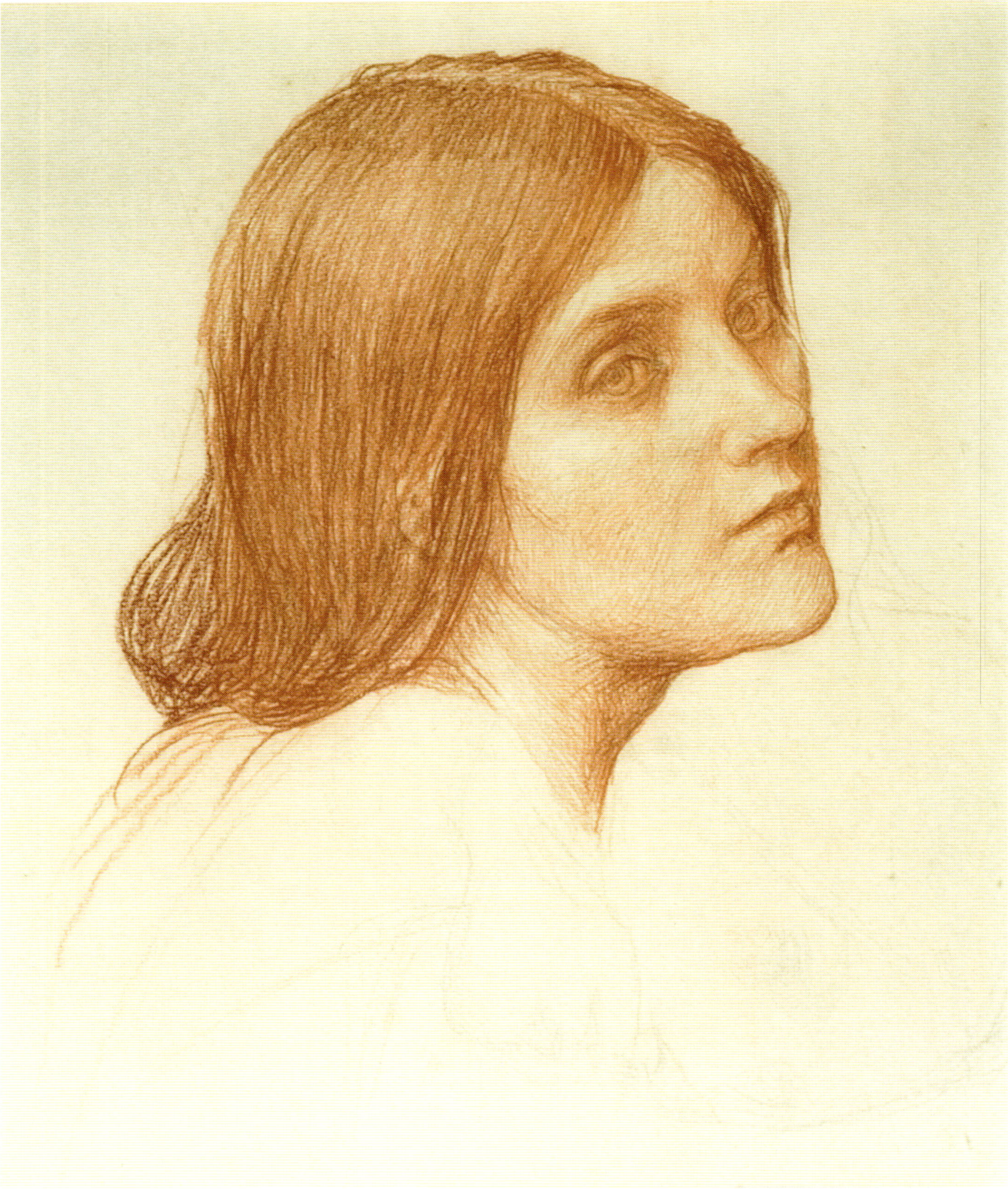

71. **Head of a Girl** c. 1915-1917

RED CHALK ON PAPER, 36 X 30 CM - PRIVATE COLLECTION

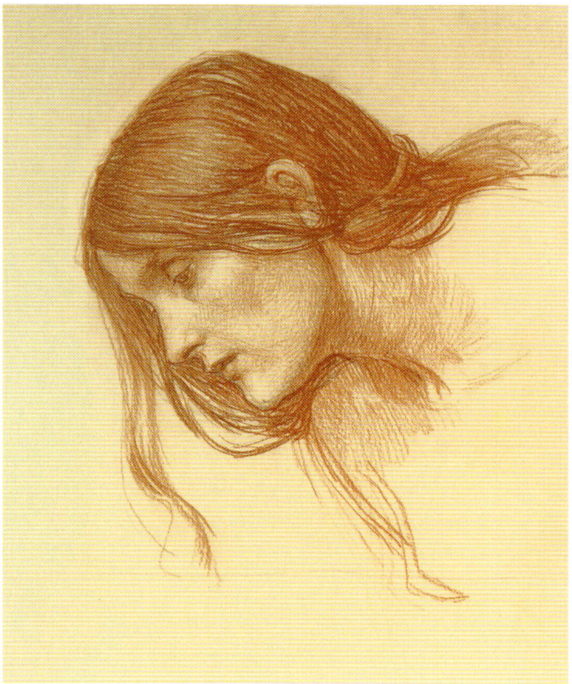

72. **Study for the Head of Phyllis in Phyllis and Demophöon** c. 1906-1907

RED CHALK ON PAPER, 30.5 X 25.4 CM - PRIVATE COLLECTION COURTESY OF CHRISTIE'S

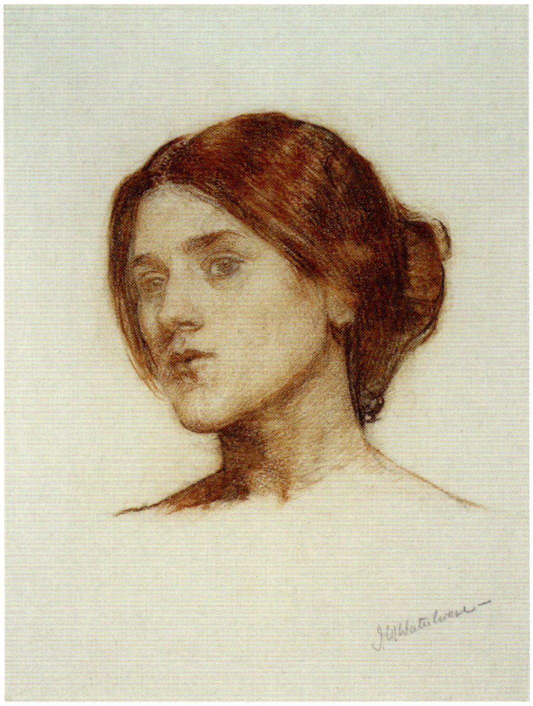

73. **Study for the Head in The Rose Bower** c. 1910

RED AND BLACK CHALK ON PAPER, 32.2 X 24.5 CM
COLLECTION DR. DENNIS T. LANIGAN, CANADA

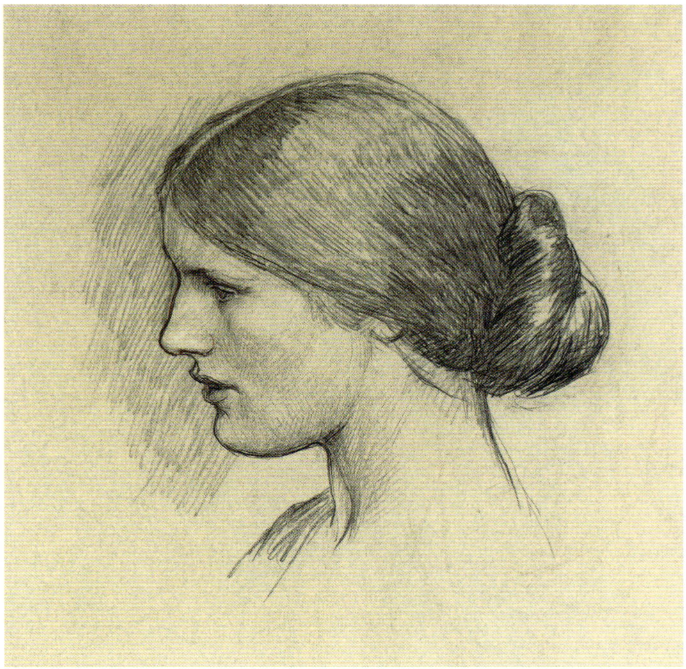

74. **Study, probably for Circe** c. 1911-1914

PENCIL, RED AND WHITE CHALK ON GREY-BLUE PAPER, 29.5 X 31.1 CM
PRIVATE COLLECTION COURTESY OF CHRISTIE'S

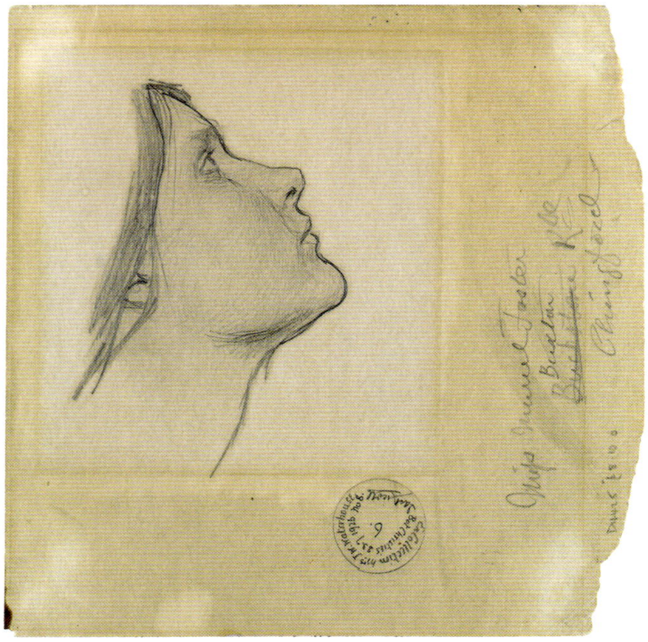

75. **Study for the Head of Lamia** c. 1904-1905

PENCIL ON PAPER, 12 X 11.5 CM - YALE CENTER FOR BRITISH ART,
NEW HAVEN, CONNECTICUT, BEQUEST OF ELIZABETH S. TOWER, 1988

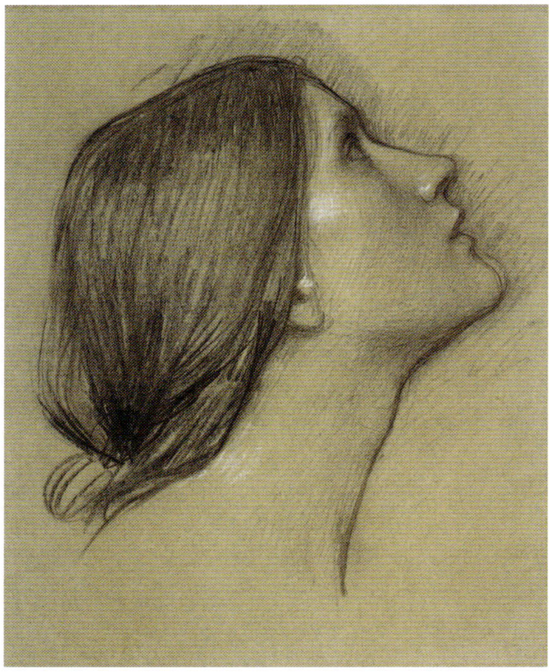

76. **Study for the Head of Lamia**
c. 1904-1905

BLACK CHALK HEIGHTENED WITH WHITE ON PAPER, 32.2 X 26.7 CM
COLLECTION DR. DENNIS T. LANIGAN, CANADA

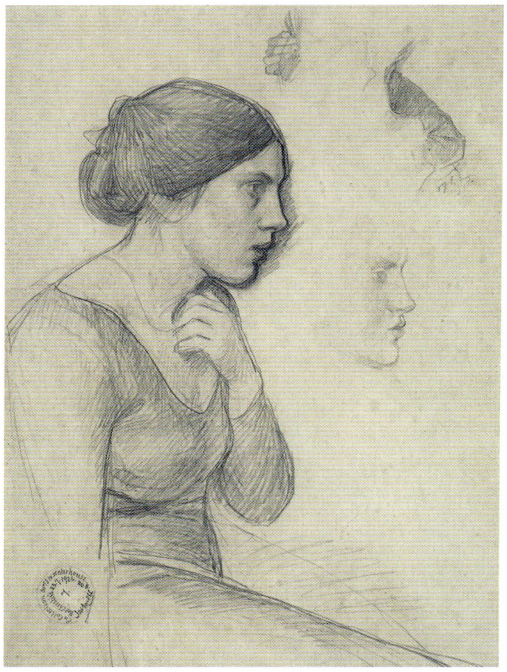

77. **Study of a Woman for The Decameron**
c. 1915-1916

GRAPHITE ON PAPER, 33 X 24.5 CM - NATIONAL GALLERY OF CANADA, OTTAWA
VERSO: STUDY OF A BRANCH WITH LEAVES
GIFT OF THE DENNIS T. LANIGAN COLLECTION IN MEMORY OF DANIEL PERRIN, 2005

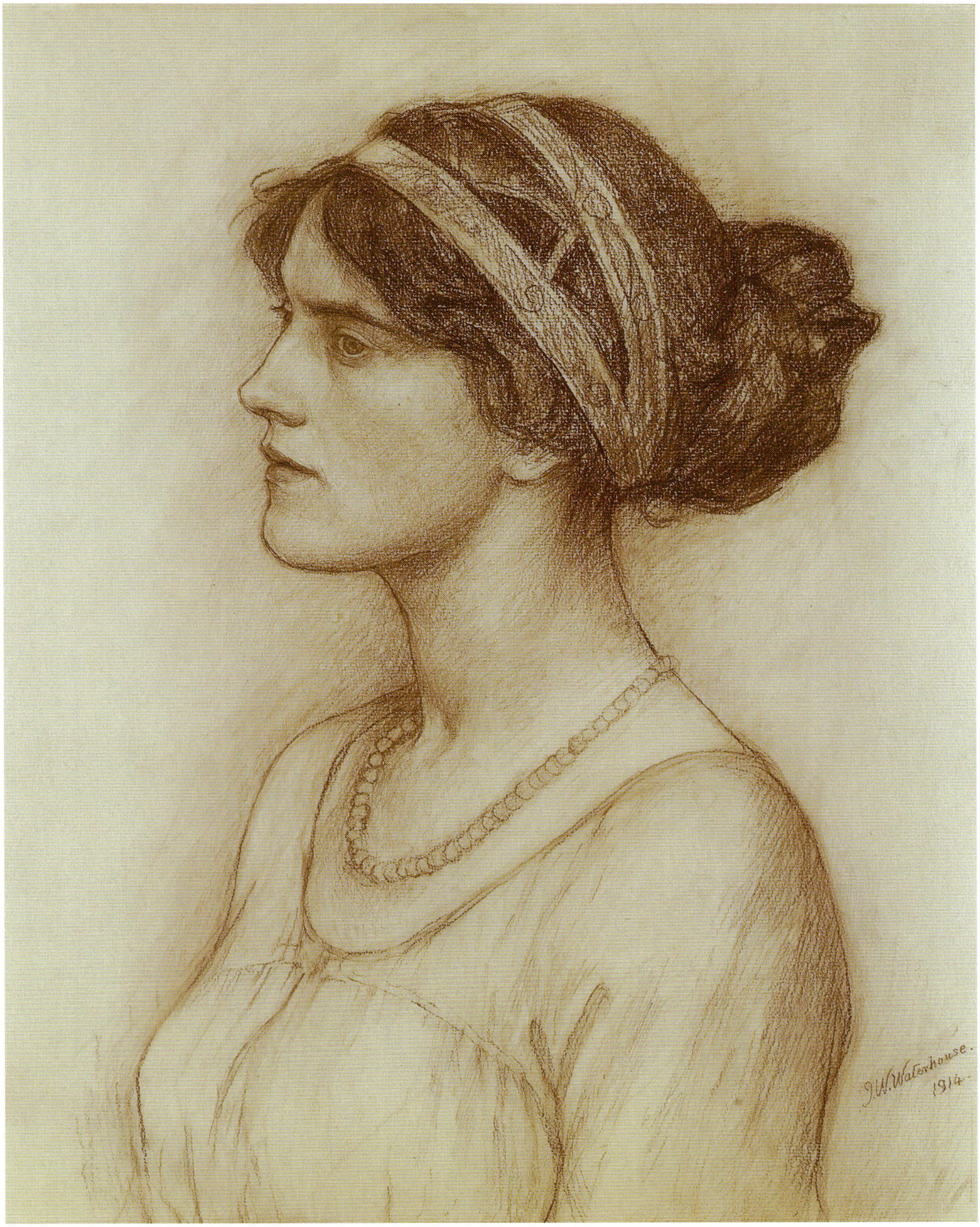

78. **Study for the Portrait of the Marchioness of Downshire** 1914

RED CHALK ON PAPER, 41.2 X 31.3 CM - PRIVATE COLLECTION

COMPOSITIONAL DRAWINGS

Studying Waterhouse's drawings offers the pleasure of watching how he modified compositions in order to maximise their beauty and dramatic impact. These adjustments were sometimes considerable, though he usually found solutions on canvas that now seem inevitable. Quite unexpected, for example, is cat. 91, an imagining of Waterhouse's 1916 *Miranda* (cat. 62) that presents the heroine not in the Renaissance garment she ultimately acquired, but in a classicised one seen in the Psyche pictures a dozen years earlier (cats 44, 45).

Drawings, of course, offer artists a place to dream, and err, in privacy. Particularly intriguing are the narratives Waterhouse conceived and abandoned, some recognisable (e.g., Perseus rescuing Andromeda) and others not at all. In view of Elizabeth Prettejohn's references to the Hermetic Order of the Golden Dawn (p. 32), we can only wonder at Waterhouse's drawing of a young woman watching the sun rise over the sea (cat. 90). Another puzzle is cat. 84, *Woman Preparing to Open a Door from Inside.* This stylistically late drawing may be a later derivation of *Mariana in the South* (cat. 33), or it may relate to the unlocated oil, *Fatima* (exhibited Royal Academy, 1911). At first we might assume Waterhouse's admiration of Mariana, the desperate lover celebrated by Tennyson, but given his fascination with women entering dangerous and unknown realms, he could have instead been thinking of Charles Perrault's story *La Barbe Bleue* (1697). Blue Beard's wife Fatima disobeys an order not to use a key to open a closet at the back of their basement. (This location might explain the staircase visible behind Waterhouse's figure.) Naturally Fatima finds there the bodies of Blue Beard's previous wives, and the plot thickens.

For those curious about how Waterhouse inter-associated various narratives, it is instructive to see which scenes appear on the same sheets. In cat. 85, for example, two women picking flowers (in keeping with Proserpina's story) share a sheet with a well-developed conception of Isolde offering the love potion to Tristram. Although we cannot be certain that Waterhouse drew on this sheet's reverse at exactly the same time, there we find a swine and two baboons related to the Circe images. Borrowed from different literary sources, all three themes have at their core the magical transformations so significant to Waterhouse.

Several of the drawings in this section show signs of having once been bound into sketchbooks, and it is likely that Waterhouse himself removed specific sheets when he needed them. Most of these date from after 1900, when the Waterhouses relocated from Primrose Hill Studios to St John's Wood. Many drawings may have been discarded during that move: a fortunate survivor is cat. 79, one of Waterhouse's few known works in sepia, a medium in which he exhibited occasionally early in his career. **PT**

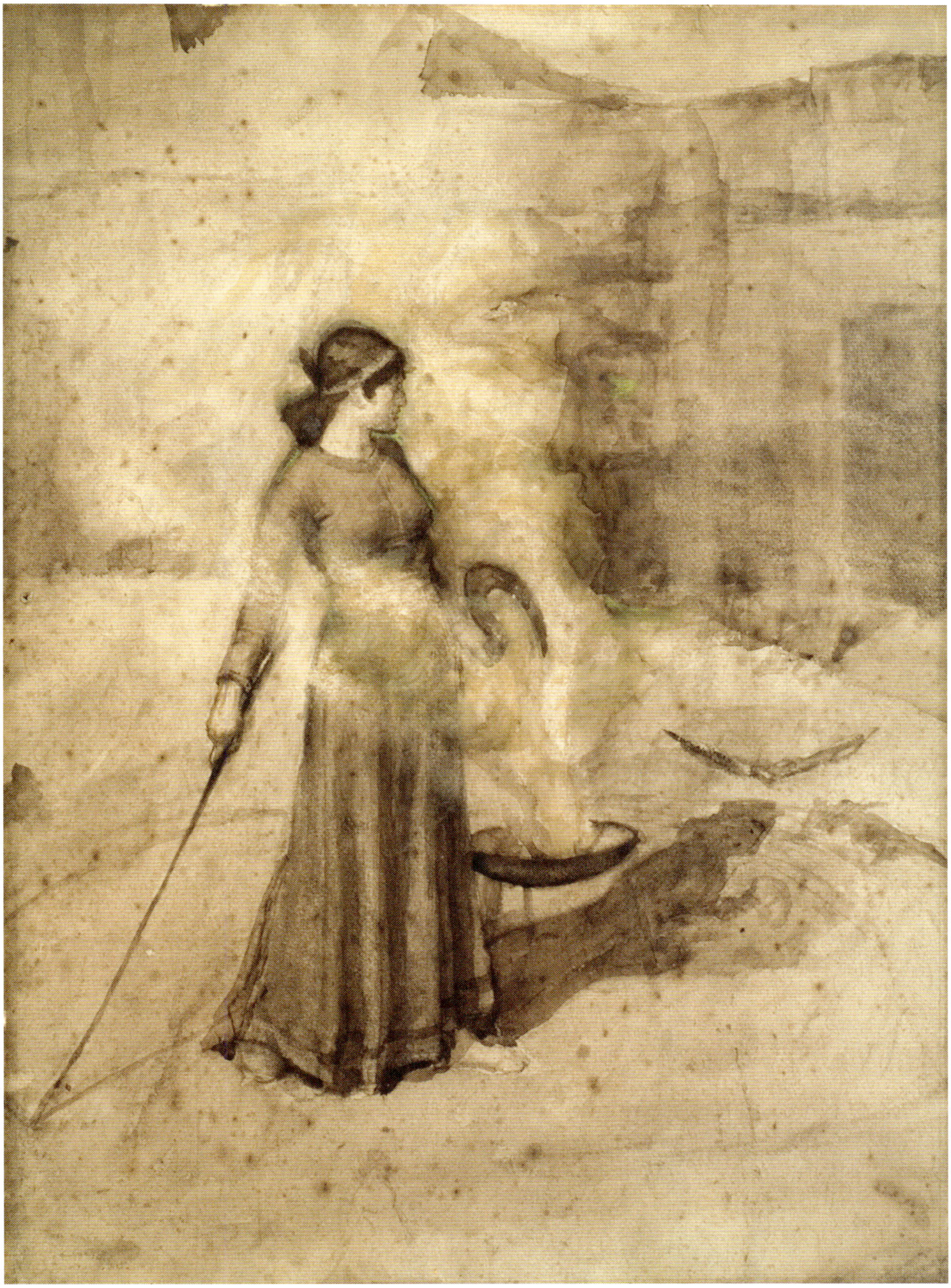

79. **Study for The Magic Circle** c. 1880-1881

SEPIA, PEN, AND INK ON PAPER, 49 X 36.3 CM - PRIVATE COLLECTION - EXHIBITED DUDLEY GALLERY, BLACK AND WHITE EXHIBITION, 1881

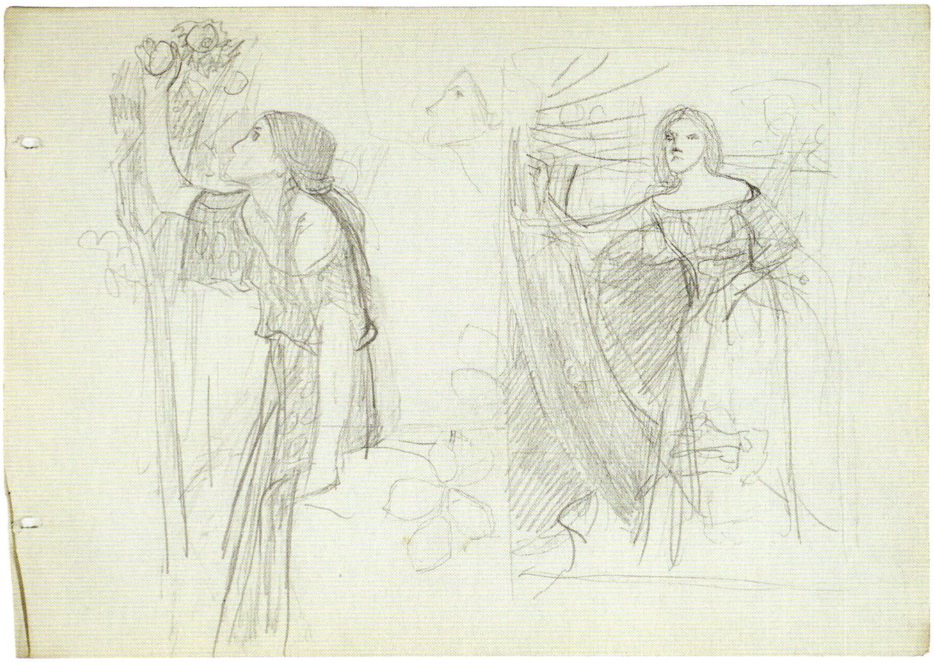

80. **Woman Picking Fruit from a Tree, and the 1910 treatment of Ophelia** c. 1910

GRAPHITE ON PAPER, 17.5 X 25 CM, VERSO: WOMAN WITH ARMS UPRAISED, BEFORE A CASTLE - COLLECTION JOHN PHYSICK

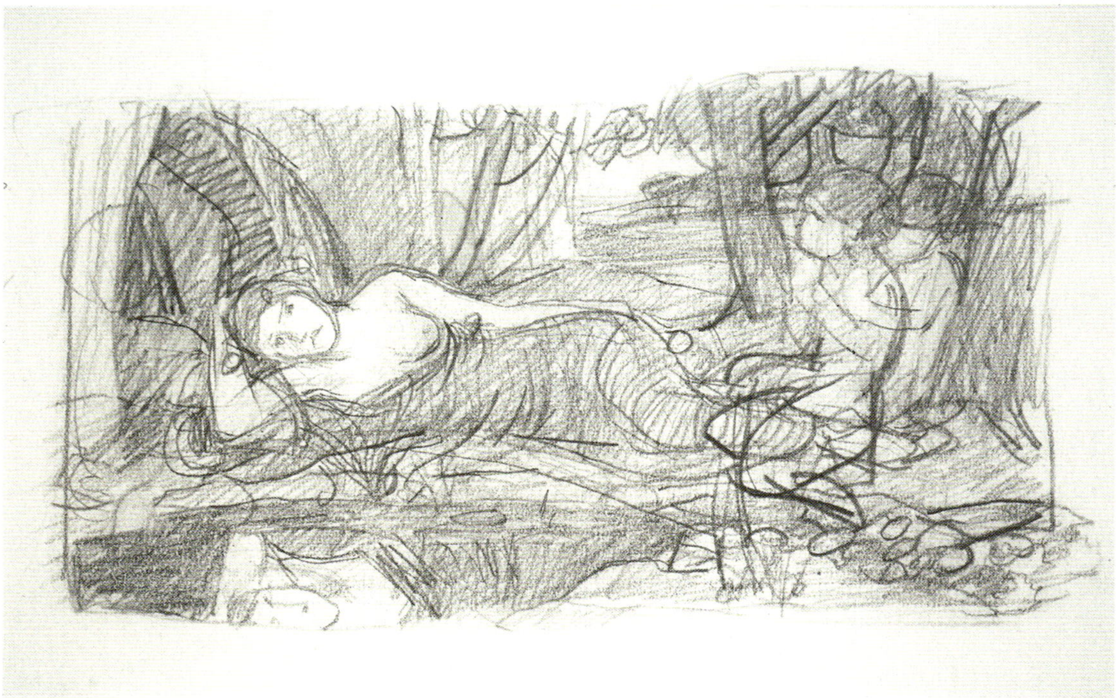

81. **Study for 'Listening to my Sweet Pipings'** c. 1910-1911

GRAPHITE ON PAPER, 17.6 X 25.2 CM, VERSO: A DRAPED FIGURE BY A TREE - COLLECTION DR. DENNIS T. LANIGAN, CANADA

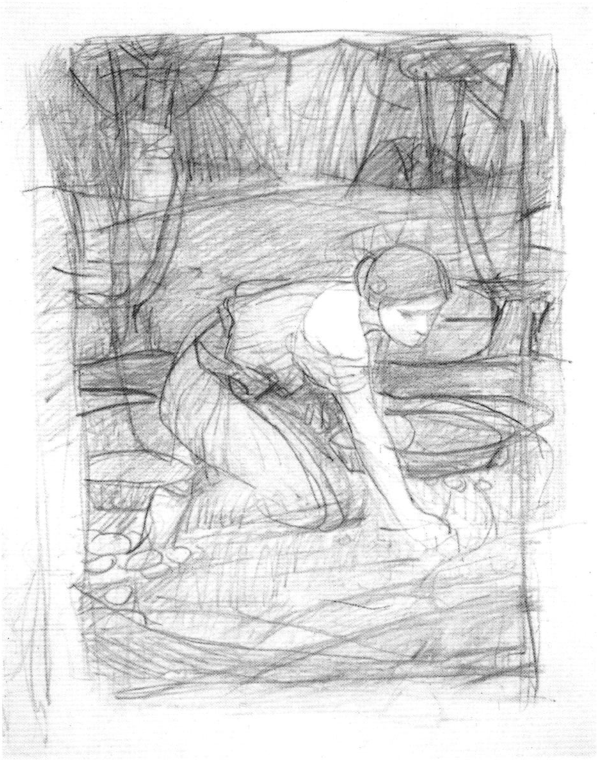

82. **Study for Maidens Picking Flowers by a Stream** c. 1911

GRAPHITE ON PAPER, 25.2 X 17.6 CM, VERSO: A WOMAN PLAITING HER HAIR
COLLECTION DR. DENNIS T. LANIGAN, CANADA

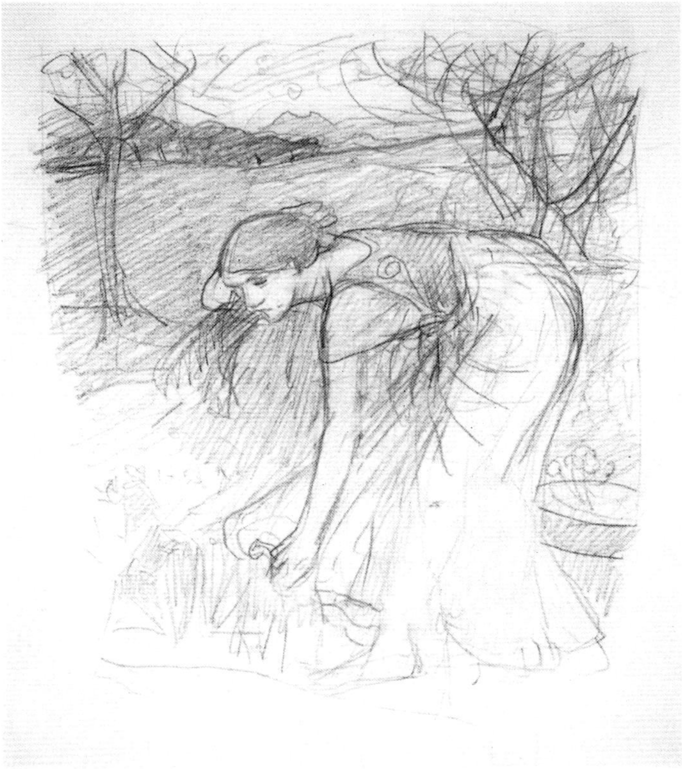

83. **Study for Narcissus or 'Gather Ye Rosebuds While Ye May'** c. 1911

GRAPHITE ON PAPER, 25.1 X 17.6 CM, VERSO: GREEK WARRIORS
COLLECTION DR. DENNIS T. LANIGAN, CANADA

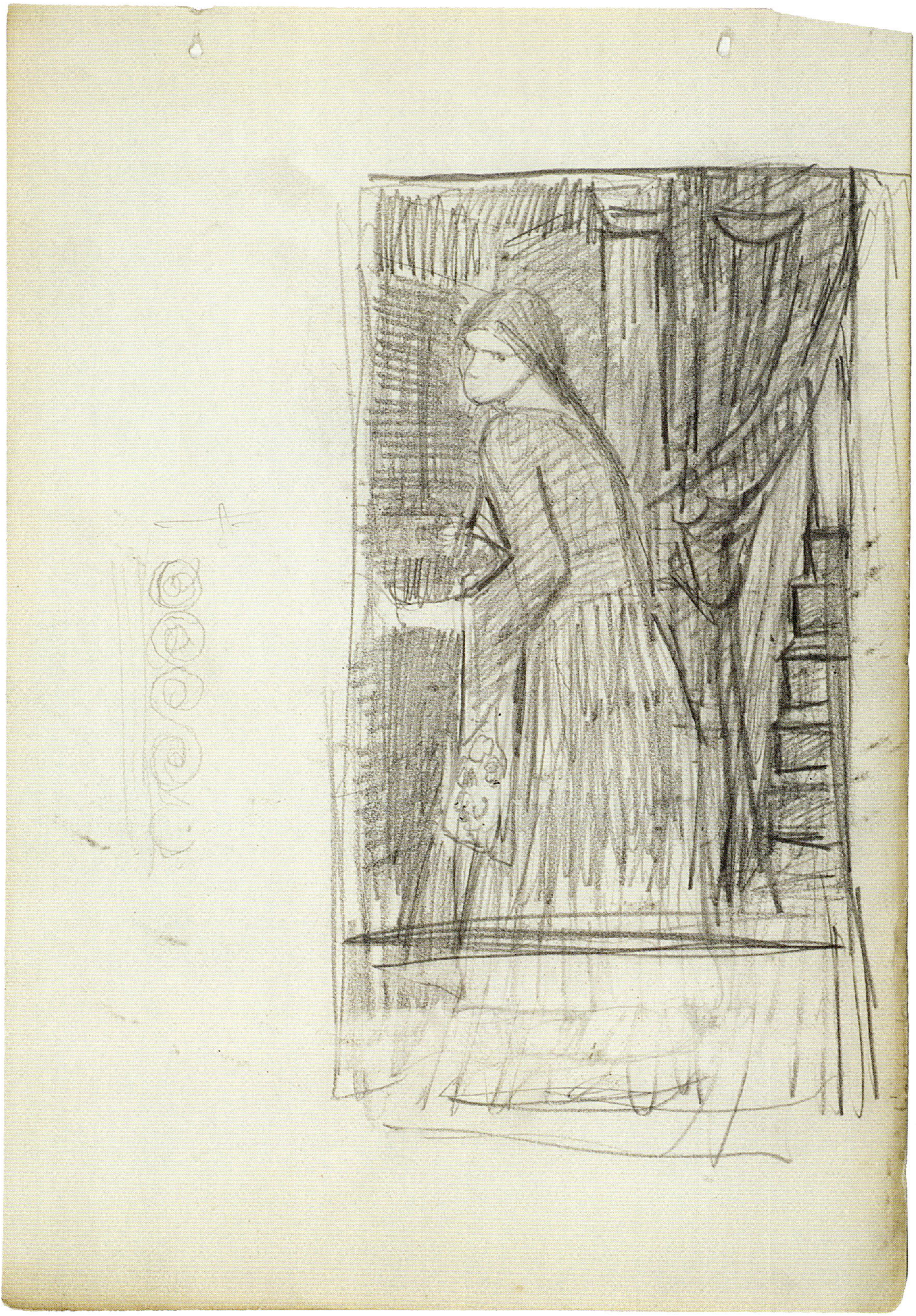

84. **Woman Preparing to Open a Door from Inside (possibly for Fatima)** c. 1911

GRAPHITE ON PAPER, 25 X 17.5 CM, VERSO: MASSIVE TREE TRUNKS WITH BRANCHES - COLLECTION JOHN PHYSICK

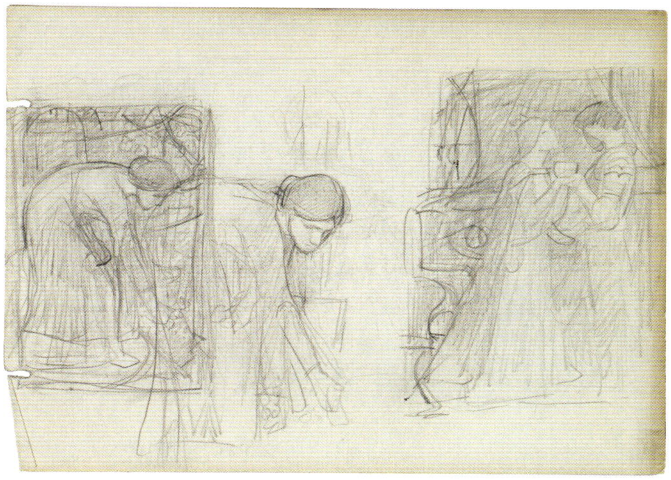

85. **Two Women Leaning Down to Pick Flowers, and Tristram and Isolde** c. 1911-1916

GRAPHITE ON PAPER, 17.5 X 25 CM,
VERSO: A SWINE AND TWO BABOONS LOOKING TO OUR RIGHT
COLLECTION JOHN PHYSICK

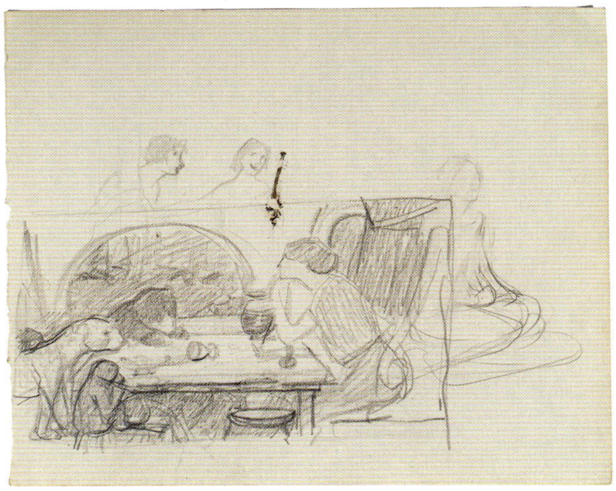

86. **Circe with Animals, and Other Figures** c. 1911-1916

GRAPHITE ON PAPER, 22.5 X 29 CM, VERSO: FAIR ROSAMUND AT HER WINDOW
COLLECTION JOHN PHYSICK

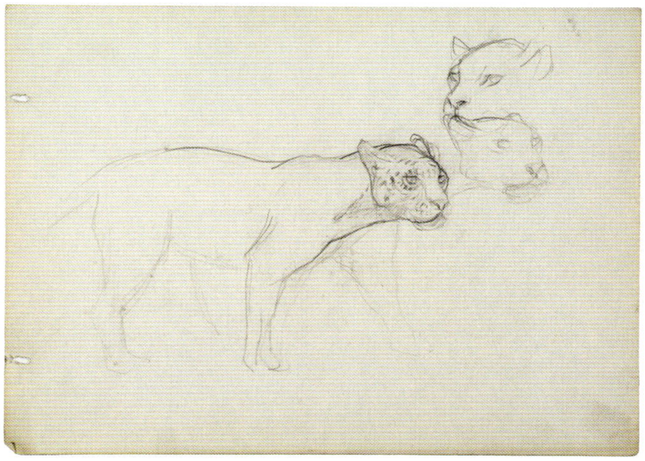

87. **Panthers** c. 1911-1914

GRAPHITE ON PAPER, 17.5 X 25 CM, VERSO: BABOONS - COLLECTION JOHN PHYSICK

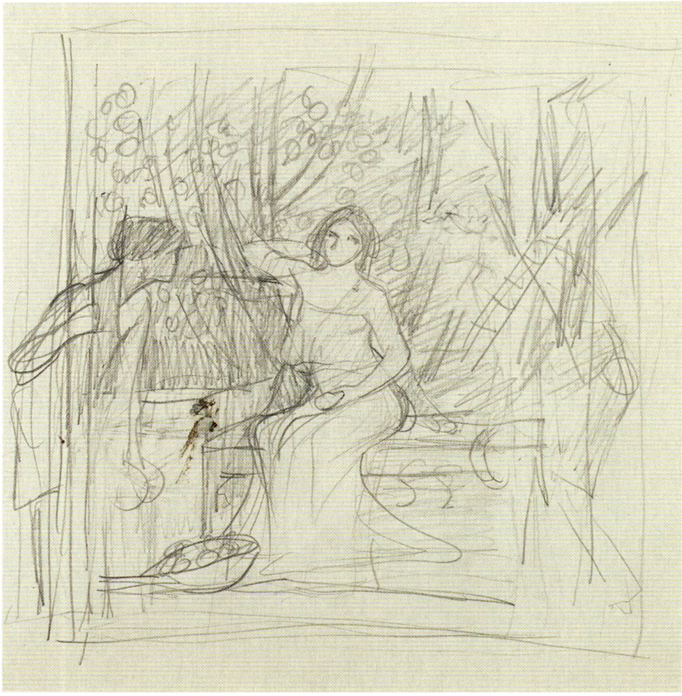

88. **Man Watching a Seated Woman Pick Fruit** c. 1912-1917

GRAPHITE ON PAPER, 22.5 X 29 CM, VERSO: WOMEN AND DEER FOR 'THE MYSTIC WOOD' (QUEENSLAND ART GALLERY, BRISBANE) - COLLECTION JOHN PHYSICK

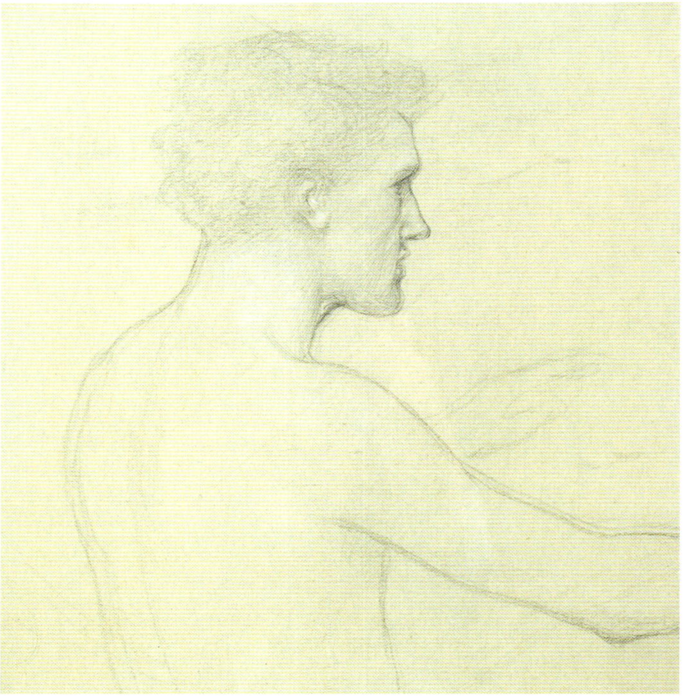

89. **Study of the Angel Gabriel for The Annunciation** c. 1913-1914

GRAPHITE ON PAPER, 31.1 X 31.1 CM - PRIVATE COLLECTION

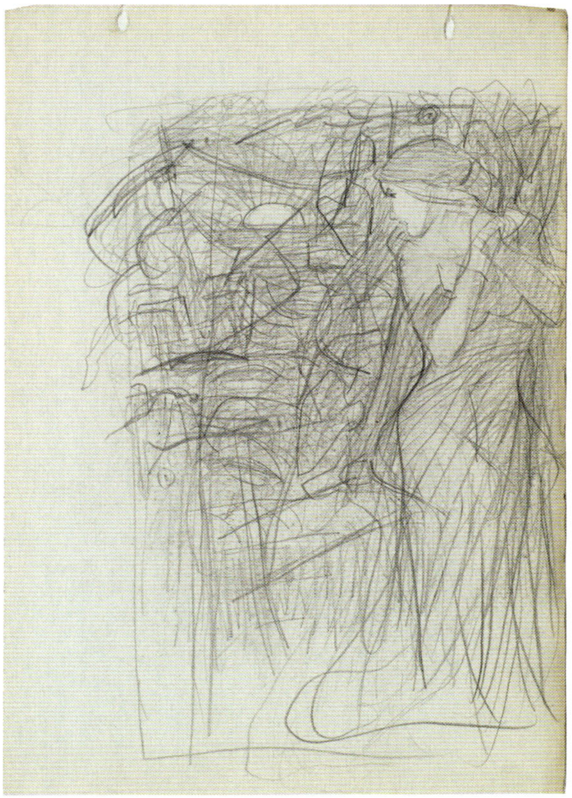

90. **Seated Girl Watching the Sun Rise** c. 1914

GRAPHITE ON PAPER, 25 X 17.5 CM
VERSO: WOMAN IN MEDIEVAL GARB HOLDING A CHALICE (POSSIBLY FOR 'THE LOVE PHILTRE')
COLLECTION JOHN PHYSICK

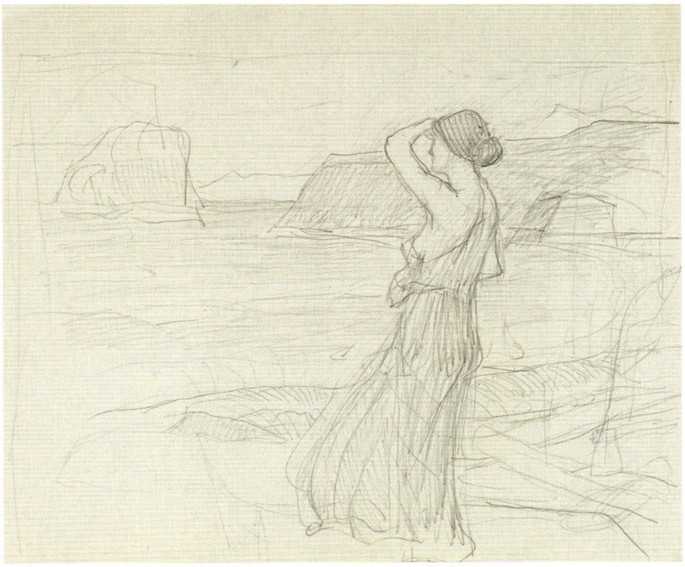

91. **Classicised Study for Miranda** c. 1914-1916

GRAPHITE ON PAPER, 22.5 X 29 CM
VERSO: TREE TRUNK, INSCRIBED 'CLIPPESBY//APRIL 1914'
COLLECTION JOHN PHYSICK

SKETCHBOOKS

These seven sketchbooks were passed down in Waterhouse's family and given to the Victoria and Albert Museum by his great-nephew, John Physick. One dates from the very beginning of Waterhouse's career (E.1109-1963, cat. 93), and includes fine-grained, painstaking drawings in hard pencil for a variety of subject types related to his student days and his earliest exhibited pictures: Orientalist figures, drawings from ancient sculptures (or casts), and studies of heads. Pages 22-23 (illustrated here) show three fine studies of ideally beautiful classical heads, clearly related to Waterhouse's first Royal Academy painting, *Sleep and his Half-Brother Death* (fig. 9); two have the sightless eyes of sculptures or casts, but the third must be a study from the living model for the haunting figure of Sleep.

Waterhouse no doubt used many more sketchbooks than are now extant; among the seven preserved at the Victoria and Albert there are none that relate to the middle period of his career, the period from the mid-1870s through to the later 1880s when he was painting scenes from ancient life and history. The remaining six sketchbooks all relate to the final phase of his mythological and poetic subjects, from the late 1880s through to the end of his life, and they show how he developed several ideas for compositions simultaneously. Indeed, the sketchbooks provide evidence of the complexity with which the subjects of Waterhouse's later phase were intertwined not only intellectually, through their references to parallel or related myths and stories, but also visually. Most of the drawings are in pencil, with occasional touches of pen and ink or black chalk. Although they range from quite rough sketches of a figure or motif to resolved drawings of whole compositions, in general they are bolder in line and more confident, evidently more quickly drawn than those of the earliest sketchbook. The sketchbooks vary in size – the later ones tend to be larger, but still transportable – and Waterhouse made drawings in all orientations, often on the same sheet. Some of the sketches are from nature (studies of the model or of landscape elements), others are designs for compositions for which a model may have been used, but not necessarily; Waterhouse had trained his own visual memory as a student, and may have been able to draw confidently without a model.[1] There is no predictable sequence to the pages in any sketchbook, as Waterhouse moves back and forth from one to another subject or motif (and he did not necessarily work systematically through the pages of the book). Although they are often attractive, the sketches are working drawings first and foremost.

One sketchbook (E.1-1949, cat. 94) records Waterhouse's experimentation from about 1888 to 1890, when he was developing the ideas for his first mythological paintings, *Ulysses and the Sirens* (cat. 22) and *Circe Offering the Cup*

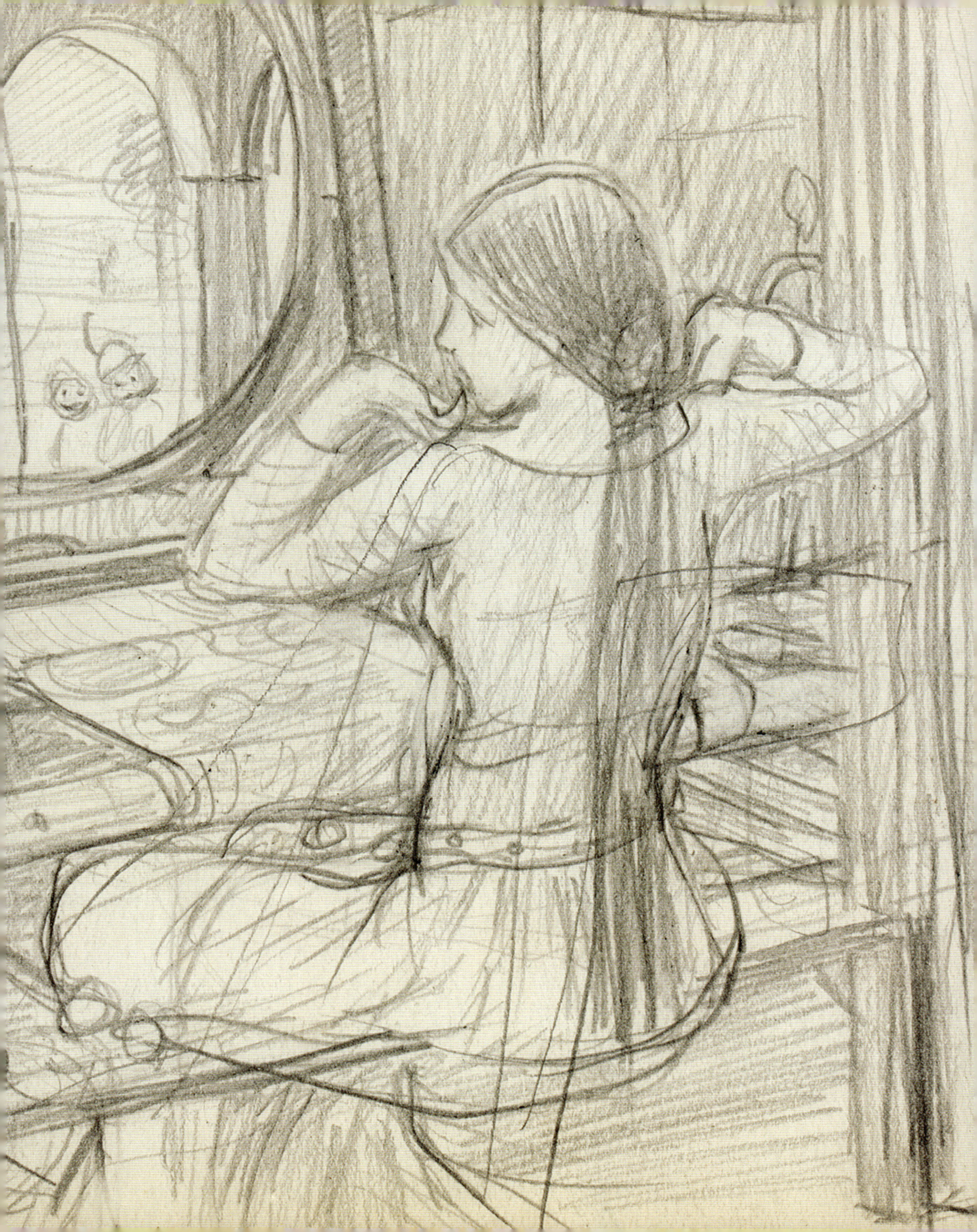

to Ulysses (cat. 21). Preliminary ideas for both paintings are interspersed with sketches of buildings and landscapes on the island of Capri, closely connected with the mythological subjects in Waterhouse's imagination at this crucial period; unusually, some of the landscapes are in watercolour, which suggests the strong impression made on the artist by the distinctive light and colour of Capri and the Bay of Naples. Other pages show the wings of birds, including eagles, which Waterhouse may have sketched in the London Zoo.[2]
Pages 26-27 (illustrated here) show how Waterhouse experimented with different orientations for the boat, in *Ulysses and the Sirens*; he tries two diagonal orientations, and adjusts the relationship between the boat and the surrounding rocks, to arrive at the final, dramatic composition with the prow heading for a narrow gap, closest to the version drawn sideways on p. 26.

Another sketchbook (E.1110-1963, cat. 95) must date from soon afterwards, and also includes sketches for *Circe Offering the Cup to Ulysses*; pp. 58-59 (illustrated here) show two different ideas for that composition. Both already feature the large circular mirror, which suggests that that element was fixed in Waterhouse's mind early on, before he had decided on the precise pose for the figure. The hauntingly faint drawing on p. 58 shows Circe in three-quarter profile, her wand in her lap, but Waterhouse eventually decided on the more dramatic composition sketched on p. 59, where Circe faces the viewer and holds the cup and wand high; already she gazes down at the viewer, but for the final painting Waterhouse again adjusted the wand to elevate it above the mirror, giving Circe an even more commanding pose. The remaining pages of this sketchbook include a variety of studies for Waterhouse's second version of *The Lady of Shalott* (cat. 30); evidently this gave him considerable trouble, for several of them are scratched out with heavy, impulsive lines. The sketchbook also includes tantalising drawings for another composition showing the Lady of Shalott's boat arriving in Camelot; Waterhouse came back to this idea a number of times in the sketchbooks, but never executed it as a painting. A number of sheets experiment with a variety of other unexecuted subjects; several obviously represent the story of Perseus and Andromeda, but others are difficult to identify.

The next sketchbook in the surviving sequence (E.1111-1963, cat. 96) includes sketches, interspersed with one another, for *The Awakening of Adonis* (fig. 19) and *Echo and Narcissus* (cat. 43), which indicates that these two subjects were developed in close concert around 1900. Pages 18-19 (illustrated here) experiment several times with the relationship between the reclining nude Adonis and Venus, bending over him; on the same page spread, towards bottom left, Waterhouse draws the reclining male nude in another pose, this time for the figure of Narcissus. Interestingly, the composition of Circe enthroned reappears in this sketchbook, apparently some years after the exhibition of *Circe Offering the Cup to Ulysses*, this time positioned before a semicircular apse; was Waterhouse meditating another version of the Circe subject? Other drawings show new ideas beginning to develop, or older ones returning for fresh treatment: the Lady of Shalott floating into Camelot on her boat, scenes of women gathering flowers, and figures with chalices that may hark back to *Circe Offering the Cup* or forward to *Jason and Medea* (cat. 48) and other pictures. The sketchbook suggests that, from about 1900, Waterhouse was increasingly developing visual ideas that might be deployed in different contexts, to create a network of links among his later paintings.

The remaining three sketchbooks all include sketches for works that were underway in the final years of Waterhouse's life, from about 1900 to his death in 1917, and they demonstrate an even more complex set of interrelationships among the compositions of that period. All of them include sketches for Waterhouse's last Lady of Shalott composition, *'I am Half-Sick of Shadows,' said the Lady of Shalott* (cat. 60), for figures picking flowers, and for a variety of other subjects of Waterhouse's later years, which seem to have been in gestation simultaneously; they also include studies of English landscapes, sometimes annotated with the names of places. One of these later books (E.2-1949, cat. 97) includes sketches for paintings exhibited soon after 1900, such as *The Crystal Ball* of 1902, *Windflowers* (cat. 42), and *Lamia* (cat. 46), so it is probably the earliest of the three. Interestingly, though, pp. 36-37 (illustrated here) show two drawings for a painting of 1903, *Psyche Opening the Door into Cupid's Garden* (cat. 45), alongside one for *'I am Half-Sick'*, not exhibited until 1916, which may indicate that the latter was in gestation for over a decade. The two Psyche drawings are quite resolved, and close to the final painting, although they experiment with two positions for Psyche's left arm (Waterhouse finally chose the one with bent elbow, as in the right-hand drawing). The drawing for *'I am Half-Sick'*, slightly rougher, contains all the elements of the final composition (figure with arms raised as if to stretch, loom, and circular mirror), but orients the figure with her back to the viewer.

A composition closer to the final version of *'I am Half-Sick'* appears in what seems to be a slightly later sketchbook (E.3-1949, cat. 98), along with sketches for many of the paintings of about 1907-1912. These include studies for two closely related paintings involving myths of women who turn into trees, *Phyllis and Demophöon* of 1907 and *Apollo and Daphne* of 1908; interestingly, the sketchbook also includes numerous studies from trees in English nature, some annotated with place names. There are also ideas for paintings that never materialised, notably one that seems to represent Orpheus with his lyre, a subject that would link *Nymphs Finding the Head of Orpheus* (cat. 41) with *Apollo and Daphne* (Apollo also carries a lyre). Pages 34-35 (illustrated here) show an early idea for *Fair Rosamund* (cat. 61) alongside a subject that has not been identified, also medieval in flavour, showing a kneeling female figure with attendants dressing her hair, and ships in the distance – could this be Isolde, preparing for her voyage from Ireland to Cornwall?

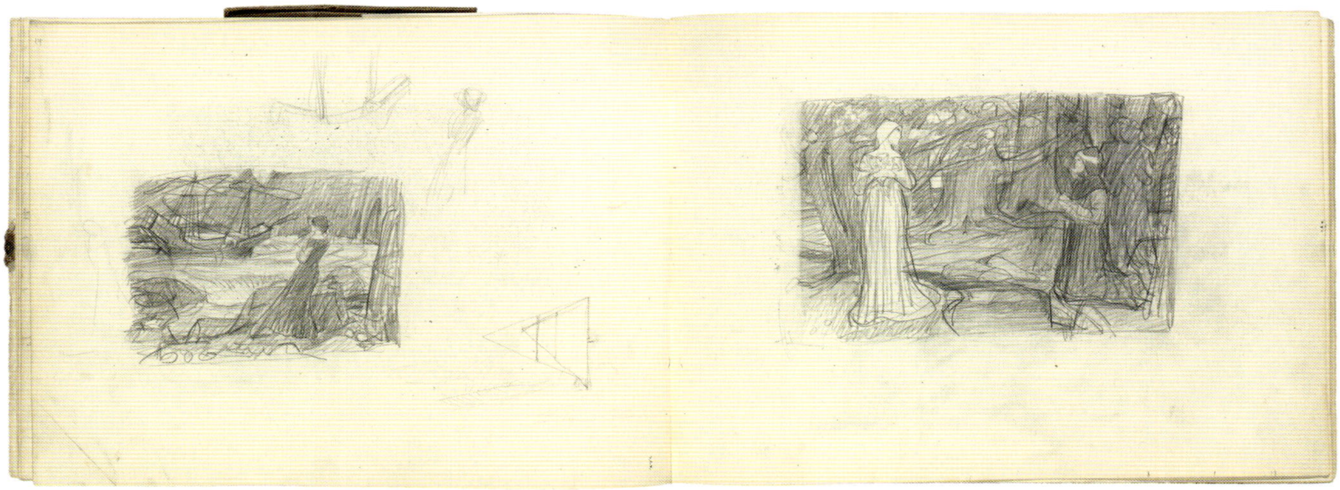

92. Sketchbook

CONTAINING SKETCHES, C. 1912-1917, RELATED TO PICTURES ON WHICH WATERHOUSE WAS WORKING IN HIS FINAL YEARS, AND SKETCHES OF ENGLISH LANDSCAPE

PENCIL, WITH SOME PEN AND INK, ON 50 PAGES (2 TORN, 1 SHEET INSERTED) OF WHITE WOVE PAPER BOUND IN CANVAS BOARDS, WITH A PENCIL HOLDER, SIZE OF VOLUME 25.4 X 36.8 CM
VICTORIA AND ALBERT MUSEUM, LONDON, E.1112-1963, GIFT OF JOHN PHYSICK
ILLUSTRATED: PP. 14-15, SHOWING DRAWINGS FOR *MIRANDA* (CAT. 62) AND *DANTE AND MATILDA* (CAT. 64)

The largest of the sketchbooks (E.1112-1963, cat. 92) seems also to be the latest; along with the ubiquitous flower-pickers and drawings for *'I am Half-Sick'*, it includes sketches for other paintings of Waterhouse's very last years. Pages 14-15 (illustrated here) show the compositions for the late version of *Miranda* (cat. 62), oil versions of which appeared in the last two Royal Academy exhibitions at which Waterhouse showed (1916 and 1917), and for *Dante and Matilda* (cat. 64), unfinished at the artist's death. Although this book includes one sketch which seems to be for the late version of *Circe* (cat. 57), most of its pages show how Waterhouse's attention had turned, in his last years, to the medieval and Renaissance worlds, in subjects from Shakespeare, Dante, and Boccaccio.

Even though these seven sketchbooks must represent only a fraction of Waterhouse's activity as a designer, they demonstrate the fertility of his imagination, the continual experimentation through which he refined his compositions, and the complex interrelationships among his various designs. A particularly notable feature is the constant presence of the Lady of Shalott throughout all six of the later sketchbooks, not only in versions of the three compositions that Waterhouse executed as paintings, but in other designs as well; sketches for the various compositions involving Circe are also frequent throughout all six books. Moreover, the sketchbooks contain ideas for at least a dozen compositions that were never executed, and many of which have still to be identified. The sketchbooks have many secrets to reveal to future scholars and students of Waterhouse's work. **EP**

1 On Waterhouse's memory training see A. Lys Baldry, 'J.W. Waterhouse and his Work', *Studio*, vol. IV, January 1895, pp. 103-104; R.E.D. Sketchley, *The Art of J.W. Waterhouse, R.A.*, Christmas Number of *The Art Journal*, 1909, p. 7.

2 Letter from Waterhouse to his patron Julia Ellsworth Ford, dated 18 March (without a year, but probably 1903 or later), Beinecke Library, Yale University, Za//Ford (Julia Ellsworth)//Corresp/Mb-Z.

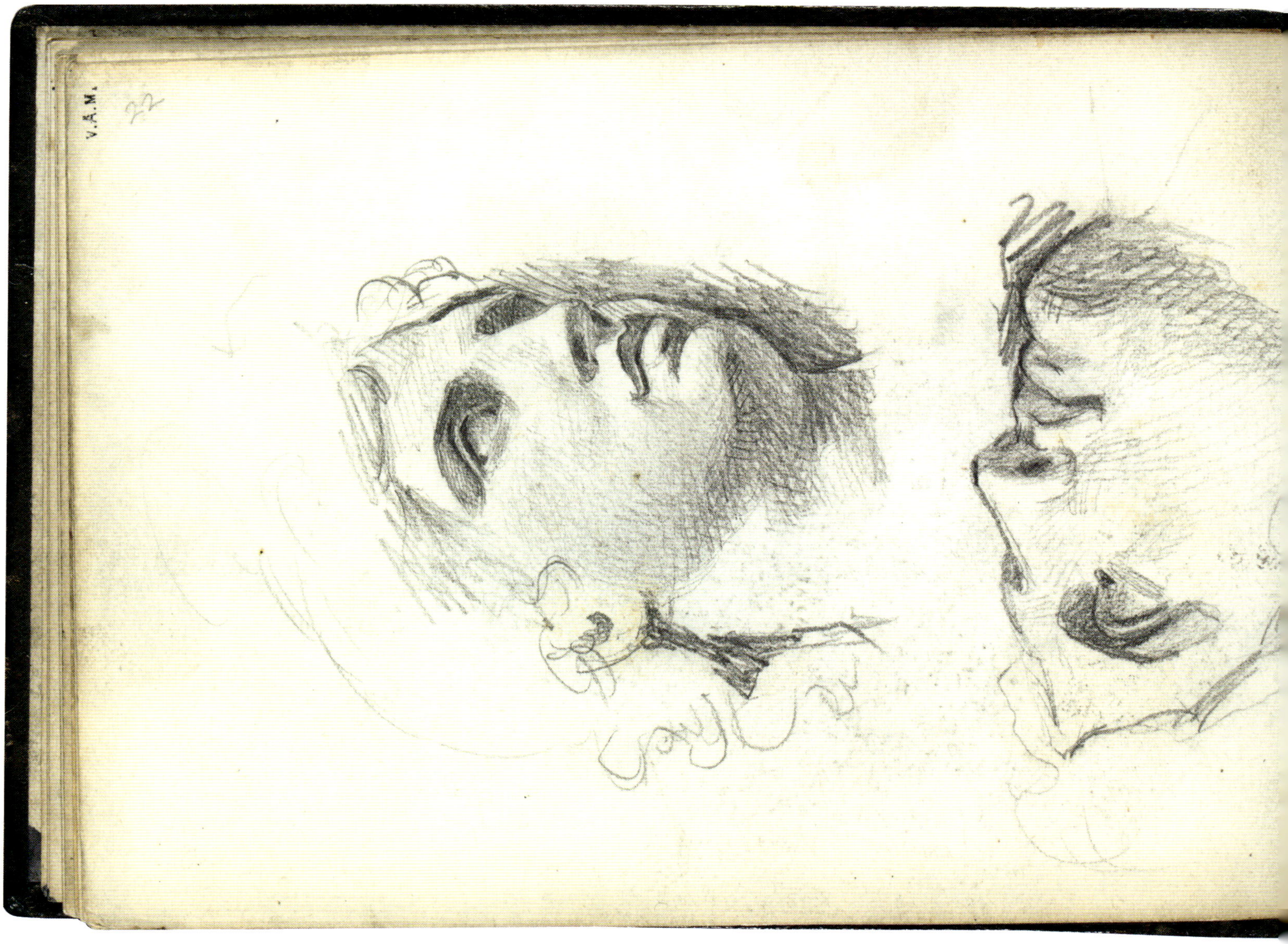
V.A.M.
22

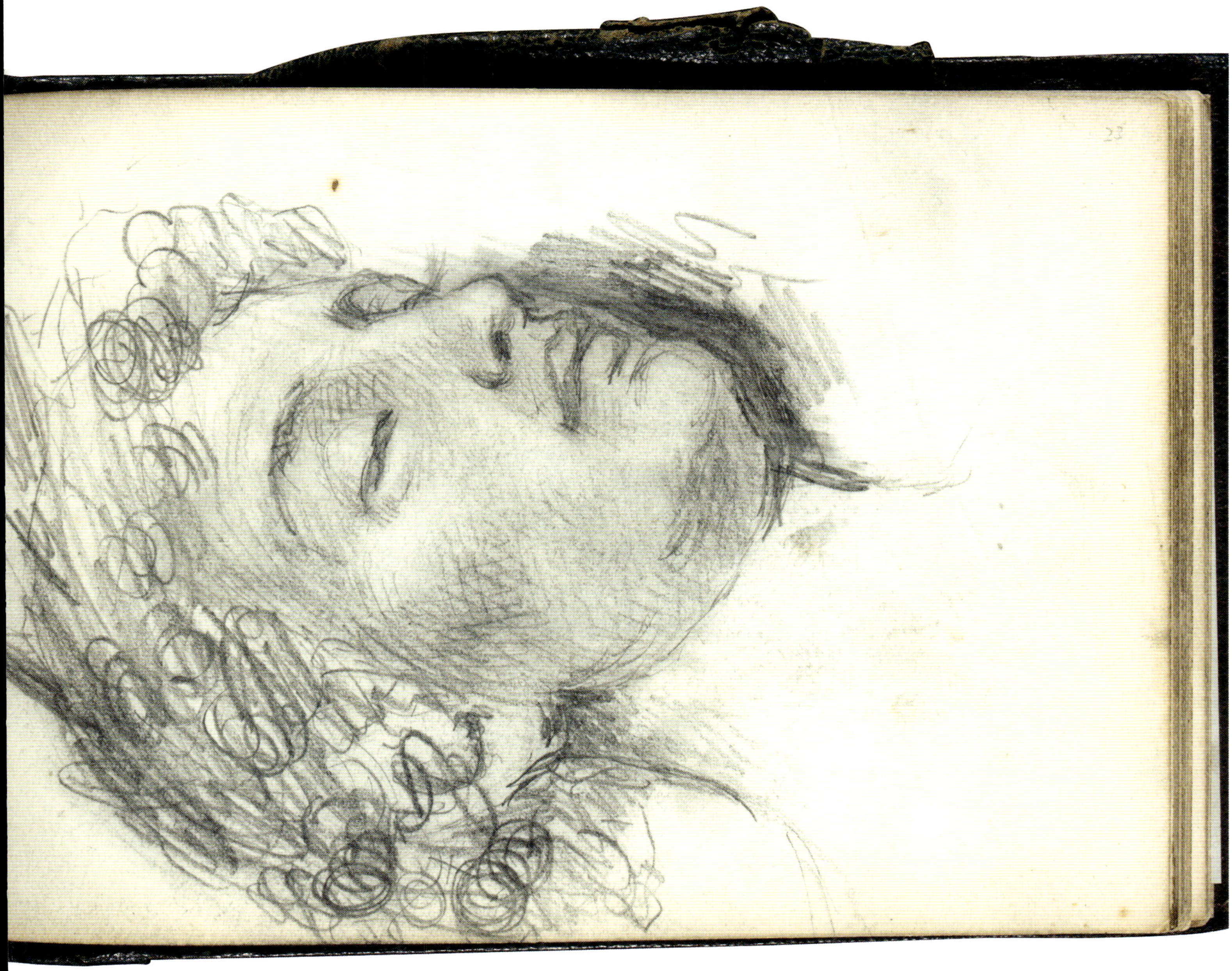

93. **Sketchbook**

CONTAINING SKETCHES RELATED TO PICTURES EXHIBITED BETWEEN 1872 AND 1874, DRAWINGS AFTER ANCIENT SCULPTURES OR CASTS, AND ORIENTALIST FIGURES

PENCIL, WITH SOME BLACK CHALK AND WATERCOLOUR, ON 62 PAGES (ONE MISSING) OF WHITE WOVE WHATMAN PAPER WATERMARKED 1872, QUARTER-BOUND IN LEATHER, CANVAS BOARDS, WITH A PENCIL HOLDER, SIZE OF VOLUME 12.7 X 17.8 CM - VICTORIA AND ALBERT MUSEUM, LONDON, E.1109-1963, GIFT OF JOHN PHYSICK, ILLUSTRATED: PP. 22-23, SHOWING DRAWINGS OF HEADS RELATED TO *SLEEP AND HIS HALF-BROTHER DEATH* (FIG. 9)

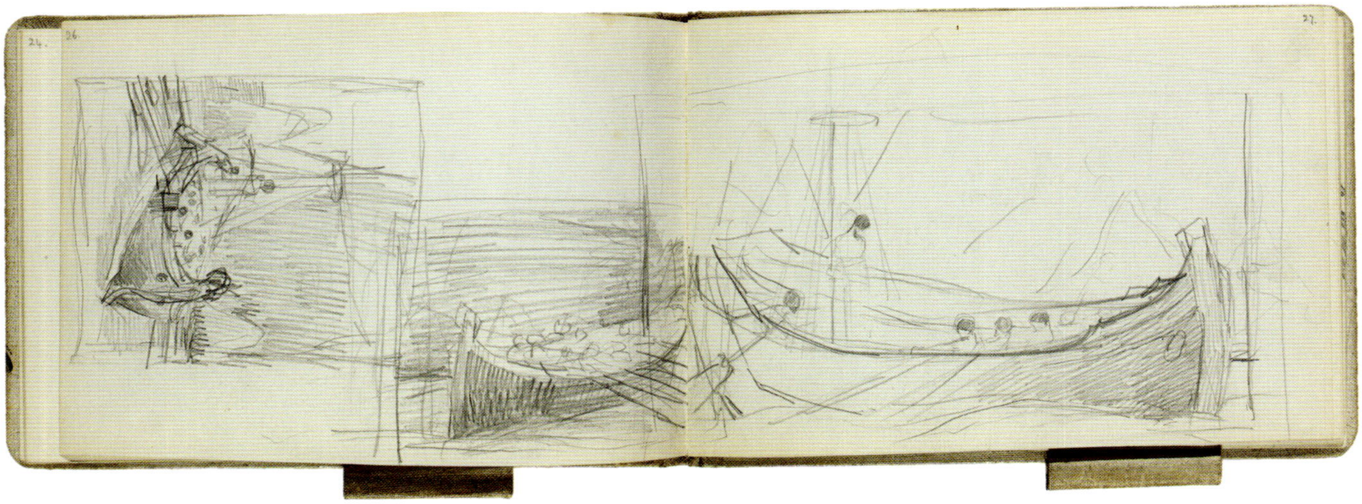

94. **Sketchbook**

CONTAINING SKETCHES RELATED TO WATERHOUSE'S EXHIBITED PAINTINGS OF 1891 AND TO HIS TRAVELS ON CAPRI

PENCIL AND WATERCOLOUR ON 56 PAGES (8 PAGES MISSING) OF WHITE WOVE PAPER BOUND IN CANVAS BOARDS, SIZE OF VOLUME 14 X 20.6 CM
VICTORIA AND ALBERT MUSEUM, LONDON, E.1-1949, GIFT OF JOHN PHYSICK
ILLUSTRATED: PP. 26-27, SHOWING THREE DRAWINGS FOR *ULYSSES AND THE SIRENS* (CAT. 22)

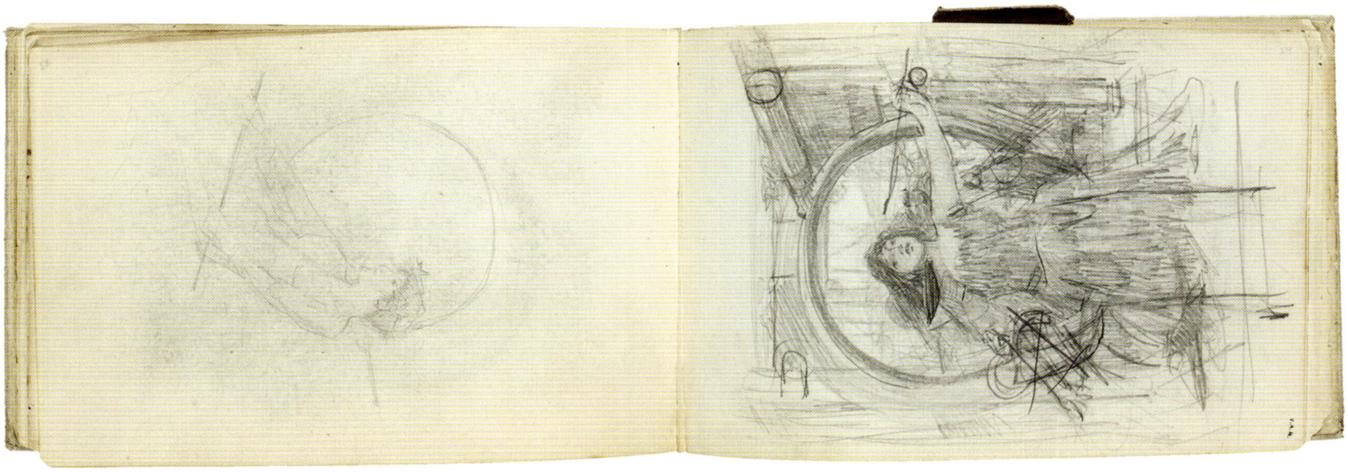

95. **Sketchbook**

CONTAINING SKETCHES RELATED TO PICTURES EXHIBITED BETWEEN 1891 AND 1894

PENCIL ON 68 PAGES (OTHERS MISSING) OF WHITE WOVE PAPER BOUND IN CANVAS BOARDS, WITH A PENCIL HOLDER, SIZE OF VOLUME 15.3 X 23.5 CM
VICTORIA AND ALBERT MUSEUM, LONDON, E.1110-1963, GIFT OF JOHN PHYSICK
ILLUSTRATED: PP. 58-59, SHOWING DRAWINGS FOR *CIRCE OFFERING THE CUP TO ULYSSES* (CAT. 21)

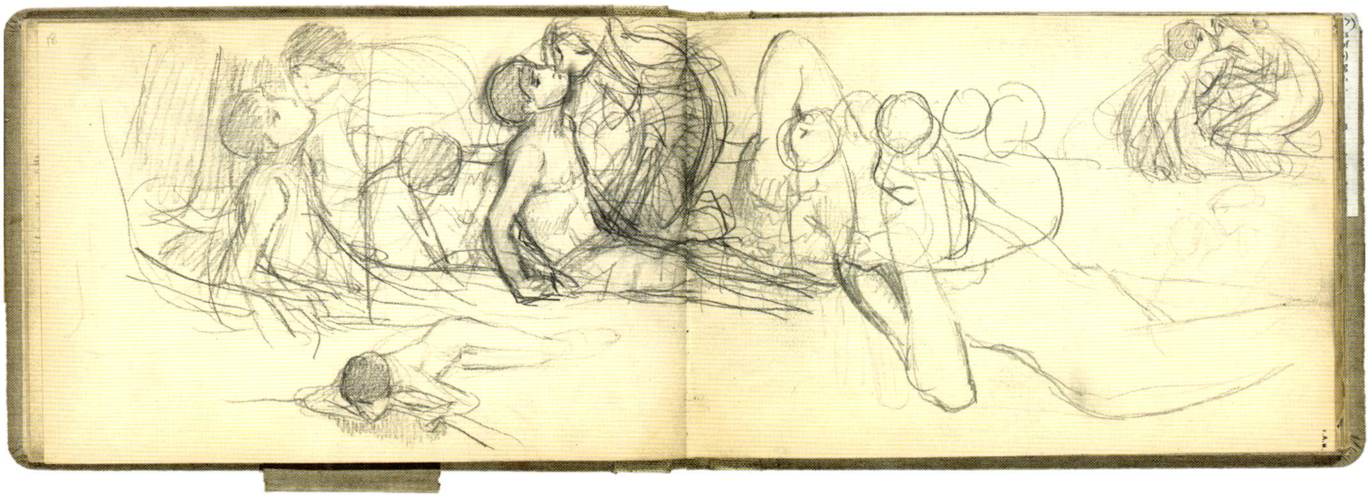

96. Sketchbook

CONTAINING SKETCHES RELATED PRIMARILY TO PICTURES EXHIBITED BETWEEN 1900 AND 1903, WITH SOME POSSIBLY RELATED TO LATER PICTURES (UP TO 1907)

PENCIL, WITH SOME PEN AND INK, ON 74 PAGES (ONE TORN) OF WHITE WOVE PAPER BOUND IN CANVAS BOARDS, WITH A PENCIL HOLDER, SIZE OF VOLUME 15.3 X 21.6 CM
VICTORIA AND ALBERT MUSEUM, LONDON, E.1111-1963, GIFT OF JOHN PHYSICK
ILLUSTRATED: PP. 18-19, SHOWING DRAWINGS FOR *THE AWAKENING OF ADONIS* (FIG. 19) AND *ECHO AND NARCISSUS* (CAT. 43)

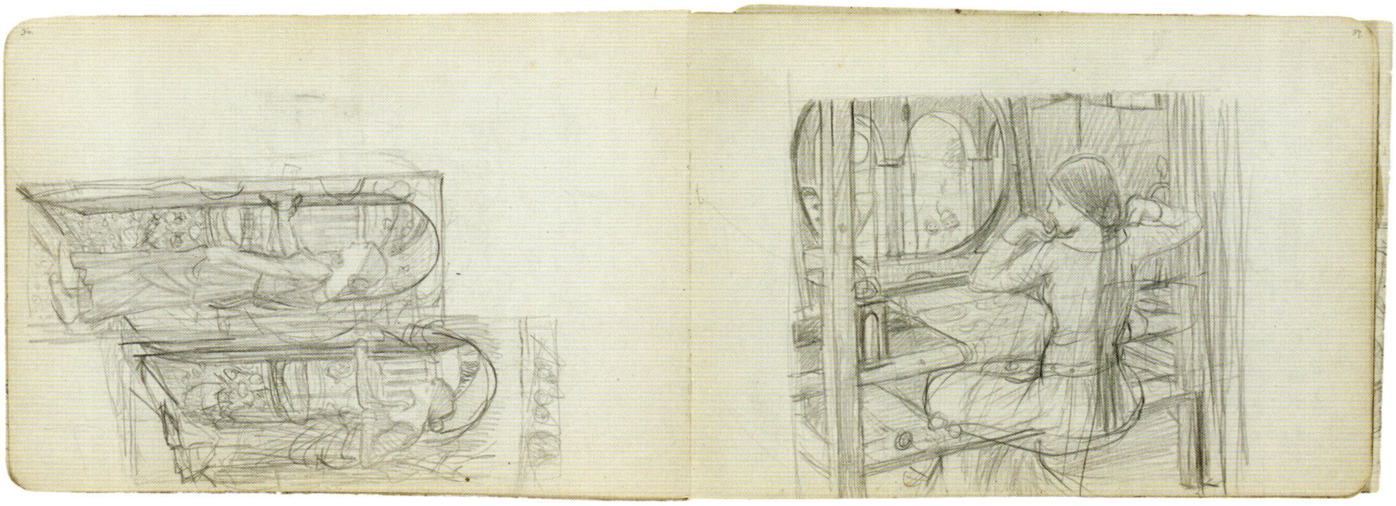

97. Sketchbook

CONTAINING SKETCHES RELATED TO PICTURES EXHIBITED BETWEEN 1902 AND 1916

PENCIL, WATERCOLOUR, AND BODYCOLOUR ON 92 PAGES OF WHITE WOVE PAPER BOUND IN CANVAS BOARDS, SIZE OF VOLUME 17.5 X 23.1 CM
VICTORIA AND ALBERT MUSEUM, LONDON, E.2-1949, GIFT OF JOHN PHYSICK
ILLUSTRATED: PP. 36-37, SHOWING DRAWINGS FOR *PSYCHE OPENING THE DOOR INTO CUPID'S GARDEN* (CAT. 45) AND *'I AM HALF-SICK OF SHADOWS,' SAID THE LADY OF SHALOTT* (CAT. 60)

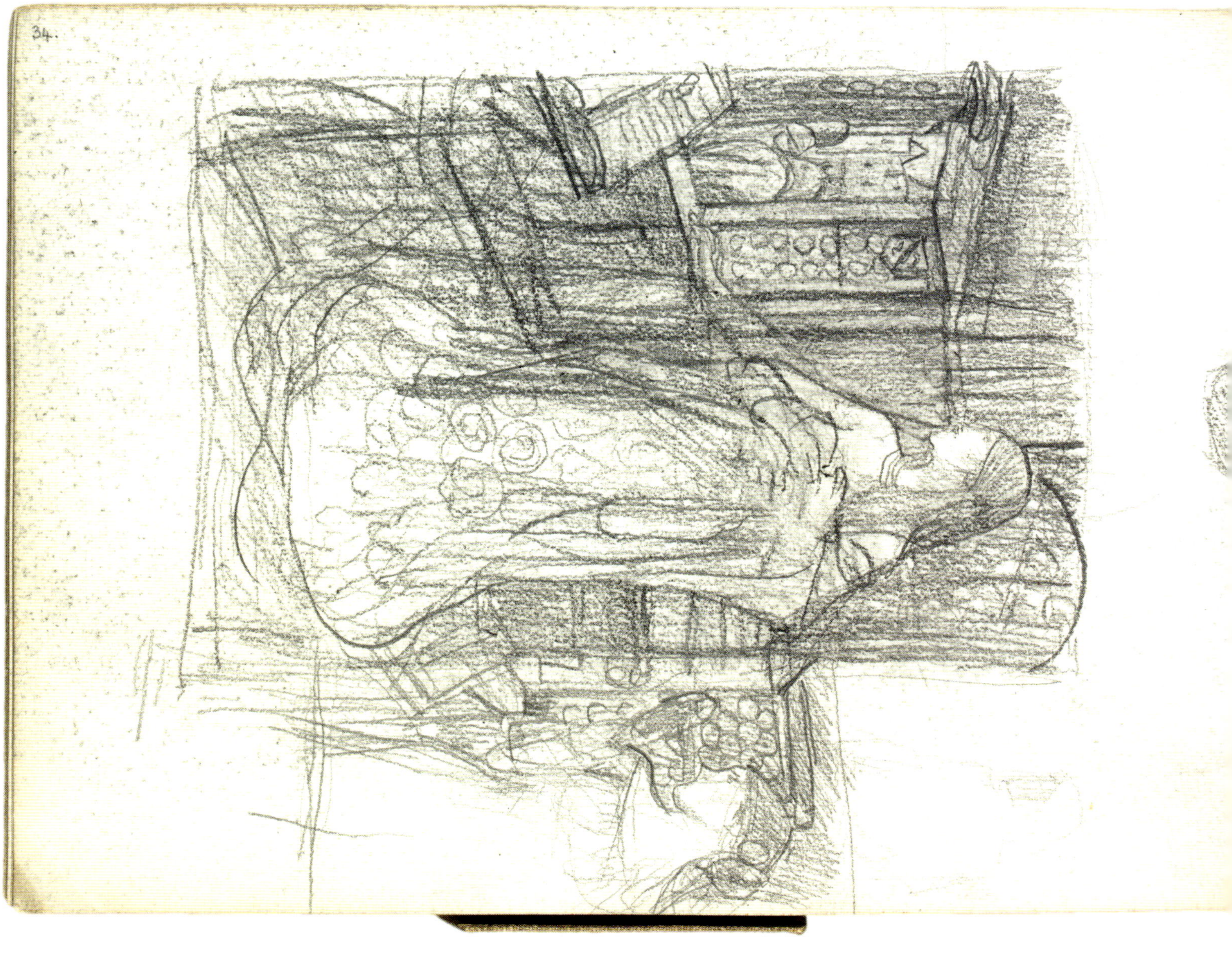
34.

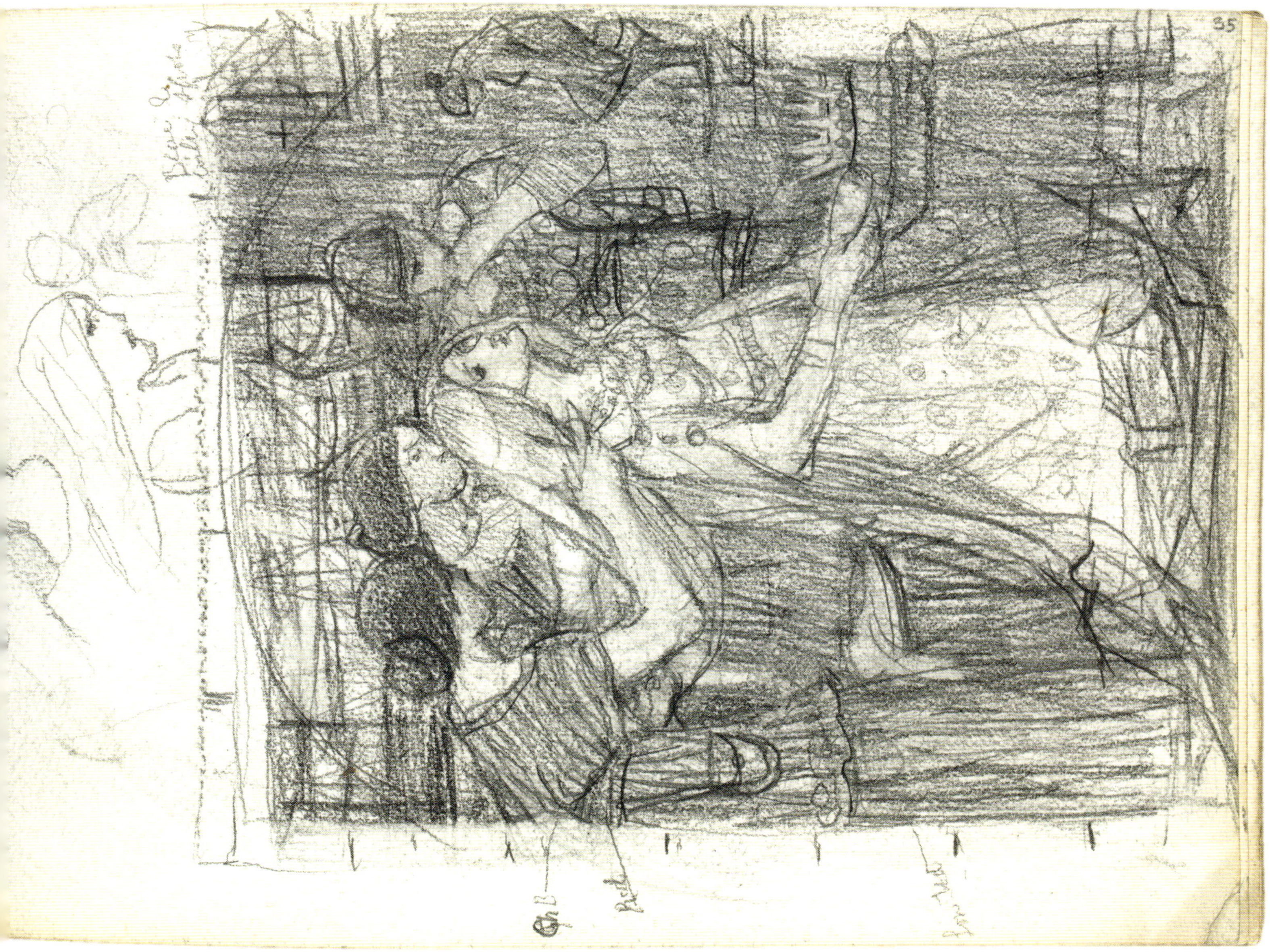

98. **Sketchbook**

CONTAINING SKETCHES RELATED TO PICTURES EXHIBITED BETWEEN 1907 AND 1917, AND STUDIES OF TREES

PENCIL, BLACK CHALK, AND PEN AND INK ON 60 PAGES OF WHITE WOVE PAPER BOUND IN CANVAS BOARDS, SIZE OF VOLUME 20.3 X 25.4 CM
VICTORIA AND ALBERT MUSEUM, LONDON, E.3-1949, GIFT OF JOHN PHYSICK
ILLUSTRATED: PP. 34-35, SHOWING DRAWINGS FOR *FAIR ROSAMUND* (CAT. 61) AND AN UNIDENTIFIED SUBJECT

RELATED WORKS

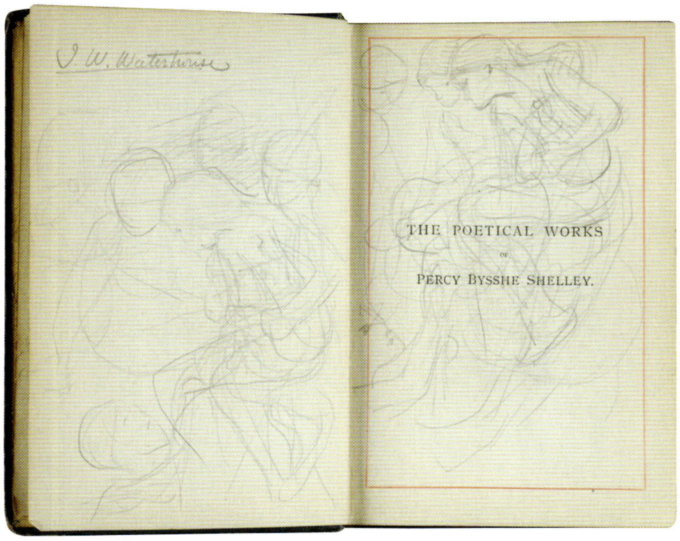

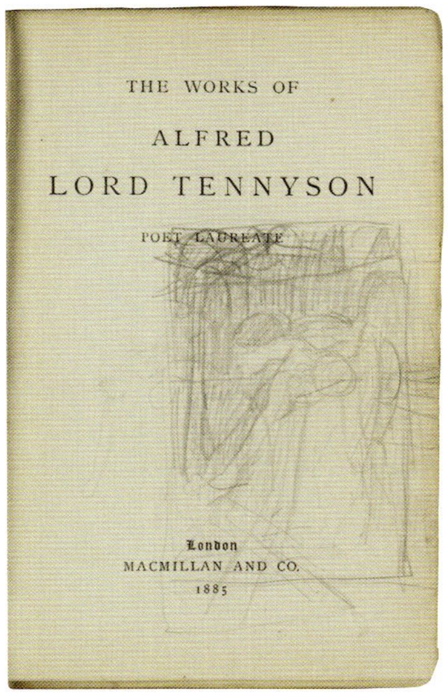

99. The Poetical Works of Percy Bysshe Shelley 1880

LONDON, GEORGE ROUTLEDGE AND SONS, INSCRIBED 'J.W. WATERHOUSE', 603 PAGES PLUS FLYLEAVES, 18 X 12 CM (PAGE SIZE), COLLECTION MICHAEL TITTERINGTON

100. The Works of Alfred Lord Tennyson, Poet Laureate 1885

LONDON, MACMILLAN AND CO., INSCRIBED 'J.W. WATERHOUSE, 3 PRIMROSE HILL STUDIOS, NW' (THUS BY 1887, WHEN WATERHOUSE MOVED FROM 3 TO 6 PRIMROSE HILL STUDIOS), 640 PAGES PLUS FLYLEAVES, 19 X 12.5 CM (PAGE SIZE), COLLECTION MICHAEL TITTERINGTON

Even a cursory glance at Waterhouse's œuvre confirms that he loved poetry, drama, and storytelling generally. Just two volumes of poetry owned by him are known, passed down through the family of his half-sister Mary ('May') until recently. These mass-produced compilations of works by Tennyson and Shelley are precious not as exemplars of printing, but for the many pencil sketches Waterhouse drew in them. It is impossible to tell exactly when specific drawings were made, as the artist may have returned regularly to these books right up until his death.

Illustrated here is the Shelley volume's title page with Waterhouse's conceptions of *The Siren*, involving as many as four girls rather than the one he ultimately painted c. 1900 (cat. 39). Also found in this volume are other conceptions for *The Siren*, as well as *Jason and Medea*, *'Listening to my Sweet Pipings'*, *The Necklace*, and *Penelope and the Suitors*. Were we to assume that Waterhouse drew these while preparing to paint the corresponding works in oil, then they date 1900-1912.

Also illustrated here is the Tennyson book's title page with Waterhouse's conception of girls leaning down to pick flowers, a theme he treated regularly from the mid-1890s (*Flora and the Zephyrs*) and especially c. 1908-1914. Also found in this volume are conceptions for *Mariana in the South*, *The Lady Clare*, *Isabella and the Pot of Basil*, *The Danaïdes*, *'I am Half Sick of Shadows', said the Lady of Shalott*, and possibly *Circe*. Were we to assume that Waterhouse drew these while preparing to paint the corresponding works in oil, then they date 1897-1916. **PT**

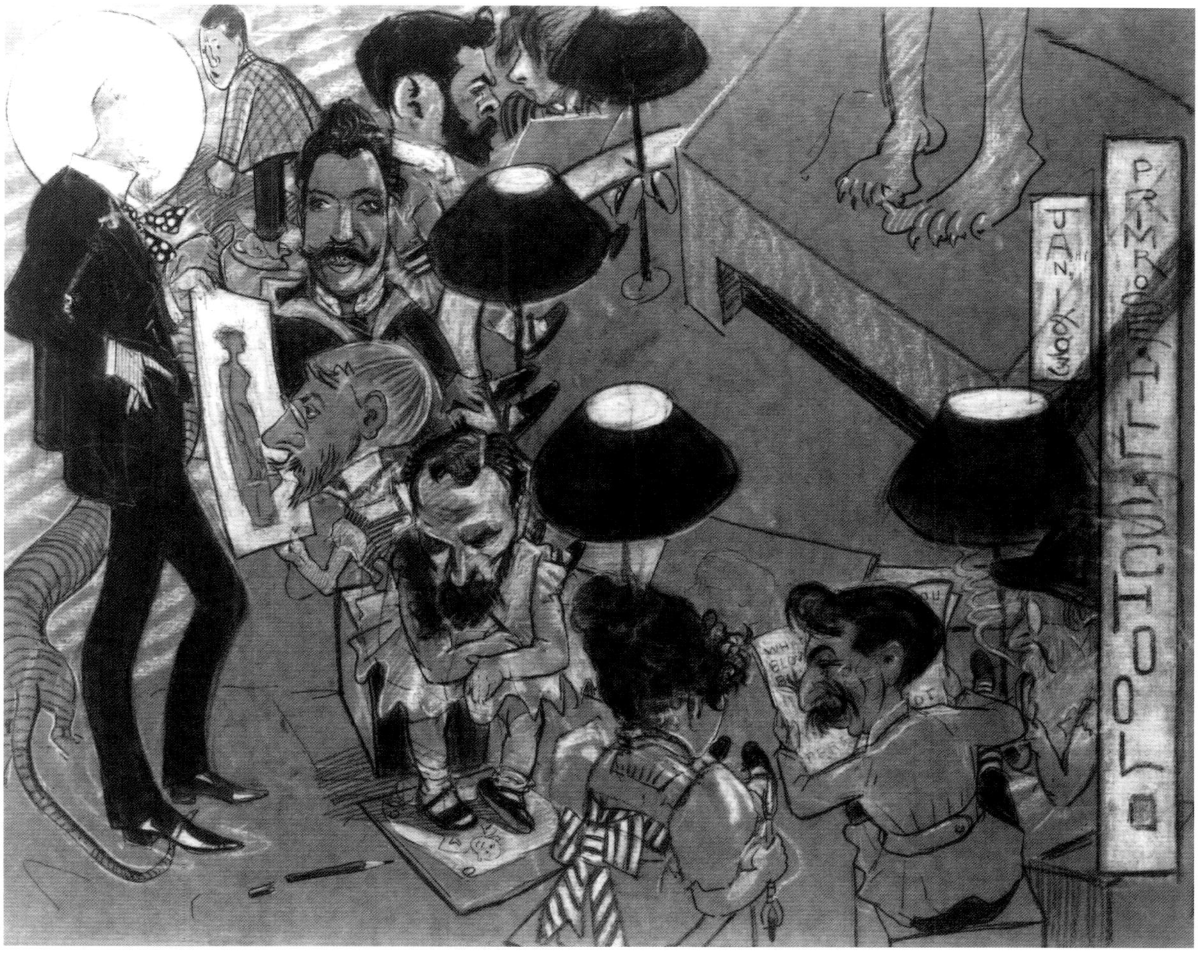

47. Unidentified artist, 'January 1893, Primrose Hill School' 1893, Chalk on paper, 54.6 x 69.5 cm, National Portrait Gallery, London, Given by Col. A.C.B. Clayton on behalf of the St John's Wood Arts Club, 1964, Presumably intended for publication (outlet unknown)

Although he was closely associated with the Royal Academy of Arts, Waterhouse's artistic and social formation was equally influenced by the friendships he made with non-Academicians in the London neighbourhood of Primrose Hill, where he took a studio in 1878. Indeed, it was not until 1900, when he was already 51, that he and his artist-wife Esther left this relatively bohemian area for the more prestigious artistic enclave of St John's Wood, also in northwest London.

This mysterious caricature offers a rare and delightful glimpse into the so-called 'Primrose Hill School' in January 1893, precisely when their landscapist-friend Ernest A. Waterlow ARA (1850-1919) was temporarily using the Waterhouses' studio while his own was being renovated. Waterlow appears in profile at the very top, with Waterhouse at the bottom centre facing the viewer. Note that he has snapped his pencil in frustration and discarded it on the floor with his aborted drawing – an intriguing hint at how intensely Waterhouse struggled with perfectionism.

In keeping with the drawing's double-edged title, most of the figures are dressed like children, with Waterhouse in girl's clothing. Because they lived so close to London Zoo in Regent's Park, the artists are sketching a primate, whose feet can be seen on the podium at top right. Waterhouse probably derived at least some expertise in depicting animals from his German-born neighbour, the naturalist-artist Joseph Wolf (1820-1899), shown in the bottom right corner, and in painting flowers from Esther, whose back is to the viewer. Some of these figures remain unnamed; identified so far are the illustrators Walter Dendy Sadler, Arthur Hopkins, Sydney Prior Hall, and the painter-educator Maurice Greiffenhagen (who gave his son the middle name 'Waterhouse'). **PT**

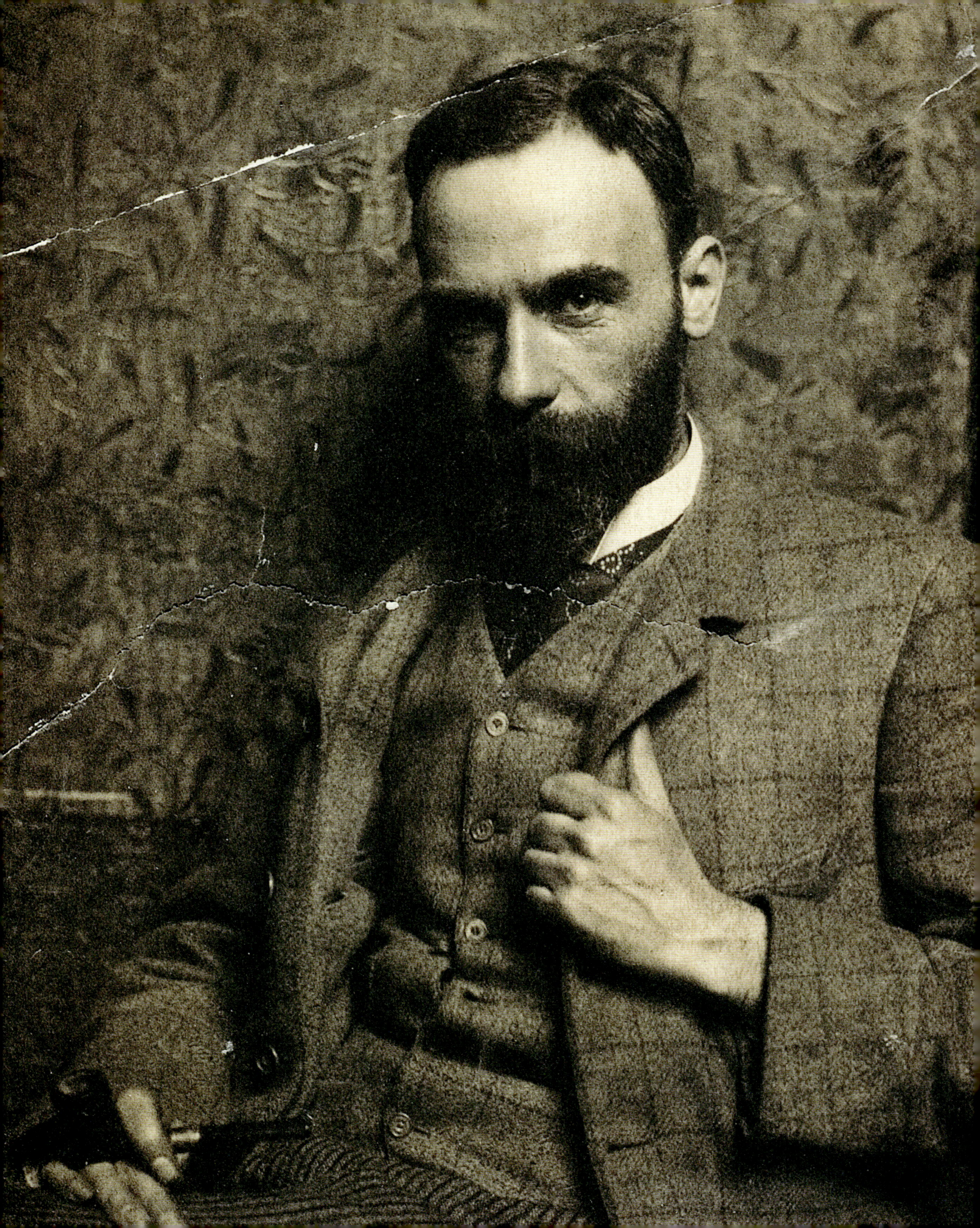

Chronology

1849
John William Waterhouse (nicknamed 'Nino') is born at Rome to British parents, both painters.

1854
Family returns to London.

1857
Mother dies of tuberculosis.

1860
Father remarries in London and starts another family.

1860s
Attends a school (unidentified) in Leeds, Yorkshire, near his father's birthplace.

1870
Admitted to Royal Academy Schools (London) as a probationer in sculpture.

1871
Admitted to Academy Schools as a full student in sculpture.

1872
Exhibits paintings at Society of British Artists (London).

1874
Exhibits a painting at Royal Academy of Arts. Does so every summer until 1917, except 1890 and 1915.

1878
Takes a studio at Primrose Hill Studios in northwest London.

1883
Marries the flower painter Esther Maria Kenworthy (1857-1944) in west London. The couple begins renting flats in Primrose Hill while working at the studio nearby. *The Favourites of the Emperor Honorius* becomes Waterhouse's first painting to enter a museum collection (Art Gallery of South Australia, Adelaide).

1885
Elected an Associate of Royal Academy of Arts after *St Eulalia* is acclaimed and purchased by the sugar manufacturer Henry Tate.

1886
The Magic Circle is acquired for the national collection (now Tate) through the Chantrey Bequest, a fund dedicated to such purchases.

1887
Begins teaching part-time at Academy Schools and does so intermittently until 1908.

1888
Exhibits his first treatment of *The Lady of Shalott* (now at Tate), still Waterhouse's most famous work and the one most closely connected to *plein-air* practices.

1889
Mariamne wins a medal at Paris's world's fair, then others at Chicago in 1893 and Brussels in 1897.

1890
Father dies. Does not exhibit at the Academy, probably due to extended travel in Italy.

1891
Ulysses and the Sirens and *Circe Offering the Cup to Ulysses* open a new phase of interest in classical myths.

1895
Elected a full Academician after *St Cecilia* is acclaimed.

1900
Waterhouses move to larger studio-house in St John's Wood, northwest London.

1909
Rose E.D. Sketchley publishes, in the Christmas Number of *The Art Journal,* the longest essay about Waterhouse prepared during his lifetime.

1917
Dies of liver cancer at home, aged 68.

1926
Esther holds a large auction of the studio's remaining contents.

1933
Esther leaves St John's Wood.

1942
Lamia (1905) sells at auction, unrecognized, for 32 guineas.

1944
Esther dies at Faversham, Kent.

1978
Retrospective exhibition mounted at museums in Sheffield and Wolverhampton.

1980
Anthony Hobson publishes the first monograph on Waterhouse.

2000
St Cecilia sells for £6.6 million – still the highest price paid for a Victorian painting at auction.

Selected Bibliography and Photographic Acknowledgements

Selected Bibliography

Asleson, Robyn, *Classic into Modern: The Inspiration of Antiquity in English Painting, 1864-1918*, Yale University Ph.D. thesis, 1993

Baker, James K., and Cathy L. Baker, 'Miss Muriel Foster: The John William Waterhouse Model', *Journal of Pre-Raphaelite Studies*, 8 (Fall 1999): 70-82
__, 'The Lamia in the Art of J.W. Waterhouse', *British Art Journal*, V: 2 (Autumn 2004), 15-22.

Baldry, Alfred Lys, 'J.W. Waterhouse and His Work', *Studio* (vol. IV, Jan. 1895): 101-115
__, 'The Late J.W. Waterhouse, R.A.', *Studio* (vol. LXXI, June 1917): 2-15
__ [probably, anonymously published], 'Some Drawings by J.W. Waterhouse, R.A.', *Studio* (vol. XLIV, Sept. 1908): 246-253
__, 'Some Recent Work by Mr. J.W. Waterhouse, R.A.', *Studio* (vol. LIII, Aug. 1911): 174-185

Barkan, Leonard, *The Gods Made Flesh: Metamorphosis and the Pursuit of Paganism* (New Haven and London, 1986)

Barlow, Paul, and Colin Trodd, eds., *Governing Cultures: Art Institutions in Victorian London* (Aldershot, 2000)

Barringer, Tim, and Elizabeth Prettejohn, eds., *Frederic Leighton: Antiquity, Renaissance, Modernity* (New Haven and London, 1999)

Barringer, Tim, *Reading the Pre-Raphaelites* (London, 1998)

Barrow, R.J., *Lawrence Alma-Tadema* (London, 2001)
__, *The Use of Classical Art and Literature by Victorian Painters, 1860-1912: Creating Continuity with the Traditions of High Art* (Lewiston, NY, Queenston, Ontario, and Lampeter, Wales, 2007)

Becker, Edwin, and others, eds., *Sir Lawrence Alma-Tadema* (exh. cat.), Zwolle: Waanders in association with Amsterdam: Van Gogh Museum and Liverpool: Walker Art Gallery, 1996

Blaikie, J.A., 'J.W. Waterhouse, A.R.A.', *Magazine of Art*, (vol. IX, 1886): 1-6

Bordass, M.E.E. (Elizabeth), 'Primrose Hill Studios 1877-1883: To What Extent Do They Reflect Their Period?', unpublished essay (1981?), Camden Local Studies and Archives Centre, Holborn Library, London

Bradstreet, Christina, 'Wicked with Roses': Floral Femininity and the Erotics of Scent', *Nineteenth-Century Art Worldwide*, spring 2007, at http://19thc-artworldwide.org.

Casteras, Susan P., and Alicia Craig Faxon, eds., *Pre-Raphaelite Art in Its European Context* (Madison, New Jersey and London, 1995)

Catalogue of the Remaining Works of the Late J.W. Waterhouse, Esq., R.A. … (London: Messrs. Christie, Manson & Woods, 23 July 1926)

Christian, John, ed., *The Last Romantics: The Romantic Tradition in British Art, Burne-Jones to Stanley Spencer* (exh. cat), London: Lund Humphries and Barbican Art Gallery, 1989

Corbett, David Peters, and Lara Perry, eds., *English Art 1860-1914: Modern Artists and Identity* (Manchester, 2000)

Dijkstra, Bram, *Idols of Perversity: Fantasies of Feminine Evil in Fin-de-Siècle Culture* (Oxford, 1986)

Eyre, A.M., *Saint John's Wood: Its History, Its Houses, Its Haunts and Its Celebrities* (London, 1913)

Frazer, J.G., *The Golden Bough: A Study in Magic and Religion* (London, 3rd ed. of 1912)

Gillett, Paula, *The Victorian Painter's World* (Gloucester, 1999)

Goldhill, Simon, 'J.W. Waterhouse and the Painting of Desire in Victorian Britain', *Ramus* 38 (2008)

Goodchild, Anne, and Anthony Hobson, eds., *John William Waterhouse R.A. 1849-1917* (exh. cat.), Sheffield: Sheffield City Art Galleries, 1978

Haskell, Francis, and Nicholas Penny, *Taste and the Antique: The Lure of Classical Sculpture 1500-1900* (New Haven and London, 1982)

Hobson, Anthony, *The Art and Life of J.W. Waterhouse RA 1849-1917* (London, 1980)
__, *J.W. Waterhouse* (London, 1989)
__, *The Life and Work of J.W. Waterhouse, R.A.*, Leicester University Ph.D. thesis, 1978

Hutton, Ronald, *The Triumph of the Moon: A History of Modern Pagan Witchcraft* (Oxford, 1999)

Jenkyns, Richard, *The Victorians and Ancient Greece* (Cambridge, Massachusetts, 1980)

Kestner, Joseph A., *Mythology and Misogyny: The Social Discourse of Nineteenth-Century British Classical-Subject Painting* (Madison, Wisconsin, 1989)

Layard, George Somes, *Tennyson and His Pre-Raphaelite Illustrators: A Book about a Book* (London, 1894)

Liversidge, Michael, and Catharine Edwards, eds., *Imagining Rome: British Artists and Rome in the Nineteenth Century* (exh. cat.), Bristol: City Museum and Gallery in association with Merrell Holberton, 1996

Macleod, Dianne Sachko, *Art and the Victorian Middle Class: Money and the Making of Cultural Identity* (Cambridge, 1996)

Mancoff, Debra N., ed., *John Everett Millais: Beyond the Pre-Raphaelite Brotherhood* (New Haven and London, 2001)

Martindale, Charles, ed., *Ovid Renewed: Ovidian Influences in Literature and Art from the Middle Ages to the Twentieth Century* (Cambridge, 1988)

Marvick, Andrew Bolton, '"Herself a Psyche": Feminine Identities in the Art of John William Waterhouse', *Journal of Pre-Raphaelite Studies* (Spring 1996): 81-94
__, *The Art of John William Waterhouse: Eclecticism in Late Nineteenth-Century British Painting*, Columbia University Ph.D. thesis, 1994

McConkey, Kenneth, *British Impressionism* (London, 1989)

McKenzie, Janet and Michael Spens, eds., 'High Art and Low Life: The Studio and the fin de siècle', *Studio International* (vol. 201, 1993)

Moore, George, *Modern Painting*, 2nd ed. (London, 1898)

'Mr. J.W. Waterhouse's Painting, "Hylas and the Nymphs"', *Studio*, (X, 15 May 1897): 242-247

'Mr. J.W. Waterhouse, R.A.: An Eclectic Painter', *The Times* (12 Feb. 1917), 6

Nead, Lynda, *Myths of Sexuality: Representations of Women in Victorian Britain* (Oxford, 1988)

Owen, Alex, *The Place of Enchantment: British Occultism and the Culture of the Modern* (Chicago and London, 2004)

Pearce, Lynne, *Woman/Image/Text: Readings in Pre-Raphaelite Art and Literature* (Toronto and Buffalo, 1991)

Phillips, Claude, 'Death of Mr. J.W. Waterhouse, R.A.', *Daily Telegraph* (13 Feb. 1917): A4

Postle, Martin, and William Vaughan, eds., *The Artist's Model: From Etty to Spencer* (exh. cat.), London: Merrell Holberton, 1999

Poulson, Christine, *The Quest for the Grail: Arthurian Legend in British Art, 1840-1920* (Manchester, 1999)

Prettejohn, Elizabeth, *Art for Art's Sake: Aestheticism in Victorian Painting* (New Haven and London, 2007)
__, *The Art of the Pre-Raphaelites* (London: Tate Publishing, 2000)

Psomiades, Kathy Alexis, *Beauty's Body: Femininity and Representation in British Aestheticism* (Palo Alto, California, 1997)

Sketchley, R.E.D., 'The Art of J. W. Waterhouse, R.A.', Christmas Number of *The Art Journal* (London, 1909)

Smith, Alison, ed., *Exposed: The Victorian Nude* (exh. cat), London: Tate Publishing, 2001

'Some Drawings by J.W. Waterhouse, R.A.' *Studio* (vol. XLIV, Sept. 1908): 246-255

Taylor, Brandon, *Art for the Nation: Exhibitions and the London Public, 1747-2001* (New Brunswick, 1999)

Trippi, Peter, *J.W. Waterhouse* (London: Phaidon Press, 2002)

Trumble, Angus, *Love and Death: Art in the Age of Queen Victoria* (exh. cat.), Adelaide: Art Gallery of South Australia, 2001

Turner, Frank M., *The Greek Heritage in Victorian Britain* (New Haven and London, 1981)

Upstone, Robert, *A Victorian Masterpiece: John William Waterhouse's* The Lady of Shalott (British Art in Focus: Patrons' Papers 2, Nov. 1999, published by the Patrons of British Art, Tate Gallery)

Helen Valentine, ed., *Art in the Age of Queen Victoria: Treasures from the Royal Academy of Arts Permanent Collection* (exh. cat.), London: Royal Academy of Arts, 1999

Wilton, Andrew, and Robert Upstone, eds., *The Age of Rossetti, Burne-Jones and Watts: Symbolism in Britain 1860-1910* (exh. cat), London: Tate Gallery Publishing, 1997

Photographic Acknowledgements

Aberdeen Art Gallery and Museums: 165, 185, 238
Amgueddfa Cymru/National Museum Wales: 191
Art Gallery of New South Wales, Sydney: 91
Art Gallery of Ontario, Toronto: 176, 189
Art Gallery of South Australia, Adelaide; South Australian Government Grant 1883: 93, 94; South Australian Government Grant 1892: 22, 121
© Birmingham Museums & Art Gallery: 53
Chi Mei Museum, Tainan, Taiwan: 85
© The Cleveland Museum of Art: 61
Collection Dr. Dennis T. Lanigan, Canada, photo: Grant Kernan: 211b, 212b, 216b, 217a, 217b
Collection John Physick CBE, FSA and Mrs Eileen Physick, photo: Ian Bavington Jones: 16a, 16b, 18, 20, 79, 216a, 218a, 219a, 219b, 219c, 220a, 221a, 221b, 234
Collection Sir Tim Rice, photo: Ian Bavington Jones: 73, 75, 76-77, 96, 124, 153
Collection Nicky and Roma Ryan, courtesy of The Maas Gallery: 6, 193
Collection Anna Sui: 179, 180
Collection Michael Titterington, photo: Lincoln Central Library: 232a, 232b
Collection Stephen and Linda Waterhouse, photo: Ian Bavington Jones: 166; photo: Kevin Noble: 97, 205
Collection Robert and Ann Wiggins, USA: 70
Dahesh Museum of Art, New York, All Rights Reserved: 197
© The De Morgan Foundation: 59
The Rob Dickins Collection courtesy of Christie's: 167
© Ronald Dreyfus, Paris: 55b
Falmouth Art Gallery Collection: 128
Reproduced courtesy of Fife Council Museums: Kirkcaldy Museum & Art Gallery: 82
Gallery Oldham: 28a, 50, 115
© Tom Haartsen, Amsterdam: 57
Harris Museum and Art Gallery, Preston: 161
Hessisches Landesmuseum, Darmstadt, photo: Sina Althöfer: 127
Kelley Gallery, Pasadena, California: 147, 187
© Leeds Museums and Galleries (City Art Gallery) U.K. / The Bridgeman Art Library: 129
© Manchester City Galleries: 24, 135, 136
Metropolitan Museum of Art, New York: 40a
Musée provincial Félicien Rops à Namur: 55a
National Gallery of Canada, Ottawa, photo: Grant Kernan: 212c
National Gallery, London: 184
National Gallery of Victoria, Melbourne: 29, 117, 118
National Museums Liverpool: 46, 157, 158, 199, 200, 203
© National Portrait Gallery: Frontispiece, 17ab, 234
Plymouth Museum & Art Gallery: 123
Private collection, photo: Ian Bavington Jones: 155, 163, 170, 206, 209b, 209c, 210, 213, 215, 220b
Private collection, courtesy of Bonhams: 32
Private collection, courtesy of Christie's: 14, 60, 111, 131, 132, 139, 160, 169, 171, 173, 182, 209a, 211a, 211c
Private collection, © Christie's Images / The Bridgeman Art Library, photo: Samuel Thompson: 58
Private collection, photo: Prudence Cuming: 141, 142
Private collection, photo: Patricia Falkner: 28b, 31, 44/2, 56, 72
Private collection, Fine Art Photographic Library, London/Art Resource, New York: 30
Private collection, by courtesy of Julian Hartnoll / The Bridgeman Art Library: 34
Private collection © The Maas Gallery, London, UK / The Bridgeman Art Library: 35
Private collection, courtesy of Peter Nahum at The Leicester Galleries, London: 175, 183
Private collection, courtesy of Nevill Keating Pictures, London: 108
Private collection, courtesy of Sotheby's: 25, 27, 33, 47, 48, 146ab, 149, 195
Private collection, photo: Foley Vereker/Original images: 122a
Prudential plc: 64, 81
© RMN (Musée d'Orsay) / Hervé Lewandowski: 49
© RMN / © René-Gabriel Ojéda: 61b
© Royal Academy of Arts, London: 122b, 145
The Schaeffer Collection, Sydney: 80
© Tate, London 2008: 36, 39, 40b, 41, 42, 43, 44a, 45, 88, 99, 100, 103, 104, 107, 113
Touchstones Rochdale Art Gallery: 68
Towneley Hall, Burnley Borough Council: 67, 151
Tyne and Wear Museums: 52, 87
V&A Picture Library, Victoria and Albert Museum, London: 19, 223, 225, 226, 228a, 228b, 229a, 229b, 230
Yale Center for British Art, New Haven: 212a

List of Works in the Exhibition

Works are by J. W. Waterhouse and are exhibited at all venues unless otherwise stated.

1. *The Unwelcome Companion: A Street Scene in Cairo*, 1873. Oil on canvas, 59 x 49.5 cm. Towneley Hall, Burnley Borough Council. Gift of Mrs Sarah Oldman, 1951
[Groningen and Montreal only]

2. *In the Peristyle*, 1874. Oil on canvas, 67.3 x 52.1 cm. Touchstones Rochdale Art Gallery. Gift of Robert Taylor Heape, 1908
[Groningen and Montreal only]

3. *Miranda*, 1875. Oil on canvas, 76 x 101.5 cm. Collection Robert and Ann Wiggins, USA

4. *After the Dance*, 1876. Oil on canvas, 76.2 x 127 cm. Collection Sir Tim Rice

5. *A Sick Child Brought into the Temple of Aesculapius*, 1877. Oil on canvas, 170 x 208 cm. Collection Sir Tim Rice

6. *Scene at Pompeii*, *c.* 1877. Watercolour on paper, 31 x 23.1 cm. Collection John Physick CBE FSA and Mrs Eileen Physick

7. *Dolce Far Niente*, 1879. Oil on canvas, 49.5 x 36.5 cm. Prudential plc
[Groningen and Montreal only]

8. *Dolce Far Niente*, 1880. Oil on canvas, 50 x 95.5 cm. Fife Council Museums, Kirkcaldy Museum and Art Gallery. Bequest of Mrs John Harly, 1927

9. *The Household Gods*, 1880. Oil on canvas, 102.6 x 74.3 cm. Chi Mei Museum, Rendei Township, Taiwan

10. *A Flower Stall*, 1880. Oil on canvas, 57.8 x 79.3 cm. Laing Art Gallery, Tyne and Wear Museums, Newcastle upon Tyne. Bequest of John Lamb, 1909
[Groningen and Montreal only]

11. *Diogenes*, 1882. Oil on canvas, 208.3 x 134.6 cm. Art Gallery of New South Wales, Sydney. Purchased 1886
[Groningen and London only]

12. *The Favourites of the Emperor Honorius*, 1883. Oil on canvas, 119.3 x 205 cm. Art Gallery of South Australia, Adelaide. Purchased 1883

13. *The Favourites of the Emperor Honorius*, *c.* 1882–1883. Sketch. Oil on canvas, mounted on board, 20 x 28 cm. Collection John Physick CBE FSA and Mrs Eileen Physick

14. *The Favourites of the Emperor Honorius*, *c.* 1882–1883. Sketch. Oil on canvas, 94 x 166.5 cm. Collection Stephen and Linda Waterhouse

15. *Consulting the Oracle*, 1884. Oil on canvas, 119.4 x 198.1 cm. Tate, London. Gift of Sir Henry Tate, 1894

16. *St Eulalia*, 1885. Oil on canvas, 188.6 x 117.5 cm. Tate, London. Gift of Sir Henry Tate, 1894

17. *The Magic Circle*, 1886. Oil on canvas, 182.9 x 127 cm. Tate, London. Purchased by the Trustees of the Chantrey Bequest, 1886

18. *Mariamne*, 1887. Oil on canvas, 259 x 180 cm. Private collection, courtesy of Nevill Keating Pictures, London

19. *Cleopatra*, 1888. Oil on canvas, 65.4 x 56.8 cm. Private collection, courtesy of Christie's
[Groningen and Montreal only]

20. *The Lady of Shalott*, 1888. Oil on canvas, 153 x 200 cm. Tate, London. Gift of Sir Henry Tate, 1894
[Groningen and London only]

21. *Circe Offering the Cup to Ulysses*, 1891. Oil on canvas, 149 x 92 cm. Gallery Oldham. Gift of Marjorie Lees, 1952

22. *Ulysses and the Sirens*, 1891. Oil on canvas, 100.6 x 201.7 cm. National Gallery of Victoria, Melbourne. Purchased 1891

23. *Circe Invidiosa: Circe Poisoning the Sea*, 1892. Oil on canvas, 180.7 x 87.4 cm. Art Gallery of South Australia, Adelaide. Purchased 1892

24. *A Hamadryad*, 1893. Oil on canvas, 159.8 x 62.1 cm. Plymouth City Museum and Art Gallery. Gift of Alfred de Pass, 1926
[Groningen and Montreal only]

25. Landscape sketch for *A Naiad*, *c.* 1892–1893. Oil on canvas, 44.5 x 34.3 cm. Private collection

26. Unidentified artist, Cover of the programme for *Pallettaria* at the Royal Academy Schools, 1895. Pen and ink on paper, 23 x 29.3 cm. Royal Academy of Arts, London
[London and Montreal only]

27. *A Naiad*, 1893. Oil on canvas, 66 x 127 cm. Collection Sir Tim Rice

28. *La Belle Dame Sans Merci*, 1893. Oil on canvas, 110.6 x 81 cm. Hessisches Landesmuseum, Darmstadt. Purchased 1964
[London only]

29. *The Lady of Shalott*, 1891–1893. Sketch. Oil on canvas, 120.5 x 68.3 cm. Falmouth Art Gallery. Gift of Alfred de Pass, *c.* 1939
[Groningen and Montreal only]

30. *The Lady of Shalott*, 1894. Oil on canvas, 142.2 x 86.3 cm. Leeds Art Gallery. Purchased 1895
[Groningen and Montreal only]

31. *St Cecilia*, 1895. Oil on canvas, 123.2 x 200.7 cm. Private collection

32. *Hylas and the Nymphs*, 1896. Oil on canvas, 98.2 x 163.3 cm. Manchester City Galleries. Purchased 1896
[Groningen and London only]

33. *Mariana in the South*, 1897. Oil on canvas, 114.4 x 72.4 cm. Private collection, courtesy of Peter Nahum at The Leicester Galleries, London
[Groningen and Montreal only]

34. *Ariadne*, 1898. Oil on canvas, 91 x 151 cm. Private collection
[Groningen and London only]

35. *A Mermaid*, 1900. Oil on canvas, 96.5 x 66.6 cm. Royal Academy of Arts, London. Diploma work presented by the artist, 1900

36. *A Mermaid*, 1892. Sketch. Oil on canvas, 33.5 x 19.5 cm. Private collection, New York

37. *Head of a Girl*, *c.* 1892–1900. Sketch. Oil on canvas, mounted on board, 34.3 x 24.1 cm. Private collection, New York

38. *Head of a Girl*, *c.* 1892–1900. Sketch. Oil on canvas on board, 35.6 x 25.4 cm. Kelley Gallery, Pasadena, California

39. *The Siren*, *c.* 1900. Oil on canvas, 81 x 53 cm. Private collection, courtesy of Sotheby's
[Montreal only]

40. *Destiny*, 1900. Oil on canvas, 68.5 x 54.6 cm. Towneley Hall, Burnley Borough Council. Purchased 1906

41. *Nymphs Finding the Head of Orpheus*, 1900. Oil on canvas, 149 x 99 cm. Collection Sir Tim Rice

42. *Windflowers*, 1902. Oil on canvas, 114 x 79 cm. Private collection
[Groningen and London only]

43. *Echo and Narcissus*, 1903. Oil on canvas, 109.2 x 189.2 cm. Walker Art Gallery, National Museums Liverpool. Purchased 1903
[Groningen and London only]

44. *Psyche Opening the Golden Box*, 1903. Oil on canvas, 117 x 74 cm. Private collection, courtesy of Christie's

45. *Psyche Opening the Door into Cupid's Garden*, 1903. Oil on canvas, 109.5 x 72 cm. Harris Museum and Art Gallery, Preston. Purchased 1908

46. *Lamia*, 1905. Oil on canvas, 146 x 90.2 cm. Private collection
[Groningen and London only]

47. *The Danaïdes*, 1906. Oil on canvas, 163.3 x 128 cm. Aberdeen Art Gallery and Museums. Purchased 1927

48. *Jason and Medea*, 1907. Oil on canvas, 134 x 107 cm. The Rob Dickins Collection, courtesy of Christie's

49. *Medea*, *c.* 1906–1907. Sketch. Oil on canvas, 61 x 53 cm. Collection Stephen and Linda Waterhouse

50. *The Soul of the Rose*, 1908. Oil on canvas, 88.3 x 59.1 cm. Private collection, courtesy of Christie's

51. *'Gather Ye Rosebuds While Ye May'*, 1908. Oil on canvas, 61.6 x 45.7 cm. Private collection, courtesy of Christie's
[Groningen and Montreal only]

52. *'Gather Ye Rosebuds While Ye May'*, *c.* 1908. Oil on canvas, 79 x 57 cm. Private collection
[Groningen and Montreal only]

53. *Lamia*, 1909. Oil on canvas, 92.5 x 57.5 cm. Private collection, courtesy of Christie's
[Groningen and Montreal only]

54. *Vanity*, *c.* 1908–1910. Oil on canvas, 66 x 68.6 cm. Private collection, courtesy of Peter Nahum at The Leicester Galleries, London
[Montreal only]

55. *'Listening to My Sweet Pipings'*, 1911. Oil on canvas, 57.8 x 102.2 cm. Collection Anna Sui

56. *Circe*, *c.* 1911–1914. Sketch. Oil on canvas, 86.3 x 77.2 cm. Private collection
[Groningen and Montreal only]

57. *Circe*, *c.* 1911–1914. Sketch. Oil on canvas, 76 x 110.5 cm. Private collection, courtesy of Peter Nahum at The Leicester Galleries, London
[London only]

58. *Penelope and the Suitors*, 1912. Oil on canvas, 129.8 x 188 cm. Aberdeen Art Gallery and Museums

59. *The Love Philtre*, *c.* 1913–1914. Sketch. Oil on canvas, 58.4 x 45.7 cm. Kelley Gallery, Pasadena, California
[Groningen and Montreal only]

60. *'I am Half Sick of Shadows', said the Lady of Shalott*, 1915. Oil on canvas, 100 x 74 cm. Art Gallery of Ontario, Toronto. Gift of Mrs Phillip B. Jackson, 1971
[London and Montreal only]

61. *Fair Rosamund*, *c.* 1916. Sketch. Oil on canvas, 60.6 x 48 cm. Amgueddfa Cymru/ National Museum Wales, Cardiff. Gift of Sir William Goscombe John RA, 1940
[Montreal only]

62. *Miranda*, 1916. Oil on canvas, laid on board, 47.5 x 60 cm. Collection Nicky and Roma Ryan, courtesy of the Maas Gallery
[Groningen and Montreal only]

63. *Tristram and Isolde*, 1916. Oil on canvas, 107.5 x 81.5 cm. Private collection, New York

64. *Dante and Matilda* (formerly known as *Dante and Beatrice*), *c.* 1916–1917. Oil on canvas, mounted on wood, 49.5 x 62.2 cm. Dahesh Museum of Art, New York. Purchased 1997
[Groningen and Montreal only]

65. *The Decameron*, 1916. Oil on canvas, 101 x 159 cm. Lady Lever Art Gallery, National Museums Liverpool. Purchased 1916
[London only]

66. *The Enchanted Garden, from Boccaccio's Tales*, *c.* 1916–1917. Oil on canvas, 115.5 x 160 cm. Lady Lever Art Gallery, National Museums Liverpool. Purchased 1922
[Montreal only]

67. *The Decameron*, *c.* 1915–1916. Sketch. Oil on canvas, 53 x 89.5 cm. Collection Stephen and Linda Waterhouse
[Groningen and Montreal only]

68. *Head of a Girl*, *c.* 1905. Chalk on paper, 37.5 x 31.1 cm. Private collection, courtesy of Christie's

69. *Head of a Woman*, *c.* 1883–1884. Chalk on paper, 21 x 21.5 cm. Private collection

70. *Head of a Girl*, *c.* 1903. Chalk on paper, 23.5 x 26 cm. Private collection

71. *Head of a Girl*, *c.* 1915-1917. Chalk on paper, 36 x 30 cm. Private collection

72. Study for the head of Phyllis in *Phyllis and Demophöon*, *c.* 1906–1907. Chalk on paper, 30.5 x 25.4 cm. Private collection, courtesy of Christie's

73. Study for the head in *The Rose Bower*, *c.* 1910. Chalk on paper, 32.2 x 24.5 cm. Collection Dr Dennis T. Lanigan, Canada

74. Study, probably for *Circe*, *c.* 1911–1914. Pencil and chalk on paper, 29.5 x 31.1 cm. Private collection, courtesy of Christie's

75. Study for the head of *Lamia*, *c.* 1904–1905. Pencil on paper, 12 x 11.5 cm. Yale Center for British Art, New Haven, Connecticut. Bequest of Elizabeth S. Tower, 1988

76. Study for the head of *Lamia*, *c.* 1904–1905. Chalk on paper, 32.2 x 26.7 cm. Collection Dr Dennis T. Lanigan, Canada

77. Study of a woman for *The Decameron*, *c.* 1915–1916. Graphite on paper, 33 x 24.5 cm. National Gallery of Canada, Ottawa. Gift of the Dennis T. Lanigan Collection in memory of Daniel Perrin, 2005
[Montreal only]

78. Study for the *Portrait of the Marchioness of Downshire*, 1914. Chalk on paper, 41.2 x 31.3 cm. Private collection

79. Study for *The Magic Circle*, *c.* 1880–1881. Sepia, pen and ink on paper, 49 x 36.3 cm. Private collection
[Groningen and Montreal only]

80. *Woman Picking Fruit from a Tree* and the 1910 treatment of Ophelia, *c.* 1910. Graphite on paper, 17.5 x 25 cm. Collection John Physick CBE FSA and Mrs Eileen Physick
[Groningen and Montreal only]

81. Study for *'Listening to My Sweet Pipings'*, *c.* 1910–1911. Graphite on paper, 17.6 x 25.2 cm. Collection Dr Dennis T. Lanigan, Canada

82. Study for *Maidens Picking Flowers by a Stream*, *c.* 1911. Graphite on paper, 25.2 x 17.6 cm. Collection Dr Dennis T. Lanigan, Canada

83. Study for *Narcissus* or *'Gather Ye Rosebuds While Ye May'*, *c.* 1911. Graphite on paper, 25.1 x 17.6 cm. Collection Dr Dennis T. Lanigan, Canada

84. *Woman Preparing to Open a Door from Inside* (possibly for *Fatima*), *c.* 1911. Graphite on paper, 25 x 17.5 cm. Collection John Physick CBE FSA and Mrs Eileen Physick
[Groningen and Montreal only]

85. *Two Women Leaning Down to Pick Flowers* and *Tristram and Isolde*, *c.* 1911–1916. Graphite on paper, 17.5 x 25 cm. Collection John Physick CBE FSA and Mrs Eileen Physick

86. *Circe with Animals*, and Other Figures, *c.* 1911–1916. Graphite on paper, 22.5 x 29 cm. Collection John Physick CBE FSA and Mrs Eileen Physick

87. *Panthers*, *c.* 1911–1914. Graphite on paper, 17.5 x 25 cm. Collection John Physick CBE FSA and Mrs Eileen Physick

88. *Man Watching a Seated Woman Pick Fruit*, *c.* 1912–1917. Graphite on paper, 22.5 x 29 cm. Collection John Physick CBE FSA and Mrs Eileen Physick
[Groningen and Montreal only]

89. Study of the Angel Gabriel for *The Annunciation*, *c.* 1913–1914. Graphite on paper, 31.1 x 31.1 cm. Private collection
[Groningen and Montreal only]

90. *Seated Girl Watching the Sun Rise*, *c.* 1914. Graphite on paper, 25 x 17.5 cm. Collection John Physick CBE FSA and Mrs Eileen Physick
[Groningen and Montreal only]

91. Classicised study for *Miranda*, *c.* 1914–1916. Graphite on paper, 22.5 x 29 cm. Collection John Physick CBE FSA and Mrs Eileen Physick
[Groningen and Montreal only]

92. Sketchbook, *c.* 1912–1917. Pencil, pen and ink on wove paper bound in canvas boards, 25.4 x 36.8 cm. Victoria and Albert Museum, London, E.1112-1963. Gift of John Physick

93. Sketchbook, *c.* 1896. Pencil, chalk and watercolour on wove Whatman paper, quarter-bound in leather, canvas boards, 12.7 x 17.8 cm. Victoria and Albert Museum, London, E.1109-1963. Gift of John Physick

94. Sketchbook, *c.* 1888–1890. Pencil and watercolour on wove paper bound in canvas boards, 14 x 20.6 cm. Victoria and Albert Museum, London, E.1-1949. Gift of John Physick

95. Sketchbook, *c.* 1891–1893. Pencil on wove paper bound in canvas boards, 15.3 x 23.5 cm. Victoria and Albert Museum, London, E.1110-1963. Gift of John Physick

96. Sketchbook, *c.* 1901–1916. Pencil, pen and ink on wove paper bound in canvas boards, 15.3 x 21.6 cm. Victoria and Albert Museum, London, E.1111-1963. Gift of John Physick

97. Sketchbook, *c.* 1906–1907. Pencil, watercolour and bodycolour on wove paper bound in canvas boards, 17.5 x 23.1 cm. Victoria and Albert Museum, London, E.2-1949. Gift of John Physick

98. Sketchbook, *c.* 1905–1915. Pencil, chalk and pen and ink on wove paper bound in canvas boards, 20.3 x 25.4 cm. Victoria and Albert Museum, London, E.3-1949. Gift of John Physick

99. J. W. Waterhouse's copy of *The Poetical Works of Percy Bysshe Shelley*. London, George Routledge and Sons, 1880. 18 x 12 cm. Collection Michael Titterington
[London and Montreal only]

100. J. W. Waterhouse's copy of *The Works of Alfred Lord Tennyson, Poet Laureate*. London, Macmillan and Co., 1885. 19 x 12.5 cm. Collection Michael Titterington
[London and Montreal only]

Index

Index

Benefactors of the Royal Academy of Arts

Royal Academy Trust

MAJOR BENEFACTORS
The Trustees of the Royal Academy Trust are grateful to all its donors for their continued loyalty and generosity. They would like to extend their thanks to all those who have made a significant commitment, past and present, to the galleries, the exhibitions, the conservation of the Permanent Collection, the Library collections, the Royal Academy Schools, the education programme and other specific appeals.

HM The Queen
The 29th May 1961 Charitable Trust
Barclays Bank
B.A.T. Industries Plc
Big Lottery Fund (formerly New Opportunities Fund)
John Frye Bourne
British Telecom
Mr and Mrs John Burns
Mr Raymond M Burton CBE
Sir Trevor Chinn CVO and Lady Chinn
The Trustees of the Clore Foundation
The John S Cohen Foundation
Sir Harry and Lady Djanogly
The Dulverton Trust
Alfred Dunhill Limited
The John Ellerman Foundation
The Eranda Foundation
Ernst and Young
Esso UK Plc
The Foundation for Sport and the Arts
Friends of the Royal Academy
Jacqueline and Michael Gee
Mr Mark Getty
Glaxo Holdings plc
Diane and Guilford Glazer
Mr and Mrs Jack Goldhill
Maurice and Laurence Goldman
Mr and Mrs Jocelin Harris
The Philip and Pauline Harris Charitable Trust
The Charles Hayward Foundation
Heritage Lottery Fund
Mr Damien Hirst
IBM United Kingdom Limited
The Idlewild Trust
Lord and Lady Jacobs
The J P Jacobs Charitable Trust
The Japan Foundation
Gabrielle Jungels-Winkler Foundation
Mr and Mrs Donald P Kahn
The Lillian Jean Kaplan Foundation
The Kirby Laing Foundation
The Kresge Foundation
The Kress Foundation
The Lankelly Foundation
The Leverhulme Trust
Lex Service Plc
The Linbury Trust
Sir Sydney Lipworth QC and Lady Lipworth
John Lyons Charity
Ronald and Rita McAulay
McKinsey and Company Inc
John Madejski OBE DL
Her Majesty's Government
The Manifold Trust
Marks and Spencer
The Mercers' Company
Mr and Mrs Minoru Mori
The Monument Trust
The Henry Moore Foundation
The Moorgate Trust Fund
Robin Heller Moss
Museums and Galleries Improvement Fund
National Westminster Bank
Stavros S Niarchos
The Peacock Trust
The Pennycress Trust
P F Charitable Trust
The Pilgrim Trust
The Edith and Ferdinand Porjes Trust
John Porter Charitable Trust
The Porter Foundation
Rio Tinto Plc
Mr John A Roberts FRIBA
Simon and Virginia Robertson
The Ronson Foundation
The Rose Foundation
Rothmans International Plc
Mrs Jean Sainsbury
The Saison Foundation
The Basil Samuel Charitable Trust
Mrs Coral Samuel CBE
Sea Containers Ltd
Shell UK Limited
Miss Dasha Shenkman
William and Maureen Shenkman
The Archie Sherman Charitable Trust
Sir Hugh Sykes DL
Sir Anthony and Lady Tennant
Ware and Edythe Travelstead
The Trusthouse Charitable Foundation
The Douglas Turner Trust
Unilever plc
The Weldon UK Charitable Trust
The Welton Foundation
The Weston family
The Malcolm Hewitt Wiener Foundation
The Maurice Wohl Charitable Foundation
The Wolfson Foundation
and others who wish to remain anonymous

Patrons
The Royal Academy is delighted to thank all its Patrons for generously supporting the following areas over the past year: exhibitions, education, the Royal Academy Schools, the Permanent Collection and Library and Anglo-American initiatives, and for assisting in the general upkeep of the Academy.

PLATINUM
Mr and Mrs John Coombe
Mr and Mrs Patrick Doherty
Mrs Helena Frost
Lady Getty
Janicke and Leif Höegh
Mr Frederik Paulsen
Mr and Mrs David Shalit

GOLD
Sir Ronald Cohen
Lady Gosling
Michael and Morven Heller
Lady Hobson MBE
Sir Sidney Lipworth QC and Lady Lipworth
Mr and Mrs Ronald Lubner
Prof and Mrs Anthony Mellows
Lady Jane Rayne
Mrs Stella Shawzin
Mr James B Sherwood
Mrs Roama L Spears

SILVER
Mrs Denise Adeane
Mrs Leslie Bacon
Alain and Marie Boublil
Mrs Gary Brass
Mrs Elie Brihi
Mrs Debbie Burks
Sir Charles and Lady Chadwyck-Healey
Sir Trevor Chinn CVO and Lady Chinn
John C L Cox CBE
Mary Moore Danowski
Benita and Gerald Fogel
Mr and Mrs Eric Franck
The Lady Henrietta St George
Jaqueline and Jonathan Gestetner
Patricia and John Glasswell
Mr and Mrs Alan Hobart
Mr and Mrs Jon Hunt
S Isern-Feliu
Mrs Raymonde Jay
Mr and Mrs Fred Johnston
Mr and Mrs Joseph Karaviotis
Mr Nand Khemka and Princess Jeet Nabha Khemka
Mrs Aboudi Kosta
Lady Lever of Manchester
Mr and Mrs Mark Loveday
Mr and Mrs Richard Martin
The Mulberry Trust
Mr and Mrs D J Peacock
Mr and Mrs Kevin Senior
The Countess of Shaftesbury
Mr and Mrs Andrew Shrager
Richard and Veronica Simmons
Jane Spack
Sir James and Lady Spooner
Mrs Elyane Stilling
Sir Hugh Sykes DL
Group Captain James Tait
Mr David Teitelbaum

BRONZE
Mr and Mrs Gerald Acher
Agnew's
Julie and James Alexandre
Mr Derrill Allatt
Mr Peter Allinson
Edgar Astaire
Jane Barker
Mrs Yvonne Barlow
Stephen Barry Charitable Settlement
James M Bartos
The Duke of Beaufort
The Bellinger Donnay Charitable Trust
Mrs J K M Bentley/Summers Art Gallery
Konrad O Bernheimer
Dame Elizabeth Blackadder RA
Sir Victor and Lady Blank
Mrs Charles Brocklebank
Jeremy Brown
Mr and Mrs Charles H Brown
Lord Browne of Madingley
Mrs Alan Campbell-Johnson
Mr F A A Carnwath CBE
Jean and Eric Cass
Mr and Mrs George Coelho
Mrs Carole Cohen
Denise Cohen Charitable Trust
Carole Conrad
Mrs Cathy Corbett
Mr and Mrs Sidney Corob
Thomas Corrigan OBE
Julian Darley and Helga Sands
The Countess of Dartmouth
Ms Davina Dixon
Dr Anne Dornhorst
Lord Douro
Sir Philip Dowson CBE PPRA and Lady Dowson
Mr and Mrs Maurice Dwek
Lord and Lady Egremont
Mary Fedden RA
Mr and Mrs David Fenton
Bryan Ferry
Mrs Donatella Flick
Mrs George Fokschaner
Lord and Lady Foley
Mrs Pamela Foster-Brown
Mrs Jocelyn Fox
Mr Monty Freedman
Arnold Fulton
Mark Glatman
Michael Godbee
Nicholas and Judith Goodison
Piers and Rosie Gough
Peter and Kate De Haan
David and Lesley Haynes
Mr Andreas Heeschen
Mr and Mrs Christoph Henkel
Mr and Mrs Jonathan Hindle
Anne Holmes-Drewry
Mrs Pauline Hyde
Sir Martin and Lady Jacomb
Harold and Valerie Joels
Fiona Johnstone
Dr Elisabeth Kehoe
Mr D H Killick
Mr and Mrs James Kirkman
Norman A Kurland and Deborah A David
The de Laszlo Foundation
Joan H Lavender
Mr George Lengvari and Mrs Inez Lengvari
Mrs Rose-Marie Lieberman
Miss R Lomax-Simpson
The Marquess of Lothian
Mr and Mrs Henry Lumley
Miss Jane McAusland
Mr and Mrs Christopher McCann
Gillian McIntosh
Andrew and Judith McKinna
Sally and Donald Main
Mr and Mrs Eskandar Maleki
Mr Michael Manser RA and Mrs Jose Manser
Mr Marcus Margulies
Mr and Mrs Stephen Mather
Zvi and Ofra Meitar Family Fund
Lakshman Menon and Darren Rickards
Mrs Michele Michell
Mrs Michael Moore
James Moores
Mrs Alan Morgan
Dr Ann Naylor
Ann Norman-Butler
North Street Trust
Mrs Elin Odfjell
Hilary O'Neill
Mr Georg von Opel
Mr Michael Palin
John H Pattisson
Mr Philip Perry
David Pike
Mrs Godfrey Pilkington
Mr and Mrs Anthony Pitt-Rivers
William Plapinger and Cassie Murray
John and Anne Raisman
Mr and Mrs Ian Rosenberg
Lord Rothschild
Lady (Robert) Sainsbury
Mrs Sirkka Sanderson
H M Sassoon Charitable Trust
Carol Sellars
Dr Lewis Sevitt
Mrs Lesley Silver
Alan and Marianna Simpson
Mr and Mrs Mark Franklin Slaughter
Brian D Smith
Mr and Mrs David T Smith
Mrs D Susman
Mrs Mark Tapley
Lord and Lady Taylor
Miss M L Ulfane
Mrs Norah de Vigier
John and Carol Wates
Edna and Willard Weiss
Anthony and Rachel Williams
and others who wish to remain anonymous

BENFACTOR PATRONS
The Peter Boizot Foundation
Mr and Mrs William Brake
Mrs Mary Graves
Mrs Sue Hammerson
The Lord Marks of Broughton
Sir Anthony and Lady Tennant

Benjamin West Patrons Group

CHAIRMAN
Lady Judge

PLATINUM PATRON
Dean Menegas

GOLD PATRON
Lady J Lloyd Adamson

SILVER PATRONS
Mrs Adrian Bowden
Mr and Mrs Paul Collins
Brian and Susan Dickie
Kim Dunn
Dr Yvonne von Egidy-Winkler and Mr Peter Philip Winkler
Charles and Kaaren Hale
Lady Judge
Scott and Christine Morrissey
Elaine and David Nordby
Mr and Mrs John R Olsen
Wendy Becker Payton
Frank and Anne Sixt

BRONZE PATRONS
Ms Ruth Anderson
Mrs Alan Artus
Tom and Diane Berger
Mrs Michael Berkner
Wendy Brooks and Tim Medland
Mrs J Morgan Callagy
Debra Cajrati Crivelli
Mr and Mrs Gunnar L Engstrom
Cyril and Christine Freedman
Mr Andrew Hawkins
Mr Roy Hill
Madeleine Hodgkin
Suzanne and Michael Johnson
Sarah H Ketterer
Mr and Mrs H A Lamotte
Charles G Lubar
Mr and Mrs Patrick Mahon
Neil Osborn and Holly Smith
Lady Purves
Carole Turner Record
Mr and Mrs K M Rubie
Sylvia Scheuer
Mr and Mrs Thomas Schoch
John and Sheila Stoller
Mrs Betty Thayer
Frederick and Kathryn Uhde
Mr John D Winter
Mary Wolridge
and others who wish to remain anonymous

Schools Patrons Group

CHAIRMAN
Mr John Entwistle OBE

PLATINUM PATRONS
Mr Campbell Rigg
Matthew and Sian Westerman

GOLD PATRONS
Mr Andrew Hanges
Mr and Mrs Paul Myners

SILVER PATRONS
Lord and Lady Aldington
Mr John Entwistle OBE
Mr Philip Marsden

BRONZE PATRONS
Ian and Tessa Ferguson
Julia Fuller and David Harding
Prof Ken Howard RA and Mrs Ken Howard
Trevor Pickett Esq
Peter Rice Esq
Anthony and Sally Salz
Mrs Inge Borg Scott
Mr Ray Treen
and others who wish to remain anonymous

Contemporary Patrons Group

CHAIRMAN
Susie Allen

PATRONS
Mr Tarek Aquizy
Mrs Alan Artus
Viscountess Bridgeman
Dr Elaine C Buck
Miss Camilla Bullus
Jenny Christensson
Mr Gus Danowski
Mary Moore Danowski
Helen and Colin David
Chris and Angie Drake
Dr Yvonne von Egidy-Winkler
Ms Lissa Engle
Lawton Wehle Fitt
Belinda de Gaudemar
Ms Soma Ghosh
Elizabeth Griffith
Mrs Selima Gürtler
Caroline Hansberry
Mrs Susan Hayden
Dr David Landau CBE
Mazen and Mireille Masri
Mrs Penelope Jane Mather
Sharon Maurice
Marion and Guy Naggar
Angela Nikolakopoulou-Koulakoglou
Barbara Pansadoro
Mr Andres Recoder and Mrs Isabelle Schiavi
Sir John Rose
Rosanna Wilson Stephens
John Tackaberry
Mr and Mrs Nicholas Whyatt
Cathy Wills
John and Amelia Winter
Manuela and Iwan Wirth
Mary Wolridge
and others who wish to remain anonymous

Trusts and Foundations

The Peter Boizot Foundation
The Bomonty Charitable Trust
The Charlotte Bonham-Carter Charitable Trust
William Brake Charitable Trust
C H K Charities Limited
The Carlton House Charitable Trust
The Coutts Charitable Trust
Alan Cristea Gallery
The Dovehouse Trust
D'Oyly Carte Charitable Trust
The Gilbert & Eileen Edgar Foundation
The Fenton Arts Trust
The Flow Foundation
Joseph Strong Frazer Trust
Goethe Institut London
Heritage Lottery Fund
Institut für Aulandsbeziehungen e.V.
Stanley Thomas Johnson Foundation
The Emmanuel Kaye Foundation
The Kindersley Foundation
Lapada Association of Art and Antiques Dealers
The de Laszlo Foundation
The David Lean Foundation
The Leche Trust
The Leverhulme Trust
The Maccabaeans
The McCorquodale Charitable Trust
Marsh Christian Trust
The Paul Mellon Estate
The Mercers' Company
The Millichope Foundation
The Mulberry Trust
The National Manuscripts Conservation Trust
Newby Trust Limited
North Street Trust
The Old Broad Street Charity Trust
P F Charitable Trust
The Peacock Charitable Trust
The Stanley Picker Trust
The Pidem Fund

Benefactors of the Royal Academy of Arts

Edith and Ferdinand Porjes Charitable Trust
Pro Helvetia
Mr and Mrs J A Pye's Charitable Settlement
The Radcliffe Trust
The Rose Foundation
The Schroder Charity Trust
The Archie Sherman Charitable Trust
The South Square Trust
Oliver Stanley Charitable Trust
The Peter Storrs Trust
The Swan Trust
Swiss Cultural Fund in Britain
Sir Jules Thorn Charitable Trust
The Patricia Turner Foundation
Albert Van den Bergh Charitable Trust
The Celia Walker Art Foundation
The Spencer Wills Trust
The Harold Hyam Wingate Foundation
Hazel M Wood Charitable Trust
The Worshipful Company of Painter-Stainers

American Associates of the Royal Academy Trust

BURLINGTON HOUSE TRUST
Mr and Mrs James C Slaughter

BENJAMIN WEST SOCIETY
Mrs Walter H Annenberg
Mr Francis Finlay
Mrs Nancy B Negley

BENEFACTORS
Mrs Deborah Loeb Brice
Mrs Edmond J Safra
Mr and Mrs Albert H Small
The Honorable John C Whitehead
Mr and Mrs Frederick B Whittemore

SPONSORS
Mrs Russell B Aitken
Ms Britt Allcroft
Mrs Katherine D Findlay
Mrs Sylvia K Hassenfeld
Mrs Henry J Heinz II
Mr Arthur L Loeb
Mr and Mrs Hamish Maxwell
Mrs Lucy F McGrath
Mrs Diane A Nixon
Mr Arthur O Sulzberger
and Ms Allison S Cowles
Mr Vernon Taylor Jr
Mr and Mrs Dave Williams

PATRONS
Ms Helen Harting Abell
Mr and Mrs Steven Ausnit
Mr Donald A Best
Mrs Edgar H Brenner
Mrs Mildred C Brinn
Mrs Benjamin Coates
Mrs Mary Sharp Cronson
Anne S Davidson
Ms Zita Davisson
Mrs June Dyson
Mrs Barbara Fox-Bordiga
Mr and Mrs Lawrence S Friedland
Mr and Mrs Leslie Garfield
Mr C Hugh Hildesley
Dr Bruce C Horten
The Hon W Eugene Johnston
and Mrs Johnston
Mr William W Karatz
The Hon Philip Lader and Mrs Lader
Mr and Mrs Daniel Leab
The Hon Samuel K Lessey Jr
Ms Barbara T Missett
Mr and Mrs Wilson Nolen
Mr and Mrs Jeffrey Pettit
Cynthia Hazen Polsky and Leon B Polsky
Lady Annie Renwick
Mr and Mrs Peter M Sacerdote
Ms Louisa Stude Sarofim
Mrs Frances G Scaife and Mr William G Dagit
Mr and Mrs Stanley De Forest Scott
Mrs Frederick M Stafford
Mr and Mrs Stephen Stamas
Ms Joan Stern
Ms Brenda Neubauer Straus
Ms Elizabeth F Stribling
and Mr Guy Robinson
Mr Martin J Sullivan
Mr and Mrs Lewis Townsend
Dr and Mrs Robert D Wickham
Mr Robert W Wilson

DONORS
Mr James C Armstrong
Mr and Mrs Stephen Bechtel
Mr Constantin R Boden
Mr and Mrs Philip Carroll
Mr and Mrs Reginald B Collier
Mr and Mrs Howard S Davis
Ms Jody Donohue
Mr and Mrs William J Doody
Mrs Beverley C Duer
Mr Robert H Enslow
Mr Ralph A Fields
Mr and Mrs Christopher Forbes
Mr and Mrs Gordon P Getty
Mrs Betty N Gordon
Mr O D Harrison Jr
Mr and Mrs Gurnee F Hart
Mr and Mrs Gustave M Hauser
Mrs Judith Heath
Ms Elaine Kend
Mr and Mrs Nicholas L S Kirkbride
Mr and Mrs Gary Kraut
Mr Henry S Lynn Jr
Ms Christine Mainwaring-Samwell
Ms Clare E McKeon
The Hon William Nitze and Mrs Nitze
Mrs Charles W Olson III
Mrs Patsy Preston
Mrs Nanette Ross
Laura Christman and William Rothacker
Mr Mark Schneider
Mrs Martin Slifka
Mrs Sharon Tedesco
Mrs Judith Villard
Mr and Mrs William B Warren

CORPORATE AND FOUNDATION SUPPORT
American International Group, Inc.
Annenberg Foundation
Bechtel Foundation
The Blackstone Charitable Foundation
The Brown Foundation
Fortnum & Mason
Gibson, Dunn & Crutcher
The Horace W Goldsmith Foundation
Hauser Foundation
Leon Levy Foundation
Loeb Foundation
Henry Luce Foundation
Lynberg & Watkins
Sony Corporation of America
Starr Foundation
Thaw Charitable Trust

Corporate Members of the Royal Academy

Launched in 1988, the Royal Academy's Corporate Membership Scheme has proved highly successful. Corporate membership offers benefits for staff, clients and community partners and access to the Academy's facilities and resources. The outstanding support we receive from companies via the scheme is vital to the continuing success of the Academy and we thank all members for their valuable support and continued enthusiasm.

PREMIER LEVEL MEMBERS
A T Kearney Limited
Accenture
The Arts Club
Bain Capital
The Bank of New York Mellon
Barclays plc
Booz & Company
CB Richard Ellis
Deutsche Bank AG
E.ON
Ernst & Young LLP
GlaxoSmithKline plc
Goldman Sachs International
Hay Group
HSBC plc
Intercontinental London Park Lane
Kleinwort Benson
LECG Ltd
Lombard Odier Darier Hentsch
Northern Trust
Schroders plc
Smith and Williamson
Standard Chartered

CORPORATE MEMBERS
All Nippon Airways
Arcadia Group plc
BGC Brokers L.P.
Bibendum Wine Limited
BNP Paribas
The Boston Consulting Group
Bovis Lend Lease Limited
British American Business Inc.
British American Tobacco
Calyon
Capital International Limited
Christie's
Citi
Clifford Chance LLP
Concateno plc
Control Risk Group
Curzon Partnership LLP
Denton Wilde Sapte
Diageo plc
Doll
Eurohypo AG
F & C Asset Management plc
GAM
Heidrick & Struggles
Insight Investment
ITV plc
John Lewis Partnership
JP Morgan
KPMG
Lazard
London College of Fashion
Louis Vuitton
Man Group plc
Mizuho International plc
Momart Limited
Morgan Stanley
Navigant Consulting
Nedrailways
Novo Nordisk
Osborne Samuel LLP
Pentland Group plc
Rio Tinto
Roger Vivier
The Royal Society of Chemistry
Skadden, Arps, Slate, Meagher & Flom LLP
Slaughter and May
Société Générale
Theo Fennell
Timothy Sammons Fine Art Agents
Trowers & Hamlins
Veredus Executive Resourcing
Weil, Gotschal & Manges
Windsor Partners Limited

SPONSORS OF PAST EXHIBITIONS
The President and Council of the Royal Academy would like to thank the following sponsors and benefactors for their generous support of major exhibitions in the last ten years:

2009
241st Summer Exhibition
Insight Investment
Kuniyoshi
Canon
Travel Partner: Cox & Kings

2008
GSK Contemporary
GlaxoSmithKline
Byzantium 330–1453
J. F. Costopoulos Foundation
A. G. Leventis Foundation
Stavros Niarchos Foundation
Travel Partner: Cox & Kings
Miró, Calder, Giacometti, Braque: Aimé Maeght and His Artists
BNP Paribas
Vilhelm Hammershøi: The Poetry of Silence
OAK Foundation Denmark
Novo Nordisk
240th Summer Exhibition
Insight Investment
From Russia: French and Russian Master Paintings 1870–1925 from Moscow and St Petersburg
E.ON
2008 Season supported by Sotheby's

2007
Paul Mellon's Legacy: A Passion for British Art
The Bank of New York Mellon
Georg Baselitz
Eurohypo AG
239th Summer Exhibition
Insight Investment
Impressionists by the Sea
Farrow & Ball
Premiums and RA Schools Show
Mizuho International plc
RA Outreach Programme
Deutsche Bank AG
The Unknown Monet
Bank of America

2006
238th Summer Exhibition
Insight Investment
Chola: Sacred Bronzes of Southern India
Travel Partner: Cox & Kings
Premiums and RA Schools Show
Mizuho International plc
RA Outreach Programme
Deutsche Bank AG
Rodin
Ernst & Young

2005
China: The Three Emperors, 1662–1795
Goldman Sachs International
Impressionism Abroad: Boston and French Painting
Fidelity Foundation
Matisse, His Art and His Textiles: The Fabric of Dreams
Farrow & Ball
Premiums and RA Schools Show
The Guardian
Mizuho International plc
Turks: A Journey of a Thousand Years, 600–1600
Akkök Group of Companies
Aygaz
Corus
Garanti Bank
Lassa Tyres

2004
236th Summer Exhibition
A. T. Kearney
Ancient Art to Post-Impressionism: Masterpieces from the Ny Carlsberg Glyptotek, Copenhagen
Carlsberg UK Ltd
Danske Bank
Novo Nordisk
The Art of Philip Guston (1913–1980)
American Associates of the Royal Academy Trust
The Art of William Nicholson
RA Exhibition Patrons Group
Vuillard: From Post-Impressionist to Modern Master
RA Exhibition Patrons Group

2003
235th Summer Exhibition
A. T. Kearney
Ernst Ludwig Kirchner: The Dresden and Berlin Years
RA Exhibition Patrons Group
Giorgio Armani: A Retrospective
American Express
Mercedes-Benz
Illuminating the Renaissance: The Triumph of Flemish Manuscript Painting in Europe
American Associates of the Royal Academy Trust
Virginia and Simon Robertson
Masterpieces from Dresden
ABN AMRO
Classic FM
Premiums and RA Schools Show
Walker Morris
Pre-Raphaelite and Other Masters: The Andrew Lloyd Webber Collection
Christie's
Classic FM
UBS Wealth Management

2002
234th Summer Exhibition
A. T. Kearney
Aztecs
British American Tobacco
Mexico Tourism Board
Pemex
Virginia and Simon Robertson
Masters of Colour: Derain to Kandinsky. Masterpieces from The Merzbacher Collection
Classic FM
Premiums and RA Schools Show
Debenhams Retail plc
*RA Outreach Programme**
Yakult UK Ltd
Return of the Buddha: The Qingzhou Discoveries
RA Exhibition Patrons Group

2001
233rd Summer Exhibition
A. T. Kearney
Botticelli's Dante: The Drawings for Dante's Divine Comedy
RA Exhibition Patrons Group
The Dawn of the Floating World (1650–1765). Early Ukiyo-e Treasures from the Museum of Fine Arts, Boston
Fidelity Foundation
Forty Years in Print: The Curwen Studio and Royal Academicians
Game International Limited
Frank Auerbach, Paintings and Drawings 1954–2001
International Asset Management
Ingres to Matisse: Masterpieces of French Painting
Barclays
Paris: Capital of the Arts 1900–1968
BBC Radio 3
Merrill Lynch
Premiums and RA Schools Show
Debenhams Retail plc
*RA Outreach Programme**
Yakult UK Ltd
Rembrandt's Women
Reed Elsevier plc

2000
1900: Art at the Crossroads
Cantor Fitzgerald
The Daily Telegraph
232nd Summer Exhibition
A. T. Kearney
Apocalypse: Beauty and Horror in Contemporary Art
Eyestorm
The Independent
Time Out
Chardin 1699–1779
RA Exhibition Patrons Group
The Genius of Rome 1592–1623
Credit Suisse First Boston
Premiums and RA Schools Show
Debenhams Retail plc
*RA Outreach Programme**
Yakult UK Ltd
The Scottish Colourists 1900–1930
Chase Fleming Asset Management

* Recipients of a Pairing Scheme Award, managed by Arts + Business. Arts + Business is funded by the Arts Council of England and the Department for Culture, Media and Sport

OTHER SPONSORS
Sponsors of events, publications and other items in the past five years:

Carlisle Group plc
Country Life
Derwent Valley Holdings plc
Dresdner Kleinwort Wasserstein
Foster and Partners
Goldman Sachs International
Gome International
Gucci Group
Rob van Helden
IBJ International plc
John Doyle Construction
Martin Krajewski
Marks & Spencer
Michael Hopkins & Partners
Morgan Stanley Dean Witter
Prada
Radisson Edwardian Hotels
Richard and Ruth Rogers
Strutt & Parker